Straight with a Twist

Straight with a Twist

Queer Theory and the Subject of Heterosexuality

Edited by Calvin Thomas

With the Assistance of Joseph O. Aimone
and Catherine A. F. MacGillivray

University of Illinois Press

Urbana and Chicago

⊖ *This book is printed on acid-free paper.*

Library of Congress Cataloging-in-Publication Data
Straight with a twist : queer theory and the subject of
heterosexuality / edited by Calvin Thomas ; with the
assistance of Joseph O. Aimone and Catherine A. F.
MacGillivray.
p. cm.
Includes bibliographical references (p.   ) and index.
ISBN 0-252-02495-8 (alk. paper)
ISBN 0-252-06813-0 (pbk. : alk. paper)
1. American literature—20th century—History and
criticism—Theory, etc. 2. Sex in literature. 3. English
literature—History and criticism—Theory, etc. 4. Sexual
orientation in literature. 5. Heterosexuality in literature.
6. Difference (Psychology) 7. Sexual orientation.
8. Heterosexuality. 9. Group identity. 10. Homosexuality.
I. Thomas, Calvin, 1956–   . II. Aimone, Joseph O.
III. MacGillivray, Catherine A. F.
PS228.S42S77   2000
810.9′353—dc21   99-6072
CIP

1 2 3 4 5 C P 5 4 3 2 1

For John Speaks
   (C.T.)

For Frances Forbes
   (J.A.)

For Merlin
   (C.M.)

Contents

Part 3: "Culture"

Acknowledgments

We would like to thank Leo Bersani, Judith Butler, and Diana Fuss for their kind words of encouragement at the beginning of this project. We would also like to thank the Department of English Language and Literature and the Graduate College of the University of Northern Iowa for their support. Cara Ullrich gets a special note of thanks for her speedy and diligent assistance, as does Richard Martin, an executive editor at the University of Illinois Press, for his judicious perserverance.

Straight with a Twist

Introduction: Identification, Appropriation, Proliferation

Calvin Thomas

You are always a different person.
—Nietzsche, *The Gay Science*

"Queer is hot"—or at least it was in May 1995, when Lauren Berlant and Michael Warner posed the question "What Does Queer Theory
Teach Us about *X*?" and pointed out that the term "queer" itself, as positive
nomination rather than hurtful slur, "is less than five years old."[1] However,
the appearance of this collection of essays—all written around 1995, all asking about queer theory, many asking what queer theory teaches us about
straights—could be taken as a sign that queer has already begun to cool
down. After all, if queer is hot, then straight is not, and it may be difficult for
some to imagine how any theoretical work that takes straightness as its
object of scrutiny could generate interest, much less excitement. The very
fact that some straights have begun to write about queer theory or perhaps
even produce theory that itself somehow lays claim to queerness—to what
Andrew Parker calls "a non-gender-specific rubric that defines itself diacritically not against heterosexuality but against the normative"[2]—might be
taken as a sign that the queer moment has passed. Indeed, the appearance
of a collection such as *Straight with a Twist: Queer Theory and the Subject of
Heterosexuality* may seem a predictable if not inevitable marker of what
Judith Butler has termed the "institutional domestication of queer thinking," that "normalizing [of] the queer [that] would be . . . its sad finish."[3]

But however boring straightness might be (even, or perhaps particularly,
to straights themselves), and whatever normalizing tendencies straights
"by definition" bring with them, some straight readers have taken a gen-

uine interest in queer theory and have found much there to be excited about. Not the least cause of their excitement may be their surprised perplexity at recognizing their own reflections in queer theory's mirror. Granted, that surprise is perhaps dulled by an overfamiliarity with post-modernism's destabilizations and decenterings of identity, its general insistence on "constitutive otherness": from Rimbaud's "Je est un autre" or the above epigraph from Nietzsche's *Die Fröliche Wissenschaft* (with its appropriately translated title *The Gay Science*), to Saussure's description of language as a differential system without positive terms (and the inclusion of subjectivity within linguistic *différance*), to the Lacanian problematic of ego-formation through mirror-stage misrecognition (and the political appropriation of Lacan in Althusser), through Foucault, Derrida, and Kristeva, to the work of Butler herself (to which several essays in this collection refer).[4]

The problem, however, for theory-savvy straights inured to the idea of constitutive otherness is probably less in being able to recognize their own identity in the scene of "the other" or to acknowledge the other's constitutiveness and more in deciding how to articulate that recognition in a productive, nonappropriative manner—or, overly wary of the charge of appropriation, deciding whether or not to articulate the recognition at all. Rather glibly, one could argue that the notion of constitutive otherness obviates the problem of appropriation anyway, and of narcissism as well: the "other" discourse that one would appropriate was never purely other to begin with, while the "same" of one's own narcissistic desire was never purely same (thus also are the boundaries of "hetero" and "homo" thrown into question). More seriously, however, it should be stated immediately that the "problem" (if it can even be called that) of straight anxiety about being charged with appropriation is completely insignificant when compared to the real problems and fears of gays and lesbians living in a society predicated on what Eve Sedgwick calls "the overarching, hygienic Western fantasy of a world without any more homosexuals in it."[5] Still, for a collection such as this one, the issue of appropriation looms large and thus warrants this prefatory discussion.

James J. Sosnoski describes appropriation as "the assimilation of concepts into a governing framework . . . [the] arrogation, confiscation, [or] seizure of concepts."[6] Tracy B. Strong relates the word appropriation to its Latin root, *proprius*, which "carries with it connotations not only of property, but also of proper, stable, assured and indeed of common or ordinary." Strong writes:

I have appropriated something when I have made it mine, in a manner that I feel comfortable with, that is in a manner to which the challenges of others will carry little or no significance. A text, we might then say, is appropriated when its reader does not find him or herself called into question by it, but does find him or herself associated with it. A successfully appropriated text no longer troubles the appropriator that it has become part of his or her understanding, and it is recognized by others as "owned," not openly available for interpretation.[7]

It is appropriation in these senses of the word that the contributors to *Straight with a Twist* have attempted to avoid (though to claim assuredly that we have succeeded in our attempt would be to demonstrate that we have failed). Whatever our success, the desire behind the essays collected here is not to assimilate ourselves into queer theory or queer theory into any governing framework; it is not to arrogate, confiscate, or seize queer theory's varied conceptual tools and put them to straight use. Even less do we desire to install ourselves in a position of "comfort" relative to queer theory or to find ourselves no longer called into question by its provocations. We are suspicious of a desire that, as Joseph Aimone has put it, wants queer theory but wants nothing from it.[8] We do not want a queer theory that "no longer troubles" us, nor do we want to let our signs of engagement or association with queerness be read as proclamations of ownership.

Rather, the engagements articulated here remain open to interpretation and contestation. They want not to appropriate queer theory but to proliferate its findings and insights. Gloria Anzaldúa, in her introduction to *Making Face, Making Soul/Haciendo Caras: Creative and Critical Perspectives by Feminists of Color*, provides a very useful distinction when she writes that "the difference between appropriation and proliferation is that the first steals and harms; the second helps heal breaches of knowledge."[9] Given this distinction, let it be said that, whatever its ungovernable effects, the purpose of this collection is certainly not to steal or to harm.

But perhaps Anzaldúa's rhetoric of healing is not exactly appropriate here either. For ultimately the political intent of *Straight with a Twist* is to do its part in the project of "mak[ing] the world queerer than ever."[10] To the extent that it helps with that project, the collection will perhaps have done so less by healing breaches of knowledge than by helping to proliferate the discovery—the fundamentally queer discovery—of identity itself as a productively unhealable breach.

The idea for this collection originated from my efforts to think through some of the implications of my previous book, *Male Matters*. That book began as a self-consciously "male feminist" project, but an early reader suggested that its topic—the construction of normative masculinity through the repression of the male body—called for greater attention to gay male criticism than the book at that point evidenced. I have to admit that my initial inclination was to resist that suggestion, partly because of the concerns about appropriation described above, but also, as I came to understand, for reasons that have everything to do with my own construction as a heteronormatively masculine subject: in other words, my resistance was a function of homophobia. But since one of the points of *Male Matters* is that whatever provokes anxiety in the masculine subject needs to be not only explored but nurtured and developed, I eventually began to follow the reader's suggestion. Though the fruits of the resulting inquiry are somewhat apparent in *Male Matters* (and I am pleased to note that to date the most positive reviews of that book have been authored by gay men), they are rather more conspicuous in *Straight with a Twist*.

The collection developed through not unusual routes: a special session at the Midwest Modern Language Association Convention in 1994, followed by a broader call for papers in the *PMLA*. I invited ten or so of the most prominent figures in queer theory to contribute and received declines with kind encouragement from three. After receiving a fair number of submissions, I eventually asked Joseph Aimone, whom I had met through the MMLA session, and Catherine MacGillivray, who had joined me as a colleague at the University of Northern Iowa, to assist me in the editorial process.

It will be noticed that there are a fair number of contributors to *Straight with a Twist* who are either doctoral candidates or recent Ph.D.'s. We make no apology for this ratio: because queer theory is such a recent development, the majority of the people working in this emergent field are graduate students (as Berlant and Warner point out). We doubt that this situation has drastically changed since 1995. Indeed, given the current crisis in the academic job market, we imagine that most people working in queer theory are either still graduate students or have not yet found the tenure-track positions that would allow them to develop their scholarship.

The collection is divided into three sections—"Theory," "Literature," and "Culture." The scare-quotes are retained to suggest the permeability of boundaries between these demarcations and to unsettle the obviousness of the divisions themselves. My essay, which begins the "Theory" section, lays out the general problematic of straight negotiation of queer theory and then specifically explores the contradictions of my own response to a particular formulation by Judith Butler that explicitly gathers antihomophobic straights under the queer rubric. Jacqueline Foertsch continues in a similar vein, examining her own relationship as a heterosexual feminist to lesbian theory. Clyde Smith writes not as a literary or theoretical scholar but as a dancer, and his essay is included for its refreshingly experiential perspective. Lauren Smith returns us to the academic, examining challenges to the reproduction of the normative at the level of "self-expression" in the composition classroom.

The "literary" essays—by Goran Stanivukovic, Richard Nemesvari, John Duvall, and Mary Wiles—range historically and textually from Shakespeare to Dorothy Allison. We think that these essays are important not only because they demonstrate the variety of literary texts that are open to queer interpretation but because they foreground the value of theoretically informed close reading, a practice that we feel the cultural left is in danger of losing to conservative scholars who pine for a return to "literature for literature's sake." Though we no longer understand what that phrase could productively mean, neither do we feel that close attention to a literary text—such as is evidenced by the essays collected here—constitutes a betrayal of the political project of intervention into power relations that animates cultural studies.[11] Indeed, we feel that the desire to read closely is indispensible to that project and that the essays included here only help to further it.

Nevertheless, in the "Culture" section, the essays do veer away from "Literature": Katherine Gantz gives us a very engaging demonstration of the queer in *Seinfeld,* while Jane Garrity offers an up-to-the-minute examination of straight/lesbian tensions in recent film and television. Joseph Aimone's essay nicely problematizes the literature/culture divide, queerly crosscutting between Yeats's poetry and the film *To Wong Foo, Thanks for Everything! Julie Newmar.*

The collection ends with a dialogue between Catherine MacGillivray and myself, an exchange that was enjoyable and productive for us as colleagues and as friends and that we hope will be interesting to our readers. One salient fact about the conversation is that it was punctuated a number of times by the pre-symbolic—indeed, pre–mirror stage—interjections of Catherine's two-and-a-half-month-old son Merlin, a boy whose mother is, as she says, determined to raise him queerly. Of course, nothing is more conventional, or straighter, than recourse to an infant—particularly a white male infant—as a general emblem of hope for the future. On the other hand, that conventionality is disrupted when it is a queer future for which one hopes. Merlin's presence can serve to remind us that political interventions such as *Straight with a Twist* aspires to be are ultimately for human beings and that the queerer world that the contributors to this volume collectively desire would, indeed, be a more human world for all.

Notes

1. Lauren Berlant and Michael Warner, "What Does Queer Theory Teach Us about *X*?" *PMLA* 110:3 (May 1995): 343.

2. Andrew Parker, "Foucault's Tongues," *Mediations* 18:2 (Fall 1994): 80.

3. Judith Butler, "Against Proper Objects," *differences* 6:2–3 (1994): 21.

4. For an elaboration of the phrase "constitutive otherness," see Lawrence Cahoone, *From Modernism to Postmodernism: An Anthology* (Cambridge, Mass.: Blackwell, 1996): "What appear to be cultural units—human beings, words, meanings, ideas, philosophical systems, social organizations—are maintained in their apparent unity only through an active process of exclusion, opposition, and hierarchization. Other phenomena or units must be represented as foreign or 'other' through representing a hierarchical dualism in which the unit is 'privileged' or favored, and the other is devalued in some way" (16). For the rest of the theoretical itinerary, see Arthur Rimbaud, "Letter to Georges Izambard," *Complete Works and Selected Letters,* trans. Wallace Fowlie (Chicago: University of Chicago Press, 1966), 304; Friedrich Nietzsche, *The Gay Science,* trans. Walter Kaufmann (New York: Vintage, 1974), 246; Ferdinand de Saussure, *Course in General Linguistics,* ed. Charles Bally and Albert Sechehaye, trans. Roy Harris (La Salle, Ill.: Open Court, 1986); Jacques Lacan, *Écrits: A Selection,* trans. Alan Sheridan (New York: Norton, 1977); Louis Althusser, *Lenin and Philosophy and Other Essays,* trans. Ben Brewster (New York: Monthly Review Press, 1971); Michel Foucault, *The History of Sexuality,* vol. 1: *An Introduction,* trans. Robert Hurley (New York: Vintage, 1990); Jacques Derrida, *Speech and Phenomena and Other Essays on Husserl's Theory of Signs,* trans. David B. Allison (Evanston, Ill.: Northwestern University Press, 1973); Julia Kristeva, *Powers of Horror: An Essay on Abjection,* trans. Leon S. Roudiez (New York: Columbia University Press, 1982); Judith Butler, *Gender Trouble: Feminism and the Subversion of Identity* (New York: Routledge, 1990) and *Bodies That Matter: On the Discursive Limits of "Sex"* (New York: Routledge, 1993).

5. Eve Kosofsky Sedgwick, *Epistemology of the Closet* (Berkeley: University of California Press, 1990), 42.

6. James J. Sosnoski, "A Mindless Man-Driven Theory Machine: Intellectuality, Sexuality, and the Institution of Criticism," in *Feminisms: An Anthology of Literary Theory and Criticism,* ed. Robyn Warhol and Diane L. Herndl (New Brunswick, N.J.: Rutgers University Press, 1993), 50.

7. Tracy B. Strong, "Nietzsche's Political Misappropriation," in *The Cambridge Companion to Nietzsche,* ed. Bernd Magnus and Kathleen M. Higgins (Cambridge: Cambridge University Press, 1996), 125.

8. Aimone made these remarks during a special session at the Midwest Modern Language Association conference in November 1994. That session bore the name of this book and was one of its origins. I would like here to mention and thank the other participants: Jon Beasly-Murray, Mary V. Dougherty, Michelle K. Ephraim, Michael Maranda, Constance Morris-Shortlidge, and Richard Morris.

9. Gloria Anzaldúa, "Haciendo cara, una entrada," in *Making Face, Making Soul/Haciendo Caras: Creative and Critical Perspectives by Feminists of Color,* ed. Gloria Anzaldúa (San Francisco: Aunt Lute Books, 1990), xxi.

10. Michael Warner, "Introduction," in *Fear of a Queer Planet: Queer Politics and Social Theory,* ed. Michael Warner (Minneapolis: University of Minnesota Press, 1993), xxvii.

11. In a recent *PMLA* forum commenting on the aversion of some practioners of cultural studies to close textual readings, Rachel Bowlby writes: "It's as though cultural studies were afraid of being sucked into a celebration of Great Works at the very mention of the word *literature*" ("Forum: Thirty-two Letters on the Relations between Cultural Studies and the Literary," *PMLA* 112:2 [Mar. 1997]: 277).

Part 1 "Theory"

1

Straight with a Twist: Queer Theory and the Subject of Heterosexuality

Calvin Thomas

> Indeed, it may be only by risking the *incoherence* of identity that connection is possible.
> —Judith Butler, *Bodies That Matter*

The final chapter of Judith Butler's *Bodies That Matter: On the Discursive Limits of "Sex"* bears the conspicuous and rather provocative title "Critically Queer." At first glance, this title could seem to be offering only the less than startling suggestion that "queers"—with the word understood as referring to lesbians, gays, or bisexuals—are or can be "critical." More interestingly, however, the title also suggests that, just as there is more than one way to be "critical," there may be many more ways than one to be "queer." This suggestion of multiple if not limitless forms of queerness corresponds with certain formulations in the work not only of Butler but of other lesbian and gay theorists engaged in the postmodern "labor of ambiguating categories of identity."[1] It also provokes no few questions.

To begin with, to what extent does critical queerness—as differentiated from some other form or forms of queerness—depend on a specific identification with the words "homosexual," "bisexual," "lesbian," or "gay" and the outlawed sexualities these terms conventionally represent? How might a lesbian, gay, or bisexual subject fail to be sufficiently critically queer?[2] Conversely, and more to the point of this discussion, to what extent could an otherwise "straight" subject elaborate a queer criticism? If, as Lauren Berlant and Michael Warner suggest, membership in "queer publics" is "more a matter of aspiration than it is the expression of an identity or a history" ("Queer Theory" 344), what accounts for, or disallows, the decidedly ambiguous labor of straight queer aspiration? What problems and possibilities are opened up by questions of straight engagement with or participation in queer theory (or, as Berlant and Warner prefer to call it, "queer commentary")?[3] What does reading queer theory tell the straight reader about being queer, about being straight, about being, about becoming, what one putatively is, what one (supposedly thereby) is not, the permeability of the boundaries between the two, the price of their maintenance? Of what, if anything, might "otherwise straight" "critical queerness" consist? What exactly would it, or should it, if anything, perform? Other than voyeurism, appropriation, theoretical trendiness, or the desire to be a "good," responsible heterosexual critic, what might the draw of queer theory for straights be? What can antihomophobic straights do to help "make the world queerer than ever"?[4]

As an "otherwise straight" subject—an academic man, a reader and professor of feminist, queer, and other theory, who has long been involved in a committed, monogamous, state-sanctioned, fully benefited, but nonetheless quite happy, childfree relationship with a female artist—I would like to explore some of these questions here. I will do so, eventually, by focusing on my own problematic but perhaps illustrative response to a particular passage in *Bodies That Matter* where Butler specifically describes (albeit in passing) the possibility of a straight affiliation with the term "queer." I will begin, however, by examining some recent formulations within queer theory that, by virtue of their antiessentialist emphasis on queerness as "resistance to regimes of the normal" (Warner, "Introduction" xxvi), would seem to invite, or at least not explicitly forbid, something like a "queer aspiration" on the part of subjects who do not identify themselves as homosexual, gay, lesbian, or bisexual—or who at least could not base such identification on particular sexual practices, corporeal stylings, or specific "bodies and pleasures." These are formulations of discursive, performative, or "dis-positional" queerness that, given the inherent instability of discourse itself, would seem to trouble the stable boundaries of sexual identity or identity politics.[5]

For example, L. A. Kauffman writes in the *Village Voice* of "a new kind of politics, a post-identity politics of sorts. Queerness, in this view, [is] more a posture of opposition than a simple statement about sexuality. It [is] about principles, not particularities. 'To me,' explained [Queer Nation/San Francisco activist Karl] Knapper, 'queerness is about acknowledging and celebrating difference, embracing what sets you apart. A straight person can't be gay, but a straight person can be queer.'"[6] In *Making Things Perfectly*

Queer, Alexander Doty writes of "cases of straight queerness, and of other forms of queerness that might not be contained within existing categories or have reference to only one established category." Although he does not elaborate on what constitutes straight "cases," Doty does suggest "that new queer spaces open up (or are revealed) whenever someone moves away from using only one specific sexual identity category—gay, lesbian, bisexual, or straight—to understand and to describe mass culture, and recognizes that texts and people's responses to them are more sexually transmutable than any one category could signify—excepting, perhaps, that of 'queer.' "[7]

Michael Warner, in his introduction to *Fear of a Queer Planet,* writes the following about shifts in self-identification from "gay" or "lesbian" to "queer":

> The preference for "queer" represents, among other things, an aggressive impulse of generalization; it rejects a minoritizing logic of toleration or simple political interest-representation in favor of a more thorough resistance to regimes of the normal. For academics, being interested in queer theory is a way to mess up the desexualized spaces of the academy, exude some rut, reimagine the public from and for which academic intellectuals write, dress, and perform. . . . For both academics and activists, "queer" gets a critical edge by defining itself against the normal rather than the heterosexual. . . . The insistence on "queer" . . . has the effect of pointing out a wide field of normalization, rather than simple intolerance, as the site of violence. (xxvi)

Unlike Knapper or Doty, Warner does not allude to straight queerness here. Like theirs, however, his formulation does leave open the possibility of straight "resistance to regimes of the normal," if only because Warner does not explicitly state what would constitute the impossibility of such a stance. For other than the (admittedly formidable) unlikelihood born of safety and privilege, what is to prevent straights from "protesting not just the normal behavior of the social but the idea of normal behavior" (xxvii), from engaging in such protest even if the straights in question themselves behave largely (if not exactly) according to the norm? What would it mean for straights really to understand (and not just theoretically toy with) the queer argument that the normative regimens they inhabit and embody are ideological fictions rather than natural inevitabilities, performatives rather than constatives? After such knowledge, what normalness?

Warner provides a way of producing such antinormative knowledge in his essay "Homo-Narcissism; or, Heterosexuality." There, Warner points out that "the modern system of sex and gender would not be possible without a disposition to interpret the difference between genders as the difference between self and Other."[8] According to this disposition, Warner writes, difference is always an allegory of gender and "having a sexual object of the opposite gender is taken to be the normal and paradigmatic form of an interest in the Other or, more generally, in others" (191). Conversely, according to this heterosexist view—particularly, for Warner, as insistently articulated in Freudian and Lacanian psychoanalysis—if one's sexual object is of the same gender as oneself, then one has "failed" adequately to discern Self and Other, to erect the proper barricades between identification and desire: homosexuality thus becomes defined as a "regressive" or developmentally "arrested" function of autoeroticism or narcissism. Warner brilliantly demonstrates how in psychoanalysis this normative view is simply and bluntly asserted by fiat, how heterosexual romance is just as implicated in narcissism as any homosexualized ego ideal, and how heteronormativity occludes its own narcissistic investments by displacing them onto the queer.

What Warner's discussion leaves open, however, is the possibility— indeed, the desirability—of a generalized resistance to this normative interpretation of sexual difference as difference itself, a resistance in which straights could conceivably participate, not by surrendering or repressing their desire for sexual objects of the opposite gender, but by questioning the dominance of the assumption that such interest constitutes the natural paradigm of interest in the Other, or in others per se. In keeping with the terms set forth elsewhere in Warner's work, such a questioning could in and of itself qualify as queer. Indeed, as the preceding examples may suggest, straights, who would be definitionally barred from the terms gay, lesbian, or bisexual, could not be excluded from the domain of the queer except by recourse to the very essentialist definitions that queer theory is often at pains to repudiate.[9]

This definitional tension manifests itself in Eve Kosofsky Sedgwick's "Queer and Now" introduction to her essay collection *Tendencies*. There, Sedgwick writes that "queer" involves "the open mesh of possibilities, gaps, overlaps, dissonances and resonances, lapses and excesses of meaning [that occur] when the constituent elements of anyone's gender, of anyone's sexuality aren't made (or *can't be* made) to signify monolithically."[10] Sedgwick gathers a number of fish into this widely thrown net, including not only some of the usual suspects—"drags, clones, leatherfolk"—but also "fantasists," "feminist men," "masturbators" (talk about a universalizing move!), and "people able to relish, learn from, or identify with such" (8). She then goes on to praise "work around 'queer' [which] spins the term outward along dimensions that can't be subsumed under gender and sexuality at all" (8–9). But Sedgwick also concedes that queer must denote "almost simply, same-sex sexual object choice, lesbian or gay," and states that "given the historical and contemporary force of the prohibitions against *every* same-sex sexual expression, for anyone to disavow those meanings, or to displace them from the term's definitional center, would be to dematerialize any possibility of queerness itself" (8). Thus, even though queer commentary such as Sedgwick's relies on the now-familiar tropes of poststructuralist decentering—gaps, dissonances, lapses, and excesses of meaning—it must also recur to a nominally essential "definitional center" without which queerness would not be what it is. Though on one level queerness as elaborated by Sedgwick, Warner, and others is complex, mobile, and open enough of a mesh not to exclude some antinormative, sympathetic, fantasizing, or masturbating straights, on another level it must also not displace "almost simple" same-sex sexual object choice, lesbian or gay. This caution against same-sex displacement seems obvious and, I would imagine, welcome enough. But the crucial question thus perhaps becomes: does the very suggestion of the possibility of including straights in the queer mesh in and of itself constitute the disavowal of certain specifically sexual meanings, the displacement of "almost simply" self-identified lesbians and gays, and consequently the dematerialization of "any possibility of queerness itself"?

Such would seem to be the conclusion of several theorists for whom the overly general inclusiveness and despecificity of the term "queer" provide grounds for its repudiation. Teresa de Lauretis, for instance, dismisses "queer theory" as a marketing ploy that "has quickly become a conceptually vacuous creature of the publishing industry."[11] Moreover, in *The Practice of Love: Lesbian Sexuality and Perverse Desire*, de Lauretis questions certain feminist (rather than queer) desexualizations of lesbianism that work to afford heterosexual feminist women access to the term. De Lauretis respects but interrogates and finds wanting both Adrienne Rich's notion of the "lesbian continuum" and psychoanalytic feminism's "figuration of a female desiring subjectivity to which all women may accede by virtue of their 'homosexual' relation to the mother."[12]

Leo Bersani, in *Homos,* also warns against the dangers of despecification and desexualization posed by the emergence of the term "queer." Citing Warner's appeal to "resistance to regimes of the normal," Bersani writes:

"This generous definition puts all resisters in the same queer bag—a univer-salizing move I appreciate but that fails to specify the sexual distinctive-ness of the resistance. I find this particularly unfortunate since queer theo-rists protest, albeit ambiguously, against the exclusion of the sexual from the political."[13] By this point in his book, however, Bersani himself has already suggested that "if homosexuality is a privileged vehicle for homo-ness, the latter designates a mode of connectedness to the world that it would be absurd to reduce to sexual preference" (10). Later in *Homos,* Ber-sani amplifies what he means by homo-ness as "connectedness to the world" when he writes that it is what he calls "self-shattering [that] is intrinsic to the homo-ness in homosexuality." Homo-ness, he goes on to say, "is an anti-identitarian identity" (101).

Readers familiar with such examples of Bersani's work as *The Freudian Body* and "Is the Rectum a Grave?" will recognize his insistence on the intrinsic self-shattering of *jouissance.* But we may also wonder why he here connects such anti-identificatory self-shattering with the *homo-ness* and not the *sex* of homosexuality. Indeed, the problem Bersani faces in his elaboration of homo-ness is that of maintaining sexual specificity while at the same time avoiding an "absurd" reduction to sexual preference. That problem is at least partially resolved by the fact that, for Bersani, sexuality quite specifically is self-shattering—or rather, what Bersani values in sex-uality, and in art, is the capacity of both to shatter that "coherent self" that for him is both the effect and condition of possibility for institutionalized heteronormativity and hence "a sanction for violence."[14] As Jonathan Dollimore points out in *Sexual Dissidence,* Bersani "sees gay male sexuality as enacting insights into sexuality *per se* which heterosexual culture has to repress ruthlessly."[15] Ultimately, I would submit, Bersani holds that gay men (in certain of their specific sexual practices) have a greater, more prob-able, perhaps even a more profound access to an antiredemptive, antirela-tional (but thereby politically salutary) self-shattering than do straight men or women but that such access is not finally exclusive to gay male sex-uality. Otherwise, Bersani would indeed be reducing the anti-identitarian mode of connectedness he advocates (in terms similar to Judith Butler's in the epigraph to this essay) not only to sexual preference but to a quite specific sexual practice: rimming. He is not making that reduction, how-ever, and when he alludes to "celebrating 'the homo' in all of us" (*Homos* 10), he means, I think, radically enough, us all.

Moreover, Bersani's comments on what he considers the intrinsic self-shattering of "sexuality *per se*" reveal what is perhaps the most salient irony of the phrase "sexual identity": its two terms are mutually incompatible, so that any attempt to use sexual specificity to ground the exclusions that constitute identity and provide its contours must come to grief or comedy. If, as Bersani has it, sexuality is inimical to identity, then identity can scarcely be based on sexuality. But if nothing can be firmly based on the specifically sexual, "sexuality *per se*" can become the "privileged vehicle" for baselessness itself, for the antirelationality and anti-identitarian identity that Bersani calls homo-ness.

Still, the question of differences in access to "sexuality *per se*," of differences between gay and straight celebrations of " 'the homo' in all of us," remains vexed. In a sense, Bersani is letting gay male sexuality and/or "sexuality *per se*" serve as "vehicles" (that is to say, metaphors) for our all connecting to the world as something radically other than autonomous, sovereign, phallicized egos willing to kill to protect the seriousness of our statements and the sanctity of our identities: he advocates an exuberant discarding of the self through sex, particularly through "de-meaning" receptive male anal eroticism. And yet, if homo-ness as self-shattering world-connectedness cannot finally be reduced to sexual preference or be said to depend on specific sexual practices, then it too, like "queer," risks becoming an utterly generalized or dematerializing signifier: Bersani might as well be calling for a celebration of "the Buddha-nature" in all of us.[16]

The danger, then, of the overly generalized deployment of such terms as "queer" or "homo-ness" is that the terms can allow the straights who are drawn to them to sidestep interrogations of their own sexual practices—or, more precisely, the mutually reinforcing relationship between their culturally sanctioned sexual practices and their privileged and valorized social identities. Although, as I will presently suggest, the problem may be less practices than privilege, less heterosexuality than heteronormativity, none of these can or should be neatly separated. The ease with which straights can assume this separation—an ease to which my own thinking in working through this essay has been susceptible—is a conspicuous marker of privilege itself: straights have had the political luxury of not having to think about their sexuality, in much the same way as men have not had to think of themselves as being gendered and whites have not had to think of themselves as raced. Straights drawn to formulations of queerness or homo-ness need to interrogate their own sexual practices and the exclusions and repressions that make them possible. At the very least, a straight male theorist who feels "able to relish, learn from, or identify with" the insights of a Bersani or a Sedgwick would need to make some attempt to understand and work through his relationship to the receptive anal eroticism that they celebrate and that the dominant culture represses and reviles.[17]

However, though heterosexuality and heteronormativity cannot be separated, Bersani's formulation of homo-ness as a self-shattering "sexuality *per se*" to which we all have putative access but that "heterosexual culture has to repress ruthlessly" (Dollimore, *Sexual Dissidence* 321) does allow an interesting if problematic distinction to be drawn between the heterosexual and the heteronormative, a distinction that could bear directly on the question of straight queer aspiration: heterosexuals may have some access to homo-ness, whereas heteronormativity is perhaps constitutively antisexual. Again, I do not mean to suggest by this assertion that heterosexuality can be unproblematically pried loose from its heteronormative moorings. Nor do I mean to posit some natural, pure, or unsullied form of sex between men and women that exists before or outside of the heteronormative institutions that produce the very cultural intelligibility of sexual practices. I do mean to suggest that, in terms of the "labor of ambiguating categories of identity" (Berlant and Warner, "Queer Theory" 345), the labor that helps "make the world queerer than ever" (Warner, "Introduction" xxvii), the problem, the obstacle, may be less straight sexual practices per se than the privileging of those practices. What queerly aspiring straights need to interrogate, challenge, and work toward changing is less their own sexual practices than their condition of possibility.[18]

I will be returning to this distinction. Here, however, I turn to Judith Butler and to the way my own troubled response to her work can help exemplify the problems in straight interrogations of heteronormativity, the problems in straight queer aspirations or identifications. Butler herself is, of course, an insistently anti-identitarian thinker, perhaps queer theory's strongest advocate of committing political and discursive "disloyalty against identity"—a disloyalty, as she puts it, "that works the iterability of the signifier for what remains non-self-identical in any invocation of identity."[19] In *Bodies That Matter*, Butler addresses the way the signifier "queer" has been reappropriated and reworked by lesbian and gay activists—transformed, so to speak, from taunt to flaunt, from a hurtful slur into an emblem of positive identification. Butler writes that "queer" has become "the discursive rallying point for younger lesbians and gay men and, in yet other contexts, for lesbian interventions and, in yet other contexts, for bisexuals and straights for whom the term expresses an affiliation with antihomophobic politics. That it can become such a discursive site whose uses are not fully constrained in advance ought to be safe-guarded not only for the purposes of continuing to democratize queer politics, but also to expose, affirm, and rework the specific historicity of the term" (230). Allow me to report that, when I first read this passage, I underlined it heavily and then wrote in the margins, just alongside the phrase concerning "straights for whom the term expresses an affiliation," the words "at last!" I confess that this "at last!" marked a small outcry of what I can now only call pleasure on my part: the pleasure of being rec-ognized, acknowledged, included, if only in this completely anonymous way. "At last," after several hundred pages, Judith Butler was finally calling me a name, interpellating or hailing me as a straight subject for whom the term "queer" does indeed express an affiliation with antihomophobic pol-itics. Or so I wanted, and still want, to think—and to argue.

And yet, though I did not quite go so far as to erase my little outburst—as if anyone were likely to be examining my marginalia anyway—I did almost immediately think better, or at least more hesitantly, of this fleeting mo-ment of jubilation before the mirror of queer theory. I began to question this "at last!" with its rather obnoxiously impatient "it's-about-time-you-mentioned-me" tone of self-congratulation and self-insistence. After all, what business had I, heterosexual male, reading a lesbian's book and desir-ing recognition, expecting acknowledgment, demanding inclusion, like Mr. Ramsay demanding sympathy in Virginia Woolf's *To the Lighthouse*? What was the meaning of this desire to be mentioned, this impatience to be named, this insistence on visibility? (Though I was not conscious of being desirous, impatient, or insistent, my spontaneous response certainly seems to suggest that I was all three.) What was this unconscious anxiety, then, in the face of reading a few hundred pages that did not seem closely to concern my particular subject position? What does that discomfort amount to when compared with the thousands of pages of straight litera-ture and theory, the countless reels of mainstream film and hours of com-pulsorily heterosexual television, that lesbians and gays have suffered through for years without finding any such specific and positive trace of recognition but only the dominant culture's silence, hatred, and derision? Where did I get off with this "at last!" when my subject position had al-ready gotten and still gets much more attention than it ever deserved?[20]

Moreover, why exactly did I think I needed to jump at the straight bait when Butler's critically queer line already had me hooked? Why did I think that it was only now, at last, with this one positive reference to queerly affiliated straights, that Butler was finally counting me in when *I*—or perhaps the instability and incompletion of the subject-formation marked by that signifier—was actually "being addressed" all along? While on one level I was apparently searching *Bodies That Matter* for some indication that the book was "also" about me, on another less apparent level *I* must have been satisfied that the book was already about me, about the constitutive exclusions that form and thereby include *me,* that it was *really me* who was being hailed, that my relationship to Butler's discourse could not be one of complete exteriority.

I should say that my interest in *Bodies That Matter* was, on the one hand, professional and academic. Familiar with *Gender Trouble* and just finishing my own book on the abjected "matters" of the male body and their potential to trouble gendered (masculine) identity, I wanted to see how Butler's latest arguments would complement or complicate my own, what fresh footnotes would need to be appended to which chapters, and so on (in other words, whether my book actually was or was not "finished").[21] On the other hand, my interest in her book while caught up in reading it was not *purely* academic but seemed rather to be affectively engaged on the unpredictable level of identification and desire; and this engagement must have been evident to me well before the phrase in which *I* found myself "named." Otherwise, I doubt I would have read so thoroughly, so emphatically, so lovingly. Sure, lovingly: for though I would stop short of saying that I "simply loved" *Bodies That Matter* (not enough bodily matters, for my peculiar tastes), I would still submit that one rarely finds any sort of book compelling unless it somehow tugs on the bonds of love. As Jonathan Culler has recently pointed out, to read "with love" is not to read uncritically or disinterestedly but rather to be caught up in or possessed by a variety of different and often contradictory psychic and libidinal investments, among which he lists "aggressivity, transference, sadomasochism, identification, or fetishization."[22]

It is the penultimate item on Culler's list that would seem most pertinent here in relation to the questions opened up by my marginalia. Or rather, what seems to pertain here is the way "identification" as an active, ongoing, potentially endless process can be reified into "identity" as a putatively finished product, the way the process always threatens to subvert the product even as the latter works relentlessly to reconsolidate, or terminate, the former. What my "at last!" seems to articulate is exactly this tension, simultaneously libidinal and semiotic, between desire-identification (in which the boundaries between the two are unpredictably permeable and mobile) and desire/identity (in which the boundaries are ostensibly stable and thus the two terms mutually exclusive): on the one hand, a desire to be engaged, to be possessed, to be liked in the affective sense; on the other, the desire to be named, to be acknowledged, recognized, made visible, counted in, to be liked in the mimetic sense of having one's *own* likeness reproduced.

The fact remains, however, that though I had for several hundred pages of reading been caught (up) in the act of queer discursivity and had been unself-consciously identifying with many of Butler's performative reiterations, it was not until I "at last" saw "myself" named as a straight "for whom the term [queer] expresses an affiliation" that I imagined I had been, finally, liked (in both the affective and mimetic senses). Now, since in the Lacanian terms that Butler adopts and reworks it is the phallus that governs the dispensation of meanings and names, my pleasure in being named by Butler might indicate a sort of acknowledgment of her "lesbian phallus" within my "morphological imaginary." So far, perhaps, so good. But perhaps I also took Butler's strap-on all too like a man. For what my jubilation over "finally" being positively "recognized" as a "*straight* queer" may also indicate is that, in the name of identity and according to its exclusionary logic, my "at last!" had to some extent just consolidated the refusal of the very queer identification that had already been happening all along. Had I not, after all, just enacted what Butler would call a "refusal to recognize [an] identification that is, as it were, already made" (*Bodies* 113)? And does not the "refusal to identify with a given position [suggest] that on some level an identification has already taken place" (113)? As Butler poses the question: "What is the economic premise operating in the assumption that one identification is purchased at the expense of another? If heterosexual identification takes place not through the refusal to identify as homosexual but through an identification with an abject homosexuality that must, as it were, never show, then can we extrapolate that normative subject-positions more generally depend on and are articulated through a region of abjected identifications?" (112).

Following Butler's questions, I would submit that my allowing her to like me only as a straight (for whom the term queer expresses . . .) could in itself have expressed my "own" dislike, my "own" heteronormative disidentification with or abjection of the very term I had, in fact, been liking. In other words, my jubilant recognition of myself in Butler's mirror-ph(r)ase concerning "straights for whom the term [queer] expresses an affiliation with anti-homophobic politics" could itself have been an expression both of antihomophobic politics, of straight queer aspiration, and of homo-

phobia at the same time. My "at last!" could mark both a politically salutary move toward a disidentificatory practice, "a disloyalty against identity" (*Bodies* 220), a desire to reiterate heterosexuality differently, to be
straight *otherwise* (which is, of course, what I want it to signify), and, at the
same time, an all-too-familiar erasure of *otherness,* a most unwelcome reas-
sertion of and insistence on "my" straight subjectivity's normative centrality (which is what I do not want it to signify but which it may despite
my best intentions).

There are, then, it seems, valid political reasons for both my desire to
identify with the phrase concerning "straights for whom the term [queer]
expresses" and my growing suspicion of that desire. I dare say that many
gays and lesbians will with justification be considerably more suspicious of
my desire than I have managed to be in this essay thus far. On the other
hand, I would like to imagine that there are no few straights who, like me,
have begun to see the need for a critical interrogation of their "own" relationship to, and problematic identification/disidentification with, the
queer theory I presume and hope they have been reading. For whatever the
level of "our" straight aspirations toward or negotiations with queer theory may be, it needs, I think, to be accounted for, to be theorized. It should
neither be simply proclaimed (for, as I hope to have just demonstrated,
there would hardly seem to be any simple way to proclaim it) nor cursorily
dismissed as "appropriation," as what James J. Sosnoski describes as "the
assimilation of concepts into a governing framework. . . . [the] arrogation,
confiscation, [or] seizure of concepts."[23]

But if there are valid political reasons for straight negotiations with
queer theory to proceed (and equally valid reasons for proceeding with
caution), such proceedings themselves raise questions about the institutional delimitations of such theoretical, political, and pedagogical projects. For example, it should be noted that just as the 1980s saw what some
consider an egregiously depoliticizing move in the academy from "feminism" or "women's studies" to "gender studies"—a move that by some
strange coincidence seemed to work largely to accommodate men like
me[24]—so this decade sees what could be considered a similarly depoliticizing shift from specifically "gay and lesbian studies" to the more general "queer theory"—a move that potentially opens the doors to straights
(again, like me).[25] In that thin volume the October 1994 *MLA Job Information List,* for example, Cornell University's English Department invited
applications for twentieth-century specialists working "in Queer Theory

or Gay and Lesbian Studies." I doubt I am the only one who noticed that "or" and pondered its implications.

I would submit, however, that these terminological shifts within the profession—from feminism to gender studies, from gay and lesbian studies to queer theory—are, while potentially dangerous, not necessarily normativizing breaks with or betrayals of the political projects inscribed in the more specific nominations: they need to be read dialectically, in Fredric Jameson's sense of containing both reactionary and utopian potential. On the more obviously reactionary hand, what these transformations could be said to underscore is the deadly gravity that threatens to pull subversive or transgressive movements back toward the mainstream, thus emptying them of their subversive, transgressive content. Like my "at last!" dissected above, these shifts could be said to reveal just how intolerable it is for "my" subject position and the structures that produce and maintain it to be denied the privileged place of absolute centrality: men must be accommodated; straights must be allowed in the door.

On the more tenuously utopian hand, however, the possibility might be left open that gender studies, queer theory, and even my "at last!" are not altogether or necessarily signs of business as usual. After all, "gender studies" can do something more and other than waste faculty positions on "'bright boys'"[26] or allow men "into" feminism (an allowance that for some erases or deradicalizes the feminist agenda): it can also designate the critical process by which (some) men learn from feminism to make subversive interventions into the reproduction of normative masculinity itself.[27] From a certain feminist perspective, such interventions into masculinity— by feminist women and men—are necessary because, as Kaja Silverman puts it, "masculinity impinges with such force upon femininity [that] to effect a large-scale reconfiguration of male identification and desire would, at the very least, permit female subjectivity to be lived differently than it is at present."[28] I would submit, however, that such a large-scale reconfiguration is unlikely without the participation of feminist-informed men who are or have been themselves the putative subjects of heteromasculine paradigms of identification and desire.[29]

Similar points can be made about queer theory. It may do more than squander rare queer faculty positions on straights (if such has ever happened) or in some other way allow straights "into" gay and lesbian studies (again, an allowance that for some would dematerialize the very possibility of queerness itself); rather, it might designate the critical process by which straights can learn from gay and lesbian theory to make interventions into the reproduction of heteronormativity or compulsory heterosexuality. To use Silverman's language, such interventions are necessary because heteronormativity impinges with such force on homosexuality that to effect a large-scale reconfiguration of heterosexual identification and desire would, at the very least, permit queer subjectivity to be lived differently than it is at present. Again, however, I would submit that any large-scale reconfiguration is unlikely without the participation of those women and men who are themselves the putative subjects of heteronormative paradigms of identification and desire but who, for whatever reason, are "able to relish, learn from, or identify with" queers and queer theory.

Perhaps, then, my own troublesome marginalia and the very fact of my writing this essay need not necessarily be read as heralds of what Butler calls the "institutional domestication of queer thinking," that "normalizing [of] the queer [that] would be . . . its sad finish."[30] After all, despite the way I glommed on to the word "straight" in Butler's phrase (in a desire for acknowledgment perhaps politically inappropriate but nonetheless difficult to eradicate), and despite the desire for a safe identity that continued to subtend the risk of identity's incoherence (so that identification was abjected and identity itself perhaps never really put at risk)—despite all of that, I would still maintain that there is something, well, queer about wanting to be recognized as a straight for whom the term "queer" expresses an affiliation with antihomophobic politics (as problematic as that desire for recognition itself might be). Though lesbians and gays may be justifiably suspicious of me as an ally, those who are our (if I can risk that possessive pronoun) most conspicuous enemies—the Christian Coalition and their Republican cohorts—would hardly mistake me for a friend.

Because I do teach their children.[31] And I do hope to participate in what bell hooks calls "teaching to transgress," in "education as the practice of freedom."[32] I believe that it is important not only for "us" to make antihomophobic politics a structural component of "our" teaching practice (along with feminism and antiracism) but that it is important—indeed, crucial—for me as a straight white man to do so. For one political irony I have noted and have asked students to note in the ten years or so that I have been professing feminism as an academic man is that I often have some modest success in making feminist interventions—that is, in getting nonfeminist-identified male and female students to recognize the social and political realities of male domination and women's oppression—precisely because I am a man, because the students are all too well trained by patriarchy to associate my male voice with that of disinterested and objective authority and truth and so, sadly enough, to accept feminism from me more readily than they would from a feminist woman. My being a man at least prevents students from dismissing, with the all-too-familiar blather about male-bashing, axe-grinding, or merely "personal" grievance, the feminist analysis I present to them (while feminist students, when I am lucky enough to have them in my classrooms, can help me see the blind spots in my own presentations).

That this irony obtains is, of course, and as I also point out to students, a clear sign of how much feminist work remains to be done. In the feminist work that I try to do, I exploit my privileged position as much as I can in a way that, arguably, only someone in such a position is able to do. Or so I like to think. But, of course, the phrase "as much as I can" is troublesome. How can I know to what extent I "exploit" my position, to what extent I "subvert" it—the old saw about "subverting from within"—and to what extent I merely preserve my straight, white male privilege and resist any real threat to it? For I, after all, can always retreat to that position of safety that I may, in fact, have never left; I can always reclaim that identity whose incoherence I may never really have risked. My body is never "really" put on the line. I have the luxury of a political unconscious.

Moreover, there is a certain tenuousness in the analogy I have been leading up to here between professing feminism as a man and in some way "doing" queer theory as a straight. On the one hand, there is some basis for the analogy in the strong connections between misogyny and homophobia that prevail within the dominant culture. Despite the complexities of these connections, the fact remains that one of the reasons for the dominant culture's hatred of gay men is that, in liking to be fucked by other men, they are perceived as behaving sexually "like women." As Catherine Waldby writes:

> Homophobic violence . . . and homophobia in general might also be ways of adjudicating the anxiety aroused in heterosexual men by their own penetrability. If a potential for passive anal pleasure is denied, its denial can be acted out as violence against or contempt for, those who are interpreted as wishing to either experience such pleasure themselves, or to "impose" it on another. In this sense the repression or elision of anal eroticism in heterosexual men can be seen to work not only along the lines of the masculine/feminine divide, but also along the homosexual/heterosexual divide.[33]

Heterosexual male derogation of "penetrable" women, then, helps consolidate and exacerbate straight hatred of, anxieties about, and violence against gay men. Conversely, the celebration of women in all human capacities—including the capacity to enjoy being fucked—can work to defuel and dissipate the hatred of men who may enjoy the same thing.[34] Not that straight male anxieties about penetrability totally account for misogyny and homophobia; not that varieties of homophobia among feminists and misogyny among gay men do not flourish; not that feminist and queer politics are automatically or necessarily the same thing: but there are compelling reasons for projecting the two as being in structural solidarity. So there would seem to be a political logic in suggesting that the project of being/teaching as a male feminist would lead necessarily to that of being/teaching as a straight for whom the term "queer" expresses . . .

And yet, on the other hand, I can teach and profess feminism until the cows come home without ever feeling myself "in danger" of being "mistaken" for or, more to the point, "treated as" a woman. In fact, given the number of films in the last ten years or more that feature men "getting in touch with their 'feminine' side"—from *Tootsie*, with Dustin Hoffman in drag, to the more recent *Junior*, which offers the spectacle of a pregnant Schwarzenegger—I would imagine that discourses of androgyny or imputations of male "femininity" are no longer particularly troublesome for many straight men—provided, of course, that "femininity" or even "maternity" imply absolutely nothing sexual. In other words, it is quite all right for straight men to "get in touch with 'the feminine side,'" to acknowledge the "woman within," provided that "she" neither "values powerlessness"—to use Bersani's words[35]—nor enjoys being fucked.

But the comfort level plunges—and conventional, exclusionary logic reels—at the more radical suggestion that the straight man might "get in touch with his queer side." After all, there is little "danger" in an untransgendered man's being literally mistaken for a woman: the mistake rarely happens and can be easily "rectified." But there can be nothing more terrifying to what Monique Wittig calls "the straight mind"[36] than being "mistaken" for a "queer." This power of horror dominates the straight mind, particularly the straight male mind, not simply because the dominant culture's most repetitive message to men is that it is infinitely preferable for them to compete with each other viciously, to batter each other violently, even to murder each other brutally than it is for them to fuck each other passionately. This terror of being mistaken for a queer dominates the straight mind, again, not simply because, since bad things do happen to "real" queers, bad things could also happen to the straight "mistakenly" or (worse) "unjustly" taken for a "queer" ("unjustly," as if, according to the same logic for which there are "innocent" victims of AIDS, the real queers who get bashed, or murdered, or infected with HIV, are simply getting their just desserts).

The terror of being mistaken for a queer dominates the straight mind because this terror *constitutes* the straight mind: it is precisely that culturally produced and reinforced horror of/fascination with abjected homosexuality that produces and maintains "the straight mind" as such, governing not so much specific sexual practices between men and women (after all, these things happen) as the institution (arguably antisexual) of heteronormativity itself. For according to some queer theorists, heteronormativity, "straightness as such," is less a function of other-sexual desire than of the disavowal or abjection of that imagined same-sex desire upon which straightness never ceases to depend. To quote D. A. Miller, the "only necessary content" of male heterosexuality is "not a desire for women, but the negation of the desire for men."[37] As Miller continues, this necessary negation is such that "straight men unabashedly *need* gay men, whom they forcibly recruit (as the object of their blows or, in better circles, their jokes) to enter into a polarization that exorcises the 'woman' in man through assigning it to a class of man who may be considered to be no 'man' at all" (135). Homophobia, then, is on one level the fear of homosexual women and men. On another level, it is the disavowal of this dependence on homosexuals, of the structurating necessity of this negation. On another level still, homophobia entails not only the fear of those who are abjectly identified (and depended on) but also the fear of being abjectly identifiable oneself: the fear, as the word most literally means, of being "the same as." This latter fear is arguably a much stronger component of homophobia than of, say, sexism or racism (despite the mechanisms of projection and abjection doubtless at work in those forms of hatred), because the sexist male or the racist white is in much less "danger" of being "mistaken" for a woman or a nonwhite than the straight is of being "mistaken" for a queer. For that reason, despite the structural, constitutive roles "femininity" and "blackness" play in constructions of "masculinity" and "whiteness," the role played by "queerness" in the construction of "straightness" is even more structural and constitutive: racism and sexism, that is, certainly help to "keep one" white and male but not in the same way or to the same extent that homophobia works to "keep one" straight.[38]

Several consequences arise from this positing of homophobia as the fear of being out of one's own keeping, an aspect of the fear of non-self-identity as such and perhaps—at least at this particular historical juncture—the dominant culture's most prominent figure for that fear. First of all, despite postmodern theory's destabilizations of such "biological" matters as sexual difference or skin pigmentation as self-evident empirical indices of gendered or racialized identity, the dominant culture itself blithely continues to behave as if such matters could be taken "for granted" as compelling or reassuring evidence of identity-formation. But the dominant culture is more suspicious, more self-suspicious—and hence more self-policing—when it comes to "proving" heterosexuality. For it is possible, after all, to "fake" the "realest" possible "evidence" of heterosexuality: man or woman, one can participate in heterosexual marriage and even help produce a brood of spawn and still "turn out" to have been "living a lie," to have been "really" gay or lesbian all along. Precisely because there is no final "proof" of heterosexuality, heterosexuality must constantly set about trying to prove itself, assert itself, insist on itself. Indeed, as Butler argues, heterosexuality as hegemonic institution is finally nothing more than its own repetitive self-insistence, nothing other than "a constant and repeated effort to imitate its own idealizations" (*Bodies* 125). Or, as Janet E. Halley puts it in regard to legalistic constructions of heterosexuality, normative heterosexuality "is a highly unstable, default characterization for people who have not marked themselves or been marked by others as homosexual." As Halley continues: "The resulting class of heterosexuals is a default class, home to those who have not fallen out of it."[39] Heteronormativity, then, has something—itself—to prove but has no other proof of itself that its own repeated efforts at self-demonstration. The structurating persistence of homophobia within heteronormativity would seem the strongest evidence not only that its best efforts have proven insufficient but that such insufficiency—and hence the relentless need for "proof"—is integral to heteronormativity's very mechanisms of self-production.

A second point arising from the notion of homophobia as fear of non-self-identity per se is that such fears can only be conflated in response to specific historical pressures that work to constrain and maintain identity-formation as such. If we follow Foucault's well-known argument in *The History of Sexuality* that it was not until the nineteenth century that a network of medical and juridical discourses produced the equation between sexual practices and the "truth" of personal identity—that it was not until the nineteenth century that the homosexual "became a personage"[40]— then we recognize that it is only after the nineteenth century that homophobia as fear of being identified as homosexual could subtend in any extensive way the fear of non-self-identity per se. In other social and historical contexts, other fears (involving class, nationality, race, or religious affiliation) could have a more dominant role in the maintenance of coherent identity boundaries or ego-syntony. However, in this particular context—by which I mean the contemporary United States—I would argue that homophobia is so dominant among the fears of non-self-identity that are currently culturally deployed to produce identity as such that the fear of being marked "different" as such is thoroughly intricated with, if not overdetermined by, the fear of being queered.

My point here is that the fear of being queered, of being out of one's own keeping, could work to "constrain in advance" the otherwise straight's queer aspiration, his or her desire to affiliate with a term that expresses antihomophobic politics, in ways the aspirant may not immediately recognize. As Bersani puts it in *Homos*: "Given the pressures and privileges intrinsic to the position one occupies on the great homo-heterosexual divide in our society, we can . . . appreciate the anxiety, on the part of those straights most openly sympathetic with gay causes, not to be themselves mistaken for one of those whose rights they commendably defend" (1). I must admit, then, that this anxiety may subtend whatever risks I may think I take as a straight professor who "does" queer theory (for I could hardly profess straightness and at the same time claim not to participate in that which I have just argued constitutes it). Certainly this anxiety is inscribed in my "at last!" in my effort to reclaim identity in the midst of a (potentially) radically disidentificatory gesture (for what is identity, after all, but the effect of having controlled, having reeled in, one's errant identifications?). With that "at last!" in other words, I seem to say that I am quite pleased and satisfied to have identified with queer discourse and even to identify with the signifier queer—so long as it is understood that I am "really" straight.

I also must confess that I confront my own fear of being queered when I encounter, in Lauren Berlant and Elizabeth Freeman's essay "Queer Nationality," the following advice from a treatise called "I Hate Straights": " 'Go tell [straights to] go away until they have spent a month walking hand in hand in public with someone of the same sex. After they survive that, then you'll hear what they have to say about queer anger. Otherwise, tell them to shut up and listen.' "[41] Although this passage is directed not at "straights for whom the term queer expresses . . ." but rather toward "straights [who] ask the gay community to self-censor, because anger is not 'productive' "—a request I have never made—the passage nonetheless leads me to face my own hesitancy to conduct the monthlong experiment it describes.[42] It suggests that, while identity may be discursively constructed, to risk identity only at the level of discourse is to risk very little indeed. It compels me to admit that "I" must, after all, be deeply afraid of being taken for a queer.

However, one important point arising from Butler's argument is that on a certain level the straight is, to use a tired phrase, always already taken for a queer, self-mis-taken for a queer, and that there is, therefore, in a sense, really no mistake at all. For as Butler might put it, to profess straightness is to claim identity within an economy that assumes that one identification can only be purchased at the expense of another. What this expensive assumption lays bare is the fact that other identifications are available for purchase but have been refused. But as Butler suggests, the refusal of an identification indicates that on some level it has already taken place. If straightness, therefore, depends structurally less on other-sex desire than on abjected queer identification, then to profess straightness is always to acknowledge that, on some level, *one must have already taken oneself for a queer.*[43]

One possible goal, then, of a straight negotiation with queer theory is to let this acknowledgment proceed. The point would be neither to appropriate the signifier queer nor to arrogate or confiscate queer theory but rather to proliferate the findings of queer theory in unexpected ways, or at least from unexpected points of enunciation, in the hope, however feeble, of reiterating heterosexuality otherwise. Such a reiteration begins with, and perhaps can be nothing more than, the recognition and acknowledgment that straightness, like all identity-formation, is an effect of constitutive exclusion and thus never ceases to depend on the excluded, the *part maudit,* the abjected itself—the recognition and acknowledgment that all along one has needed "the queer" that one really is(n't) to be "the straight" that (no) one (ever) really is. Such a recognition would constitute a challenge— a limited challenge, granted, but a challenge nonetheless—to an institutional heterosexuality that imagines itself safely ensconced within its own "natural" self-sufficiency, that reiterates itself as solely and transparently a function of other-sex desire, that presents itself as what Diana Fuss calls "a practice governed by some internal necessity" rather than by constitutive exclusion. For if, as Fuss writes, compulsory heterosexuality "secures its self-identity and shores up its ontological boundaries by protecting itself from what it sees as the continual predatory encroachment of its contaminated other,"[44] then radical heterosexuality or self-conscious straightness—which is to say, other-conscious straightness, straightness that recognizes and somehow acknowledges its dependence on the queerness in which it does(n't) participate—would not protect but rather open itself to the possibility of its own structural dependence on its constitutively excluded other. It would, in other words, own up to the exclusions by which it proceeds, as well as to the ultimate unownability of its own or any other idealizations. For if heteronormativity (or institutional heterosexuality) is nothing more than the effort to live up to its own relentlessly reiterated ideals, "a constant and repeated effort to imitate its own idealizations" (*Bodies* 125), then self(-as-other)-conscious straightness—straightness, that is, with a twist[45]—is not and can never exactly be the "ideal" (institutional, compulsory) way for heterosexuality to reiterate or imitate itself. Straightness *with a twist* would, rather, work to mitigate, or militate against, those institutional, compulsory ideals, those compulsory performances. As Butler puts it:

> Insofar as heterosexual gender norms produce inapproximable ideals, heterosexuality can be said to operate through the regulated production of hyperbolic versions of "man" and "woman." These are for the most part compulsory performances, ones which none of us choose, but which each of is forced to negotiate. I write "forced to negotiate" because the compulsory character of these norms does not always make them efficacious. Such norms are continually haunted by their own inefficacy; hence the anxiously repeated effort to install and augment their jurisdiction. The resignification of norms is thus a function of their inefficacy, and so the question of subversion, of *working the weakness in the norm,* becomes a matter in inhabiting the practices of its rearticulation. (*Bodies* 237)

Of course, like any other form of postmodern "subversion," the political value of "working the weakness in the norm" is open to question. But if there is any political value in straight queer aspiration, in straight disloyalty to straight identity, it may be only this: to assist in working the weakness in the heterosexual norm, to inhabit the practice of heterosexuality's rearticulation and inhibit its hegemonic dominance. If heterosexual norms are, as Butler puts it, "continually haunted by their own inefficacy," then perhaps the work of the straight theorist with queer aspirations is somehow to be that inefficacious ghost in the house of heteronormativity.

As I hope to have suggested here, however, such work, such haunting, can be conducted only from critical positions that are themselves constrained by culturally produced anxieties that may be acknowledged after the fact but cannot always be known and mastered in advance. As Butler would argue, however, it is exactly this lack of mastery, this productive failure to master the terms of identity, anxiety, and desire, that needs to be safeguarded and promoted in the interest of proliferating critical queerness, of risking identity's incoherence. What and how much straights can do to proliferate queerness, to make the world queerer than ever, remains to be seen, and I hope here to have opened a question rather than to have offered any final words. But I would submit that whatever any of us do, however we perform (and whomever we perform with), the extent to which our actions and performances are "critically queer" may be the extent to which we promote connections—erotic and political, with others and with the world—that indeed seem possible only if identity and identity politics are allowed to be put at risk.

Coda

Butler writes: " 'Queer' derives its force precisely through the repeated invocation by which it has become linked to accusation, pathologization, insult. This is an invocation by which a social bond among homophobic communities is formed through time. The interpellation echoes past interpellations, and binds the speakers, as if they spoke in unison across time. In this sense, it is always an imaginary chorus that taunts 'queer' " (*Bodies* 226).

As a straight, I know that I have most likely in some way (though I cannot recall specific instances) lent my voice to this chorus. But I have also heard it singing and thought that it was singing to me. Two choral incidents, or echoes of past interpellations, both well before the possibility of my considering any "straight" affiliation with the signifier "queer": I am sixteen or so, standing with a group of men in the grocery store where, working for my father, I spent no small part of my childhood and adolescence. I have managed to "establish" my heterosexuality, letting the fact of my being "sexually active" with my "girlfriend" be known, participating in the heteromasculinist rituals of ogling and "rating" women shoppers, and so forth. And yet, when a woman passes by pushing a shopping cart laden with screaming kids, and I casually remark that I do not really like children very much, one of the men (he worked in the meat market) turns to me. Eyes narrowed to slits, he says: "What are you, some kinda queer?"

He did have a point. That is, he spoke the logic of heteronormativity with a relentless precision. For the imperative behind the norm is not simply to enjoy having sex with women but (since we are using the Althusserian language of interpellation here) to reproduce the conditions of production. Heteronormative sex is teleologically narrativized sex: sex with a goal, a purpose, and a product. The ends—children—justify the means, which are otherwise unjustifiable. The child, then, is not simply the outcome of but the justification for having engaged in sex. As Bersani puts it: "There is a big secret about sex: most people don't like it" ("Rectum" 197). That is, most "people" do not like sex because, again, as Bersani has it, sex is inimical to personhood, incompatible with the self as a structured (heteronormatively structured) ego. So perhaps, as I suggest in passing in the body of this essay, heteronormativity is antisexual in that it will only tolerate sex as a means toward the reproduction of "the person"—both in terms of "the child" and the ego. Perhaps heteronormativity, then, is abrogated whenever people actually like sex. And perhaps people who do like sex (the childfree het couple, for example) are, in a sense, "queer" (the man in the grocery store certainly thought as much). Correspondingly, perhaps people who fuck in the name of identity, who make an identity out of whom they fuck, who fuck to reproduce "the person," are fucking heteronormatively—are, in a sense, "breeders"—even if "the person" or "identity" thereby reproduced is "homosexual."

Second incident/interpellation: It is ten years or so later, and I am walking in daylight through my neighborhood in Atlanta: Midtown, an area so well known to have a large gay male population that goon squads from the suburbs and hinterlands would often drive through looking for gays to taunt and bash. So it is no surprise when a car pulls up from behind, and slows down, and the chorus sings: "Hey, *queer!*"

I *turned.* Perhaps not in the full "one-hundred-and-eighty-degree physical conversion" described by Althusser in his example of interpellation as turning in response to being hailed by the policeman who says: "Hey, you there!"[46] But I did turn. Had it been night, I might have had to turn and run, since I am not sure what I might have done to "prove" that they had "the wrong man," had "mistaken" my "identity." After all, I had turned. I was walking in a "gay" neighborhood. I was wearing "gay" clothes: jeans and a shirt. And I do not think the postmodern argument that all identity is a mistake, a "necessary error" (Butler, *Bodies* 229), would have been much help even if I had even known anything about such notions at the time. Fortunately for me, the car sped on, with a great squealing of tires on the hot Georgia asphalt, and I was left only with the knowledge that I had turned—a vague knowledge, a recognition, with which I did not exactly know what to do. Twenty years and a whole lot of theory later, I do not know in the name of what I would say that it was not "really me" who was really "meant by the hailing," that it was not "me" who was "really" being addressed.

Notes

An earlier version of this chapter appeared in *Genders* 26 (1997): 83–115 and is used here by permission of New York University Press.

1. Lauren Berlant and Michael Warner, "What Does Queer Theory Teach Us about *X*?" *PMLA* 110:3 (May 1995): 345. Subsequent references to this work will be included parenthetically in the text.

2. "Critical" in this usage obviously invokes political investment, as Andrew Parker's discussion in "Foucault's Tongues" would suggest: commenting on "the genealogy of queerness as a non-gender-specific rubric that defines itself diacritically not against heterosexuality but against the normative," Parker goes on to say that this distinction is "captured neatly in what I think is a pretty fair joke: 'What's the difference between gay and queer?' 'There are no queer Republicans'" (*Mediations* 18:2 [Fall 1994]: 80).

3. In "What Does Queer Theory Teach Us about *X*?" Berlant and Warner write: "In our view, it is not useful to consider queer theory a thing, especially one dignified by capital letters. We wonder whether *queer commentary* might not more accurately describe the things linked by the rubric, most of which are not theory. The metadiscourse of 'queer theory' intends an academic object, but queer commentary has vital precedents and collaborations in aesthetic genres and journalism. It cannot be assimilated to a single discourse, let alone a propositional program" (343).

4. Michael Warner, "Introduction," in *Fear of a Queer Planet: Queer Politics and Social Theory*, ed. Michael Warner (Minneapolis: University of Minnesota Press, 1993), xxvii. Subsequent references to this work will be included parenthetically in the text.

5. I take the word "dis-positional" from Ed Cohen's essay "Are We (Not) What We Are Becoming? 'Gay' 'Identity,' 'Gay Studies,' and the Disciplining of Knowledge," in *Engendering Men: The Question of Male Feminist Criticism*, ed. Joseph A. Boone and Michael Cadden (New York: Routledge, 1990), 160–75. There, Cohen answers the question of identity politics with the hearty cry, "'Fuck identity.' Or perhaps more accurately, let's not make an 'identity' out of whom we fuck" (174). Cohen goes on to counsel "abjuring our hard-won gay and lesbian 'identities' in favor of more relational, more mobile categories: 'gay dis-positions' or 'lesbian attitudes,' for example" (174). See also Cohen's "Who Are 'We'?: Gay 'Identity' as Political (E)motion (A Theoretical Rumination)," in *Inside/Out: Lesbian Theories, Gay Theories*, ed. Diana Fuss (New York:

Routledge, 1991), 71–92, where he asks: "How can we affirm a relational and transformational politics of self that takes as its process and its goal the interruption of those practices of differentiation that (re)produce historically specific patterns of privilege and oppression?" (89).

6. L. A. Kauffman, "Radical Change: The Left Attacks Identity Politics," *Village Voice*, 30 June 1992, 20.

7. Alexander Doty, *Making Things Perfectly Queer: Interpreting Mass Culture* (Minneapolis: University of Minnesota Press, 1993), xvii–xix.

8. Michael Warner, "Homo-Narcissism; or, Heterosexuality," in *Engendering Men*, ed. Boone and Cadden, 191. Subsequent references to this work will be included parenthetically in the text.

9. Although the question of exclusion seems prominent in my discussion thus far, I do not intend this essay as some inane lament that straights are being excluded from an interesting new theoretical project or that the contributions of straights to this project are not being adequately recognized. I do attempt to address the problematic of my own desire for inclusion, recognition, and visibility later in the essay, but here I would stress that my purpose is not to whine about exclusion but to explore the productive definitional tensions opened up by new reworkings of the term "queer."

10. Eve Kosofsky Sedgwick, *Tendencies* (Durham, N.C.: Duke University Press, 1993), 8. Subsequent references to this work will be included parenthetically in the text.

11. Teresa de Lauretis, "Habit Changes," *differences* 6:2–3 (1994): 297.

12. Teresa de Lauretis, *The Practice of Love: Lesbian Sexuality and Perverse Desire* (Bloomington: Indiana University Press, 1994), xvii. For negative or "critique-al" readings of queer theory that concern not its sexual overinclusiveness but its conspicuous failure to produce Marxist revolution, see Rosemary Hennessey, "Queer Visibility and Commodity Culture," *Cultural Critique* 29 (Winter 1994–95): 31–75; Don Morton, "Birth of the Cyberqueer," *PMLA* 110:3 (May 1995): 369–81. Hennessey's essay is for the most part a salutary reminder of the need to consider queer theory in terms of the relations between sexuality and capitalism; however, she seems overly eager to reduce all queer theory to an academic marketing ploy, to "capital's insidious and relentless expansion," to a "gay visibility aimed at producing new and potentially lucrative markets," and thus to strategies in which "money, not liberation, is the bottom line" (32). Morton similarly but less convincingly collapses all queer theory into a ludic postmodernism that he judges to be nothing but (*quel surprise*) the latest ruse and symptom of late capitalism. See also Don Morton, "The Politics of Queer Theory in the (Post)Modern Moment," *Genders* 17 (1993): 121–50. For a response to Hennessey, see Dennis Allen, "Lesbian and Gay Studies: A Consumer's Guide," *Genders* 26 (1997): 23–50.

13. Leo Bersani, *Homos* (Cambridge, Mass.: Harvard University Press, 1995),

71–72. Subsequent references to this work will be included parenthetically in the text.

14. Leo Bersani, "Is the Rectum a Grave?" *October* 43 (Winter 1987): 197–222. Subsequent references to this work will be included parenthetically in the text.

15. Jonathan Dollimore, *Sexual Dissidence: Augustine to Wilde, Freud to Foucault* (Oxford: Oxford University Press, 1991), 321. Subsequent references to this work will be included parenthetically in the text.

16. Actually, one could argue that in a strange way Bersani's arguments do resonate with certain Buddhist deconstructions of the self, but that would require another essay altogether. For discussion of "discarding the self" as the objective of Buddhist practice, see Mark Epstein, *Thoughts without a Thinker: Psychotherapy from a Buddhist Perspective* (New York: Basic Books, 1995).

17. For an interesting extension of Bersani's points about anal eroticism to the specific question of straight male sexuality, see Catherine Waldby's excellent "Destruction: Boundary Erotics and the Refigurations of the Heterosexual Male Body," in *Sexy Bodies: The Strange Carnalities of Feminism,* ed. Elizabeth Grosz and Elspeth Probyn (New York: Routledge, 1995), 266–77. Waldby writes: "Anal eroticism carries disturbingly feminizing connotations. Part of the significance of intercourse understood in its ideological aspect is its assertion not just of the woman's penetrability but of the man's impenetrability, the exclusive designation of his body by its seamless, phallic mastery. . . . But the possibilities of anal erotics for the masculine body amount to an abandonment of this phallic claim. The ass is soft and sensitive, and associated with pollution and shame, like the vagina. It is non-specific with regard to genital difference in that everybody has one. It allows access into the body, when after all only women are supposed to have a vulnerable interior space. All this makes anal eroticism a suasive point for the displacement of purely phallic boundaries" (272). Given Waldby's comments, it may seem a tremendous evasion on my part to say that exploring the relationship between *my* straight male identity and *my* anal eroticism (digital, relatively shallow, and largely solitary) is beyond the scope of this essay. I do, however, rather extensively consider the question of the anus as a site of significant leakage for masculine subjectivity in *Male Matters: Masculinity, Anxiety, and the Male Body on the Line* (Urbana: University of Illinois Press, 1996), though even there, because I focus more on "productive" than receptive anal eroticism, I remain open to the charge of keeping my ass covered.

18. I find problematic, anyway, the notion that subjects can voluntaristically "change" their sexual practices. Certainly, change is possible; but such voluntarism plays all too well into the right-wing religious rhetoric of homosexuality as a perverse but alterable "lifestyle choice" and pseudotherapeutic efforts to convert gays and lesbians to "healthy" heterosexuality. Moreover,

though I agree with Bersani that there are salutary political *possibilities* inscribed in anti-identitarian sexuality per se, it is not clear to me, or to him, that any specific sexual practice has an intrinsic political value in itself nor, correspondingly, that any change in sexual practice has intrinsic political value.

19. Judith Butler, *Bodies That Matter: On the Discursive Limits of "Sex"* (New York: Routledge, 1993), 220. Subsequent references to this work will be included parenthetically in the text.

20. Judith Roof makes some comments that are pertinent here in her review essay "Hypothalamic Criticism: Gay Male Studies and Male Feminist Criticism," *American Literary History* 4:2 (Summer 1992): 355–64. Referring to Boone and Cadden's *Engendering Men,* Roof writes: "this anthology's biggest anxieties (and most annoying tics) are linked to problems of recognition: . . . to the proper acknowledgement of male feminist efforts, to the continual reminder of the presence of 'right-thinking,' well-meaning men. This is not to say that anxieties about visibility are necessarily harmful or appropriative; it is to question how the specific stake in visibility shapes the interrelation among connected but diverse critical practices" (356–57). My aim here is to interrogate my own anxiety, not to insist on visibility or to engage in what Roof calls "the struggle for the right kind of visibility [that] continues among men in a battle that seems to shift the stake of identity politics from authenticity and a 'right' to speak to the crucial importance of being seen speaking" (357). The unavoidable irony, of course, is that I am here visibly offering my self-interrogation up for recognition (or at least for reading).

21. See Thomas, *Male Matters.*

22. Jonathan Culler, "Lace, Lance, and Pair," *Profession 94* (New York: Modern Language Association, 1994), 5.

23. James J. Sosnoski, "A Mindless Man-Driven Theory Machine: Intellectuality, Sexuality, and the Institution of Criticism," in *Feminisms: An Anthology of Literary Theory and Criticism,* ed. Robyn Warhol and Diane L. Herndl (New Brunswick, N.J.: Rutgers University Press, 1993), 50. Concerning "appropriation": while I fully understand the sentiment that straight affiliations with queer theory can pose the threat of "appropriation" in the sense of an arrogant confiscation that negates difference and works to erase signs of the real social presence of lesbians and gays, it seems problematic to me that in some discursive contexts merely to *charge* appropriation—without having demonstrated where and how the appropriation takes place (a demonstration that would necessarily depend on some attention to specific existing articulations)—is to *prove* appropriation. This is politically understandable, perhaps even strategically desirable, and certainly the burden of proof should be placed largely on the subject supposed to appropriate. But the charge of appropriation can function as an expedient way of not actually having to consider or contest the legitimacy or validity of a specific interpretation or argument. As for myself, I

admire the distinction Gloria Anzaldúa makes—in her introduction to *Making Face, Making Soul/Hacienda Caras: Creative and Critical Perspectives by Feminists of Color* (San Francisco: Aunt Lute, 1990)—between "appropriation" and "proliferation." I would like, but do not expect, this essay to be received as an example of the latter.

24. In a 1994 interview, Rosi Braidotti characterizes gender studies as "the take-over of the feminist agenda by studies on masculinity, which results in transferring funding from feminist faculty positions to other kinds of positions. There have been cases . . . of positions advertised as 'gender studies' being given away to [i.e., wasted upon] the 'bright boys.' Some of the competitive take-over has to do with gay studies. Of special significance in this discussion is the role of the mainstream publisher Routledge who, in our opinion, is responsible for promoting gender as a way of deradicalizing the feminist agenda, re-marketing masculinity and gay male identity instead" (Judith Butler, "Feminism by Any Other Name," *differences* 6:2–3 [1994]: 44–45). Although she has valuable things to say in other portions of this interview, here Braidotti seems to see not just queer theory but all gay studies only as a marketing ploy with no other purpose than the erasure of feminism. This view is problematic in that it occludes the fact that, as Joseph Allen Boone points out, "many of the men in the academy who are feminism's most supportive 'allies' *are* gay" ("Of Me[n] and Feminism," in *Engendering Men,* ed. Boone and Cadden, 23). See also Craig Owens, "Outlaws: Gay Men in Feminism," in *Men in Feminism,* ed. Alice Jardine and Paul Smith (New York: Methuen, 1987), 219–32. Braidotti also ignores the fact that some "studies of masculinity" have been conducted by feminists: for example, Kaja Silverman's *Male Subjectivity at the Margins* (New York: Routledge, 1992). Finally, Braidotti's formulation is also a bit disingenuous in that it pretends that feminism and the careers of certain feminist theorists have not been helped by the marketing strategies of "mainstream" publishers such as Routledge.

25. Does a straight male's engagement with feminism *necessarily* lead to a negotiation with queer theory? That is, can the gender system be investigated by anyone without a consideration of the hetero/homo divide, or, as Eve Kosofsky Sedgwick contends in *Epistemology of the Closet* (Berkeley: University of California Press, 1990), would anyone's investigation of any aspect of modernity be "not merely incomplete, but damaged in its central substance to the degree that it does not incorporate a critical analysis of modern homo-heterosexual definition" (1). Conversely, as some feminists have charged, might a move toward queer theory, with its emphasis on sexualities, provide a convenient means of neglecting feminism's insistent focus on sexual difference and gender asymmetry?

For discussions of the problematic relationship between feminism and queer theory, see the *differences* issue entitled "More Gender Trouble: Feminism Meets Queer Theory" (6:2–3 [1994]), particularly Judith Butler's essay "Against Proper Objects" (1–26) and her interview with Braidotti, "Feminism by Any Other Name" (27–61). For a discussion of the way queer theory's emphasis on sexualities can work to efface or ignore gender, see Biddy Martin, "Sexualities without Genders and Other Queer Utopias," *diacritics* 24:2–3 (1994): 104–21. As for the question of a necessary connection between male feminism and queer theory, I should say that my own work, as exemplified in *Male Matters*, began as a more or less self-consciously "male feminist" project but was pushed toward the question of queer theory not by my own desire to be theoretically trendy but by readers of the manuscript who suggested that the absence of attention to gay male criticism was its major blind spot. I have to confess that, for this straight male feminist, the push toward queer theory— a push against my own initial resistance and indifference—was a function more of the relatively autonomous velocity of an intellectual project than of my own conscious desire.

26. See Braidotti's comments in note 24.

27. Along with Boone in "Of Me(n) and Feminism," I still consider Alice Jardine's essay "Men in Feminism: Odor di Uomo or Compagnons de Route?" in *Men in Feminism*, ed. Jardine and Smith, 54–61, to contain the best practical advice for such men.

28. Kaja Silverman, *Male Subjectivity at the Margins* (New York: Routledge, 1992), 2–3.

29. And yet this "male feminist" participation is unlikely to reconfigure anything at all if it "redefin[es] feminist method as a politics of visibility . . . which then applies to males as *equal* victims of an oppressive, obscuring gender system" (Roof, "Hypothalmic Criticism" 356; emphasis added), or if "the turn to gender obfuscates or denies the asymmetrical relation of sexual difference" (Butler, "Against Proper Objects" 49). To say that the gender system is oppressive, and to suggest that within that system "masculinity" is no less of a gendered position, no less of a "social category imposed upon a sexed body" (Joan Scott, *Gender and the Politics of History* [New York: Columbia University Press, 1988], 32), than is "femininity," is not to say that the two positions are symmetrical nor that the system oppresses both genders equally—as some critics of the "turn to gender" suggest that the turn itself implies. For example, in Butler's interview "Feminism by Any Other Name," Braidotti states that "the focus on gender rather than sexual difference presumes that men and women are constituted in symmetrical ways. But this misses the feminist point about masculine dominance. In such a system, the masculine and the feminine are in a structurally dissymmetrical position: men, as the empirical referent of the masculine, cannot be said to have a gender; rather they are expected to carry the Phallus—which is something different. They are expected to exemplify abstract virility, which is hardly an easy task" (38).

Though I would certainly grant Braidotti's last point, I fail to understand how the exemplification of abstract virility that is expected of masculinity is not gender, particularly if gender is understood in de Lauretis's terms as "the process of assuming, taking on, identifying with the positionalities and meaning effects specified by a particular society's gender system" ("Habit Changes" 302). To insist, then, on masculinity as gender, and on the politically salutary contributions of men to gender studies, is, again, not to presume that "men and women are constituted in symmetrical ways." Therefore, I would disagree with Braidotti's point "that gender studies presumes and institutionalizes a false 'symmetry' between men and women" (Butler, "Feminism by Any Other Name" 38).

30. Butler, "Against Proper Objects," 21.

31. I turn this particular phrase to allude to comments reportedly made recently by America's favorite demagogue (and, as Al Franken has recently called him with great accuracy, "big fat idiot"), Rush Limbaugh: "When lampooning an academic who had written about 'male lesbians,' [Limbaugh] sternly offered this warning: 'This woman is teaching your kids.' When a caller told him, 'I'm gonna be a conservative professor,' Limbaugh responded, 'We need every one of you that we can get' " (Jeff Klinzman, "Life with Dittohead; or, How I Learned to Stop Worrying about Right-Wingers and Just Dig the Beat," *Wapsipinicon Almanac* 5 [1995]: 47). Now, I am not sure exactly which of us academics it was who had written about "male lesbians" (though a likely candidate would be Jacquelyn Zita, "Male Lesbians and the Postmodern Body," *Hypatia* 7:4 [1992]: 106–27), nor do I know exactly what a male lesbian would be, other than a male-to-female transsexual who has sex with women. But there are, I think, reasons for the designation to be attractive, not as a marker of identity—and let me clearly state that while I might include the term in a general rubric of straight queer aspiration, I do not claim to identify or "style" myself as a male lesbian—but rather as a signifier that might strategically assist in "the labor of ambiguating categories of identity" or in resisting "regimes of the normal." Not the least reason for the term to be compelling is its rhetorical power to appall, irritate, and mystify a Rush Limbaugh.

On the other hand, the umbrage that the term might cause some lesbians themselves, who have certainly been irritated enough, is sufficient reason to let it drop. Ed Cohen, for example, mentions "male lesbians" in "Are We (Not) What We Are Becoming" (174), and Judith Roof is not amused, calling Cohen's phrase "a jest perhaps, but too close to the truth of habitual masculinist assumptions to be really funny" ("Hypothalamic Criticism" 362). Butler, however, in *Bodies That Matter*, apparently is not joking when she asks: "And if [a] man desires another man, or a woman, is his desire homosexual, heterosexual, or even lesbian? And what is to restrict any given individual to a single identification?" (99). It is, of course, salutary to ask about the grounds for restriction. But one might also ask what, exactly, would constitute a man's sexual desire for a woman as "lesbian"? What, for that matter, constitutes lesbian desire as lesbian? In *The Practice of Love,* de Lauretis writes about the problematic relationship between lesbian and certain feminist identifications. She writes that "the seductiveness of lesbianism for feminism lies in the former's figuration of a female desiring subjectivity to which all women may accede by virtue of their 'homosexual' relation to the mother. . . . Without denying for a moment that the relation to the mother has a fundamental influence on all forms of female subjectivity, I will argue that woman-identification and desire or object-choice do not form a continuum, as some feminist revisions of Freud would have it. The seduction of the homosexual-maternal metaphor derives from the erotic charge of *a desire for women which, unlike masculine desire, affirms and enhances the female-sexed subject and represents her possibility of access to a sexuality autonomous from the male.* But in the great majority of feminist psychoanalytic writings (Rose, Doane, Silverman, Sprengnether, Gallop, Jacobus, etc.), such access is paradoxically secured by erasing the actual sexual difference between lesbians and heterosexual women" (xvii; emphasis added).

I do not want to address the larger terms of de Lauretis's argument here. Even less do I want to erase the actual sexual difference between lesbians and heterosexual men by suggesting that the two groups "have something in common"—that is, women as objects of desire. What I do want to suggest is that, since there is nothing natural or inevitable about "masculine desire," there is no reason why heterosexual men could not adopt or aspire toward the emphasized description above as a sort of ethics (provided, of course, that the word "autonomous" is read in terms of subjective sexual agency rather than in the exclusive sense of separation). What I am suggesting, in other words, is the possibility of obversing the "masculinization of the lesbian" that obtains in classical, normative psychoanalysis and working toward what might be called a "lesbianization" of masculine desire. Or, rather, working toward a version of masculine desire, call it whatever, that, unlike the one de Lauretis names, affirms and enhances female-sexed subjectivity.

32. bell hooks, *Teaching to Transgress: Education as the Practice of Freedom* (New York: Routledge, 1995).

33. Catherine Waldby, "Destruction: Boundary Erotics and the Refigurations of the Heterosexual Male Body," in *Sexy Bodies,* ed. Grosz and Probyn, 272–73.

34. On cultural assumptions about the incompatibility between penetrability and power—both male power/authority and female or feminist empowerment—see Bersani's "Is the Rectum a Grave?" Commenting on the notions of "moral incompatibility between sexual passivity and civic authority" that

Foucault detected in ancient Greek thought, Bersani writes that "the moral taboo on 'passive' anal sex in ancient Athens is primarily formulated as a kind of hygienics of social power. *To be penetrated is to abdicate power*. I find it interesting that an almost identical argument—from, to be sure, a wholly different moral perspective—is being made today by certain feminists" (ibid. 212). The feminists Bersani goes on to name are, of course, Catharine MacKinnon and Andrea Dworkin. In her critique of MacKinnon in *Beyond Accommodation: Ethical Feminism, Deconstruction, and the Law* (New York: Routledge, 1991), Drucilla Cornell also examines the putative incompatibility between having power and being fucked: "In order to challenge MacKinnon's apparatus of gender identification, we also need to challenge the two kinds of selves, rigidly designated as male and female, that are produced by it. Under MacKinnon's view of the individual or the subject, the body inevitably figures as the barrier in which the self hides and guards itself as the illusionary weapon—the phallus—in which 'it' asserts itself against others. But why figure the body in this way? Why not figure the body as threshold or as position of receptivity. As receptivity, the body gives access. To welcome accessibility is to affirm *openness* to the Other. To shut oneself off, on the other hand, is *loss* of sensual pleasure. If one figures the body as receptivity, then 'to be fucked' is not the end of the world. The endless erection of a barrier against 'being fucked' is seen for what it 'is,' a defence mechanism that creates a fort for the self at the expense of *jouissance*. . . . My suggestion is . . . that it is only if one accepts a masculine view of the self, of the body and of carnality, that 'being fucked' *appears* so terrifying" (154).

Cornell's formulation—tying the terror of being fucked with a masculine view of the self, a view that necessarily masculinizes or phallicizes power—resonates with Bersani's definition of phallocentrism: "the temptation to deny the . . . strong appeal of powerlessness, of the loss of control. Phallocentrism is exactly that: not primarily the denial of power to women (although it has obviously also led to that, everywhere and at all times), but above all the denial of the *value* of powerlessness in both men and women" ("Rectum" 217). I reproduce at such great length these comments from Bersani and Cornell not to suggest that straight men need necessarily to rush out and get fucked to prove their antimisogynist/antihomophobic mettle. What I would submit is that straight men need to recognize the way their fears of being fucked, their anxieties about anal eroticism, and their participation in the devaluation of powerlessness all help constitute heteromasculine subjectivity. Such recognition could perhaps help reconfigure that subjectivity or at least help prevent the projections and disavowals that fuel misogynist and homophobic violence.

35. See note 34.

36. Monique Wittig, *The Straight Mind* (Boston: Beacon Press, 1992).

37. D. A. Miller, "Anal *Rope*," in *Inside/Out*, ed. Fuss, 128. Subsequent references to this work will be included parenthetically in the text.

38. In *Homos*, Bersani writes: "Unlike racism, homophobia is entirely a response to an internal possibility. Though racism and homophobia both include powerful projective energies, the projections are quite different. A white racist projects onto blacks some lurid sexual fantasies of his own, but essentially his version of 'the nature of blacks' . . . is a response to what he sees as an external threat, a threat to personal safety, economic security, and the achievements of white civilization. Blacks are a dangerous and inferior race, and they may destroy us. But not even racists could ever fear that blacks will seduce them into becoming black. Homophobia, on the other hand, is precisely that: to let gays be open about their gayness, to give them equal rights, to allow them to say who they are and what they want, is to risk being recruited" (27).

39. Janet E. Halley, "The Construction of Heterosexuality," in *Fear of a Queer Planet*, ed. Warner, 83, 85.

40. Michel Foucault, *The History of Sexuality*, vol. 1: *An Introduction*, trans. Robert Hurley (New York: Vintage, 1990), 43.

41. Lauren Berlant and Elizabeth Freeman, "Queer Nationality," in *Fear of a Queer Planet*, ed. Warner, 201.

42. I should stress that my hesitation is not about holding a man's hand but about doing so in public, and for a month, particularly in the exceedingly small and achingly backward Iowa town (it is not even the relatively queer-friendly Iowa City) where this essay was written. One does not have to be gay to be afraid, and justifiably so, of homophobic violence. In any case, the point of the "I Hate Straights" treatise is less to compel straights to prove their commitment by putting themselves in harm's way but rather to demand that straights recognize their own privilege, their ability to take for granted their own safety in public displays of physical affection or desire.

43. I like the auto- and homoeroticism implied in the expression "to take oneself." I sometimes tell students that anyone who has ever masturbated—which is to say, everyone—is "queer" in the sense of having participated in what is necessarily a form of same-sex activity, whatever the heteroerotics of one's reveries or visual aids. A silly enough point, perhaps, but you would be surprised how uncomfortable it makes the frat boys, who are, typically, the last ones to deny masturbation but also the ones most at pains to reiterate themselves as hets. And perhaps the homo-ness of masturbation as a universal form of self-shattering self-relation is partly what Bersani has in mind when he writes of " 'the homo' in us all" (*Homos* 10). For as he asks: "Who are you when you masturbate?" (103). Compare again Sedgwick's inclusion of "masturbators" on her queer list in *Tendencies* (8).

44. Diana Fuss, "Inside/Out," in *Inside/Out*, ed. Fuss, 2.

45. In *The Self and Its Pleasures: Bataille, Lacan, and the History of the Decentered Subject* (Ithaca, N.Y.: Cornell University Press, 1992), Carolyn J. Dean writes that "Bataille remains, to be sure, a man, but a different sort of man; he remains heterosexual, but he is a straight man with a twist" (240).

46. Louis Althusser, *Lenin and Philosophy and Other Essays,* trans. Ben Brewster (New York: Monthly Review Press, 1971), 174.

2

In Theory If Not in Practice: Straight Feminism's Lesbian Experience

Jacqueline Foertsch

In the window of a leather shop at the back of Bourbon Street one day, a T-shirt I had seen once or twice on campus caught my attention. It was black (of course) and stretched tightly over the impressive breasts of the female mannequin on display. In elaborately feminine, almost too-flowery-to-discern script were the words "Everybody Thinks I'm Straight." "Me, too," I said to my (straight-identified) self, though actually addressing the "lesbian" in the window. "Don't you hate that?"

My encounter with this message brought to mind a position advanced by a favorite lesbian theorist, Judith Butler, who wrote a few years back, "identity categories tend to be instruments of regulatory regimes, whether as the normalizing categories of oppressive structures or as the rallying points for a liberatory contestation of that very oppression. This is not to say that I will not appear at political occasions under the sign of lesbian, but that I would like to have permanently unclear what that sign signifies."[1] Butler's construction "would like to have" suggests that it is up to her or any of us to decide what our respective "signs" will mean, yet she later seriously questions whether it is possible to enjoy what Carol-Anne Tyler calls an "indexical"[2] relation to the names attached to us: "Can sexuality even remain sexuality once it submits to a criterion of transparency and disclosure, or does it cease to be sexuality precisely when the *semblance* of full explicitness is achieved?" (Butler, "Imitation," 15; emphasis added). Our very constitution as sexual selves, she argues, depends on an "opacity designated by the unconscious" that prevents the meaning of our respective sexualities from ever fully manifesting itself.

A decidedly more conscious opacity operates at the political level in a straight society that cannot see homosexuality as other than an outrage when it does not "disappear" altogether "into the presumptive universal"[3] of a heterosexual consciousness. Yet the assumption of straightness about a lesbian person, while dehumanizing and thus infuriating, is only marginally more problematic than mainstream society's assumption of my own straightness: it is not that we assume certain people are straight who in fact are not; it is that we assume straightness in *every* person.

Back in front of the leather shop, I contemplate entering to make a purchase. I am, after all, as bothered as any gay activist by society's automatic gender assigning and consider for a moment buying every such shirt in the store—distributing them to my similarly inclined straight and gay colleagues and suggesting we wear them to all our classes on the first days of school next semester. Our students will immediately be thrown into a mental confusion whose every outcome will provide an enlightening insight for themselves and a positive, campuswide political effect: either "there are sure a lot more gay people in this world than I ever thought there were" (in some cases this number will be up from zero); or "these teachers cannot all be gay; surely there must be something about gender identity that I cannot simply read on the surface."

Gay and lesbian student organizations on my campus and others have already developed such an incisive strategy, sponsoring an annual "Jeans Day" during which all students supportive of gay and lesbian lifestyles wear their jeans to demonstrate this support. The choice of this clothing item as political code-for-a-day is fiercely clever: not only does it enable gay-affirmative straight students to use what is already "in their closets" to make a vital political statement; it likewise allows still-closeted or just-coming-out students to show their support for or even identification with the group in a manner that is nonpressurized and, at the level of fashion, universally accepted. The greatest coup of all, however, is the "outing" of the "straightest," most entrenched conservatives on campus, for whom jeans are a no-funny-business sartorial staple. Not even aware that it is "Jeans Day," much less aware of the radical message their pants are giving out about them, otherwise homophobic students are enlisted in a cause anathema to them, "counted" in the fight for gays' and lesbians' civil rights without ever putting down their *National Reviews*. Again, the mere replication of such a fashion "statement," body after body across the campus, turns it into a fashion "question" with important ramifications, both political and theoretical: what *is* the relationship between these jeans (or T-shirts) that are everywhere and the "limits" of queer identity, between the exterior and interior of one's gendered self?

It occurs to me that, within an activist agenda, I would have greater effect wearing my jeans and that black T-shirt than would some of the lesbians I know. In fact, the shirt would not "look right" on any lesbian who chose to wear it, since the message was designed to coincide with the look of a particular wearer—the femme who passes more or less easily for straight in the first place, as opposed to the butch who would fool nobody except maybe Jesse Helms.[4] Like my lipsticked sisters in the lesbian realm, I can more easily infiltrate a group that assumes that I, like them, am indifferent to the advancement of gay and lesbian rights, as removed from queer worlds as any "normal" person would be. In the past I have enjoyed whipping out lesbian-authored scholarship and creative works on a plane or at the beach, hooking the eyes of those around me on the provocative titles and artwork; the T-shirt, exposed after removing a seemingly innocent jacket or sweater, would only complete the picture.

Yet further recollection of Butler's theory suggests that buying this shirt would be a waste of my money, wearing it a waste of my effort (as it takes, of course, exhausting amounts of courage to put on such a shirt for any reason), since while "Everybody Thinks I'm Straight, No One Really Believes It After All." Butler refers to all gender roles as "repeat performances," a restaging of that which is without an original run yet is also always a minute variation, making gendered identity a temporal proposition, a condition that evolves with us throughout our lives and reflects our individual histories.[5] Heterosexuality, however, is not only performative but *compulsory,* thus illusory, a tightrope act that is really a magic act, ultimately impossible to sustain: "if heterosexuality is compelled to *repeat itself* in order to establish the illusion of its own uniformity and identity, then this is an identity permanently at risk, for what if it fails to repeat, or if the very exercise of repetition is redeployed for a very different performative purpose?" ("Imitation" 24).

Butler is asking two different questions at the end of this quotation: the second, regarding the "redeployment" of repetition, refers to the activity of gays and lesbians who adopt cross-dressing or exaggerated straight roles to subvert the traditional order; but the first, regarding the mere "failure to repeat" that is the heterosexual's own self-subversion, the permanent risk presented by his or her "psychic excess," prompts the answer that I, that all of us who identify as straight, waste our time trying to sustain the illusion that it is a straight world out there (and in here) when in fact it is anything but. That we are ultimately aware of our abysmal mistakenness on this issue accounts for the virulence of homophobia in our society yet more immediately provides the impetus to keep me moving down the sidewalk, away from that T-shirt in the window: the preposterous falseness of my heterosexual "identity" will out without the accompanying fashion statement—will "out" all of us in the end.

Yet other forces move me down the sidewalk, as well. I know very well that to many in the lesbian community my wearing of that shirt would constitute an enormous travesty, a betrayal of the tenuous bond our shared positioning on the feminist continuum affords us, and thus undo any political or psychic good I may have tried to work in the first place. I am fascinated by a remark, made by Diana Fuss in a later essay from *Essentially Speaking,* that "in general current lesbian theory is less willing to question or to part with the idea of a 'lesbian essence' and an identity politics based on this shared essence. Gay male theorists, on the other hand, following the lead of Foucault, have been quick to endorse the social constructionist hypothesis and to develop more detailed analyses of the historical construction of sexualities."[6] Fuss chalks up the difference between these modes of theorization to the difference between gay men's and lesbians' respective levels of oppression: although victimized by homophobia in many respects, gay men are still *men* and thus enjoy not only more privileges in an androcentric society but also more "air time" in discursive and thus philosophical and psychological registers as well. Even the taxonomizing and pathologizing of the gay male "specimen" in earlier centuries, often to the obscuration or total exclusion of his lesbian counterpart, at least fed the ontologic validity of gay men, the "right" of them to exist at all, and eventually led to the wealth of much more historically and philosophically astute discourse on "the homosexual" (man) that has followed in our own century.

Fuss identifies this greater oppression as the cause of lesbian "insecurity" and suggests that such insecurity is the impetus for an emphasis on essentialism and identity politics as practiced by any group. I question, however, whether it is insecurity or in fact an exact opposite that best describes the position of lesbians in contemporary culture. Fuss herself argues that " 'lesbian' is a historical construct of comparatively recent date" (*Essentially Speaking* 45), and we must understand that she sees this term (let alone, for the moment, the woman it is said to represent) as "recently constructed" compared to discursive markers for gay men, straight women, and straight men. Of these four bluntly divided groups, then, there is indeed an extremity of lesbian representation—an ultimate "invisibility" if one reads this extremity negatively, or an ultimate extradiscursivity if one reads it in a more liberating sense.

Straights—the most heavily culturally represented, encoded, celebrated, but also confined—stand at the opposite, originating end of this spectrum, gay men somewhere in the middle, enjoying an existence in the Symbolic register somewhere between the dawn of human sexuality and the current moment.[7] Lesbian subjectivity, a relative neophyte in the represented universe, may offer an outsider like myself an especially productive moment for intersubjective interaction before centuries of "diagnoses," legal statutes, manifestos, and critical victories coalesce around and solidify it; or it may (as Fuss suggests it does) emphatically remove itself from the interaction I am suggesting by withdrawing into an unbreachable "essential experience" it neither can nor wants to move beyond at this point.

Thus, while Butler has often wondered whether Aretha Franklin could be singing "You Make Me Feel Like a Natural Woman" to her, I am fairly certain that that T-shirt, while perhaps teaching, reminding, scolding, or warning me, is surely not "singing" to me. While I am definitely its target consumer in one respect, it is the message that some other, more proper owner of that shirt bears toward me on her chest, not the shirt itself, that is being marketed to me. Thus my relationship to the "lesbian in the window," though more importantly to the "lesbian in the T-shirt," remains at the level of the discursive: I can read (or listen to) what she has to say, but I cannot walk a mile in her shirt.

Yet even discursive relations between lesbian and straight gender theorists can get one into trouble, given the entirely troublesome nature of gendered identity to begin with. For a conference on sexuality and gender sponsored by Tulane University a few years ago, I considered the nature of my position—as a straight-identified feminist within lesbian theory—recognizing that my interface with the novels, poetry, philosophies, and political texts of favorite lesbian writers was arguably a "lesbian experience" yet one in urgent need of further exploration. What had I to offer this engaging body of work that coincided with straight feminism at so many crucial intersections but that remained a body significantly different from mine, attractive and exciting but not at the explicitly sexual level by which lesbians enter and find voice? What were the dimensions and boundaries of this position that, perforce, could not identify itself as lesbian yet presumed, as "lesbian theorist" nevertheless, to describe my experience inside gay women's texts as an effectively lesbian one? While *her* position was broader and deeper, enunciative at multiple levels, was not mine, by virtue of its roots in whatever we might term the "not-lesbian," not accessible to her and therefore worth the delineation?

I flirted with the ambiguity of the term "lesbian theorist," arguing that the Foucauldian impasse[8] posed by the double question—"Does she *do* lesbian theory?" or "*Is* she a lesbian with broader, perhaps completely other, theoretical interests?"—characterized the fluid nature of lesbian identity itself. I recalled for my audience the now-famous "lesbian continuum" described by Adrienne Rich and the chance but emphatic remark made by Judith Butler at Tulane shortly before the conference that "we are *all* lesbians."[9] I pointed out that both these feminists, while occupying opposite poles of a radical/deconstructive spectrum, were arguing for a notion of identity so unrestricted and liberating that they invited and even forced us to reconsider the makeup of lesbian positionalities and gender constructions as a whole.

Made brave by a wealth of statements such as these, I dared to assume for myself a lesbian identity, different from that of the "practicing lesbian" yet particular to lesbian experience and thus contributory to lesbian theory just the same. In explicating the ideas of several major lesbian theorists, my aim was to point to a curious contradiction that ran through much of the debate: these theorists and others, arguing from both essentialist and deconstructive positions (sometimes within the course of the same essay), claimed that identity assumptions of the type I was attempting were either fruitless (if not harmful) or not only beneficial but inevitable. Several claimed that the only position from which to do gender studies was from outside the hegemonic "heterosexual contract," leaving committed gender scholars no other role to take on, or at least attend to in unprecedented ways, than that of the theoretical lesbian.

My audience's response following the reading was spirited though hardly congratulatory. My attempt to cross this significant boundary, I realized, had challenged some to defend a position that many of us in the straight feminist movement had long ago left behind—that of the eternal and transcendent Woman, recast here as the "essential lesbian" that Fuss identifies above—a position unchanging and impervious, if not to the inevitable vicissitudes of a poststructurally rendered language, at least to the likes of upstart "squatters" like myself whose motives were highly suspect. We were soon divided into two camps, though each consisted of straight- and gay-identified audience members—the essentialists enforcing a boundary between lesbian experience and whatever was "other" to it, the deconstructors insisting that binaries like that did not even exist.

I would like now to restate the core of my original argument, then return to the discussion begun between my audience and myself, mediated at this point, however, by a more complex terminology and theoretical approach set forth in recent writings that may enable us to find some common ground.

In her important 1988 essay for *Signs,* Linda Alcoff opens the debate triangulating essence, history, and agency by arguing that gender, while absolutely constituted through discourse, also provides the necessary point of political departure, the footing without which political action is impossible. Alcoff contends that to acknowledge membership in a traditionally oppressed group when you have been previously culturally assimilated is to practice effective "identity politics." Her example is an assimilated Jew who henceforth chooses to be Jewish-identified as a strategy against anti-Semitism. Alcoff adds the examples of black men and of women of all races to make clear that all oppressed groups can claim their marginal identities and turn a once-victimizing situation into a politically powerful one. In the same way, a claim to lesbianism made by someone who has never identified herself as such before may make an equally powerful political move—indeed, even more powerful, as the act of coming out presents devastating risks that emphasizing an African-American or Jewish identity does not.

We notice that the white Euro-American male is decidedly excluded from this strategy, no matter how he might try to distance himself from a hegemony he knows to be oppressive and unjust. I note that I, as a white Euro-American female, have only one more point of entry than he; and, indeed, Alcoff directs her definition of identity politics to those who are simply more victimized, who have greater need for the strategies it may afford them. Yet both of us Euro-Americans, recognizing the profound uncertainty that inevitably follows from careful consideration of gender's utterly mediated presence, could not so much "claim" as "assume" for ourselves (and by this I mean "let the assumptions of others do the work") a homosexual identification—as queer theorists, as members of ACT UP, or as sign-carrying participants in a gay rights parade—as a way to practice "identity politics" the way Alcoff suggests.

Even more tempting to an outsider like myself is Alcoff's later formulation describing identity politics as the litmus test for feminism itself. She distinguishes the feminist and the antifeminist by "the affirmation or de-nial of our right and our ability to construct and take responsibility for our gendered identity, our politics, and our choices"[10]: if I have the ability to construct a lesbian identity and can bring positive political change out of such a construction, to fail to do so is to deny my feminism.

Yet in two other highly influential, lesbian-authored essays, such self-questioning flares into self-cancellation through an assertion that as a "straight feminist," I am an oxymoron, an ontological impossibility—a position I find both supremely threatening and thrillingly liberating. In *Technologies of Gender,* Teresa de Lauretis applauds the efforts of Jean Ken-nard to reserve a lesbian reading practice that is not subsumed under a "universal female." She herself agrees that "lesbians read differently from committedly heterosexual women as well as men,"[11] and I will assume for my argument that her opinion attaches itself to many important elements of lesbian existence, significantly differentiating lesbians from straight women.

Elsewhere in this same essay, however, de Lauretis describes the "hetero-sexual contract" that keeps heterosexual women, however ideologically aware they are, in a comparative—and thus subservient—relationship to heterosexual men: a heterosexual perspective on gender is a perspective on "gender *difference,*" and this is undeniably a reinscription of traditional gender roles and their traditionally assigned asymmetric values. To pose an effective challenge to this hegemonic construction of gender, de Lau-retis argues late in the essay, we must take up a position "elsewhere"—not in a utopian, metaphysical realm of objectivity but in the "space off," the chinks and cracks of the hegemonic (heterosexual) discourse—that will share the same pitfalls of constructedness but emphasize a contradiction that will keep the discussion dynamic and inclusive.

While de Lauretis does not state it directly, the "elsewhere" to the hetero-sexual contract can only be the lesbian or gay alternative—the hom(m)o-sexual disrupted by the homosexual, to use Irigarayan terms. De Lauretis does not simply oppose these two but holds them in contradiction, insist-ing that answers to gender questions can only be found by "crossing back and forth of the boundaries" that construct "sexual difference(s)" (*Tech-nologies* 25). As does Alcoff, de Lauretis expands this gender discussion to define feminism itself, arguing that "the movement in and out of gender as ideological representation, which I propose characterizes the subject of feminism, is a movement back and forth between" (26) these boundaries. Thus I am bound to "live this contradiction"—to cross back and forth between the boundary dividing the hegemonic from the other—if I am to practice effective feminism. We all must pursue such a project; and, in de Lauretis's terms, it seems not only possible but absolutely necessary.

If we are uncomfortable with the terms I set up in the beginning of this essay—straight and lesbian as opposed to de Lauretis's hegemonic and other—perhaps it is due to the still-radical reaction attending what Sue-Ellen Case has termed the "emergence of the lesbian subject" in conventional feminist discourse. In her essay "Towards a Butch-Femme Aesthetic," Case demands this very emergence if gender issues are ever to be studied extrahegemonically. She begins with the de Lauretis thesis outlined above, rephrasing it provocatively: "Because she is still perceived in terms of men and not within the context of other women, the subject in heterosexuality cannot become capable of ideological change."[12] Once again, the straight gender theorist finds herself trapped in the heterosexual contract, disabling her against the male-centered ideology she tries to challenge.

Case calls de Lauretis's conclusion her starting place and argues that the butch-femme couple is feminism's new "dynamic duo," particularly because it allows the lesbian subject in feminist theory to come out of the closet. Case has argued elsewhere that when she refers to a "subject," she (like Butler) means "subject-in-discourse," performing and not expressing an essential gender identity, once again inviting traditionally oriented women like myself to flirt with a positioning within this "dynamic" and politically enlightened community.

Yet later in this same essay, Case harshly critiques "heterosexual feminists who metaphorize butch/femme roles, transvestites, and campy dressers" ("Butch-Femme" 62), a tactic that eliminates the historical impact from the practicing lesbian existence. She is quite right to argue that this appropriating of a cultural particularity disempowers it immediately, draining any subversive potential from the "strangeness" it poses. Yet it is hard to determine whether Case is only faulting heterosexual women who transgress this way (and if my proposed gender-bending is among such transgressions) or whether she argues that heterosexual feminists by virtue of their heterosexuality are bound to offend in this manner. If the latter, then she leaves little space in which straight gender theorists may practice: we cannot escape ideology as heterosexual women, yet we cannot access a lesbian position of critique, because our efforts always co-opt unfairly and detrimentally, discounting our theories. As we recall, de Lauretis poses a similar catch-22 when she argues that there is an innate difference in the lesbian reader but warns that women who cannot live this difference cannot inhabit that politically charged "elsewhere"—that is, cannot be feminists.

In the dissolution of these contradictory remarks, I find the summation that embodies both this self-annihilating threat and liberating thrust: straight women and lesbian theory just do not mix. If heard as threat, certain of these gender theorists are saying that straight women should simply stay away from gender studies, especially lesbian studies, because their position is always reinscriptive of heterosexual hegemony and too essentially different from that of lesbians for them to ever entertain notions of crossing over. Worse yet, straight women, unsalvageable victims of the heterosexual contract, should unburden themselves of the illusion that they can be feminists at all, should recognize that lesbian theory, with the newfound articulation of its insightful and subversive political strength, is not just the new feminism but the true feminism, the discussion that has at long last ejected the violence and inequality (but also the unacknowledged desirability) of the phallus from its main field of inquiry. Yet if heard as invitation, as I indeed do choose to hear it, do I not find myself approaching the neighborhood of that very "psychic excess" that Butler warns (or promises) is lying just beneath the surface of my crazily assembled heterosexed worldview?

This debate between essentialist and deconstructive notions of gender has been rephrased more recently and much more encouragingly—by de Lauretis herself[13] and other feminists—not as an *opposition* but as the *relationship* between the psychic realm and the historic realm, the psyche presenting a more sophisticated mapping of the territory marked by biological sexual difference and historicism encompassing a wider range of social phenomena than the narrowly (theoretically) conceived "deconstruction." De Lauretis describes a "body-ego"[14] that she would set against Butler's Foucauldian-inspired "radical delegitimation of the subject"[15]; while Biddy Martin, also suspicious of overstrenuous interpretations of Foucault, argues that "neither the psyche nor the body are direct or simple effects of internalized norms" and that the "givenness of bodies and psyches in history" is the point of departure for social change.[16] Meanwhile, Charles Shepherdson distinguishes between "*the subject* in psychoanalysis" and "the constructed *subjectivity* of historicism, understood as a discursive formation," drawing "a distinction . . . between the *question* posed by the analyst . . . and the *answer* that is *given in advance* by science and the law."[17] In each of these more recent arguments, agency is rescued from a totalizing Foucauldian paralysis while the psyche is recognized as the site that not only produces this agency but softens the opposition between body and culture into the complex and imbricated relationship it more correctly is.

An emphasis on *agency*—flexible, particular, powerful—instead of the limited and limiting *agent* herself finds helpful articulation in Walter Benn Michaels's insistence that identity theorists separate questions of "what I do" from those of "who I am" by radically suspending the second half of the equation. Fuss has argued that "constructionism . . . really operates as a more sophisticated form of essentialism" (*Essentially Speaking*, xii), and Michaels has recently, helpfully, elaborated on this view: "this essentialist commitment to the primacy of identity is in no way avoided by what are hopefully described as anti-essentialist accounts . . . that emphasize the complex, conflicted, mobile, and so on nature of identity. There are no anti-essentialist accounts of identity. The reason for this is that the essentialism inheres not in the description of the identity but in the attempt to derive the practices from the identity—we *do* this because we *are* this."[18] I contend that my interaction with lesbian theory will open a position within gender studies that, by virtue of my very occupation of it, does just this—derives an "I" that as straight feminist no longer is. "Am" no longer, "what I do"—action, in this case, activism[19]—remains; while it may be ultimately impossible to identify the locus of agency in a region of the psyche beyond our grasp, it should be possible to identify the effect—and enjoy the rewards—of such psychic work in the kind of de-essentialized doing-without-being I propose inhabiting here. Instead of the self-annihilating verdict ("get lost!") that straight feminists might hear lesbian theorists handing them in the theories I review above, here is an undoing of the self that, equally difficult, may generate terrifically productive ends.

In the conference version of this essay, I speculated on "using" a lesbian subject position to advance a career in a politically progressive English or cultural studies program, recognizing queer theory as a "hot topic" in the same way as are African-American, postcolonial, and other "minority" literatures. I now regard this tactic as largely misguided—*not* because this kind of career strategy, however respectably packaged, is ineffective or rarely employed *nor* because, as it was suggested that day, queer theory is a marginalized and persecuted cultural field that rewards no effort to establish oneself therein but instead because this approach provoked a lengthy, emphatic, multivoiced attack—on my false position of authority, my invalid claim to the victim experience—that ultimately occluded the main thesis of this argument: flirt with gender positionality as I will, my position is and has always been incontestably that of a lesbian *in theory,* as removed and excluded from whatever we might understand as "traditional" lesbian experience as my most essentialist detractor could assert.

When I argue, then, that my position as straight feminist inside lesbian texts will be a "lesbian experience" nonetheless, I am attesting not only to the power and influence of the texts themselves but also to the tenuousness—might we say absurdity?—of the boundary constituting the hetero/homo binary in ways lesbians reading lesbian texts never could. Finally, we must recognize my real transgression not as an attempt to appropriate someone else's voice but to create an equation inside lesbian studies that does not—perforce cannot—include the perspective, input, and presence of sexually practicing lesbians. If this attempt has indeed transgressed, has in fact weakened or displaced the lesbian discussant in her position of experience, persecution, and authority, then this is the point on which we must focus and attempt resolution. For I do not wish to silence long-awaited and much-needed lesbian voices, yet neither will I dissolve my relationship to a body of knowledge that has so far been only theoretically illuminating and politically inspiring.

Notes

1. Judith Butler, "Imitation and Gender Insubordination," in *Inside/Out: Lesbian Theories/Gay Theories,* ed. Diana Fuss (London: Routledge, 1991), 13–14. Subsequent references to this work will be included parenthetically in the text.

2. Carol-Anne Tyler, "Passing: Narcissism, Identity, and Difference," *differences* 6:2–3 (1994): 216.

3. My reference here is again to Tyler, who argues on a parallel plane (that of race identification as opposed to gender identification) so effectively for my purposes here (see ibid. 215).

4. Butler, in describing Helms's attack on National Endowment for the Arts funding of gay artists, notes that it was many months before Helms even recognized the existence of lesbian artists—that is, directed his virulence against their funded projects as well: "oppression works not merely through acts of overt prohibition, but covertly, through the constitution of viable subjects and through the corollary constitution of a domain of unviable (un)subjects—*abjects,* we might call them—who are neither named nor prohibited within the economy of the law. . . . Lesbianism is not explicitly prohibited in part because it has not even made its way into the thinkable, the imaginable, that grid of cultural intelligibility that regulates the real and the nameable" ("Imitation" 20).

5. Several critics have pointed to the temporal, evolving qualities of gendered identity, deepening the spatial notion of a gendered "position" to include the movements of history and our personal "time zones" as well. See Diana Fuss, *Essentially Speaking: Feminism, Nature, and Difference* (New York: Routledge, 1989), 104; Teresa de Lauretis, "Habit Changes," *differences* 6:2–3 (1994): 302; Tyler, "Passing," 221.

6. Fuss, *Essentially Speaking*, 98. Subsequent references to this work will be included parenthetically in the text.

7. My range is so broad in this designation because, as Fuss has also pointed out, the exact time of "birth" of the gay man in Western civilization is still widely contested (see ibid. 107–8).

8. In *The History of Sexuality*, Foucault points to a distinction between discrete sexual acts and the "incorporation of perversions" that arose in the nineteenth century and has been the subject of debate ever since. For Foucault, this phenomenon of the "homosexual bec[oming] a personage, a past, a case history and a childhood" was not more than part of the "new persecution of the peripheral sexualities"; yet for many gay theorists and rights activists, a gay identity is asserted over a gay "choice" as a means of confronting heterosexism and identity issues. See Michel Foucault, *The History of Sexuality*, vol. 1: *An Introduction*, trans. Robert Hurley (New York: Vintage Books, 1990), 42–43.

9. Adrienne Rich, "Compulsory Heterosexuality and Lesbian Existence," *Signs* 5:4 (1980): 631–60. Along the same lines as Rich and Butler, Eve Kosofsky Sedgwick has described the male homosocial bonds that structure *all* culture, suggesting that, at least in "relations of [economic/kinship] exchange," there is a little male homosociality in all of us. Indeed, an elemental structure of Sedgwick's argument has always been the homosocial continuum, that which controls economic and social relations *between* men and, even more interestingly, accounts for the psychic violence (always eventually directed outward in the form of homosexual panic) *within* men. In considering the homosocial continua operating between and within *women*, we may lose the emphases on economics and social control (and, I would argue, violence) yet retain the ultimate connectedness of women—those we would identify on the "other side" of the gendered divide, and those versions of ourselves we would consign to pre-Oedipal youth or the confusion of dreams. See Eve Kosofsky Sedgwick, *Between Men: English Literature and Male Homosocial Desire* (New York: Columbia University Press, 1986), 88–90, and *Epistemology of the Closet* (Berkeley: University of California Press, 1990), 182–88.

10. Linda Alcoff, "Cultural Feminism versus Post-Structuralism: The Identity Crisis in Feminist Theory," *Signs* 13:3 (1988): 432.

11. Teresa de Lauretis, *Technologies of Gender* (Bloomington: Indiana University Press, 1987), 22. Subsequent references to this work will be included parenthetically in the text.

12. Sue-Ellen Case, "Towards a Butch-Femme Aesthetic," *Discourse* 11:1 (1988–89): 56. Subsequent references to this work will be included parenthetically in the text.

13. It is interesting that over the course of the last decade de Lauretis and others have, in fact, reversed the terms of this debate over the possibility and location of agency. Whereas now, influential authors like Joan Copjec have questioned "historicist" (or Foucauldian) approaches to feminist analysis, in the mid-1980s, materialist feminists like de Lauretis emphasized history as a way outside the web of power—specifically, the Lacanian (psychoanalytic) web of the phallic Symbolic. "Consciousness," wrote de Lauretis in 1986, "therefore, is never fixed, never attained once and for all, because discursive boundaries change with historical conditions" ("Feminist Studies/Critical Studies: Issues, Terms, and Contexts," in *Feminist Studies/Critical Studies*, ed. Teresa de Lauretis [Bloomington: Indiana University Press, 1986], 8–9). In a 1990 collection, Mary Ann Doane appeals to a 1984 de Lauretis essay to make the point that "this is not a naive appeal to history (all agree that history must be theorized) but it is an invocation of history designed to counter certain excesses of theory (especially psychoanalytic theory) and the impasse resulting from those excesses. History is envisaged as a 'way out' " ("Remembering Women: Psychical and Historical Constructions in Film Theory," in *Psychoanalysis and Cinema*, ed. E. Ann Kaplan [New York: Routledge, 1990], 48).

14. De Lauretis ("Habit Changes," 303) defines this "body-ego" as that which, while not a "preexisting subjectivity" or "original materiality," is, nevertheless, the site of sexuation and subjectivation and is constituted through primal or original fantasies (the Freudian *Urphantasien*). Thus, it has an originary quality to it and may be understood as the seat of one's identity, one's basis for taking social action. Beyond its primacy in the examples of de Lauretis, Martin, and Shepherdson that I give here, the discussion exploring the relationship between the "new" psyche and the "old" historicism has become the cornerstone to almost any discussion of gendered identity and agency in recent years. See also Fuss, *Essentially Speaking;* Judith Butler's interview of Rosi Braidotti, "Feminism by Any Other Name," *differences* 6:2–3 (1994): 27–61; Joan Copjec, *Read My Desire: Lacan against the Historicists* (Cambridge, Mass.: MIT Press, 1994), 10–18 (in another impassioned defense of psychoanalysis, this time against the naïveté of the Foucauldian "multiple subject"), and "*m/f,* or Not Reconciled," in *The Woman in Question: m/f,* ed. Parveen Adams and Elizabeth Cowie (Cambridge, Mass.: MIT Press/October Books, 1990), 10–18. For an early reading of what is now a renewed inquiry into the psychic-historicist dynamic, see Gayle Rubin, "Thinking Sex: Notes for a Radical Theory of the Politics of Sexuality," in *Pleasure and Danger: Exploring Female Sexuality,* ed. Carole S. Vance (Boston: Routledge and Kegan Paul, 1984), 267–319.

15. De Lauretis, "Habit Changes," 302.

16. Biddy Martin, "Extraordinary Homosexuals and the Fear of Being Ordinary," *differences* 6:2–3 (1994): 123.

17. Charles Shepherdson, "The *Role of Gender* and the *Imperative of Sex*," in *Supposing the Subject*, ed. Joan Copjec (London: Verso, 1994), 162. Shepherdson spends much of this essay building an opposition between psychoanalysis and historicism, describing an array of polarized positions inhabited by, pertaining to, or influencing chiefly psychoanalysis and historicism, perpetuating the "enormous gap" (170) between them: the "real of embodiment" versus a "fantasy [or imaginary] body," desire versus demand, the ego-ideal versus primary narcissism in Freud, the masculine versus feminine in Lacan's sexuation formulae. Despite these many enumerated differences, Shepherdson comes to the surprising, perhaps only obligatorily Derridian, ultimately correct realization early in the piece that "it would . . . be a mistake to engage in the familiar polemic between 'psychoanalysis or history' . . . because psychoanalysis is in no way simply *opposed* to history, as though psychoanalysis were simply 'ahistorical', or as though there were a contradiction between them, obliging us to choose one or the other" (166).

18. Walter Benn Michaels, "Race into Culture: A Critical Genealogy of Cultural Identity," *Critical Inquiry* 18 (Summer 1992): 684n. Michaels goes on to define "anti-essentialism" as that which "must take the form not of producing more sophisticated accounts of identity (that is, more sophisticated essentialisms) but of ceasing to explain what people do or should do by reference to who they are" (684n).

19. As a community service volunteer in several "real world" fields, I find it difficult to define activism as ever occurring within the ivory tower of academia, even in teaching, especially with respect to scholarly production. Still, there are front lines against racism, sexism, homophobia, and misunderstanding in general among humanities scholars as within any group, and I feel it is possible to define the battle conducted on these lines as its own form of activism.

3

How I Became a Queer Heterosexual

Clyde Smith

This is the story of how I became a queer heterosexual. It begins in North Carolina, where I spent most of my life till I was twenty-nine. There, I developed a flexible conception of gender and an openness to others' sexual orientation but held on to binaries of male and female, hetero and homo. The bulk of my story focuses on a three-year period spent in San Francisco, where I was immersed in a queer milieu. There I learned a great deal about further possibilities for sexual and gender identity that went beyond rigid binaries. Much of this learning occurred in queer territory and led, simultaneously, to my alignment with that identity and my initial inability to claim such a title. I close with my experiences after leaving San Francisco and my eventual coming out as a queer heterosexual. Though this account follows a linear path through time, I know my development to be complex, unpredictable, and not fully reproducible. The story of how I came to claim the identity of a queer heterosexual—a story with neatly fitted details—could only be written in retrospect.

As my story unfolds, I will relate what a queer heterosexual might be, but I must begin by clarifying my use of the word "queer." I draw on Keith Hennessy's definition from a pamphlet entitled *Addressing the Queer Man's Role in the New World Anarchy and the Future of the Men's Movements in the Dis/United States:* "Queer: an umbrella term which embraces the matrix of sexual preferences, orientations, and habits of the not-exclusively-heterosexual-and-monogamous majority. Queer includes lesbians, gay men, bisexuals, transvestites/transgenders, the radical sex communities, and many other sexually transgressive (underworld) explorers."[1] While I will not discuss my own practices, I include myself in this broad definition, with the modifier of "heterosexual" following "queer."

Though one might think of such a term as simply relating to sexuality, the emergent use of the term "queer" also indicates radical notions regarding gender. In both aspects, queer emerges from the opposition to and subversion of such binaries of sexuality as hetero/homo and of gender as male/female. My understanding of queerness includes Kate Bornstein's redefinition of transgender as "transgressively gendered" and her call for a gathering of queer forces "that would include anyone who cares to admit their own gender ambiguities . . . that includes all sexualities, races and ethnicities, religions, ages, classes and states of body."[2] This redefining of transgender is another articulation of queerness as it has emerged in the 1990s. My story focuses on the experiences and encounters I had that formed a curriculum in queer identity encompassing both sexuality and gender.

North Carolina

In North Carolina, I learned much that laid a foundation for my experiences in San Francisco. At the University of North Carolina at Greensboro, where I studied dance and theater arts, I encountered a wide variety of gay men yet also spent much time in dance classes where I was the only male. Most of my teachers at that time were either women or gay men. This experience resulted in my growing to accept homosexuality as a reasonable orientation and expanded my sense of gender possibilities in that movement choices did not have to align themselves with traditional notions of masculinity and femininity.

After college, in Raleigh and Durham, North Carolina, I made art on a community level with a commitment to left political activism. I read about and discussed feminist theory and practice. This activity included dialogues with lesbian women and led me to a critique of male dominance, white supremacy, and heterocentrism. Though earlier I approached sexuality and gender as personal choices within a restrictive social setting, at this point I began to recognize the political nature of such choices. However, I also developed a "politically correct" attitude about gender and sexuality. This attitude required a rejection of what I considered traditionally masculine movement choices, including strong, forceful, explosive action on my part. It also meant that certain forms of sexuality—such as S/M, even in consensual adult relationships—were simply wrong and reinforced dominant ideologies of oppression.

In the mid-1980s, during a year of movement studies at the University of Washington in Seattle, I began to reclaim aspects of my moving self that I had rejected as forms of machismo. This learning happened in a strong group of women where again I was the only male. My teachers encouraged me to explore a full range of movement possibilities and themselves embodied movement tendencies associated with both masculinity and femininity. With them, I regained a sense of the flexibility of gender and began to reject the rigidity of both hegemonic and politically correct gender roles. Yet, for the rest of my time after my return to North Carolina, I held on to restricted notions of sexuality. My beliefs were to be radically altered in San Francisco.

San Francisco

In the summer of 1989, as I was about to turn thirty, I moved to San Francisco, a city that I experienced as a life laboratory for the exploration and social re/construction of sexuality and gender. Shortly after I arrived, I attended a trailblazing conference organized by and for bisexuals and their supporters that awakened me to their marginalized status in both gay and straight discourse. Neither one nor the other, bisexuals resist the binary restrictions society attempts to impose on them. In claiming such a destabilizing identity, bisexuals establish a feature of queer terrain. The conference and related reading sensitized me to the prejudices faced by bisexuals and provided an early lesson in the broader possibilities for sexual identity.

After a few months, I joined a men's dance company called The High Risk Group, directed by my longtime friend Rick Darnell, and began to make a place for myself in San Francisco. I was the only hetero-identified member of a company that performed primarily in alternative art spaces and at gay and lesbian events. Through The High Risk Group, I gained entry into social settings with which many people, whatever their sexual identity, are totally unfamiliar. My experiences with The High Risk Group were at the core of my discoveries regarding sex and gender. This was the only time I felt like an integral part of a group of gay and bisexual men. Of course, this integration did not occur immediately. The first months were a testing period to see if I would stay with the group, which itself faced many interpersonal and organizational obstacles.

Because we were a small group and often danced in difficult physical

situations—in clubs, on sidewalks, and in other nontraditional settings—
we grew to know each other very well. The other members of the company, whose membership shifted periodically, gradually revealed more of
themselves as I showed myself to be open, nonjudgmental, and generally
intrigued with their behavior. Their self-revelations usually took narrative
form, including both anecdotal references to and lengthy accounts of sexual experiences. These stories educated me into the world of radical queer
sex in San Francisco, which includes but is not limited to group activities,
anonymous encounters, exhibitionism, S/M, and other pursuits counter-
posed to the so-called "vanilla sexuality" of most hetero and homo cit-
izens. Such practices expand sexuality into other dimensions "devoted to
intensifying the act of sex itself" in which one "make[s] use of every part of
the body as a sexual instrument."[3] My education deepened as I asked for
more specifics or inquired about technical details ranging from the use of
cockrings to safe-sex practices in extreme situations.

Though one may think of certain districts in San Francisco as debauched
playgrounds where everyone indulges in erotic experimentation, such activities seem more a limited but highly visible aspect of Bay Area culture,
even assuming that what is visible is only a small part of the overall activity. I also knew gay men who found much of what my friends were into
rather disturbing. The transgressive element of their activities is one aspect
of queer as a category other than gay, though queer is certainly grounded
in homosexual opposition to hetero hegemony. Of course, the original
appropriation of "gay" as a term was much more powerful than its current
usage.[4] My friends' practices are another way in which queer expands sexuality and destabilizes hetero/homo binaries.

My understanding was also extended by the traditional form of information dispersal known as gossip. Over time, I discovered that many of
the people I met in the alternative arts scene had various kinks that one
might not identify without behind-the-scenes knowledge. This devoted
couple were swingers, that straight-identified person was on his knees at
the Church of Priapus, and so forth. Gossip provided a glance backstage at
the behavior of people I knew only casually. Though gossip allows for a
high degree of inaccuracy and certain of my cohorts had well-deserved
reputations as unreliable narrators, I began to piece together a sense of
what was not visible in a city where so much was already on display. Not
only was I learning that things are not as they seem and that human sexual activities are complex in ways that go beyond labels such as gay and
straight but that many if not most of us have unrevealed potentials for

experimentation. Perhaps in a restrictive society there are a wide range of folks who would not claim queerness but whose practices include many queer elements.

Yet much was not hidden. I saw many performances in addition to other artworks that were a part of the emergence of queerness. Elsewhere I have written on men's performance in San Francisco, including the work of The High Risk Group, Keith Hennessy, Jules Beckman, and Jess Curtis.[5] These performances explored various possibilities for male existence that included much queer material, particularly in the work of Rick Darnell and increasingly in that of Keith Hennessy. But of all the performances I saw it was Kate Bornstein's play "Hidden: A Gender" that caused me to begin a serious questioning of binary gender.[6]

"Hidden: A Gender," which I saw fairly early in my time in San Francisco, was written and directed by Bornstein and performed by her, Justin Bond, and Sydney Erskine. This production featured a man playing a young girl who discovered she was biologically male (Bond), a woman playing a man who had once been a woman (Erskine), and a male-to-female transsexual playing a man (Bornstein). "Hidden: A Gender" problematized gender in a way that emphasized its constructed nature and undermined biological assumptions. More than any other art work I experienced in San Francisco, this show really pushed me toward an understanding that gender is socially constructed. But the implications went beyond simply analyzing the construction of gender to offering radical possibilities for creating new gender identities.

This show also introduced me to a broader understanding of transgender behavior and an expanded notion of the drag queen. Justin Bond, one of the performers, was a drag queen who I would see at various events or in the local media. I saw him perform only in "Hidden: A Gender," but he was a noticeable presence wherever he appeared. Whether Justin was in full drag or in less-transgendered wear, there was always a femme elegance about him. His presence and way of being in the world helped me to understand that drag was not always about appearing to be the opposite sex. In fact, I rarely saw most of the drag queens I came to know in anything like the popular media image of crossdressers. While some of them performed in that sort of drag, I knew most of them in more boyish wear; yet their way of being signaled transgender identity. These encounters and friendships caused me to realize that transgender behavior was not so much about crossdressing as about genderfuck.

In a recent letter, my queer friend Jonathan Meyer explained his conception of genderfuck, writing that it "has at least 2 meanings for me—the first, more obvious, is fucking with gender—distorting, twisting, inverting, playing with, challenging—but still (potentially) retaining and honoring the beauty in any expression of gender/sexuality, etc. . . . But the other is fucking gender: making love to gender. . . . it is as much a source of inspiration, joy, anguish, beauty, & entrapment as any other aspect of human existence & human culture."[7] The concept of genderfuck opens queer further to the playful possibilities of destabilizing rigidly gendered boundaries. My own awareness was expanded by the wide variety of genderfuckers I encountered in my daily life in San Francisco.

Of course, all these experiences caused me to wrestle with my own identity. Though a brief label cannot sum up human experience, I still desired a term that at least referenced my own complex nature and my kinship with these folks. At the time, queer was just emerging as a term for militant gay/lesbian/bi/transgender activists and appearing in the media through public actions by such groups as Queer Nation. Though Keith Hennessy's definition of queer included me, I had not yet read his pamphlet. Queer still seemed too strongly identified with same-sex sexuality for me to claim it. Consequently, there was no ready label for my identity, and so I settled for considering myself a fellow traveler in the queer revolution.

After California

In the fall of 1992, I left San Francisco to become a graduate student in dance and performance studies. Along the way, I discovered an article by Ann Powers in the *Village Voice* in which she discussed the emergence of the "Queer Straight, that testy lovechild of identity politics and shifting sexual norms." At first glance, this was the idea for which I was looking. Her definition of inclusion in the queer world did not require "the fundamental acts of intimacy that ground homosexual identity." Rather, she spoke of "the projection of a queer attitude [as] enough to claim a place in homosexual culture." This form of "passing" becomes "a passage into a whole new conception of the self." Yet Powers's definition of queerness is ultimately grounded in same-sex sexuality, and so she feels that heterosexuals cannot "claim a wholly queer identity."[8] Nonetheless, my reading of her article planted a seed and inspired the possibility of another hybrid, not the oxymoronic queer straight, but the queer heterosexual who is queer without having to pass for homosexual.

My master's thesis, written at the University of North Carolina at Greensboro, focused on an evening of men's dance called "Mandala." This work was created and performed by Keith Hennessy, Jess Curtis, and Jules Beckman, then the male members of Contraband, a San Francisco–based dance/performance company. When I was gathering material about this show, Hennessy passed along the aforementioned pamphlet in which I encountered his definition of queer. Though I did not speak of it publicly, I began to think of myself as a queer heterosexual. However, I did not come out as such until I reached my next institutional home, Ohio State University.

At Ohio State, while working on a collaborative unpublished project with physical educator and sport historian Gary Joseph and tracing how I came to understand gender as a realm of multiple possibilities, I identified myself as a queer heterosexual. Though this semipublic maneuver frightened me, it also felt like the right thing to do. I contextualized this label with Hennessy's definition, Ann Powers's concept of the queer straight, the work of Kate Bornstein, and my own immersion in queer culture. The juxtaposition of the terms queer and heterosexual startled those in attendance at our presentation and led to a discussion of both terms and their combination. From that discussion, it became clear that this juxtaposition was a powerful device to shake up established notions about the boundaries of queerness and of heterosexuality.

Back when I was first dancing with The High Risk Group in San Francisco, I publicly identified myself as straight—out of insecurity as much as any stated reason. Once I recognized what I was doing, I stopped looking for opportunities to proclaim my heterosexuality except when the point needed to be made that straight and gay men could work together. At these moments, such an intervention was an attempt to trouble the hetero/homo divide while maintaining my own sense of identity within this particular group. Claiming queer heterosexuality is an extension of that earlier positionality as I now pursue more individual work. This maneuver also allows me to remain connected to queerness in environments that are less supportive than San Francisco.

I claim the identity of queer heterosexual to further my own desires for a world of multiple possibilities rather than as a means of benefiting from queer chic. Such a world would be one in which we are not restricted by binaries of sex and gender or by the balkanization of identity groups. Yet we would not erase differences and would respect the need for boundaries as deemed necessary for both individual and group autonomy. Such a world would allow for the "mobility" that Leo Bersani speaks of in *Homos*, which "should create a kind of community, one that can never be settled, whose membership is always shifting . . . a community in which many straights should be able to find a place."[9] Temporarily, at least, I have a home in the shifting community of queerness as a queer heterosexual.

Notes

1. Keith Hennessy, *Addressing the Queer Man's Role in the New World Anarchy and the Future of the Men's Movements in the Dis/United States* (San Francisco: Abundant Fuck Publications, 1992), 11.

2. Kate Bornstein, *Gender Outlaw: On Men, Women, and the Rest of Us* (New York: Routledge, 1994), 98.

3. Michel Foucault, *Politics, Philosophy, Culture: Interviews and Other Writings, 1977–1984*, ed. Lawrence Kritzman (New York: Routledge, 1990), 298–99.

4. With the emergence of Gay Liberation in the late 1960s, the term *gay* came to mean, as Michael Silverstein recounts, "far more than the original fact of our homosexuality." For Silverstein, "Gayness is revolutionary because it requires the end of capitalist society and the creation of a society in which Gay people can live" ("The History of a Short, Unsuccessful Academic Career," in *Men and Masculinity*, ed. J. Pleck and J. Sawyer [Englewood Cliffs, N.J.: Prentice-Hall, 1974], 107, 122).

5. See Clyde Smith, " 'Mandala' and the Men's Movements in the Light of Feminism" (master's thesis, University of North Carolina at Greensboro, 1995) and "Men's Rowdy Dances Making Gender Trouble," *Contact Quarterly* 21:2 (Summer–Fall 1996): 26–30.

6. "Hidden: A Gender" was originally performed in November 1989 at Theater Rhinoceros in San Francisco. The text has since been published in Bornstein's *Gender Outlaw.*

7. Jonathan Meyer, personal communication, August 1996.

8. Ann Powers, "Queer in the Streets, Straight in the Sheets: Notes on Passing," *Village Voice*, 29 June 1993, 24, 30–31.

9. Leo Bersani, *Homos* (Cambridge, Mass.: Harvard University Press, 1995), 9.

4

Staging the Self: Queer Theory in the Composition Classroom

Lauren Smith

In one of my composition classes, I assign a personal essay and receive, among other things, a paper entitled "Just Do It," an essay about how the author came to believe that he could "be all that he could be" if he just "kept his eyes on the prize." In another class, a student writes movingly about a gay-bashing incident at a local McDonald's and her still-nascent struggle to understand how such violence could exist in her community. Assuming that at least one purpose of a liberal education in general and a writing class in particular is to help our students develop, as Henry Giroux puts it, a "critical citizenship," then it is arguable that the first essay represents a probable failure of such development and the second, a potential success.

In my composition classes, I make assignments that elicit personal responses because of my background in and continued reliance on expressivist pedagogies. I am aware, however, that expressivism has become one bogeyman in postmodern discussions about composition. Expressivism has been accused, among other things, of (re)authorizing an apolitical individualism in the guise of a liberatory politics, of contributing to the creation of quiescent subjects of consumer capitalism. While the criticism of expressivism by postmodern thinkers has been valuable and convincing, it seems clear to me that the personalist discourse that is the center of the expressivist movement can produce both quiescent and resistant subjects. I would like to argue here that one vital postmodern discourse—

queer theory—might help us understand the double nature of personal writing in our courses and help us enhance its critical potential.

Criticism of the use of personal writing, especially in expressivist classrooms, focuses on the construction of the student-subject as an isolated and apolitical being. Freshmen are encouraged to look to the "self" for knowledge outside of any sense of that self's relationship to the historical, the social, the political. Susan Miller argues, for example, that the emphasis on self-reflexivity in expressivist composition theory takes part in a history of composition practices that sought to separate the academic, intellectual work from profane or utilitarian concerns—and that sought to separate students according to their social class. Nineteenth-century emphases on modes of writing rather than purposes or subjects pushed formal concerns to the center of writing instruction and concerns about subject matter to the side. The goal, according to Miller, was to produce students who "were writing only for a surface gentility, only about 'personal' experiences that immediately exposed their genteel or more humble origins."[1] The subjects created in such exposition were expressly apolitical and, ideally, cooperative with class structures as they were then constituted.

Miller continues to argue that, while less focused on surface perfection or "gentility," expressivism likewise creates a subject primarily concerned with cultivating and presenting certain desirable qualities *as an individual*. Such a student is invested in seeing him/herself as working in a sphere above, beyond, at the very least separate from, the practical and political spheres. S/he (and here Miller quotes Terry Eagleton) "is sensitive, receptive, imaginative and so on . . . *about nothing in particular*" (*Textual Carnivals* 91). Such a self perceives itself as powerless in and/or alienated from the public sphere and, of course, any kind of political action, engagement, or analysis. Freshman composition, Miller argues, "further[s] the end of neutralizing the public participation of its students" (91).

James Berlin makes a similar argument. He traces expressivism back to a Romantic belief in writing as a gift of individual genius, a gift that to the Romantics was rare but that the expressivists popularized. Though the exclusivity of "genius" changed, Romantic beliefs in the "inherent goodness of the individual"[2] and the corruption of public space, social groups, and politics remained the same. He argues that whatever politics have been available in expressivist pedagogy have been, after the demise of more radical and experimental expressivists of the 1960s and the 1970s, resolutely individualist: "While the reality of the material, the social, and the linguistic are never denied, they are considered significant only insofar as they serve the needs of the individual" (484). Thus, Berlin argues, while the message of much expressivist pedagogy is resistance to current social constructions, that resistance is always understood to take place on the private level. It is always understood to bypass or enter sideways into the social or political.

Richard W. France makes a related argument in more revealing terms in his article "Assigning Places: The Function of Introductory Composition as a Cultural Discourse." Like Miller and Berlin, France argues that "when we teach students to construct an 'authentic' self and to subordinate that self to the rules of a dominant discourse, we are reproducing ideological formulations of truth, whether we intend to or not."[3] In other words, he argues—like other postmodern critics of expressivism—that the selves that expressivist teachers want students to reveal in their writing are really selves created in social disciplinary practices that include the composition class, that include the "discipline" of writing. For this reason, France argues, expressivism functions as an unself-conscious and uncritical form of social control. Especially, the selves created in these classrooms cooperate with individualist and consumerist ideologies because they participate in "the flight from politics—the privatization of rhetoric" (593).

France chooses *What Makes Writing Good,* an anthology of student writing edited by Coles and Vopat,[4] as the focus of this portion of his argument, pointing out that the collection is resolutely apolitical, that it emphasizes individualism, and that it "claims to have 'no party line . . . for a teacher to . . . feed to students' " ("Assigning Places" 595). He argues rightly that the model writing assignments and essays included in the collection generally assume a writing self posed against a social world that is either beyond the students' kens and concerns or is hopelessly chaotic—in any case, alien (598). France could have similarly critiqued Peter Elbow's *Writing without Teachers* for its apolitical outlook. In the first sentence of the first chapter, Elbow makes an oblique reference to the social movements contemporary with his writing of the book: "Many people are trying to become less helpless, both personally and politically."[5] Once again, Elbow, who wrote this book in the early 1970s, never mentions political concerns, never refers to the social movements of his day. He goes on to assert that people need to have power over their writing, ignoring, among other things, the possibility that some people already have more power to speak or write than others, that the question of voice is political, that the composition classroom has any political function.

Clearly, such an approach to the teaching of composition is undesirable for those of us committed to, at the very least, acknowledging the politics of writing, of "voice," and of language both inside and outside the university. In this regard, I agree with France's assessment of *What Makes Writing Good* and the expressivist movement more generally. However, at least two things strike me as problematic in France's critiques of the Coles and Vopat anthology and, by extension, of the expressivism his essay participates in. The first is France's failure to account for those student essays that do address issues that might be understood as public. The Coles and Vopat anthology includes, for example, an essay by Teri Cor entitled "Autobiographical Sketch," in which she writes that Armageddon, in her education, was equated with the victory of communism: "That was how we would know the Communists were coming. First the river of blood, then the invincible soldiers, jeering with unholy glee, and finally the tortures."[6] Hers is not a sophisticated treatise on the relationship between Christianity and nationalism. But not only is Cor critical in this essay of the sadistic element of her Catholic education; she also notices and critiques the anticommunist, nationalist sentiments that were, in her experience, associated with it. Michael Canlon's "A Great Way of Life," also included in the Coles and Vopat collection, criticizes the misrepresentation of air force life, which was much more miserable and oppressive than he was led to believe it would be. And Curtis Buhman's brief "Street Scene/Mall Scene" offers startling observations about the manipulative nature of mall architecture and, implicitly, about the consumerist culture malls participate in.

While none of these student essays offers the kind of thoroughgoing, historical or political critique we might most like to see, it is unfair to categorize them as purely personal. Cor, Canlon, and Buhman record their private responses to what they see, but they are responding to distinctly public institutions—the church, the military, the mall. Furthermore, it ought to be easy for us to break down the binary opposition of private and public. When, after all, is the private not also public and political? When is the private not structured by public discourses? When does the public cease to be experienced as private? Furthermore, while none of these student writers shows any historical awareness of the institutions they experience and expose, their experiences themselves are historically situated. The *I* is necessarily structured by the historical forces that bring it into being in the first place. It has no nature, no existence, outside of those historical forces. If history is understood as public while these structured-within-history, individual life experiences are understood as private, then the public/private opposition is meaningless in any case.

Queer theorists have helpfully attacked the kinds of binary oppositions that definitively mark the personal off from the political. Judith Butler's "Imitation and Gender Insubordination," for example, deconstructs the binary oppositions "in" and "out" that the metaphor of the closet sets up. According to Butler, the image of the closet relies on the idea that the closeted space is dark, limited, marginal, and different from the "fresh air" and "light of illumination" on the outside.[7] When someone is *"in* the closet," their true identity—and, by implication, the *truth*—is hidden; and when that person is *"out* of the closet," that true identity is revealed. Among the problems with the idea that a person can come "out of the closet" is precisely the expectation that complete revelation, complete knowledge, is possible. This expectation, and the image of the closet itself, relies on the idea that identity is a preexisting thing outside of its position in the social.

Similarly, Diana Fuss argues in the introduction to *Inside/Out* that the coming out trope constructs gay and lesbian identities rather than revealing identities that are already there. And, conversely, it constructs the closet in the act of coming out: "the first appearance of the homosexual as a 'species' rather than a 'temporary aberration' also marks the moment of the homosexual's disappearance—into the closet."[8] Ironically, according to Fuss, the out gay or lesbian ostensibly becomes what is excluded; s/he asserts the identity of an outsider. But, she argues, the assertion itself is a claim to power that undermines the outsider status of the claimant because declaring an identity at all is declaring a position within the social: "To be out, in common gay parlance, is precisely to be no longer out; to be out is to be finally outside of exteriority and all the exclusions and deprivations such outsiderhood imposes. Or, put another way, to be out is really to be in—inside the realm of the visible, the speakable, the culturally intelligible" (4). The metaphor of coming out of the closet, and the ideology that surrounds it, tends to obscure the ephemeral nature of the marginal, that to speak the marginal is to bring it to the center, that marginality is never absolute or essential: "The problem of course with the inside/outside rhetoric . . . is that such polemics disguise the fact that most of us are both inside and outside at the same time" (5).

In any case, and this is perhaps more to the point, "in" and "out" are not separate concepts but concepts that are dependent on each other for definition—as are the terms "heterosexual" and "homosexual." Fuss points out that the idea of heterosexuality only makes sense when posed in opposition to the idea of homosexuality (and vice versa): "The homo in relation to the hetero . . . operates as an indispensable interior exclusion . . . a transgression of the border which is necessary to constitute the border as such" ("Inside/Out" 3). Butler writes more or less the same thing: "being 'out' always depends to some extent on being 'in'; it gains its meaning only within that polarity" ("Imitation" 16). In other words, the borders around heterosexuality cannot exist unless there is something outside of those borders. In this sense, the excluded second term is contained within the first term itself (and vice versa). The dependence of heterosexuality on homosexuality, however, is always masked. The very nature of a heterosexual or homosexual identity requires the negation of the other on which it is posited. We might say that each term "closets" the other inasmuch as it asserts its own self-identity, its own independence. Or perhaps what is "closeted" is the very instability of the terms themselves. To be "out of the closet," then, as either gay or straight, according to Fuss and Butler, is always to contain or cover up another closet.

The bearing that all of this has on personalist discourse in composition classes is, I imagine, not immediately obvious. Not, that is, unless we consider that the discourse surrounding closets, closeting, and coming out of the closet is generally about the revelation of *self*. And the self is precisely what students are asked to reveal in expressivist composition essays. France points out again and again the degree to which self-disclosure is the dominant trope of *What Makes Writing Good,* in which essays are praised for their honesty and authenticity. We might say, then, that what we ask students to do in many of our expressivist classrooms is to come "out of the closet" in relation to any number of aspects of their lives.

It should not be surprising, then, that Butler's and Fuss's critiques of inside/outside bear some resemblance to France's critique of the narratives included in *What Makes Writing Good.* France argues, among other things, that the self created in expressivist discourse and in expressivist student writings is a self already mortgaged to conservative political ends because it is so resolutely private, because its gratification is structured as private and consumerist. The upshots of Butler's and Fuss's arguments are very similar. The self created in the coming-out narrative is more submissive to heterosexist norms than it seems to be. Both argue, in essence, that the very notion of confession that both narratives depend on is a ruse, that the self-disclosure in coming-out/composition narratives is really the construction of the self that is supposedly being revealed. More importantly, Fuss and France both insist that the creation of such selves is not necessarily desirable because it participates in a humanist understanding of the self as a discreet, knowable, and controllable thing or, more accurately, because these narratives are exercises in social control.

Interestingly, however, despite the suspicion with which queer theory regards coming out, even the most postmodern theorists do not dismiss the coming out story or the social trope of coming out as entirely useless or utterly conservative. About those discourses that create and maintain homosexual identity as an identity, Foucault argues that they can cut both ways: "There is no question that the appearance in nineteenth-century psychiatry, jurisprudence, and literature of a whole series of discourses on the species and subspecies of homosexuality . . . made possible a strong advance of social controls into this area of 'perversity'; but it also made possible the formation of a 'reverse' discourse: homosexuality began to speak in its own behalf."[9] Clearly, the possibility that homosexuality might "speak in its own behalf" is desirable for Foucault. Similarly, Butler writes: "It is possible to argue that . . . there remains a political imperative to use these necessary errors or category mistakes . . . to rally and represent an oppressed political constituency" ("Imitation" 16). She suggests, in other words, that it might still be politically useful to "come out" and organize under the signs "gay" and "lesbian."

In *Essentially Speaking,* Fuss argues more forcefully that the consolidation of identity that coming out represents remains useful. The problem with the kind of consolidated, humanist self created in, for example, coming out narratives, she argues, is that it has functioned to grant some people power over others and to maintain that power once it was established. The rationality and self-possession of the (Western) self justifies the power exercised over others. It is one thing, however, to want to deconstruct the identities of people who have had access to power; it is another to deconstruct the identities of people who have not traditionally had access to power: "women [subaltern peoples and lesbians] do not necessarily have the same historical relation to identity . . . and they do not necessarily start from a humanist fantasy of wholeness." The subject denied power "*begins* fragmented and dispersed."[10] The deconstruction of identity, then, can only be understood as politically useful when differences in power are also being dismantled. It may be "radical" for someone who has had access to a clear sense of self, to voice and presence, to give these things up; but for someone who already understands herself to be without self, voice, presence, such a sacrifice is politically meaningless.

Furthermore, such narratives are simply inescapable. Judith Butler's understanding of their necessity is especially instructive. Her argument in the essay "Imitation and Gender Insubordination" is that gender and sexuality are roles we act out, that they are both a kind of mimicry. The conventional, heterosexist view is that homosexuality is a distorted copy of heterosexuality, that gay men—especially queens—imitate "real women" both socially and sexually, and that lesbians—especially butch dykes—imitate men. In other words, heterosexuality is the original and homosexuality a kind of failed copy, and homosexuality is thus dependent on heterosexuality. Really, Butler argues, the copy as copy verifies the existence of the original as original. Therefore, the copy exists as the guarantee of the original, as a necessary condition of the existence of the original as original. In any case, this play is, according to Butler, inescapable. We simply do not exist outside of our construction as gendered and sexual: "I do not mean to suggest that drag is a 'role' that can be taken on or taken off at will. There is no volitional subject behind the mime who decides, as it were, which gender it will be today. On the contrary, the very possibility of becoming a viable subject requires that a certain gender mime be already underway" (24). Therefore, according to Butler, we cannot get outside of those identities to deconstruct or in some other way elude them. Any means we might use to resist the ideologies that constantly hail us must come from *inside* those very ideologies. Butler's answer to the question Audre Lorde asked so many years ago—"Can the master's tools dismantle the master's house?"—is both no and yes.

While it is true that for Butler we and anything we might do or say is always already implicated, always already part of systems we might purport to work against, that constant implication is in some ways an advantage. It is access to the structures we want to take apart, structures that are, after all, permanently unstable. As Butler writes: "I'm permanently troubled by identity categories, . . . [and] even promote them, as sites of necessary trouble" ("Imitation" 14). She proposes that we take advantage of this instability, and, in "Imitation and Gender Insubordination," she takes gay and lesbian *identity* as a model of resistant subjectivity: "It is important . . . to affirm that gay and lesbian identities are not only structured in part by dominant heterosexual frames, but that they are not for that reason determined by them. They are running commentaries on those naturalized positions as well, parodic replays and resignifications of precisely those heterosexual structures that would consign gay life to discursive domains of unreality and unthinkability" (23). Drag, especially, manages to undermine the system of gender identification.

More than twenty years ago, Esther Newton argued in *Mother Camp* that drag signified an awareness that "all of life is role and theatre—appearance" and that camp queens could, through humor, "neutralize the sting" of homophobia.[11] Butler takes this argument further, insisting that camp does much more than make "life a little brighter" (Newton, *Mother Camp* 110) for the gay community; it actually works against the "stinging" categories of gender and sexuality. The drag queen does not try to escape social constructions of identity—an attempt that would be misleading and disingenuous. Instead, s/he plays these constructions out in an exaggerated fashion and, in so doing, marks their function, makes them more apparent: "In imitating gender, drag implicitly reveals the imitative structure of gender itself—as well as its contingency."[12] The difference between the drag queen and a writer who more unself-consciously takes up a particular identity is not one so much of content as of style. Both the camp artist and, for example, the author of a coming-out narrative fashion themselves in culturally set terms because they have no choice. The camp artist, however, wears his mask as a mask while the author of the coming out narrative treats the mask as if it were the truth. The camp artist, in other words, stages the self as a production, as a construction; and this self-consciousness undermines the construction/production as natural.

It is important to point out, though, that the camp artist does not do away with personal narrative. Newton, for example, understands camp as an expression of identity. With camp, a gay man can "defin[e] a positive homosexual identity" (*Mother Camp* 110). But camp is not a straightforward "definition"; instead, it is a dramatization of self that is aware of (it)self *as* drama. It is self-conscious, self-critical, and—on some level—aware of its historical presence as drama. As Newton puts it: "drag implies that sex role and, by extension, role in general is something superficial, which can be manipulated, put on and off again at will" (109). Hence, it is a personal narrative that is profoundly critical of the social dynamics that bring it into being, one that confounds the distinction France makes between the personal and the public.

One thing we can understand from a reading of queer theory, then, is that personal narrative in the composition classroom and elsewhere need not necessarily work toward conservative ends. On at least one fundamental level, this seems obvious. Much of the new knowledge produced by the gay rights movement, as well as the women's rights and civil rights movements, came out of personal experience and was transmitted via personal narratives delivered at rallies, collected in anthologies, published in small journals, and so forth. The personal narratives produced in these movements have been profoundly disruptive of American social and political life. The stories our students tell have similar disruptive potential.

Many of my colleagues report their experiences with student personal narratives that they found to be profoundly disruptive on one level or another. I began this essay, for example, by invoking a piece of freshman writing that demonstrated a valuable intellectual and critical effort. The writer of that piece—a young, straight, white woman from a small Midwestern town—tells the story of her own homophobia and how she came to question it. She traces her feelings about gays and lesbians back to her older brother's attitude, reinforced by her peers at school, an attitude that she unquestioningly accepts as her own. When she befriends a young gay man from her high school, someone she works with at McDonald's, she begins to see the pain homophobia causes this young man. She interrogates herself, her community, and her brother. With some disclaimers (she resists concluding that homosexuality is "right"), the writer decides that her community's homophobia—and especially the violence associated with it—is wrong.

What impresses me about this essay is not just the writer's change in attitude; rather, it is her developing awareness of the social dynamics of homophobia. She becomes more aware, for example, of the kind of group-think that engendered her attitude toward gays and lesbians from the beginning. Her realization that she learned fear and hatred of gays and lesbians from her brother and her peers immediately denaturalizes her prejudice. For her, homophobia is no longer a natural reaction to an obvious aberration of nature. She comes to see it, rather, as part of a network of social beliefs that she can resist. And, again, she does not see the "mistake" she made when she accepted her brother's homophobia as a glitch in individual logic. On the contrary, she clearly sees herself as part of a social world that, if it is not depicted as having a clear historical situatedness, nevertheless has some sense of locality. She depicts the place she comes from as having limitations, boundaries.

It is arguable that the essays included in the Coles and Vopat anthology that I defended several pages earlier have a less developed critical awareness. Curtis Buhman's "Street Scene/Mall Scene," for example, argues that the interior of the mall echoes the street scene outside the mall so that the mall can inspire "the sort of trust . . . that we willingly give to the downtown."[13] The downtown, he argues, was shaped by the community to meet its own needs, but the mall only looks like it was shaped by the community. But Buhman stops there, suggesting only in the most oblique way any connection between his observations and larger social or political issues. Likewise, Teri Cor's "Autobiographical Sketch" demonstrates a relatively limited critical perspective on the Roman Catholic Church. The sadistic elements of her education are attributed primarily to one nun "who was intrinsically aware of the extreme impressionability of very young children" (177). Again, Cor only suggests the relationship between the Catholic Church as a larger institution and the cruelty elements of the stories she was told at Catholic school; she only hints at the relationship between the Catholic Church and anticommunist nationalism in the United States. Finally, it could be argued that Michael Canlon's "A Great Way of Life" is almost exclusively solipsistic in its concerns, spends the larger part of its intellectual energy on the personal discomforts Canlon experienced while enlisted, and pays little attention to anything ethically problematic in the structure of the military as an institution.

Nevertheless, these three student essays are quite strong as freshman pieces and have a great deal of potential. Curtis Buhman might have simply followed his own line of thinking a little further. Why do mall architects wish to create a sense of trust and comfort? Why does it matter that this is so? Likewise, Michael Canlon might have expanded his view to include his experience of the air force as an institution. How did that institution lure Canlon and others like him in the first place? How did it ensure their continued cooperation? And Teri Cor might have delved further into her experiences with Catholic school without having to take her thinking in a different direction. How important a part of her education were the violent stories and scare tactics she reports in her essay? How else do they reverberate in her adult life and in the lives of those around her? Even if we insist on the shortcomings of these student essays, we must at least admit that each contains the seeds of a truly impressive critique.

In other words, despite their failings, these essays represent a good start and interesting intellectual/critical work for students in their first semesters of college. Of course, critics of expressivism are not targeting student writers anyway. France is critical of the assignments that elicited the essays in *What Makes Writing Good,* and so am I, to some degree. The assignments collected in the Coles and Vopat anthology are thoughtful and, I imagine, provocative for students. They are also taken out of the context of the classes for which they were designed, and this leaves them vulnerable to misreading. Having acknowledged this, however, I must also point out that many of the assignments included in the anthology eschew the kind of critical commitment at issue here.

Robert Holland's assignment, for example, fosters exactly the kind of individualist thinking for which expressivism is criticized. His assignment asks students to tell the story of a barrier overcome, but the kind of barrier Holland has in mind is a phantasmic one. Students are to choose a " 'known' limit" that "was not real" and explain how they came to see and, therefore, overcome it.[14] What is interesting to me in this assignment is not that Holland fails to encourage students to consider the sociohistorical elements of "limits" but that he actively *dis*courages such consideration. Rosemary Deen's assignment is interesting for similar reasons. She tells students to imagine that they have "just made a remark about something that is important to [them]" and that someone responds in an "outrageous, thoughtless, or reductive" way to that remark.[15] Deen is asking students to write polemic, a form most often deployed in pointedly political ways. Interestingly, however, she discourages the development of sociohistorical consciousness by asking students to write from within the context of an *imaginary* conversation; students are, in a sense, expected to *have an argument with themselves.*

Many of the contributors to the Coles and Vopat anthology focus on the "honesty" of the student writer, praise "natural" or "naive" voices, and even explicitly dismiss student political concerns; but not everything these teacher-contributors write is as politically or materially bereft as France would have us think, however. James Sledd, for example, writes about the need for English teachers and students to understand different forms of the English language in their own historical contexts and praises a colleague who asks students to wonder "whether it is possible or even desirable to be just one integrated self and not some number of different selves at once, whether honesty is relative, and whether the truth of a statement can be judged without regard to the situation where it's made."[16] Likewise, Ira Schor makes the connections between the personal and political in his classes explicit. Students write about "material from their daily lives" not to escape from the social, political, or historical but to "gain critical awareness of themselves as individuals connected to a larger social picture."[17] Throughout the collection, furthermore, students understand themselves in relation to different contexts, different audiences, different disciplinary parameters.

My point is simply this: the limitations of some expressivist assignments do not implicate all such assignments and certainly do not extend to all assignments of personal writing in the college classroom. We should, however, be aware of the potential problems of personal writing, should struggle to come up with assignments and ways of talking about personal writing that prompt our students toward the critical awareness we would like them to have. My thinking on this issue is relatively new (some of it done in the process of writing this paper), but I do have a few practical suggestions. The assignment that generated the paper about homophobia, for example, is one that I think works in the right direction. This assignment asks students to trace the history of their thinking about something. The assignment, sometimes called "A History of My Thinking," asks students to reconstruct the contexts within which they came to hold a particular belief. I ask them to try to imagine when they might have first come to believe as they do, to explain how the belief was affirmed, whether it was ever modified, and so forth. I also ask a number of specific questions that probably helped the student in the essay on homophobia locate her brother as one source of her feelings about gays and lesbians. I ask whether their belief developed in relation to family, friends, community members, church. I ask if any particular events influenced their thinking, things they had seen on the news, things that had happened to them personally or to their friends. Finally, I ask students the current status of the belief in question.

I find this assignment especially effective as a first or early assignment in a composition class for a number of reasons. To begin with, it is compelling for many students. It asks them to use their analytical skills, but it asks them to apply those skills to a subject they already know something about. Also, though the assignment asks students to think—in relatively new ways—about abstract concepts and their own beliefs, the students are beginning from a place of relative comfort. Finally, the generally straightforward narrative structure allows students to explore their ideas in the context of a relatively manipulable format.

A second assignment that also works well, though not as uniformly so far, is a personal narrative about a conversation. For this assignment, I ask students to interview another person on the history of his or her belief about something. As before, the students are asked to analyze a personal experience, but this time the subject under consideration is something they know less about, an external "text." The construction of the paper is also more complicated because it does not necessarily make sense to write it in chronological order. What is important in this assignment is for students to convey both a sense of respect for the interviewee and a sense of the historical context within which s/he came to have his/her position on the issue in question. This is a more difficult assignment for students; but when it works, it works very well. When it does not work, students nevertheless get the opportunity to explore another person's perception in a way that confounds the distinction students and the rest of us tend to make between the intellectual and the personal.

Generally speaking, I get a number of strong responses to both of these assignments. I also get essays, however, more like the second essay I mentioned in my introduction. This essay was a patchwork of clichés and advertising slogans. It was the story of how the author confirmed for himself what he had always believed anyway, that he could "be all that he could be" if he just "kept his eyes on the prize." In some ways, this essay was itself a kind of masculine drag. The slogans the author chose to use in his writing were clearly invocations of masculinity. He primarily used, I think, rhetoric from sports or military advertising; but the writer was very unconscious of the role he was playing. The vocabulary and the stock of slogans and images he employed were, for him, completely natural.

I would go so far as to say that, while I have significantly better results with the "History of My Thinking" and with the interview assignment than with the more traditional personal writing assignments I used in the past, the larger part of my students still hand in essays that show only slightly more self-awareness than this last student. Often, my students treat the essays I assign them as rote. They write essays like "How I Came to Believe in the Importance of Seatbelts" or "How I Know I Shouldn't Drink as Much as I Did Last Night." My students show a marked preference for avoiding critical thinking. They do not necessarily want to know about those social and political dynamics, knowledge of which might call on them to live their lives differently. To return to Judith Butler's metaphor, students do not necessarily want to see gender or any of the other roles they play as a mime, do not want to see their own social actions and relationships as anything other than natural.

How do I further counter such resistance? How, within the confines of my own institutional role, might I wake students up to a greater awareness of the social/sexual/gender roles they play? How might I move students further in the direction of disruptive or self-conscious narratives and away from naturalized representations of self and world? I am not sure. So far, I have moved more and more toward an emphasis on critical writing that I elaborate in the context of extended attention to the social and historical position of the "self." Besides the assignments I describe, I ask students to write about their relationships with particular vocational or avocational discourses, to critique the ideas of professional writers within those discourses, and to engage in a conversation with a series of printed texts. I try to contextualize and problematize.

However, I now think—and these are ideas I have barely had the opportunity of testing on my classes—that I might push the development of critical thinking a little further by expressing more self-consciousness about my own role. What might it mean to go "in drag" as a teacher? I do not, at this moment, mean teacher as knuckle-slapping upholder of institutional mores, though certainly the limitations of my institutionalized position are worthy of exploration and exposition. I am thinking, at the moment, of the role I am playing now: teacher as moral guardian, teacher as enlightener. At conferences, I have heard over and over again the accusation that teachers with progressive agendas are acting like missionaries—an accusation that more often than not comes from the ranks of progressives themselves and that is educated, in any case, by progressive rhetoric. In the past, I have found this accusation irritating and easy; but suddenly, it seems helpful.

It seems to me that I have thus far been very much "in the closet" in relation to my classes. My concern about encouraging students to develop critical perspectives is often covered over by my more traditional concerns about style, organization, and rhetorical modes. That is, I tend to make assignments I hope will push students to critique the world around them, but then I talk primarily about organization, focus, rhetorical modes, surface errors—things that are important but clearly not my only object. Obviously, part of my reason for this secrecy is my own sense of vulnerability. After all, to expose my own program is to reveal that, indeed, I have a program and am not the universal and objective teaching subject. Without pretending to abjure the institutional power that, in fact, I cannot abjure, perhaps I should be more open about what it is I hope to see happen in the classroom and why. After all, progressive teaching has a history, too, as do the choices of individual teachers. If I pick up a particular mantle at least partly because I worry about my children, myself, my species, it might not be a bad idea to stage that anxiety.

I think I did just that (by accident) a few days ago. The last assignment I give in my advanced writing course is a problem-and-solution paper. I tell students they can write about anything that might, even loosely, be defined as a problem, but I encourage them to think about social problems in their own community or in the professional community that they wish to be a part of. This time, out of frustration with student apathy, I introduced the assignment with an in-class personal essay that we discussed at some length. I asked students to write about what they would like to see change in the world during the 720 or so months they have left here. I asked them to explore their personal stake in the problem(s) they were writing about, and, finally, I asked them to break their problem down into chunks small enough for an individual to grapple with in some concrete way. The hours they have, I pointed out, are not endless, and those they spend in my classroom should not be thrown away. They could use the class, use the paper, to think through an issue of concrete importance to them, to the people they care about, and/or to the people they will work with. They could use their class time to come up with a plan of action.

My students certainly took the assignment more seriously, as much I think because of what I exposed about myself as because of anything I might have exposed about their own situations. What was I exposing? What could they see about me that day? That I have anxieties and desires? That I *would* like to use the hours I have left for something other than the production of competent writers for consumption by scholarly, corporate, or political machines? Could they see the role I assign myself? That I would like to see myself as something other, and something more, than the marker "civil servant" suggests? I got a couple of satirical writings, a mildly hostile essay, and quite a few very earnest and thoughtful pieces in response to this assignment, this plea, this staging of my pedagogical desires. The point is, though, that I was playing in earnest the role that I have developed a habit of hiding. I was more open to student critique, and those students who resisted had to play their roles more openly, too. It became, I think, more possible for us to discuss what is at stake in the theater of the classroom.

Notes

1. Susan Miller, *Textual Carnivals: The Politics of Composition* (Carbondale: Southern Illinois University Press, 1991), 61. Subsequent references to this work will be included parenthetically in the text.

2. James Berlin, "Rhetoric and Ideology in the Writing Class," *College English* 50:5 (1988): 484. Subsequent references to this work will be included parenthetically in the text.

3. Alan W. France, "Assigning Places: Introductory Composition as a Cultural Discourse," *College English* 55:6 (Oct. 1993): 593. Subsequent references to this work will be included parenthetically in the text.

4. William E. Coles Jr. and James Vopat, ed., *What Makes Writing Good* (Lexington, Mass.: Heath, 1985).

5. Peter Elbow, *Writing without Teachers* (London: Oxford University Press, 1973), 7.

6. Teri Cor, "Autobiographical Sketch," in *What Makes Writing Good,* ed. Coles and Vopat, 179. Subsequent references to this work will be included parenthetically in the text.

7. Judith Butler, "Imitation and Gender Insubordination," in *Inside/Out: Lesbian Theories, Gay Theories,* ed. Diana Fuss (New York: Routledge, 1991), 16. Subsequent references to this work will be included parenthetically in the text.

8. Diana Fuss, "Inside/Out," in *Inside/Out,* ed. Fuss, 4. Subsequent references to this work will be included parenthetically in the text.

9. Michel Foucault, *The History of Sexuality,* vol. 1: *An Introduction,* trans. Robert Hurley (New York: Vintage, 1978), 101.

10. Diana Fuss, *Essentially Speaking: Feminism, Nature, and Difference* (New York: Routledge, 1989), 95.

11. Esther Newton, *Mother Camp: Female Impersonators in America* (Englewood Cliffs, N.J.: Prentice-Hall, 1972), 108, 111. Subsequent references to this work will be included parenthetically in the text.

12. Judith Butler, *Gender Trouble: Feminism and the Subversion of Identity* (New York: Routledge, 1990), 137.

13. Curtis Buhman, "Street Scene/Mall Scene," in *What Makes Writing Good,* ed. Coles and Vopat, 59.

14. Robert Holland, "Assignment," in *What Makes Writing Good,* ed. Coles and Vopat, 12.

15. Rosemary Deen, "Assignment," in *What Makes Writing Good,* ed. Coles and Vopat, 114.

16. James Sledd, "Commentary," in *What Makes Writing Good,* ed. Coles and Vopat, 35.

17. Ira Schor, "Commentary," in *What Makes Writing Good,* ed. Coles and Vopat, 168.

Part 2 "Literature"

5

"Kissing the Boar": Queer Adonis and Critical Practice

Goran V. Stanivukovic

At a crucial moment near the end of William Shakespeare's *Venus and Adonis,* disoriented by despair for the loss of Adonis, Venus recounts Adonis's death in his encounter with the boar in the following way:

> But this foul, grim, and urchin-snouted boar,
> Whose downward eye still looketh for a grave,
> Ne'er saw the beauteous livery that he wore;
> Witness the entertainment that he gave.
>> If he did see his face, why then I know
>> He thought to kiss him, and hath killed him so.
>
> 'Tis true, 'tis true; thus was Adonis slain:
> He ran upon the boar with his sharp spear,
> Who did not whet his teeth at him again,
> But by a kiss thought to persuade him there;
>> And nuzzling in his flank, the loving swine
>> Sheathed unaware the tusk in his soft groin. (1105–16)[1]

This is a familiar death scene in the early Shakespeare. Its origins are in Ovid, but Shakespeare adds erotic ambiguities. While Ovid's Adonis dies as a hunter, in Shakespeare's poem Adonis dies as a lover in a violent clash represented as a passionate union; this is how Venus imagines Adonis's death to be, projecting her own erotic desire onto the boar. The boar's kiss, not found in Ovid, is Shakespeare's invention. In classical mythology, Adonis does get gored by the boar. In rewriting Ovid, however, Shakespeare ambivalently transforms the death scene by adding a kiss to the boar's clash with Adonis, associating the touch of the boar's snout with an intimate gesture. However, as Venus repeats twice (109–10, 103), the kiss was not intended to kill Adonis; his death is an accident.[2] The wound in Adonis's groin, both in Ovid and Shakespeare, is also charged with erotic symbolism. The boar-Adonis encounter is further complicated by Shakespeare's identification, through the masculine pronoun "he," of the two protagonists as male. Therefore, the semantic shift from the man-animal to the man-man dynamics turns the death scene into an allegory of violent union between two men. In the Renaissance etiology of love, especially in Neoplatonism, the kiss symbolized an exchange of souls, a completion of a desired union. Thus, by mixing the intimate with the destructive, combined with the meiosis of the boar's bite as a mortal kiss, Shakespeare adds a masculine component to the death scene. The fact that the death of Adonis is located in the context of male erotics is of particular interest in regard to the ambivalent erotic politics in the poem. What motivates this association of death with male erotics?

In Renaissance love poetry, the hunt is associated with amorous pursuit and seduction.[3] Thus, Adonis's hunt of the boar, his seductive pursuit of a desired object, becomes a sign of male yearning for union with another man. Adonis does not want just to hunt the boar; he says he wants to be with his friends (" 'I am,' quoth he, 'expected of my friends' " [718]). The clash with the masculine boar is, therefore, part of the scene of Adonis's homosocial bonding with other men. Could it be, then, that Arthur Golding, an adamant Puritan, spotted something illicit in the death scene when in his most influential translation of *Metamorphoses* in the Renaissance he decided to delete the wound in the groin?

The association of Adonis with erotic transgression, which is what I argue is the issue in the death scene in *Venus and Adonis,* also occurs in book 3, canto 6 of Edmund Spenser's *Faerie Queene.* In stanza 48, for example, Spenser tells us that after Venus has "firmly emprisoned" in a cave the castrating boar who threatened Adonis, Adonis continues to "liueth in eternall bliss, / Ioying his goddesse, and of her enioyd." Yet this hetero-erotic bliss is immediately interrupted in stanza 49, where Spenser represents the dalliance of Adonis and the idle Cupid:

There now he liues in euerlasting ioy,
With many of the Gods in company,
Which thither haunt, and with the winged boy
Sporting himselfe in safe felicity:
Who when he hath with spoiles and cruelty
Ransackt the world, and in the wofull harts
Of many wretches set his triumphes hye,
Thither resorts, and laying his sad darts
Aside, with faire *Adonis* playes his wanton parts.[4]

The "wanton parts" that Cupid plays with Adonis most likely suggest erotic parts, and Spenser's confusion of pronouns adds to the sexual mystery of this stanza. The obscuring in fact plays part in the erotic transgression that is at stake in this stanza.[5]

By linking eroticism with violence in the death scene, Shakespeare transcribes this male-male union as destructive. But I further want to argue that the homoerotic implications in the scene of Adonis's death suggest the way Shakespeare employs a classical developmental narrative to disrupt heteroerotic desire. Thus, *Venus and Adonis* suggests complications that surround the representation of heteroerotic masculinity in the Renaissance.

Criticism of *Venus and Adonis* has either altogether neglected the homoerotic component in the poem or, when it has tackled this subject, treated it as a category of identity.[6] In such ahistorical approaches to the erotics in the poem, homoeroticism (or any other *sexual* identity) is considered a separate identity, clearly defined and linguistically marked. In the Renaissance, however, homosexuality was not recognized as such; and, therefore, its literary representations are not easy to decipher.[7] In *Venus and Adonis,* sodomy is rhetorically inscribed into character as part of a larger strategy of the construction of erotic identity. Renaissance sodomy, as Gregory Bredbeck suggests, represents the "potentiality" of a textual—not social—subjectivity.[8] Contrary to the treatment of homoeroticism as the psychological component of a character, a queer approach to erotics that recognizes sexuality as the rhetorical sublime of the social[9] illuminates more clearly the sociosexual problems that surrounded the Renaissance conceptualization of homoeroticism. In *Venus and Adonis,* this discursive construction of the erotic is underlied by the early modern anxiety about sodomy as a gross sin. Thus, I suggest that both the fixation on identity and the heterosexual assumptions about sexuality have led traditional critical practice to examine *Venus and Adonis* almost exclusively around the axis of male-female sexuality. However, this criticism has not acknowledged anything erotic in the only union that is actually achieved in the poem: Adonis's union with the boar. And even though this union is fatal, it nevertheless represents a union that is desired and accomplished, unlike Venus's pursuit of Adonis, suggesting a desire for a union that is denied. Yet the linguistic ambiguities that characterize Adonis's articulation of desire problematize his sexuality precisely at those moments in the poem that reflect social anxieties about male-male erotics in the Renaissance.

Adonis and the boar are figures associated with homoerotic desire in the poem. With its relatively stable, archetypal signification of lust contained in overbearing masculinity, the boar clarifies the rather ambivalent figure of Adonis in the erotic economy in the poem.[10] Furthermore, while Venus's sophistic rhetoric of seduction attempts to glorify her erotic power, the failure of her eloquence implies the instability of the (hetero)erotic ideals represented in Venus. Thus, Venus's rhetorical failure opens up the possibility for Adonis to set out on *his* seductive pursuit of the boar. Adonis's flirtation with Venus earlier in the poem, without any attempt to give in to her desire, and his need (" 'I know not love . . . nor will not know it / Unless it be a boar, and then I chase it' " [409–10]) to pursue the masculine boar suggest his ambivalent attitude toward the heterosexual norm. Adonis's erotic agency in these episodes reveals what Harold Beaver calls a "double-dealer," a sexually ambivalent figure that moves almost invisibly, "incognito through a heterosexual world."[11]

The signs of Adonis's queerness, which undercut the sociosexual, generative role he is supposed to play, are numerous in the poem. First, Venus's construction of Adonis as effeminate denies his masculinity at the beginning of the poem. Venus refers to Adonis as "more lovely than a man" (9). However we read this line—either as "lovelier than a man, hence like a woman," or as an "ideal man"—it identifies Adonis with the hyperbolized praise of a woman in Petrarchan poetics. Here, Shakespeare substitutes the ideal Petrarchan woman with Adonis, applying the conventional, female attributes to Adonis, the young god of fertility. Further, Venus refers to Adonis's " 'soft hands, sweet lips and crystal eyne, / Whose full perfection all the world amazes' " (633–34) and to his "soft bosom" (81), all of which suggest emasculation. The Renaissance inherited from Aristotle the belief that men with hairless bodies, especially chests, are sexually feeble.[12] And the effeminate male was considered in the Renaissance "an ideal type of human beauty."[13] Yet Shakespeare's association of Adonis with male eroticism undercuts this ideal of human beauty by turning it into an anxious and tragic yearning. By representing Adonis as passive and effeminate, Shakespeare constructs Adonis as the body that, by avoiding heterosexual union, reveals the other side of masculinity, that which tragically shuns an active role in procreation. Praised in feminine terms, Adonis is constructed as an ambiguously gendered body, much like the fair youth in Shakespeare's sonnets. As Roland Barthes notices, the narrator's "bad faith *indicates* (by referring it to a woman) the model's lack of virility; his lie is thus an inductor of truth."[14] The ambiguous construction of Adonis's body as both beautiful and tragic is further articulated in Venus's lines: " 'For he being dead, with him is Beauty slain, / And, Beauty dead, *black Chaos comes again*' " (1019–20; emphasis added). These lines are particularly disturbing because the death of Adonis, as Venus reports, implies tragic consequences outside the realm of the private. Venus laments her own loss of consummation, and this denial of consummation threatens to destabilize the order of the universe. Combined with sodomy, which violates the procreative principle that the poem attempts to install, effeminacy has particularly threatening implications. Effeminization suggests the lack of masculine powers; it denies procreation and, according to Renaissance assumptions, thus threatens the social order. The death of the effeminized Adonis, the removal of the threat he personifies, represents an attempt to restore order, both social and sexual.

Adonis expands the representation of sexuality in the poem by simultaneously belonging to two worlds, male and female. As Venus says: " 'Thing like a man, but of no woman bred! / Thou art no man, though of a man's complexion, / For men will kiss even by their own direction' " (214–16). The androgynous figure in these lines denies a clear definition of gender and, therefore, opens up other possibilities for gender inscription. Thus, Adonis emerges as a queer figure in the sense in which Eve Kosofsky Sedgwick defines "queer," as the "open mesh of possibilities, gaps, overlaps, dissonances and resonances, lapses and excesses of meaning when the constituent element of anyone's gender, of anyone's sexuality aren't made (or *can't be* made) to signify monolithically."[15] The tragedy of Adonis's physical union with the masculine boar renders his ambivalent desire as sodomy.

The masculine symbolism of the boar further complicates his connection with Adonis in the sexual economy of the poem. The cultural tradition—heraldic representations, emblems, painting, and literature—of the boar's symbolism links this animal with virility and masculine power. The

phallic imagery that characterizes the boar episode in the poem, combined
with threat in Venus's construction of the boar, associates male sexual
potency with aggression and death. So, the boar's "snout digs sepulchres
where'er he goes" (622); he kills with his "crooked tushes" (624) and "bris-
tly pikes" (620); he has "hairy bristles" (625) and a "short thick neck"
(627). Here, the boar allegorically represents the male body in the state of
sexual arousal, which Adonis's "spear's point" (626), his phallic weapon,
cannot defeat.[16] The queer relation to sexual politics, in which both male
sexual potency and male-male erotics are constructed as subversive, underlies the scene that depicts the boar's clash with Adonis. Venus says:

> "The picture of an angry chafing boar
> Under whose sharp fangs on his back doth lie
> An *image like thyself*, all stained with gore;
>> Whose blood upon the fresh flowers being shed. . . ."
> (662–65; emphasis added)

The boar and Adonis have exchanged positions in the death scene, as the
boar looks down on Adonis's dead "image," which evokes the narcissistic
trope of homoeroticism, whereby the reflection the male sees in the mirror
and falls in love with is not only himself but another man. Adonis's quest
for union with the bestial other, symbolically rendered as his same-sexed
half, suggests the classic psychoanalytic theory that sees the pairing of the
beautiful and the monstrous as fundamentally a homosexual doubling, a
paranoid projection of the other.[17] In this doubling, the masculine boar
suggests the physical embodiment of the same-sexed other with which
Adonis seeks union. Shakespeare's version of Adonis's story, therefore, exploits the ambiguous part of Ovid's heteroerotic narrative in a way that
both constructs and defies, through Adonis's death, homoerotic pleasure
in the narrative of heterosexual seduction.

* * *

Attention to erotics in my reading of the death of Adonis challenges rou-
tinely "desexualizing readings" of this episode.[18] The death of Adonis represents the point at which Shakespeare's radical expansion of the myth
violates Renaissance sexual normativity. In this sense, the poem enables,
through Adonis and the boar, a discourse of homoeroticism in a poem
about the formation of heteroerotic desire. Recent gay historiography has
demonstrated that the hetero- and homosexual division along sharply
distinguished lines does not reflect the ways in which the Renaissance

viewed (homo)sexuality. The category of homosexuality did not mean the same thing then as it does for modern times, and it was textualized in rhetorically ambiguous signs.[19]

Adonis's death suggests the Renaissance anxiety concerning sodomy, seen, in Jonathan Goldberg's words, as "the most fundamental malaise of Elizabethan society."[20] Similarly, Bruce R. Smith suggests that sodomy was heavily stigmatized in the Renaissance, where it covered different sorts of heterosexual behavior.[21] Much has been written about Renaissance sodomy already. But I would like to summarize the matter to point to some crucial differences in modern critical attitudes toward Renaissance sodomy. Clarifying these differences is important for my argument about the ambiguities—realized along the binary opposition of pleasure-peril—in textualizing sodomy in *Venus and Adonis.*

There have been attempts in gay historiography to view the English Renaissance as less homophobic than it actually was. On the one hand, Stephen Orgel considers the Renaissance to have been more tolerant about homosexuality than ordinarily considered because the period lacked the conceptual categories of both homo- and heterosexuality, lacked a taxonomy that defined sexual behavior.[22] On the other hand, Alan Bray, in his classic study *Homosexuality in Renaissance England,* acknowledges an almost morbidly problematic attitude toward sodomy in the Renaissance. Bray's identity-oriented approach to sodomy allows for the construction of subjectivity only if the sodomitical act is not named, if it is kept secret and practiced as "merely casual and undefined."[23] Bray suggests that Renaissance sodomy was rendered as a behavior that was impossible to articulate since, subjectively, it was realized only as silence. While Bray argues that this was very likely a strategy that helped a Renaissance man "to avoid the psychological problems of a homosexual relationship or a homosexual encounter" (76), his argument about this psychological strategy raises the issue of the textual articulation of sodomy in Renaissance literature. Thus, Bray posits a methodological problem for a queer project that approaches sodomy as a rhetorically constructed subjectivity within a particular ideological realm. I want to point at the methodological possibilities for, and difficulties in, applying Bray's primarily sociohistorical study to an examination of the ways sodomy was inscribed in Renaissance literature.

In the Renaissance, sodomy was taken to include a vast array of transgressions (not necessarily sexual) that disrupted normativity. But any behavior rendered sodomitical was considered profoundly threatening to social order and procreation. Sodomy was usually considered an additional sin to go with some other debauchery that the Renaissance considered to be sodomitical. Religious heresy, for example, was frequently associated with sodomy, as in Thomas Lodge's *Wits Miserie, and the Worlds Madnesse* (1596).[24] In this treatise, Lodge defines sodomy as "peruerting the order of nature"; he says the same of religious sins. In pre-Enlightenment culture, as Ed Cohen suggests, sodomy often "constituted a transgression against the word/law of God."[25] Correspondingly, in Lodge, sodomy leads to chaos in Christendom. Seen in the light of Lodge's work, Venus's lament that Adonis's death invokes chaos associates carnal sin with public disaster. And Alan Bray suggests that the closest substitute idea for the Renaissance sodomite would be that of a traitor.[26] Indeed, what else but treason, broadly conceived as a violation of the public norm of any kind, could be more disruptive for Elizabeth I's England, totally invested in controlling the social and political order of its rising state.[27] It is also worth remembering that the stability of the Elizabethan state—since Machiavelli associated the power of masculinity with the courtier-warrior, this became true of the Renaissance state in general—was invested in powerful masculinity, as the examples of Shakespeare's Claudius and Richard III demonstrate.

In my discussion of the Adonis-boar connection, I use the term sodomy in the sense in which Goldberg defines it as "a sexual act, anything that threatens alliance—any sexual act . . . that does not promote the aim of married procreative sex" (*Sodometries* 19). Furthermore, in subverting procreation—hence denying the socially promoted normativity of marriage— sodomy, as Goldberg suggests, negates "marriage [as] the social institution whose regulatory functions ramify everywhere" (19). In *Venus and Adonis*, sodomy in the death scene, on the one hand, ironically undercuts the argument for marriage in violating the spiritual as well as physical demand for a heterosexual union. On the other hand, again ironically, the death of Adonis renders sodomy as a tragedy of the character who has violated the sanctified realm of pleasure. Thus, the sexual politics of homoeroticism in *Venus and Adonis* displays male-male erotics as fatal, as a disorderly sodomy that cancels both sexual and social regularity.[28]

* * *

In the long cultural tradition of the complex myth of Adonis, this figure symbolizes uncorrupted sexuality and represents both the order of nature and the powers of renewal.[29] By extension, Adonis's death suggests sexual impotence and the violation of the order of nature. At the climactic point in Shakespeare's narrative—the moment of Adonis's death—the myth underscores the power of desire by condemning the yearning for sodomy. Thus, by undercutting the narrative of normative sexuality, Shakespeare queers the myth of Venus and Adonis in the sense in which Judith Butler defines the queer project as a "linguistic practice whose purpose has been the shaming of the subject it names or, rather, the producing of a subject *through* that shaming interpellation."[30] Homoeroticism, constructed as sodomy, not only denies heterosexual normativity and the procreative order but also undercuts the love-beauty binarism often discussed as central to Shakespeare's epyllion.

Critical accounts of *Venus and Adonis* have either evaded the subject of Shakespeare's (homo)erotic subversion in the death scene, or they have merely scratched the surface of the subject. In one of the classic essays on the poem, A. C. Hamilton defines the boar as concupiscence or the mortal effect of concupiscence. Furthermore, Hamilton suggests that the meaning of the boar cannot only be "moral"; but, in a manner characteristic of much of normative heterosexual scholarship, he interprets the significance of the boar only because it affects the procreating agency of Venus. That part of the poem—Hamilton sees it as its center—in which Adonis does not yield to Venus's seduction, Hamilton reads as "mystery."[31] For Hamilton, the boar represents a destructive force that ruins both Venus, identified with love, and Adonis, identified with beauty and "nature in its unfallen state" ("Venus" 7). Yet Hamilton's Neoplatonic interpretation of the death scene is only partial. It avoids discussion of Shakespeare's transformation of the source through emphasis on Adonis's corporeality and the boar's violation of Adonis's body. The way Shakespeare renders Adonis's masculinity as problematic in the death scene, however, illuminates our understanding of Venus's futile attempts to seduce Adonis. Hamilton's account is representative of the kind of criticism that interprets Adonis only as a symbol of the sexual metaphysics, as an abstraction elevated to the level of a mythical erotic symbolism. In *Venus and Adonis*, however, myth and masculinity are intricately connected. By displacing Adonis from the realm of erotics—specifically, male erotics (where his mythological roots lie)—the existent criticism of the poem assumes only one desire, heterosexual desire.

Among the critics who discuss sexuality in the poem, A. T. Hatto is one of the few who have attempted to associate the boar with the powers of destructive masculinity.[32] Hatto sees the boar as the symbol of overbearing masculinity and as Venus's rival in her attempts to seduce Adonis. But Hatto's argument stops at this point. Moreover, by neglecting the agency of the boar in the death scene, Hatto's criticism narrows the symbolical implication of the scene for the interpretation of the sexual economy in the poem. Hatto examines the poem under the assumption that heterosexuality represented a stable category in the Renaissance. Continuing where Hatto stopped, William E. Sheidley addresses the subject of the boar's phallic implications. Sheidley, however, uses the phallic implications of the boar as a strategy to remove Adonis from the episode of his erotic coupling with the boar and thus, like Hamilton, to locate Venus in the center of the episode. For Sheidley, "the dislocation of phallic potency predicates the frustration of Venus and brings about the destruction of Adonis. Properly placed, in Adonis, if that were possible, it might have rendered all well. The case of Adonis . . . demonstrates that manhood must be *displayed* in other ways than by going hunting. As a boar-hunter, Adonis perversely pursues to its end a policy of self-castration."[33] The rhetoric of Sheidley's account, with its insistence on what would be "proper" in the death episode, reflects the heterosexual assumption that underlies Adonis's relation to Venus, although the narrative demonstrates that Venus is here only as a passive reporter of a completed act in which she did not participate.

Even those critics who acknowledge the homosexual component of the myth deny its relevance for the erotics in *Venus and Adonis*. For example, William Keach observes that there is nothing overtly homoerotic in Orpheus's presentation of Adonis.[34] We may question this both when it applies to Ovid and certainly when it refers to Shakespeare's representation of Adonis. The fact that in *Metamorphoses*, it is Orpheus, the patron of homosexuality, who tells the story of Adonis's death locates Adonis in the realm of homosexuality. But the point I would like to make here is that the problem with this line of criticism is not so much that it does not acknowledge a separate homoerotic discourse embedded within the recognizable discourse of normative sexuality. The problem is that, by creating an argument around an assumption of desire that is clearly defined along the clear-cut lines of binary oppositions, such criticism assumes only the heterosexual aspect of the construction of desire in the poem. Thus, such criticism not only misreads the representation of desire in *Venus and Adonis*, but it also misreads the signification of the erotic art to which the poem belongs. In this kind of art, as Foucault remarks, "pleasure is not consid-

ered in relation to an absolute law of the permitted and the forbidden . . .
but . . . in relation to itself."[35] The question, then, is not how the poem
relates to the valorized models of sexual relations but how *eros* as such can
be represented regardless of the norms that attempt to valorize it.

Hamilton and Hatto, and to a greater extent Sheidley too, represent the
kind of criticism that considers only one, singular and safe line of the
poem's symbolism. In that interpretation, *Venus and Adonis* displays the
clash between the Ovidian and the Neoplatonic conceptualization of love;
lust ruins beauty. Critics who discuss Adonis within the Neoplatonic paradigm of love deny Neoplatonic discourse of love the capacity to legitimate
homoerotic desire.[36] The homoerotic component of Neoplatonism, which
originates in Plato and is elaborated by Marsilio Ficino, permeates, for
example, the sonnets of Shakespeare and Richard Barnfield.[37] Adonis's rejection of Venus's seduction and his tragic end in the union with the boar
suggest the ironic subversion of the Neoplatonic quest for the union with
one's other—usually same-sexed—half, as Aristophanes suggests in Plato's
Symposium. As an erotic body framed within the poem's Neoplatonic discourse, Adonis may be said to characterize what Foucault calls "a kind of
interior androgyny, a hermaphroditism of the soul" (*History* 53). Therefore, the Neoplatonic decorum in *Venus and Adonis* is violated by the sodomitical undercurrent that underlies the amorous narrative of the quest
for an object of desire not clearly defined.

As an erotic narrative composed of two divergent story lines about two
different kinds of sexual longing, *Venus and Adonis* doubles the possibilities for interpreting the sexual politics that are the subject of the poem's
narrative. Recently, there have been attempts to explore desire in the poem
in more open terms. Catherine Belsey, for example, suggests that *"Venus
and Adonis* is a poetic record of the originating moment of desire."[38] Jonathan Bate interprets the poem as "a celebration of sexuality even as it is
a disturbing exposure of the dark underside of desire."[39] Both Bate and
Belsey make a leap forward in considering desire in *Venus and Adonis* as a
power that has more than one definition. However, while both authors
examine desire as a broadly encompassing phenomenon that either identifies subjectivity (Bate) or motivates the character's psycholinguistic nature (Belsey), neither considers the symbolical implication of *eros* as a force
that disrupts, by its very uncontrollable force, the ideology of procreative
order that is being disrupted in the poem.

Adonis's rejection of Venus closes down sexual possibilities for her; but at the same time, it opens up other erotic possibilities for him, possibilities enabled by his pursuit of the boar. To examine the poetic version of the myth of desire within the context of the polymorphous Renaissance sexuality only in terms of heterosexual opposition is to narrow, even to misrepresent, the negotiation of sexuality in *Venus and Adonis*. The rhetorical ambiguities in which Adonis's desire is articulated—and, furthermore, the sexual ambivalences of his attitude toward Venus and the boar—construct his homoerotic desire as an evasive, almost invisible, category. Adonis is realized as a figure that simultaneously contains and transgresses sexual meaning. He is constructed in terms that, as Barthes says, suggest that "the symbolic and the operative are non-decidable, subject to the rule of an *and/or*" (*S/Z* 77).

* * *

The sexual politics of *Venus and Adonis,* in which revulsion characterizes the (homo)eroticized body, rests on the discourse of an elusive sexuality that gay historiography associates with the discourse of sodomy in the Renaissance. What reveals the sodomite in Adonis is his need to construct his difference in the rhetorically ambiguous yet assertive terms of the rejection of heterosexual seduction. So he says:

> "I know not love . . . nor will not know it,
> Unless it be a boar, and then I chase it.
>
> . . . .
> My love to love is love but to disgrace it;
> For I have heard it is a life in death. . . ." (409–13)

> "Fair queen, . . . if any love you owe me,
> Measure *my strangeness* with my unripe years;
> Before I know myself, seek not to know me. . . ." (523–25; emphasis added)

In these lines, linguistic ambiguity becomes a sign of Adonis's sexual ambivalence. The *sprezzatura* of this passage—Adonis's disdainful playfulness with the idea of love—represents a rhetorical performance that constructs Adonis as the sodomite who articulates his sexuality as a linguistic mannerism that avoids clear definitions.[40] Adonis's wordplay suggests how something that is denied is at the same time brought out through the rhetorical strategy of concealment. As Judith Butler says, "what is 'performed' works to conceal, if not to disavow, what remains opaque, uncon-

scious, unperformable" (*Bodies* 234). Adonis's rejection of Venus's seduction (409–10), based on the argument that he has not yet reached sexual
maturity, represents an ironic strategy that closes down options for her but
opens them for himself. " 'Before I know myself, seek not to know me' "
suggests that the politics of sexuality constructs sodomy not only as a
rhetorical ambivalence but also as a psychological (developmental) ambivalence. Adonis is on the way to masculinity but is not there yet; and,
therefore, he is not ready for the heterosexual love embodied in Venus. Yet
the argument against her seduction is undone in his *love* for the boar hunt.
Thus, irony becomes a trope of the recognition of a character, offering an
insight into Adonis's hidden discourse. Shakespeare's queer irony empow-
ers Adonis with the weapon to resist Venus's heterosexual onset. The con-
ceited linguistic signs suggest in the Renaissance erotic discourses a sexual
dissent into the homoerotic.[41]

The concealment of "otherness" in the linguistic performance represents the way in which Renaissance desire is rhetorically constructed as
contingent, multifaceted, and—like other Renaissance discourses—polymorphous in meaning. At this point in Shakespeare's narrative, however,
Adonis's language suggests his distance from the regulatory sexuality of Venus. Thus, the politics of sexuality constructs sodomy as a discursive ambivalence, not as a characteristic of an identity (as Coppelia Kahn would
want to see it).[42] Namely, Kahn assumes sodomy to be a clearly defined
manifestation of sexual behavior in the Renaissance. Yet Adonis's language
does not support this, since it avoids any precise sexual definition. Kahn
imposes a contemporary meaning of sodomy as anal penetration onto a
discourse that constructs desire in a way that avoids gender identification.
In the Renaissance, as Goldberg suggests, sodomy was considered "not a
self-evident category" but a sexual activity that is "incapable of exact definition" (*Sodometries* 18).

Adonis's delight in the boar hunt, and his rhetorical evasiveness, an
avoidance to define the object of his desire, represents a speech-act that is
realized, in Sedgwick's terms, as "closet." As a sign of transgression, "closet"
is, according to Sedgwick, "a silence that accrues particularitly . . . in relation to the discourse that surrounds and differentially constitutes it."[43] As a
sign of the formation of self-knowledge, Sedgwick's closet frames Adonis's
homoerotic character within the discourse that denies Venus's (hetero)-
sexual seduction and constructs a discourse that allows what David Van
Leer calls the "possibility of homosexual meaning." For Van Leer, Sedg-

wick's closet is profitable for the examination of Renaissance polymorphous sexuality since the Renaissance does not assume homosexuality to
posit the problem of either self-identification or self-acceptance.[44]

* * *

To locate within the context of current gay historiography the queer reading of Shakespeare's *Venus and Adonis* means to redefine the relationship
between the male-male erotics in the poem and the ideological and social
contexts that surround it. Shakespeare's queer inflection of the myth of
Venus and Adonis also undercuts the sociosexual context of the male aristocratic culture—more particularly, the Earl of Southampton and his circle
of male friends and the noblemen of the Inns of Court—that the poem
addresses.

Yet this social aspect of the poem's disruptive potential has been neglected in criticism precisely because critical practice has often dissociated
the socioideological from the aesthetic aspect of the poem. Criticism has
also neglected the fact that classical stories in the Renaissance were neither
mere sources for new narratives, nor did those ancient texts, as Elizabeth
Story Donno suggests about Ovid's *Metamorphoses,* provide Renaissance
writers with material to indulge in copiousness.[45] The Renaissance emu-
lated and redefined ancient texts so that they could serve practices of the
humanist reading of classical stories, practices primarily concerned with
seeking instruction for private life and domestic concerns. Thus, the complex relationship between the humanist practical needs and classical texts
in the process of reading was considered an active process in adopting
morals and preparing for action.[46] As part of the Renaissance habits of
reading, however, this process sometimes worked in reverse. As Lisa Jardine and Anthony Grafton argue, some real-life events and outcomes of
events established a connection between writing and reading processes.[47]
The question, then, is how to relate the dynamics between the negotiation of homoerotic desire in the remodeled myth of Venus and Adonis in
Shakespeare's poem to the pleasure of reading for private purposes in the
case of the Earl of Southampton, Shakespeare's patron, to whom the poem
is dedicated. How does a poem that allegorizes both the pleasure and peril
of male erotics relate to Southampton's private experience?

Gabriel Harvey recorded that it was "the younger sort" that took "much
delight in Shakespeares Venus, & Adonis."[48] Southampton did not leave,
as far as we know, any record of his reading of either Ovid or Shakespeare.[49]
While we have no traces yet of Southampton's reading habits, we do have

records of his alleged erotic behavior. One of Southampton's contemporaries refers to him in a context that suggests the young nobleman's sybaritic taste for illicit sex.

An allegation about Southampton's odd way of dealing with friends appeared several years after the poem had been published, but it refers to the time of its publication in 1593. The allegation, which involves one Piers Edmonds, comes from William Reynolds, a public troublemaker and, as Katherine Duncan-Jones suggests, one of the first misreaders of Shakespeare's poem.[50] In his 1593 letters to the Privy Council, Reynolds identifies himself with the reluctant Adonis and Queen Elizabeth with the rapacious Venus. But in a 1601 letter to Robert Cecil, in which he slanders Southampton, Reynolds claims that, when Southampton was in the queen's service in Ireland, Piers Edmonds used to "eate & dranke at his [Southampton's] table and lay in his tente, [and when] the earle of Sowthamton gave him a horse, *which* edmones refused a 100 markes for him, the earle Sowthamton would cole and huge him in his armes and play wantonly *with* him" (qtd. in Duncan-Jones, "Much Ado" 485). Reynolds also reports that Edmonds wanted to seduce him in the same way he himself was seduced by Southampton but that he, Reynolds, rejected him. What can we make of this homosocial dalliance that Southampton was supposed to have indulged in when posted as a soldier in Ireland?

Katherine Duncan-Jones warns us that William Reynolds was very likely a "paranoid schizophrenic" and that, therefore, his manic ramblings should be taken with caution ("Much Ado" 484). Whether Reynolds's allegations are true or false is difficult to prove. Yet the rhetorical phrasing of his letter, framed around the subject of homosocial bonding and the pleasure that it yields in the private and exclusively male space of a soldier's tent, signals the contemporary culture's anxieties about the "wanton play" of men. Thus, Reynolds's account constructs a homosocial setting within which a homoerotic union is possible. (Like the soldier's tent, the all-male St. John's College, Cambridge, where Southampton studied, also provides a homosocial space within which homoeroticism is a potentiality in Southampton's life.) And one wonders whether Reynolds, who referred to *Venus and Adonis* in two of his 1593 letters, made deliberately slandering insinuations about Southampton's sexual practices, insinuations meant to harm Southampton's public standing precisely at the time when he, Reynolds, realized that he could not be Adonis but that Southampton, to whom Shakespeare dedicated the poem, could. The homosocial context that is evoked both by Reynolds's correspondence and by Shakespeare's dedication to Southampton—and, by extension, to other aristocratic, male readers—provides a background against which to explore the ambiguities in the construction of masculinity and sexuality in *Venus and Adonis*.

In his correspondence, Reynolds also mentions the Earl of Essex "and his men," presumably his friends, among whom, as Akrigg and Bray remark, we find Antonio Perez, a former secretary of King Philip II of Spain who fled to England after the Inquisition charged him with being a sodomite, heretic, and traitor (Akrigg, *Shakespeare* 36–37; Bray, *Homosexuality* 4–8). Perez lived loosely in England too, socializing with Essex, until one day he disappeared from the country after being charged for sodomy yet again. We can only speculate whether Southampton, who knew Essex and was involved in Essex's Rebellion against Queen Elizabeth in 1601, also befriended the notorious Perez at some point. But I am establishing a connection between the homosocial context of Southampton's ambiguous youth spent in the company of men and the homosocial culture invoked by Shakespeare in his dedication of *Venus and Adonis* to Southampton.

There were other riddles in Southampton's youth, however, that may help us contextualize the homoerotic undertones of *Venus and Adonis*. Southampton's scandalous refusal to marry Lady Elizabeth Vere, granddaughter of William Cecil, First Lord Burghley and Master of the Wards and Lord Treasurer of England, was still fresh in the memory of early modern London when Shakespeare dedicated his poem to Southampton. Lord Burghley was, "next to Queen Elizabeth, the most powerful person in the realm" (Akrigg, *Shakespeare* 31–35).[51] Again, we have no direct records of the causes for Southampton's obduracy, though his resentment of marriage as such, as Akrigg suggests, may have been the reason for the rejection (32). But this is a speculation. However, it would have been unusual for a young nobleman not to marry if the marriage meant a particularly profitable enterprise. And Lady Vere was doubtless one of the best bridal opportunities in England at the time. Moreover, the scandal of Southampton's refusal to marry coincided with the publication, in 1591, of John Clapham's Neo-Latin poem *Narcissus*, the first work dedicated to Southampton (Akrigg, *Shakespeare* 33). Clapham was Lord Burghley's clerk, and he would have likely been familiar with the circumstances surrounding the Southampton affair. Clapham's poem neither celebrates marriage nor advocates sex and procreation; rather, it is centered around the theme of Adonis's scoffing of Venus's love.[52] Yet, more interestingly, Clapham's subject is Narcissus, with whom Adonis is most closely associated in *Venus and Adonis*, and who was symbolically linked in the Renaissance with male-

male erotics. Containment of sodomy, which denies procreation and in turn undermines marriage (seen in the Renaissance as a social, political, and economic alliance), seems a good strategic move on the part of Shakespeare, who has just obtained patronage from a nobleman who refused a promising marriage arrangement. By insisting on the avoidance of Venus, embodied as a woman, and by sending Adonis off in quest of masculinity, allegorized in the boar, Shakespeare captures in *Venus and Adonis* some of the ambiguities of Southampton's private life. The power of the poem's narrative to manipulate desire and exclude woman from the realm of erotic fulfillment establishes, through the act of reading, a homosocial union of Shakespeare with his fictitious male readers. Yet Shakespeare's other eye, the one that often seems to look for finding ways of satisfying the normative moralism of the age, makes sure that Adonis's violent death appears threatening enough to aristocratic male readers who might find transgressive sexuality appealing. The eradication of the Adonis-sodomite at the end of the poem, therefore, suggests the final victory of normative moralism over illicit desire.

In the penumbra of the early modern transformations of Ovid's narrative into new humanist narratives, the formation of homoerotic discourse represents only one way in which Ovid was used in the Renaissance to enable various new discourses of sexuality. The transformative nature of the mythical bodies in *Metamorphoses* suggested to Renaissance writers a similar mutative quality and flexibility that their times associated with sexuality. Ovid's bodies in flux in *Metamorphoses* symbolically revealed to Renaissance writers the instabilities that underlied their own perilous fantasies about the vulnerability of the body and the slipperiness of sexuality (Orgel, "Nobody's Perfect" 16). As Shakespeare's poem suggests, the cleavage between the body and beauty in the myth of Venus and Adonis enabled an allegory of contemporary anxieties about the disruptiveness of homoerotic desire.

A queer reading of *Venus and Adonis* suggests that the poem does not lament the lack of male-female unity but, on the contrary, that the futile give-and-take erotic play between Venus and Adonis denies the celebration of heteroerotic normativity. Alternative sexual possibilities that emerge out of the narrative of procreation are strategically textualized in a subjectivity constructed as a temporary identification of the self as other, as sodomite. The sodomite, inscribed in the archetypal figure of Adonis as a symbol of beauty and repressed sexuality, becomes, ironically, a surreptitious sign of sexual dissidence, which destabilizes both aesthetic meaning and societal norms. Thus, the sodomite—associated in the Renaissance with the figure of the nobleman and inscribed in Southampton's closet—represents a disturbing category in a narrative about the formation of heterosexuality. The figure of the sodomite suggests that homoerotic desire is a contingent part of the formation of heterosexual desire. The sodomite represents a metamorphic sign that troubles meaning, a sign whose elusive textualized body has proved invisible to the long critical tradition of *Venus and Adonis*.

Notes

1. William Shakespeare, *The Narrative Poems*, ed. Maurice Evans (Harmondsworth, Eng.: Penguin, 1989).

2. In Ovid, Adonis's death is an accident, but there is no kiss. So: "protinus excussit pando venabula rostro / sanguine tincta suo trepidumque et tuta petentem / trux aper insequitur totosque sub inguine dentes / abdidit et fulva moribundum stravit harena" (X. 713–16). Ovid, *Metamorphoses*, adapted and trans. Frank Justus Miller. Loeb Classical Library, vol. 2 (Cambridge, Mass.: Harvard University Press; London: William Heinemann, 1968). In Arthur Golding's moralized, copious rendering of this passage (published in 1567), the detail of the boar's wounding Adonis in the groin is censored. Golding translates: "The Boare streyght with his hooked groyne the huntingstaffe out drew / Bestayned with his blood, and on *Adonis* did pursew, / Who trembling and retyring back to place of refuge drew, / And hyding in his codds his tuskes as farre as he could thrust / He layd him all along for dead uppon the yellow dust." Quoted in *Narrative and Dramatic Sources of Shakespeare*, ed. Geoffrey Bullough. Vol. 1 (London: Routledge and Kegan Paul; New York: Columbia University Press, 1957), 168. Melville translates the same passage as: "quick with its curved snout / The savage beast dislodged the bloody point, / And charged Adonis as he ran in fear / For safety, and sank its tusks deep in his groin / And stretched him dying on the yellow sand" (X. 713–17). See Ovid, *Metamorphoses*, trans. A. D. Melville (Oxford: Oxford University Press, 1986).

3. For example, as an allegorized seduction, the hunt is a theme of Sir Thomas Wyatt's poems "Who So List to Hunt" and "They Flee from Me."

4. *Spenser: Poetical Works*, ed. J. C. Smith and E. de Selincourt (London: Oxford University Press, 1975).

5. Frank Whigham has noticed but not explained the confusing pronouns in this stanza in his essay "Reading Social Conflict in the Alimentary Tract: More on the Body in Renaissance Drama," *English Literary History* 55 (1988): 349n18.

6. The list of studies that examine sexuality in the poem but do not analyze the homoerotic discourse in it is too long to be quoted here. Some of the crucial studies I refer to in this essay include works such as William Keach, *Elizabethan*

Erotic Narratives: Irony and Pathos in the Ovidian Poetry of Shakespeare, Marlowe, and Their Contemporaries (New Brunswick, N.J.: Rutgers University Press, 1977), 52–84; A. C. Hamilton, "Venus and Adonis," *Studies in English Literature, 1500–1900* 1 (1961): 1–15; A. T. Hatto, " 'Venus and Adonis'—and the Boar," *Modern Language Review* 41 (1946): 355–61; William E. Sheidley, " 'Unless It Be a Boar': Love and Wisdom in Shakespeare's 'Venus and Adonis'," *Modern Language Quarterly* 1 (1974): 3–15. Homoeroticism as an identity component is examined in Coppelia Kahn, "Self and Eros in *Venus and Adonis*," *Centennial Review* 20 (1976): 351–71, reprinted in a revised version in Kahn, *Man's Estate: Masculine Identity in Shakespeare* (Berkeley: University of California Press, 1981), 21–46; Jonathan Bate, *Shakespeare and Ovid* (Oxford: Clarendon, 1994), 49–65.

7. See Gregory Bredbeck, "Tradition and the Individual Sodomite: Barnfield, Shakespeare, and Subjective Desire," in *Homosexuality in Renaissance and Enlightenment England: Literary Representation in Historical Context,* ed. Claude Summers (New York: Haworth Press, 1992), 41–62; Alan Bray, *Homosexuality in Renaissance England* (London: Gay Men's Press, 1982); Bruce R. Smith, *Homosexual Desire in Shakespeare's England: A Cultural Poetics* (Chicago: University of Chicago Press, 1994); Jonathan Goldberg, *Sodometries: Renaissance Texts, Modern Sexualities* (Stanford, Calif.: Stanford University Press, 1992).

8. Bredbeck, "Tradition and the Individual Sodomite," 43. Subsequent references to this work will be included parenthetically in the text.

9. Donald B. Morton, "The Politics of Queer Theory in the (Post)Modern Moment," *Genders* 17 (1993): 121. For the relationship between sodomy and society in the Renaissance, see Jonathan Goldberg, "Introduction," in *Reclaiming Sodom,* ed. Jonathan Goldberg (New York: Routledge, 1994), 1–22.

10. Ad de Vries, *Dictionary of Symbols and Imagery* (Amsterdam: North Holland, 1974), 56–57. I thank Thomas Rendall for suggesting some of the cultural symbolism of the boar in early modern times.

11. Harold Beaver, "Homosexual Signs (In Memory of Roland Barthes)," *Critical Inquiry* 8 (1981): 103.

12. Aristotle, *On the Generation of Animals,* trans. A. L. Peck. Loeb Classical Library (Cambridge, Mass.: Harvard University Press; London: William Heinemann, 1963), 4.5.774b. See also Jacques Ferrand's 1623 treatise on erotic melancholy, entitled *De la maladie d'amour ou melancholie erotique,* translated as *A Treatise on Lovesickness* by Donald A. Beecher and Massimo Ciavolella (Syracuse, N.Y.: Syracuse University Press, 1990), 284.

13. Keach, *Elizabethan Erotic Narratives,* 67. Subsequent references to this work will be included parenthetically in the text.

14. Roland Barthes, *S/Z,* trans. Richard Miller (New York: Hill and Wang, 1974), 74. Subsequent references to this work will be included parenthetically in the text.

15. Eve Kosofsky Sedgwick, *Tendencies* (Durham, N.C.: Duke University Press, 1993), 8.

16. Here, Venus indirectly mocks Adonis's masculinity by denying the phallic potency suggested by the word "spear." Contrarily, for example, Marlowe constructs Tamburlaine's heroic masculinity around the phallic symbolism of the spear in Tamburlaine's "quivering lances" in part 1 of *Tamburlaine the Great* (2.3.18).

17. Sigmund Freud, "On Narcissism: An Introduction," in *The Standard Edition of the Complete Psychological Works of Sigmund Freud,* ed. James Strachey. Vol. 14. (London: Hogarth Press, 1957), 73–102. Julia Kristeva, *Tales of Love,* trans. Leon S. Roudiez (New York: Columbia University Press, 1987), 121, discusses the quest for the same-sexed other as a yearning that invariably results in death.

18. Goldberg, *Sodometries,* 21. Subsequent references to this work will be included parenthetically in the text.

19. Smith, *Homosexual Desire;* Goldberg, *Sodometries;* Stephen Orgel, "Nobody's Perfect; or, Why Did the English Stage Take Boys for Women?" *South Atlantic Quarterly* 88:1 (1989): 7–29.

20. Jonathan Goldberg, "Sodomy and Society: The Case of Christopher Marlowe," *Southwest Review* 69 (1984): 371.

21. Bruce R. Smith, *Homosexual Desire in Shakespeare's England: A Cultural Poetics* (Chicago: University of Chicago Press, 1994), 11–12.

22. Orgel, "Nobody's Perfect," 19–20. Subsequent references to this work will be included parenthetically in the text.

23. Bray, *Homosexuality in Renaissance England,* 76. Subsequent references to this work will be included parenthetically in the text.

24. Lodge associates the heretic-sodomite with bestiality and with "Mollities"—those who frequented the private brothels, called "molly houses," reserved for male-male sex—who perform "voluntary pollution"; Lodge represents such a figure as a grotesque body with "monsters eies . . . hanging down, as if ashamed to behold t[he] light, [and] in his browes are written, *signu[m] reprobationis,* the mark of reprobatio[n]." Lodge's heretic sodomite is possessed by the Devil. See Thomas Lodge, *Wits Miserie and the Worlds Madnesse: Discovering the Devils Incarnat of This Age* (London, 1596, sig. Hiij^r-Hiij^v).

25. Ed Cohen, "Legislating the Norm: From Sodomy to Gross Indecency," *South Atlantic Quarterly* 88:1 (1989): 185, reprinted in revised form in Cohen, *Talk on the Wilde Side: Toward a Genealogy of a Discourse on Male Sexualities* (New York: Routledge, 1993), 103–25.

26. Alan Bray, "Homosexuality and the Signs of Male Friendship in Elizabethan England," *History Workshop Journal* 29 (1990): 9.

27. Political repercussions of sexual treason associated with sodomy are best illustrated in Marlowe's play *Edward II.*

28. Mario DiGangi, "Asses and Wits: The Homoerotics of Mastery in Satiric Comedy," *English Literary Renaissance* 25 (1995): 183.

29. For the complexity of the myth of Adonis, see Marcel Detienne, *The Gardens of Adonis*, trans. Janet Lloyd (Princeton, N.J.: Princeton University Press, 1994).

30. Judith Butler, *Bodies That Matter: On the Discursive Limits of "Sex"* (New York: Routledge, 1993), 226. Subsequent references to this work will be included parenthetically in the text.

31. Hamilton, "Venus and Adonis," 7–9. Subsequent references to this work will be included parenthetically in the text.

32. Hatto, " 'Venus and Adonis'—and the Boar," 355–61.

33. Sheidley, " 'Unless It Be a Boar,' " 11 (emphasis added).

34. Keach, *Elizabethan Erotic Narratives*, 67.

35. Michel Foucault, *The History of Sexuality*, vol. 1: *An Introduction*, trans. Robert Hurley (New York: Vintage, 1990), 57. Subsequent references to this work will be included parenthetically in the text.

36. Stephen O. Murray, "Homosexual Acts and Selves in Early Modern Europe," *Journal of Homosexuality* 16 (1988): 464. Murray's examples are the sonnets of Michelangelo and Benedetto Varchi.

37. Bredbeck, "Tradition and the Individual Sodomite," 41–68.

38. Catherine Belsey, "Love as Trompe-l'Oeil: Taxonomies of Desire in *Venus and Adonis*," *Shakespeare Quarterly* 46 (1995): 258.

39. Bate, *Shakespeare and Ovid*, 65.

40. In his New Cambridge Shakespeare edition of *Venus and Adonis*, John Roe interprets the lines 412–13 as Shakespeare's rhetorical performance (William Shakespeare, *The Poems* [Cambridge: Cambridge University Press, 1992], 101). Roe glosses line 412 as: "My only regard for love is to render it contemptible. The force of 'disgrace' is 'to disdain' rather than to bring shame upon by one's own improper behaviour. 'Disgracing' is the translation Hoby finds for Castiglione's famous word *sprezzatura* . . . to suggest that the performer appears to disdain or make light of his own skill or excellence."

41. Gregory W. Bredbeck, *Sodomy and Interpretation: Marlowe to Milton* (Ithaca, N.Y.: Cornell University Press, 1991), 21.

42. Kahn, "Self and Eros in *Venus and Adonis*," 366.

43. Eve Kosofsky Sedgwick, *Epistemology of the Closet* (Berkeley: University of California Press, 1990), 3.

44. David Van Leer, "The Beast of the Closet: Homosociality and the Pathology of Manhood," *Critical Inquiry* 15 (1989): 596.

45. Elizabeth Story Donno, ed. *Elizabethan Minor Epics* (London: Routledge and Kegan Paul, 1963), 9.

46. For a lucid discussion of the strategies of reading in the Renaissance, see Lisa Jardine and Anthony Grafton, " 'Studied for Action': How Gabriel Harvey

Read His Livy," *Past and Present* 129 (1990): 30–78; Lorna Hutson, "Fortunate Travelers: Reading for the Plot in Sixteenth-Century England," *Representations* 41 (1993): 83–103.

47. Jardine and Grafton, " 'Studied for Action,' " 39–40.

48. Quoted in Virginia F. Stern, *Gabriel Harvey: His Life, Marginalia, and Library* (Oxford: Clarendon, 1979), 127.

49. Harvey, however, left substantial records, in the form of the marginal annotations of his reading of the classics, especially Livy. See Jardine and Grafton, " 'Studied for Action' "; Stern, *Gabriel Harvey.*

50. See Katherine Duncan-Jones, "Much Ado with Red and White: The Earliest Readers of Shakespeare's *Venus and Adonis* (1593)," *Review of English Studies,* n.s., 44:176 (1993): 485; Bray, "Homosexuality and the Signs of Male Friendship," 8; G. P. V. Akrigg, *Shakespeare and the Earl of Southampton* (Cambridge, Mass.: Harvard University Press, 1968), 180–82. Subsequent references to all these works will be included parenthetically in the text.

51. Elizabeth Vere was two years Southampton's senior. Despite the failure of the first attempt to marry his granddaughter to the smart and wealthy Southampton, Burghley did not give up the thought that Southampton might eventually marry Vere. Therefore, he continued postponing her marriage until 1595, when he finally conceded defeat and had her marry the Earl of Derby. Shakespeare's poem was written and published in 1593, during that waiting period.

52. Charles Martindale and Colin Burrow, "Clapham's Narcissus: A Pre-Text for Shakespeare's *Venus and Adonis?" English Literary Renaissance* 22 (1992): 151. Martindale and Burrow tentatively consider Clapham's poem a pre-text for *Venus and Adonis.*

6

Robert Audley's Secret: Male Homosocial Desire and "Going Straight" in *Lady Audley's Secret*

Richard Nemesvari

Elaine Showalter has characterized Victorian sensation novels of the 1860s as "a genre in which everything that was not forbidden was compulsory."[1] Thus, much to the chagrin of many contemporary reviewers, these works focused on murder, attempted murder, bigamy, adultery, and a series of "lesser" transgressions that shocked and titillated their audience. Sensation fiction also tended to present sexual irregularities as being behind the crimes that drove its plots, something that played no small role in reinforcing its popularity.

There was, however, one "forbidden" sexual topic that could not be addressed directly, even within the risqué confines of these novels, and that was homosexuality. Nonetheless, the origins and themes of sensation novels allowed them to explore this taboo subject in ways unavailable to most other forms of "mainstream" mid-nineteenth-century literature. In *The History of Sexuality,* Foucault asserts that, as far as the categorization of homosexuality is concerned, "Westphal's famous article of 1870 on 'contrary sexual sensations' can stand as its date of birth."[2] The concept of "homosexual" as it has come to be understood in the twentieth century was therefore being formulated at almost the exact historical moment sensation fiction first achieved notoriety. As queer theorists have pointed out, however, the creation of this newly formulated "category" gave rise to an equally unprecedented sexual identification: that of the "heterosexual." It is perhaps not surprising that sensation authors found ways to explore the tensions produced by these provocative new distinctions in their texts—which, after all, were intended to startle, if not appall, their audience.·

Thus, in *Lady Audley's Secret* (1862), one of the earliest and most successful examples of sensation fiction, Mary Elizabeth Braddon explores the anxieties produced in Victorian men by the development of male homosocial bonds. Eve Kosofsky Sedgwick's hypothesis of "the potential unbrokenness of a continuum between homosocial and homosexual—a continuum whose visibility, for men, in our society, is radically disrupted"[3]— becomes particularly evocative for this novel. By portraying her putative hero, Robert Audley, as driven by repressed homoerotic desires, Braddon exposes the denial that underlies Victorian society. The subtextual revelation of the unspeakable secret of male homosocial desire is essential to the text as, through his conflict with, and destruction of, Lady Audley, Robert determines his "proper" place on the sexual continuum and therefore learns to "go straight."

It has become something of a critical commonplace to describe sensation novels as "domesticated Gothic," since one of their most effective devices is the transferal of Gothic events and emotions from exotic and romantic locales into the heart of respectable, nineteenth-century Britain. In discussing Gothic fiction, Sedgwick makes the following observations:

> The ties of the Gothic novel to an emergent female authorship and readership have been a constant for two centuries, and there has been a history of useful critical attempts to look to the Gothic for explorations of the position of women in relation to the changing shapes of patriarchal domination. A less obvious point has to do with the reputation for "decadence": the Gothic was the first novelistic form in England to have close, relatively visible links to male homosexuality. (*Between Men* 91)

The critical furore that surrounded the Victorian manifestation of this older genre and that led it to be judged as "more pernicious than its gothic and romantic ancestors"[4] was generated by sensation fiction's insistence that even the sanctified realm of Victorian domesticity provided no real barrier to the "deviant" criminal/sexual urges that seemed waiting to overwhelm it. By tapping directly into a series of Victorian uncertainties about gender roles and sexual identification, uncertainties that became increasingly difficult to repress as the century proceeded, these novels provided an expression of the "desperation and dissent" (Hughes, *Maniac* 36) underlying middle-class assumptions and values. For a writer like Braddon, then, this neo-Gothic form holds obvious attractions: as part of its literary inheritance, it already possesses the potentially subversive elements outlined by Sedgwick, while at the same time it provides an opportunity to bring them, both literally and figuratively, "home."

The disruptive threat posed by the novel's main female character, Lady Audley, is founded on her physical appearance and assumed personality, which so closely match the Victorian ideal of the "angel in the house" that they effectively cloak a willful character ready to dare bigamy and attempted murder to get what she wants. Along with a seemingly "amiable and gentle nature always . . . light-hearted, happy, and contented under any circumstances,"[5] she possesses "soft blue eyes" (6) and "the most wonderful curls in the world—soft and feathery, always floating away from her face, and making a pale halo round her head when the sunlight shone through them" (8). Braddon undercuts gender stereotypes by demonstrating that "the dangerous woman is not the rebel or the intellectual, but the pretty little girl whose indoctrination in the feminine role has taught her deceitfulness almost as a secondary sex characteristic."[6] Interestingly enough, however, the voluntary adoption and manipulation of this rigid cultural ideal by "Lucy Graham" illustrates a perhaps even more threatening characteristic: her elastic ability to define and redefine herself.

The string of names by which Braddon's female lead is identified throughout the text indicates a protean talent for escaping the constraints of a society that attempts to restrict women's social movement and definition. As Helen Maldon, daughter of an impoverished, half-pay naval officer, she quickly learns that if her situation is to improve, she must use her looks to achieve an advantageous marriage. When, as Helen Talboys, her new husband has his income cut off by his disapproving father and then abandons her for the goldfields of Australia, she reinvents herself as the governess Lucy Graham and takes the post that brings her into contact with Sir Michael. When he proposes to her, she hesitates only momentarily at the prospect of bigamy and then accepts him and her next identity as Lucy, Lady Audley. When word reaches her that her first husband has returned, she fakes the death of "Helen Talboys" to prevent the discovery of her crime and ensure the security of her new status; and when that first husband confronts her after accidentally discovering her fraud, she tries to kill him by pushing him down a well. Her final "incarnation," as Madame Taylor, is imposed on her by Robert Audley after he exposes her and expels her from England, locking her into an identity just as he locks her into a French *maison de santé*. This act thus symbolizes both his victory over her and his neutralization of the dangerous potential for unrestrained female autonomy she represents.

Lady Audley's refusal to accept the limited roles of impoverished daughter, deserted wife, and toiling governess acts as a covert critique of the narrow, unfulfilling roles available to women in general. More significantly, however, Lady Audley's fluid identity, her masculine insistence on self-determination, threatens a class hierarchy dependent on the assurance that women remain *passive* objects of exchange through which men determine and create their own status. By aggressively attempting to advance her own social standing—and, indeed, succeeding in that attempt—Lady Audley challenges her society's assumption that "the power relationships between men and women [are] dependent on the power relationships between men and men" (Sedgwick, *Between Men* 25). It is Robert Audley's task to meet and beat back the threat posed by Lady Audley by reestablishing the homosocial bonds she has disrupted. In doing so, however, Braddon has him reveal more about himself and the society he represents than he is willing to recognize.

When the reader is first introduced to Robert, he seems an unlikely candidate for the role of social guardian. Braddon goes out of her way to provide a description that would have been problematic to a Victorian audience—and problematic in some very specific ways:

> Robert Audley was supposed to be a barrister. . . . But he had never either had a brief, or tried to get a brief, or even wished to have a brief in all those five years, during which his name had been painted upon one of the doors in Fig-tree Court. He was a handsome, lazy, care-for-nothing fellow, of about seven-and-twenty; the only son of a younger brother of Sir Michael Audley. . . . Sometimes, when the weather was very hot, and he had exhausted himself with the exertion of smoking his German pipe, and reading French novels, he would stroll into the Temple Gardens, and lying in some shady spot, pale and cool, with his shirt collar turned down and a blue silk handkerchief tied loosely about his neck, would tell grave benchers that he had knocked himself up with overwork. (32)

Clearly, Robert has no real reason to work for his living, and his aristocratic background, even if he is not in its direct lineage, allows him to indulge in a leisured existence. Nonetheless, as a barrister, he is an official caretaker and defender of his society's laws. His social/sexual "development" throughout the text will be measured by a growing awareness of his responsibility to ensure that their authority is maintained, but his position before that realization takes hold is more interesting. David Skilton suggests that in *Lady Audley's Secret* "the use of French fiction is suggestive of a certain moral and intellectual atmosphere. . . . Audley's failing according to Victorian standards is a quite 'Continental' lack of moral concern and energy in relation to the serious issues of life. . . . But this lack of English moral fibre is vague and his amoral outlook quite unfocussed."[7] Thus, on one level, Braddon begins her text by providing a hero who is apparently in need of some kind of moral reform. However, the question of just how much his "English fibre" has been shaped by "Continental" influences needs to be explored further.

While Skilton is right to note that Robert's "amorality" never finds an explicit expression within the text, I think he has missed the implied significance of Robert's style of dress, his mannerisms, and his attachment not only to French fiction and German pipes but also, as Braddon later writes, to "Turkish tobacco" (113). Robert's tendency toward a laconic, drawling irony in his speech and his complete lack of skill and interest in fox hunting on his uncle's estate provide a foreshadowing of Wilde's quip about the unspeakable in full pursuit of the uneatable, and this anachronistic connection between the two is not completely strained. At the very least, a Victorian audience would have associated Robert's habits with the kind of Romantic decadence against which the period defined itself. But by the time Braddon comes to write her novel, the very word "decadence" has taken on a more specific connotation, as Sedgwick's previously quoted statement about Gothic fiction indicates. In outlining her exploration of potential reader responses to evocations of homosexuality, Sedgwick is careful to make clear how tentative any conclusions drawn from such generalizations must be, and I can only echo her cautions here. Still, her observations are helpful in this context:

> With respect to homosocial/homosexual style, it seems to be possible to divide Victorian men among three rough categories according to class. The first includes aristocratic men and small groups of their friends and dependents, including bohemians and prostitutes; for these people, by 1865, a distinct homosexual role and culture seem already to have been in existence in England. . . . It seems to have constituted a genuine subculture, facilitated in the face of an ideologically hostile dominant culture by money, privilege, internationalism, and for the most part, the ability to command secrecy. . . . This role is closely related to—is in fact, through Oscar Wilde, the antecedent of—the particular stereotype that at least until recently has characterized American middle-class gay homosexuality;

its strongest associations, as we have noted, are with effeminacy, transvestitism, promiscuity, prostitution, continental European culture, and the arts. (*Between Men* 172–73)

Clearly, Robert does not fit all the characteristics presented here, or even perhaps most of them, but then I am not arguing anything so simplistic as that he "is" homosexual. Rather, Braddon has associated him with a recognizable aristocratic type possessed of, by this historical moment, clear homosocial/homosexual overtones. His equivocal social status—as a member of an aristocratic family fulfilling the middle-class role of a barrister—makes that association even more provocative in that it hints at the possible transference of this "style" from one class to another. From Robert Audley's first introduction in the text, therefore, Braddon subtly implies that her hero's most intense bonds will be between himself and other men, something that the novel's events bear out.

In particular, this view of Robert helps explain his reaction to the plot development that initiates the conflict in the text: George Talboys's return to England from Australia. When the two accidentally encounter each other, Robert is momentarily startled out of his air of supercilious detachment:

> "Be so good as to look where you're going, my friend!" Robert remonstrated, mildly, to the impetuous passenger; "you might give a man warning before you throw him down and trample upon him."
>
> The stranger stopped suddenly, looked very hard at the speaker, and then gasped for breath.
>
> "Bob!" he cried, in a tone expressive of the most intense astonishment; "I only touched British ground after dark last night, and to think that I should meet you this morning!"
>
> "I've seen you somewhere before, my bearded friend," said Mr. Audley, calmly scrutinising the animated face of the other, "but I'll be hanged if I can remember when or where."
>
> "What!" exclaimed the stranger, reproachfully, "you don't mean to say that you've forgotten George Talboys?"
>
> "*No I have not!*" said Robert, with an emphasis by no means usual to him; and then hooking his arm into that of his friend, he led him into the shady court, saying with his old indifference, "and now, George, tell us all about it." (34–35)

That Robert reacts "with an emphasis by no means usual to him," before his affected persona reasserts itself, demonstrates an attachment to George that has been elicited by no other character thus far in the book. The description that follows, however, is equally significant:

Robert Audley was for starting off immediately for the Crown and Sceptre, or the Castle, Richmond, where they could have a bit of dinner, and talk over those good old times when they were together at Eton. But George told his friend that before he went anywhere, before he shaved, or broke his fast, or in any way refreshed himself after a night journey from Liverpool by express train, he must call at a certain coffee-house in Bridge Street, Westminster, where he expected to find a letter from his wife. (35)

This is the first time—but certainly not the last—in which George's wife is going to come between Robert and his friend, and his response to the information that George is married is more than a little revealing: " 'The idea of you having a wife, George; what a preposterous joke' " (35). The text's passing reference to Eton provides the clue to Robert's reaction, for the attachments formed there were often more than platonic, and "candid accounts agree that in most of the public schools, the whirlwinds of the soul were often acted out in the flesh" (Sedgwick, *Between Men* 176).

It is hardly surprising, therefore, that when George receives the devastating news that his wife is dead and misses the boat that would have returned him to Australia, he "once more threw himself upon Robert Audley's hospitality," and "the barrister received him with open arms" (46). The potential disruption posed by George's "preposterous" wife is momentarily nullified, and the homosocial relationship Robert so clearly craves is reestablished when the two end up sharing his rooms. However, with George's mysterious disappearance, Robert is forced into the role of reluctant detective and into a confrontation not only with Lady Audley but with his own suppressed feelings. Throughout much of the rest of the novel, until the mystery is seemingly (re)solved, Robert finds himself both wanting and not wanting to pursue the various clues that present themselves. This ambivalence is paradigmatic of sensation fiction, for it "is a characteristic of Robert Audley's hunt . . . as of Walter Hartright's in *The Woman in White* and Pip's in *Great Expectations,* that revelation of truth will overwhelm the world of the hunter and of those he loves" (Skilton, "Introduction" xxi). But in *Lady Audley's Secret,* the protagonist's reevaluation of self is more potentially threatening than in the novels by Collins and Dickens because it entails questions of sexual identity. Braddon describes Robert's reaction to George's disappearance in the following passage:

If any one had ventured to tell Mr. Robert Audley that he could possibly feel a strong attachment to any creature breathing, that cynical gentleman would have elevated his eyebrows in supreme contempt at the preposterous notion. Yet here he was, flurried and anxious, bewildering his brain by all manner of conjectures about his missing friend, and, false to every attribute of his nature, walking fast.

"I haven't walked fast since I was at Eton," he murmured, as he hurried across one of Sir Michael's meadows in the direction of the village; "and the worst of it is that I haven't the most remote idea of where I am going." (82)

This second reference to Eton again hints at the reason for Robert's intensity of response, and his perplexity about why he is acting this way and about "where [he is] going" suggests that on some level he does not *want* to analyze too closely the motives that are driving him. If it is in Robert's own interest to avoid the kind of sexual self-knowledge that seems poised to overwhelm him, however, at least one character in the novel possesses enough insight to make the most overt statement on this topic in the entire text. Alicia Audley, Robert's cousin, holds the distinction, along with her dog, of being the only character to dislike and distrust Lady Audley from the beginning. Her description of her new stepmother as a "wax-doll" (56) indicates an awareness of Lady Audley's calculated artificiality as well as a rejection of the angel-in-the-house stereotype that she wields so effectively. More significantly, Alicia's unrequited love for Robert apparently gives her a deeper perception of his passions than even he possesses. As Robert's uneasiness about George increases, and as he becomes more and more fixated on his friend's unexplained departure, Alicia sarcastically exclaims: " 'What a dreadful catastrophe! . . . since Pythias, in the person of Mr. Robert Audley, cannot exist for half an hour without Damon, commonly known as George Talboys" (84). An illustration from Cicero's *De Officiis,* the story of Damon and Pythias—in which Damon stands as a hostage for Pythias, with his life forfeit if his companion does not return in time for his own execution—was for the Victorians representative of trust, devotion, and perfect friendship. Yet given the original setting of the tale, the Greek court and culture of Dionysius I of Syracuse, the association of Robert and George with Pythias and Damon has additional implications. An interesting parallel reference occurs in a letter that Arthur Henry Hallam sent to fellow "Apostle" Richard Milnes in 1831:

Whether it may not be better for you to take me on these terms, and to give up cheerfully the theory to which you have been visibly labouring to accommodate me, and which depends on the pleasant postulate that Arthur Hallam was once an enthusiast, and worthy to be the Pythias of that new Damon, Richard Milnes, but that all of a sudden the said AH became a reprobate, and is now grovelling on

some "Alcian field," afar from everything ideal, beautiful and true, and consequently from the aforesaid Richard, this I leave you to consider.[8]

Richard Dellamora interprets this passage as Hallam taking "the opportunity to deny for the record that his earlier confidences may have included the fact that he 'was once an enthusiast': a term that Shelley, Hallam's father, and later Pater use to denote a male committed to sexual and
emotional relations with other males" and further suggests that "in referring to Damon and Pythias, two heroic Greek lovers . . . Hallam specifies
the context of Milnes's investments in male relationships" (*Masculine Desire* 27).

By alluding to a historical moment in which the homosocial bond between men was often initiated and confirmed by sexual relations and then
directly connecting this allusion to her central male characters, Braddon
briefly exposes the foundational "secret" of masculine desire that both
Robert and his society attempt to elide. Alicia's accurate evaluation of Lady
Audley lends credence to her "revelation" about Robert, and although the
primary text never explicitly confirms her apparently passing remark, subsequent events in the plot certainly suggest its subtextual aptness. What
Alicia has perceived, quite rightly, is that George is her *rival*, and eventually
she will indeed lose Robert to "him," although in a way that leaves the
homoerotic nature of their relationship safely unspoken.

The further Robert proceeds in his investigation of George's disappearance, the more agitated he becomes. He experiences a series of disturbing
dreams and is much given to the kind of self-questioning that might lead
him to give up his role as detective: " 'Why do I go on with this,' he said,
'when I know that it is leading me, step by step, day by day, hour by hour,
nearer to that conclusion which of all others I should avoid? Am I tied to a
wheel, and must I go with its every revolution, let it take me where it will?' "
(157). Although Robert tends to couch his reluctance in terms of the effect
his disclosures may have on his uncle, it is not difficult to see in quotations
such as this a personal fear of self-exposure. In *Epistemology of the Closet*,
Sedgwick notes that "because the paths of male entitlement, especially
in the nineteenth century, required certain intense bonds that were not
readily distinguishable from the most reprobated bonds, an endemic and
ineradicable state of what I am calling homosexual panic became the normal condition of male heterosexual entitlement."[9] This nicely describes
the situation Robert finds himself in, for the further he proceeds, the more

panicked he becomes about what he may uncover. Braddon's text therefore reveals the way in which a growing awareness of the homosocial may incite homophobia, as Robert desperately, and at times angrily, struggles to deny the significance of his reactions. Finally, having reached such a psychological impasse that he is ready to abandon his search for the "truth," he decides that he will approach George's family for guidance. And it is here that he finds the resolution to his dilemma in the figure of George's sister, Clara.

Robert's interview with Mr. Talboys does not go very well, for George's father sees his son's disappearance as a ploy to create alarm and worry, thus forcing an eventual reconciliation with his rich and estranged parent. Further, George's sister remains silent during the exchange between Robert and Mr. Talboys and therefore seems to accept her father's cold response to the suggestion that her brother has been murdered. Robert takes their supposed indifference as a warrant for dropping his role as detective:

> "Thank God!" thought Robert Audley—"thank God! it is over . . . I shall not be the means of bringing disgrace upon those I love. It will come, perhaps, sooner or later, but it will not come through me. The crisis is past, and I am free."
>
> He felt an unutterable relief in this thought. His generous nature revolted at the office into which he had found himself drawn—the office of spy, the collector of damning facts that led on to horrible deductions.
>
> He drew a long breath—a sigh of relief at his release. It was all over now. (196)

Once again, the extremity of Robert's reaction suggests that the "disgrace" he has been saved from deducing is more personal than he might like to admit; but, as it turns out, he is given the opportunity to pursue the external element of his search while leaving its internal motives securely unexamined. Clara Talboys, following Robert's departure, runs after his carriage: " 'Oh, let me speak to you,' she cried—'let me speak to you, or I shall go mad. I heard it all. I believe what you believe; and I shall go mad unless I can do something—something towards avenging his death' " (197). From this point on, it is Clara whom Robert will perceive as the driving force behind his investigation; she all but literally becomes the hand of fate "beckon[ing] him onwards to her brother's unknown grave" (253). The key point for my purposes, however, is Robert's perception, and the text's constant declaration, that Clara is exactly like her brother.

Robert's first perception of Clara is "that she was young, and that she was like George Talboys" (187). After this opening statement, we are told "she is like George" (189), that she has "brown eyes, like George's" (197), that "she was so like the friend whom he had loved and lost, that it was impossible for him to think of her as a stranger" (202), that her handwriting possesses a "feminine resemblance to poor George's hand; neater than his, and more decided than his, but very like, very like" (209), and that she has his "lost friend's face" (258). Clara provides Robert with the perfect object of transference and offers him the opportunity to turn his illicit homosocial desire for George in a socially acceptable direction. Indeed, Braddon goes out of her way to portray almost the exact moment of that transference; sitting alone in his rooms, Robert ponders his situation: "'It's comfortable, but it seems so d——d lonely tonight. If poor George were sitting opposite to me, or—or even George's sister—she's very like him—existence might be a little more endurable" (208). From here on, Robert's pursuit of Lady Audley receives an increased impetus, because the possibility of being forced to confront his own homoerotic responses is safely evaded. He is on the way to being "straightened out" as, through his detections, he relievedly (dis)covers his "true" sexual orientation.

Nonetheless, given the tensions the novel has been exploring, it is hardly surprising that Robert's eventual (and inevitable) proposal to Clara is more than a little conflicted. Having banished Lady Audley to France and having discovered that her attempt to murder George failed, Robert offers to search for him in Australia:

"You are very good and generous, Mr. Audley," [Clara] said, at last, "and I feel this offer too much to be able to thank you for it. But—what you speak of could never be. By what right could I accept such a sacrifice?"

"By the right which makes me your bounden slave for ever and ever, whether you will or no. By the right of the love I bear you, Clara," cried Mr. Audley, dropping on his knees—rather awkwardly it must be confessed—and covering a soft little hand he had found half-hidden among the folds of a silken dress, with passionate kisses.

"I love you, Clara," he said, "I love you . . . and I shall love you for ever and ever, whether you will or no. . . . Clara, Clara!" he murmured, in a low pleading voice, "shall I go to Australia to look for your brother? . . . Shall we both go, dearest? Shall we go as man and wife? Shall we go together, my dear love, and bring our brother back between us?" (440–41)

The conflation here of Clara with George, of marrying the sister with searching for the brother, might leave even the most conventionally romantic of readers feeling a little uncomfortable. And Braddon drives home her point by never showing Clara actually consenting to Robert's proposal—or, indeed, saying another word for what remains of the novel.

Instead, there is a break in the text, followed by an interview between Robert and Mr. Talboys that concludes with this statement by George's father: " 'You are going to look for my son. . . . Bring me back my boy, and I will freely forgive you for having robbed me of my daughter' " (441). With Lady Audley gone, women are securely back in their place as passive and silent objects of exchange, while the men are free to work out the (at this point safely heterosexualized) homosocial relationships that determine society's structures.

The final chapter of *Lady Audley's Secret,* which describes events two years after the main action, is so overdetermined that it can only be read as an ironic statement on what the novel has "revealed." George—who, as it turns out, went to New York instead of Australia after surviving Lady Audley's murderous attack—returns in time to prevent Robert and Clara from setting out on what would have been a fruitless search. Robert, a "rising man on the home circuit" (445), has established a "fairy cottage . . . between Teddington Lock and Hampton Bridge" (445) for his new family, which now includes a baby, and George "lives there with his sister and his sister's husband" (445). "Madame Taylor" dies of a *"maladie de langueur"* (446), and Audley Court, the scene of Lady Audley's sphere of influence, is shut up. The other main characters, while proceeding with their lives, are apparently centered on the blissful domesticity established by Robert, in which "the gentlemen sit and smoke in the summer evenings . . . [until] they are summoned by Clara and Alicia to drink tea, and eat strawberries and cream upon the lawn" (446). But this idyllic scene is undercut by the subtextual secrets that remain unaddressed. The nature of Robert's detections, which uncover just enough to banish the threatening female presence while concealing the male desire that cannot be named, has been "outed" sufficiently that the novel destabilizes the heterosexual norm of its closure. Robert has learned his lesson and been rewarded for it, but the text reveals the way in which homo- and heterosexual slide into each other and therefore subverts the rigid distinctions on which this type of categorization depends.

Victorian sensation fiction became popular at a time when there was a growing perception "that knowledge meant sexual knowledge and secrets sexual secrets, [and when] there had in fact developed one particular sexuality that was distinctively constituted as secrecy" (Sedgwick, *Epistemology* 73). Thus, *both* of the main characters in *Lady Audley's Secret* have guilty secrets that are revealed; but, within the text, only the one is called on to pay for her transgressions. Because Lady Audley's criminal activities of bigamy and attempted murder embody challenges to a male-constructed social order, she cannot be allowed to "go straight" and survive. Robert Audley, on the other hand, successfully negotiates the movement from "queer" to "straight" that his society demands be made by successful men. Braddon, by revealing this *as* a "negotiation," undercuts the kind of essentialist paradigm being generated at this particular historical/cultural moment and opens the disturbingly sensational possibility that sexual identity is not fixed but fluid. *Lady Audley's Secret* thus manages to be both feminist and queer at the same time, a combination that could be counted on to provoke some of the most basic anxieties and resistances of its mid-Victorian audience.

Notes

An earlier version of this essay appeared as "Robert Audley's Secret: Male Homosocial Desire in *Lady Audley's Secret*," *Studies in the Novel* 27:4 (Winter 1995): 515–28, and is used here by permission of the University of North Texas.

1. Elaine Showalter, *A Literature of Their Own: British Women Novelists from Brontë to Lessing* (Princeton, N.J.: Princeton University Press, 1977), 158.

2. Michel Foucault, *The History of Sexuality*, vol. 1: *An Introduction*, trans. Robert Hurley (New York: Random House, 1980), 43.

3. Eve Kosofsky Sedgwick, *Between Men: English Literature and Male Homosocial Desire* (New York: Columbia University Press), 1–2. Subsequent references to this work will be included parenthetically in the text.

4. Winifred Hughes, *The Maniac in the Cellar: Sensation Novels of the 1860s* (Princeton, N.J.: Princeton University Press, 1980), 5. Subsequent references to this work will be included parenthetically in the text.

5. Mary Elizabeth Braddon, *Lady Audley's Secret* (Oxford: Oxford University Press, 1987), 5. Subsequent references to this work will be included parenthetically in the text.

6. Elaine Showalter, "Desperate Remedies: Sensation Novels of the 1860s," *Victorian Newsletter* 49 (Spring 1976): 3.

7. David Skilton, "Introduction," in *Lady Audley's Secret*, Braddon, xiii–xiv. Subsequent references to this work will be included parenthetically in the text.

8. Quoted in Richard Dellamora, *Masculine Desire: The Sexual Politics of Victorian Aestheticism* (Chapel Hill: University of North Carolina Press, 1990), 26–27. Subsequent references to this work will be included parenthetically in the text.

9. Eve Kosofsky Sedgwick, *Epistemology of the Closet* (Berkeley: University of California Press, 1990), 185. Subsequent references to this work will be included parenthetically in the text.

7

Cross-Confessing: Updike's Erect Faith in *A Month of Sundays*

John N. Duvall

A Month of Sundays, Roger's Version, and *S* serve as John Updike's sustained meditation on and recasting of Hawthorne's canonical novel. Arthur Dimmesdale's well-known problem for most of *The Scarlet Letter* is his inability to confess his adultery, but Updike's versions of Dimmesdale, Roger Chillingworth, and Hester Prynne (Thomas Marshfield, Roger Lambert, and Sarah Worth) produce a stream of confessional texts—journals and letters—that openly portray their extramarital sexual encounters and erotic fantasies, often in graphic detail. Hawthorne's tale is a dark tragedy of death, guilt, and denial, but Updike's Arthurs, Hesters, and Rogers muddle through their upper-middle-class lives with no guilt attaching to their sexual exploits, since these bodily acts are identical to their stumbling toward God.

But even to characterize briefly *The Scarlet Letter* with the word "denial" is to invoke a particular construction of Hawthorne—that of psychoanalytic criticism. As Jane Tompkins has pointed out in her reading of the politics of Hawthorne's literary reputation, the radical discontinuity of each generation's reading of *The Scarlet Letter* means that in a certain sense readers from these different periods are not reading the same text.[1] Despite the recent work of Sacvan Bercovitch and others to produce a more historicized *Scarlet Letter,* the modernist-psychoanalytic construction of Hawthorne's novel still forms an important part of Hawthorne studies.[2] In such interpretation, the unstable manifest text points to a stable latent text; in other words, the triangulated desire of Arthur, Hester, and Roger is yet another instance of transhistorical Oedipal conflict. Updike's appropriation of *The Scarlet Letter* is complicated by the difficulty in locating his project: his mode of representation is primarily realist, his technique of layered textuality is modernist mythological method, and his sense of subjectivity is incompletely postmodernized by his limited reading of poststructuralist theory. I would argue that Updike is able to employ *The Scarlet Letter* as an instance of American mythology precisely by calling on the modernist-psychoanalytic interpretation of it. *The Scarlet Letter* thus becomes usable by providing both Updike and his reader with an ahistorical model of triangulated desire; the assumption of a modernist Hawthorne, however, leads Updike to thematize psychoanalytic categories and content despite his stated distaste for Freudianism in literature.[3] There are, however, specific historical connections implicit in Updike's reading (and the professional reading of Updike) that urge a self-conscious and provisional use of a psychoanalytic reading strategy in the name of nonessentializing.

During the fourteen-year period from the publication of *A Month of Sundays* in 1974 to that of *S* in 1988, Updike was also reading and writing about Hawthorne in nonfictional contexts.[4] In one of these other forums, the "Special Message" to the Franklin Library's First Edition Society printing of *Roger's Version*, Updike curiously insists on the heterosexuality of Hawthorne and *The Scarlet Letter*. Updike calls *The Scarlet Letter* "the one classic from the lusty youth of American literature that deals with society in its actual heterosexual weave," a formulation that implicitly denies that there also might be an actual homosexual weave in the fabric of American society. For Updike, this famous American novel is but an emblem of its author: "Hawthorne, indeed, of our classic writers, seems to be, recessive and shadowy as he was, the one instinctive heterosexual."[5]

Updike's urge to construe Hawthorne as a heterosexual is repeated by the desire of certain Updike scholars regarding their man. A few years ago I wrote an article on *Roger's Version* that suggested this novel draws on the homoerotic possibility of the Dimmesdale-Chillingworth relation in portraying the relationship of a middle-aged professor of theology, Roger Lambert, bent on undermining the faith of a graduate student who is determined to prove the existence of God through computer modeling and who also is having an affair with Lambert's wife.[6] Subsequently, James Schiff published a book-length treatment of Updike's trilogy that, while acknowledging my article, attempts to contain the threat of my reading; according to Schiff: "Updike suggests a homoerotic element to the relationship between the Chillingworth and the Dimmesdale figures. . . . Though Updike's characters are decidedly heterosexual, adulterous configurations offer them the otherwise taboo pleasures of homoeroticism without the public visibility."[7] Not to worry, Schiff assures us: the homoerotic is merely an exotic spice that Updike adds to the steak and potatoes of what is at base an unambiguous heterosexuality. Schiff's comments suggest why it might be useful in the contemporary moment to deploy a psychoanalytic model of surface and depth to produce a dissident reading of Updike's textuality/sexuality.[8] The symbolic logic of *A Month of Sundays*, I believe, repeatedly challenges and complicates Updike's notion of "instinctive" heterosexuality.

In his trilogy of *The Scarlet Letter*, Updike attempts to direct our attention to a *Scarlet Letter* that is safe for heterosexuality; however, Updike's construction of Hawthorne constantly is undone by a web of intertextuality that simultaneously overwhelms Updike's desire to fix our gaze on *The Scarlet Letter* and fills his texts with queer possibilities. This insistence on the heterosexuality of *The Scarlet Letter* seems curious, particularly if one thinks of the weak, effeminate Dimmesdale or of how much the relationship between the minister and Chillingworth excludes Hester. Neither man wishes to admit his relation to her. Chillingworth's revenge may be stated simply: you violated my wife, so now I violate you. Arthur's literal penetration of Hester is repaid by Roger's thrusts into the minister's psyche. The concluding chapter of *The Scarlet Letter* obliquely hints at what may be at stake in Chillingworth's affect; commenting on Roger's withering away following Dimmesdale's death, the narrator notes: "It is a curious subject of observation and inquiry, whether hatred and love be not the same thing at bottom. Each, in its utmost development, supposes a high degree of intimacy and heart-knowledge; each renders one individual dependent for the food of his affections and spiritual life upon another; each leaves the passionate lover, or the no less passionate hater, forlorn and desolate by the withdrawal of his object."[9] Updike's Marshfield, the Dimmesdale figure of *A Month of Sundays*, would agree with Hawthorne; gesturing briefly to Freud's notion of the meaning of primal words, Marshfield notes: "Freud's darkest truism: opposites are one."[10] Eve Kosofsky Sedgwick has written extensively on Hawthorne's "curious subject"—the homoerotic possibilities that reside in relations between men who identify themselves as heterosexual—and her work on "homosexual panic" suggests that the homoerotic is embedded in, not opposed to, masculinity. Homosexual panic posits that male heterosexual "identity" is intimately tied to a definitional crisis since "male friendship, mentorship, admiring identification, bureaucratic subordination, and heterosexual rivalry all involve forms of investment that force men into the arbitrarily mapped, self-contradictory, and anathema-riddled quicksands of . . . male homosocial desire."[11] Simply put, in a culture such as ours that emphasizes male bonding in a number of institutional contexts, homosexual panic polices heterosexuality by forcing individual men to speculate uneasily whether their relations with other men may shade into the homoerotic and to recoil in horror at the possibility of being identified (by others, by oneself) as homosexual.

Updike clearly is unafraid of directly representing actual heterosexual couplings in his fiction, yet the male-male desire between Updike's "instinctive heterosexuals" in *A Month of Sundays* and *Roger's Version* disrupts masculine identity.[12] The passionate theological debate between Thomas Marshfield and Ned Bork, which is repeated by Roger Lambert and Dale Kohler in *Roger's Version,* creates a certain attraction within these two male-male pairs. The confessional texts of both Marshfield and Lambert show how they use their wives as units of exchange in a symbolic economy that effects a metaphorical consummation that is strictly between men, to borrow the title of Sedgwick's earlier study.[13] Not surprisingly, then, the masculinity that Marshfield and Lambert seek to confirm through their reading of the unconscious shows the extent to which that "identity" is an unstable multiplicity shaped by homosexual panic.

The homoeroticism of Updike's male agons oddly parallels Updike's relationship to Hawthorne's text, where Harold Bloom's anxiety of influence becomes panic. The writer is always already a reader, already penetrated by the word of the Other, as Updike's relation to Hawthorne makes clear. If to read is to be penetrated, how can a man retain a male heterosexual "identity"? Updike's solution seems to take the offensive through the very act of writing the trilogy; like Marshfield and Lambert, Updike wants to come out on top in his theological grappling with Hawthorne. One reading of the trilogy accounts for Updike's difference from Hawthorne by pointing to Updike's reading of the Swiss theologian Karl Barth. Donald J. Greiner, for example, sees Updike rejecting Hawthorne's "tendency to separate the body and soul," since such a separation "warps consideration of the erotic."[14] From Greiner's perspective, Hawthorne's concern for the realm of morality and ethics is revised by Updike's Barthian concern for the difficult matter of faith in contemporary America ("Body" 487). To the extent that this reading is correct, there arises an interesting contradiction in Updike's characterization of Hawthorne. Updike's instinctively heterosexual Hawthorne becomes associated with a theology that Updike's *A Month of Sundays* tropes as "limp-wristed," one instance of the stereotypical characterization of male homosexuality that recurs throughout the trilogy.

Against this interpretively fruitful intertextual trio (Hawthorne, Barth, Updike), I would interpose a Barth with a difference, suggesting instead another triangle: Hawthorne, Barthes, Updike. Between his writing of *A Month of Sundays* and *Roger's Version,* Updike wrote a series of reviews of Roland Barthes's work—*S/Z, The Pleasure of the Text, Sade/Fourier/Loyola,* and *New Critical Essays.* Updike's review of *S/Z* and *The Pleasure of the Text* appears in the November 12, 1975, issue of the *New Yorker* and is contemporaneous with reviews of *A Month of Sundays.* Whether Updike read Barthes's texts as he was completing the first novel of his trilogy is not really the issue; for, in reviewing Barthes, Updike surely recognized the shared project of both *The Pleasure of the Text* and *A Month of Sundays—*the construction of an erotics of the text. But while Marshfield focuses on the writer's seduction of the reader, Barthes's project questions and collapses the difference between reading and writing, emphasizing the playful power the reader can exert on the text even as the text seduces the reader. In Updike's review of *The Pleasure of the Text,* there is a moment of gender identification as telling as his insistence on Hawthorne's heterosexuality. Addressing the point in Barthes's text where he calls the text a fetish and characterizes as a castrating gesture the interpretive urge to create unity of meaning within a text, Updike responds: "Whether or not Freud was correct in supposing females to feel the lack of a penis keenly enough to braid themselves one (a custom rarely observed along the Eastern Seaboard), Barthes's critical approach seems specifically manly—insisting on readerly activity rather than passivity."[15] Since Barthes's reader is active, Updike characterizes Barthes's theory as masculine ("manly"), which implies an opposite—feminine passivity, a redundancy in Updike's world. In short, we are left, in Updike's figuration, with a heterosexual Hawthorne promoting fag theology and a homosexual Barthes advocating manly reading.

In his nonfictional writing, then, Updike is unable to denote unambiguously gendered identity because his figurative language works at cross purposes with his declarations. Updike's problem is shared by the narrators of *A Month of Sundays* and *Roger's Version.* The confessional textuality of Marshfield and Lambert depends on a series of unstable oppositions that create a number of homologous possibilities:

writer	reader
male (penetrator)	female (penetrated)
consciousness	the unconscious
faith	good works/ethics

Part of my argument, then, is that Updike's male narrators, contra Barthes, seek to essentialize a hierarchized difference between writer and reader; analogously, these narrators hope to stabilize their heterosexual masculine identity by penetrating their unconscious thoughts, by becoming penetrating readers of their uncontrolled self. The panic? If real identity lies elsewhere than consciousness, what can be done to master this shadowy region of the feminized unconscious?

Perhaps chief among the many intertextual links that simultaneously signal identity and difference between *A Month of Sundays* and *The Scarlet Letter* is the claim Hester Prynne makes to Arthur Dimmesdale in the forest regarding their adulterous relation: "What we did had a consecration of its own" (133). Updike's fictive premise might be stated as follows: What if Dimmesdale did not, on his return to the community, recoil in horror from Prynne's position? What if, following her injunction in the forest to preach, write, and act, he did precisely that, becoming the ministerial advocate of adultery?

Thomas Marshfield finds himself in a resort-style recovery house for fallen clergymen in the Arizona desert. The woman named Prynne who manages this facility points to an ostensible reversal of power relations from Hawthorne to Updike. Hawthorne's Hester is subject to the dictates of the all-male authority of the Puritan ministers and magistrates, while Updike's Prynne subjects her male charges to the regimen of their days. Prynne directs Marshfield, as well as the other ministers, to write in a journal for half of each day of his one-month stay. There is a clear Freudian presumption in this scenario—the writer's movement from consciousness to self-consciousness and the hope that this confrontation with self will prove therapeutic. Like Dimmesdale, Marshfield has committed adultery, though frequently and with several of his women parishioners.

Following a distinction in narratology running from the Russian formalists to Gérard Gennette, one might speak of the (hi)story and the discourse of Marshfield's journal. The novel's metafictional aspect, foregrounding Marshfield's discursive production, of course underscores the twin logics of textuality (chronological and synchronic), but this self-conscious narration also suggests a doubled sexuality in which the homoerotic always shadows the heterosexual act. Although the history Marshfield tells of himself—the series of adulterous relations he engaged in that led to his being sent away for rehab—focuses exclusively on his heterosexual exploits, his discourse produces a figurative countercurrent of homoeroticism that runs throughout his relation with his curate, Ned Bork. The homoeroticism of this relationship in part sheds light on Marshfield's compulsion to commit adultery, namely, the minister's need to confirm his heterosexual identity. The site of the production of this text—his "hotel" room in Arizona—reveals that the discourse itself is the occasion of another plot, his attempt to seduce Ms. Prynne, the supposed reader of his text; this second plot subverts the intention of those who sentenced Marshfield to the desert for a month of reflection precisely because it subverts the intended therapeutic repudiation of his adulterous self. Like Hester, Tom transforms his punishment into a form of self-justification so that, once again, the scarlet letter does not do its office.

As a result of this Dimmesdale-like, double-speak language, Marshfield's relation to Ned Bork in the story parallels the minister's relation to Prynne in the discourse. In both, Marshfield is engaged in a struggle in which theological and doctrinal matters serve as a double to the erotic charge of these relationships; he plots in both to come out on top, a fact that points to the basis of Updike's Christian faith, which seems finally to depend on, at least figuratively, the ability to have an erection. And although Marshfield loses with Bork, the telling of his tale allows Marshfield an opportunity to recoup that loss.

In Marshfield's presentation of himself, his religious identity as an advocate of Karl Barth's theology is intimately wed to his masculine identity. Like his minister's, Updike's own theology draws heavily on Barth: "The real God, the God men do not invent, is *Totalier aliter*—Wholly Other. We cannot reach Him; only He can reach us. This He has done as the Christ of Biblical Revelation."[16] What seems arbitrary here is the way in which faith is associated with masculinity; for traditionally, reason, logic, and ethics have been marked in Western culture as masculine against a feminine belief in the supernatural. Updike has Marshfield transform Barth's faith, which seems passive ("only He can reach us"), into the active. In *A Month of Sundays,* this transformation is effected by Marshfield's figuration of a Christianity that favors good works (which might reasonably be seen as active) as either androgynous or homosexual, which results in liberal Christianity being constellated with femininity. For example, Marshfield identifies his curate as effeminate and calls his socially activist theology "limp-wristed" (18). To stop the play of difference, Marshfield must absolutize the opposition between faith and good works. And in stopping the play of difference in the theological, he simultaneously would absolutize the erotics of sexual and textual difference. In both realms, however, he fails. Marshfield's failure constantly erupts through his language's connotative excess.[17]

Marshfield's identity in marriage proclaims him a masculine backslider. His marriage has rendered him androgynous to the extent that he is aware that he and his wife, Jane, have come to look like each other (61), and to be androgynous points to the possibility of homosexuality by a logical relation of implication. This implication is reinforced by Marshfield's understanding that his profession is not taken to be manly. He knows, for example, how the men of his congregation view him: "The blue-suited businessmen regarded me with guarded but approbatory grimace as a curious sort of specialist, while musk arose thicker than incense from between the legs of their seated wives" (35). Marshfield later posits that his women parishioners were drawn to him in part because of "the traditional sexual ambiguity of the priest, with his swishing robes and his antistoical proclamation of our pain and sickness and sickly need" (161).

Other self-representations point to a strangely configured sense of self that perhaps helps explain his desire to identify effeminacy in other males. His voice, Marshfield tells us, "is really half-octave too high for the ministry" (14). Among the several reasons he gives for only wearing pajama tops, one is "to send an encouraging signal to the mini-skirted female who, having bitten a poisoned apple at the moment of my father's progenitive orgasm, lies suspended within me" (16). Even after the discovery of his multiple adulteries, he tropes himself into a strange figuration of himself vis-à-vis Gerry Harlow, a church deacon with whose wife, Frankie, Marshfield has had a sexual relation. Marshfield writes of Gerry's leaving his office: "How sad I felt, seeing Harlow leave, his shoulders square as those of a young soldier who has just acquitted himself well with an ingenious and more than her trade demands affectionate whore" (211).

Thus, before his adultery with Alicia Crick, the church organist, Marshfield exists in a state of religious doubt that doubles, even as it disguises, his deeply concealed doubts about his sexual identity, a fact not lost on Crick, who points to a central figural strategy of the novel. In a conversation between Tom and Alicia, she answers his question about what makes him unhappy in a way he was not expecting: "I assumed she would answer,

Your theology. Instead she said, 'Your marriage'" (40). The novel posits a kind of figurative equation between theology—as the formal inscription of doctrine—and marriage—as the social contract that legitimizes heterosexual union. Against this substitutable pair of terms stands another, faith and sex, so that we might see this larger novelistic equation: theology is to faith as marriage is to sex. Theology and marriage are the institutional ghosts of living faith and vibrant sex. Therefore, if Marshfield's sexuality is structurally ambivalent because of his ministerial role, he has two routes available to him to secure heterosexual identity—heterosexual acts and professions of faith.

Alicia serves Tom in a double fashion; in bed, he tells us, she "was a revelation" (43), so much so that his restoration of his masculine identity is identical with his renewal of faith: "thus I attained, in the bound of a few spring weeks, a few illicit lays, the attitude which saints bear toward God . . . that is, of forgiving Him the pain of infants, the inexorability of disease, the wantonness of fortune, the billions of fossilized deaths, the helplessness of the young, the idiocy of the old, the craftsmanship of torturers, the authority of blunderers, the savagery of accident, the unbreathability of water, and all the other repulsive flecks on the face of Creation" (48–49). This conjunction of sexuality and faith recurs in Marshfield's relation with Frankie Harlow, despite the fact that he is impotent with her precisely because of her faith. In their final tryst, Marshfield makes an impassioned plea against the possibility of God in an attempt to overcome his impotence, concluding: "'You can't think there's a God. You know you can't. What's your reason? Give me one reason, Frankie.'" Her reply, "'You,'" causes Marshfield to have an enormous erection, and though he is unable to have an orgasm because "repentant tenderness overtook me" (186), the scene is significant for what it says about Updike's creed, which is primarily figured as a form of genital worship.

Turning from Marshfield's sexual relations with women to his relation to his curate, Ned Bork, the doubling of religious belief and sexuality continues but with a different emphasis. With the women with whom he had sexual relations, the sex itself served as the sign of religious faith; but with Marshfield's relation to Bork, their doctrinal differences serve to mask Marshfield's homoerotic affect.

There are a curious series of likenesses between and among Tom, Jane, and Ned. Tom and Jane look alike; Jane and Ned think alike. Describing himself and Jane during their courtship, Tom says: "She was liberal and ethical and soft, I Barthian and rather hard" (61). Marshfield, in his initial description of Bork, finds all of his curate's physical features and habits "odious," particularly noting his "limp-wristed theology, a perfectly custardly confection of Jungian-Reichian soma-mysticism swimming in a soupy caramel of Tillichic, Jasperian, Bultmannish blather, all served up in a dime-store dish of his gutless generations' give-away Gemütlichkeit" (18-19). This figuration of Bork's theology—a double of Jane's—points back to Tom's original desire for Jane—"to *eat* her, to taste, devour, and assimilate" (61).

From the above discussion of Marshfield, one can understand why he might wish to see effeminacy not in himself but in another male, to identify queerness as elsewhere. The oral figuration above perhaps sheds light on his confession regarding the odious Bork: "Actually, I liked him too. / And wanted him to like me" (19). Tom wants to taste Bork (or at least his confectionary theology) too to assimilate him. Frequently in Updike's representations of women, their mouths or voices are associated with their vaginas. As a child, Marshfield notes that "my mother's singing voice was, for me her sex; that I transferred in my childish innocence to her lower mouth" (27). But at a particular moment in one of their doctrinal disputes, Marshfield employs a similar figure that points to the homoerotic content of his relation with Bork: "Threatened, [Bork] tilted back his head, so his lips showed through his beard, pink and ladylike" (85); thus, Bork's fag theology issues from his cunt mouth.

This particular doctrinal dispute is calculated on Marshfield's part: he hopes to create distance between himself and his curate so that Bork will be more willing to consider a sexual relation with Jane. Marshfield hopes that if Jane and Ned have an affair, it will serve as a cover for his affair with Alicia. Thus does Marshfield plot against his doctrinal/sexual enemy in a way that, as the elder mentor figure to Bork, makes Tom at times more Chillingworth than Dimmesdale.[18] But this attempt to manipulate Bork also carries an erotic charge that must be seen again in relation to Bork's vaginal mouth. After confiding in his curate that Jane is not fulfilled in her marriage to him, Marshfield parts with Ned: "He stands at the door, teetering a touch. Streetlight strikes a gleam from his glassy eyes. His beard makes his face hard to read. The mouth a mere hole, with a sinister drawgate of teeth. . . . Even his ears, if they showed, might be a clue to his heart. His centrally parted hair is enough like a woman's to tip my insides toward kissing him. I teeter also. I tug back the abhorrent impulse and yank its leash savagely" (78). The clue to the curate's heart that Marshfield ostensibly seeks is what Ned's feelings are toward Jane; but, as the preceding discussion suggests, the sought-after clue is at least as much Tom's desire to know how Bork feels about Jane's androgynous double—Marshfield himself. Tom's panic and homophobia reveal themselves in his relation to the feared and fantasized "abhorrent impulse" vis-à-vis Bork's *vagina dentata*.

But Updike's Dimmesdale's attempt to be Chillingworth is frustrated when Alicia Crick asserts her agency. She begins an affair with Bork, an act Marshfield takes as a message to him. Alicia's action comes at a time, Marshfield notes, "when my fantasy of Ned's homo- or asexuality was inching from the realm of faith into a kind of negative verification" (99). Alicia effectively intervenes with Marshfield's plan; giving Jane to Ned was not only to have been a way to hide his affair but also a displaced consummation of his relation with Ned. Alicia's intervention nevertheless still consummates the relationship between Tom and Ned, but not with Marshfield in the "masculine" (controlling, authorizing) position as he had imagined. When, instead of having sex with Marshfield's wife, Ned has sex with the minister's mistress, a striking reversal occurs in the two men's figurative relation.

This reversal points directly to the epigraph from *The Scarlet Letter* that begins this section; here, Hawthorne speculates on the intimacy of Chillingworth's relationship with Dimmesdale. With recent confirmation of Ned's heterosexuality, Marshfield sees Bork differently:

> he moved in my vision with the unhealthy phosphorescence of a raised corpse. His body, that is, had blindly entered a charmed circle. I was still his superior, and my knowledge of his secret, where he had none of mine, improved my advantage. But the sum of all this was intimacy. Heaven forbid, I began to love him. Or at least began to listen. His views, which I had earlier dismissed as hopelessly compromised by topical fads, as the very image of the tower of Babel Barth says our merely human religiosity erects, now had some interest for me. (104–5)

As we shall see, the reference to the raised corpse is crucial to an adolescent conceit Updike plays with in Marshfield's sermons. Both Christ's resurrection and the resurrection of the dead figure the erect phallus. From the deadness of effeminacy, Bork has risen to heterosexual masculinity, which allows him to now come out on top in his debate with Marshfield. Bork's language is now imagistically phallic; and, given the metaphorical equivalence of sex and religion in the novel, the erections of religiosity are but a half-step removed from those of sexuality. When Ned directly attacks Barth, Marshfield confides: "My love for this man took a submissive form. I wanted him to be wise. I wanted him to grow. There were a dozen ledges in his exposition where one could stage an argument . . . , but I went feminine and shrugged" (109). Evidence of Ned's heterosexuality seems to unman Marshfield: figuratively, in his inability to defend his beloved Barth; literally, in his impotence with Frankie. Tom's desire to inhabit the "feminine" (passive) position indicates the way that he vacates the Chillingworth position and reverts to Hawthorne's Dimmesdale, allowing Ned to assume the position of mentor.

Marshfield's gesture here points back in his history to an earlier mentor figure, Jane's father, the Reverend Wesley Augustus Chillingworth. As Marshfield's ethics professor in divinity school, Chillingworth is another embodiment of the doctrine Marshfield finds odious: "His course epitomized everything I hated about academic religion; its safe and complacent faithlessness, its empty difficulty, its transformation of the tombstones of the passionate dead into a set of hurdles for the living to leap on their way to an underpaid antique profession" (63). In this regard, Chillingworth becomes a surrogate father; and, in a rare moment of insight on this matter, Marshfield sees how his marriage to Jane may be implicated in something more than instinctive heterosexual attraction: "To what extent, you may well ask, did I seduce this good stately girl as an undermining and refutation of the polymath's theology, his wry dimness worse than Deism, in which I recognized, carried some steps further by a better mind, my father's terrifying bumbling at the liberal Lord's busywork? Chillingworth would dustily cough beneath us at the oddest moments, so often in synchrony with orgasm as to suggest telepathic discomfort. I was slaying him that the Lord might live" (68). Stated more bluntly, Marshfield repays Chillingworth's attempt to penetrate his subjectivity and doctrinal orientation by literally penetrating his daughter. Woman here is once again a go-between in a displaced game of male erotics. But if Marshfield is capable of this insight regarding his relation to Chillingworth, he is unable to carry that insight through to its homoerotic implications that reside in his relationship with Bork. Some time after he "went feminine" in his relation with Bork, Marshfield is still obsessed with the curate's sexuality. In the context of Ned's progressive usurpation of more and more power within the congregation, Marshfield notes: "Ned's queerness . . . was, in the developing pan of his new confidence, becoming less shadowy, emerging as a faintly fussy and rococo edge for his gestures and dress. . . . My own miserably heterosexual example may have helped him here" (171). As always, Marshfield secures his sexual identity by identifying queerness elsewhere.

In the story Marshfield tells, then, Ned's fag theology wins. Marshfield is disgraced; and Ned, the embodiment to Marshfield of "the androgynous homogenizing liberals" (240), will be installed as the new minister in Marshfield's church. But in the discourse, Marshfield as the teller of his tale has a chance to rewrite the failed ending of his story through his relationship with his reader, Ms. Prynne. If Marshfield has been feminized by Bork's rise to heterosexuality, the reader—in Updike's textual erotics—is always already feminized in relation to the writer's activity.

It is, therefore, in Marshfield's relation to Ms. Prynne that *A Month of Sundays* comes to parallel most closely Barthes's concerns in *The Pleasure of the Text*, particularly as Updike's text meditates on the possibility of desire between author and reader. For Barthes, of course, "the author is dead" in terms of a final authority of textual meaning, "but in the text, in a way, *I desire* the author: I need his figure (which is neither representation nor his projection), as he needs mine (except to 'prattle')."[19] Updike seems nervous about Barthes's reader, who is free "to skim or to skip certain passages (anticipated as 'boring') in order to get more quickly to the warmer parts of the anecdote" (Barthes, *Pleasure* 11), because such a "manly" reader has usurped authority and condescends to the writer (Updike, "Barthes" 582). But Marshfield's nervousness is more acute, for he is unsure whether or not he has a reader. In Updike's erotics of the text, the reader is the shadowy, disembodied possibility, and Marshfield intensely desires a reader's acknowledgment. In his penultimate journal entry, Marshfield's increasing desire for Prynne manifests itself in this plea: "You are yet the *intelligens entis,* of my being, insofar as I exist on paper. Give me a body. Otherwise I shall fall through space forever" (261).

Marshfield imagines that Prynne is the sole reader of his daily typing; however, except for a brief textual presence of her handwriting—if it is hers—after his fourth sermon, Prynne exists solely as Marshfield's construction of her as the ideal reader.[20] In this regard, Ms. Prynne is a figuration of Marshfield's attempt to master his (feminine) unconscious, the space where "identity" can never be verified, since it is never fully present to itself. Her title (Ms.) is, as others have noted, the abbreviation for manuscript, but her title and patronymic together suggest that Ms. Prynne is literally the misprint. She is, then, a code for his manuscript's typos, which Marshfield reads—with good Freudian suspicion—through a series of metacritical footnotes as possible messages from his shadowy unconscious, even as he devalues the unconscious as "Freud's stumblebum God" (139). This is clearly a gesture of control, one that forestalls his reader's possible interpretations of his unconscious. The most extreme manifestation of this controlling urge occurs once even after he has already erased the textual trace of his typo; he nevertheless feels compelled to provide commentary in the following footnote on his typescript's reference to "his upraised phallus": "The first time, believe it or not, I typed 'unpraised'—my uxorious lament in an uninvited consonant" (43). The only readings of this dark space of his psychic life that Marshfield will allow are his own.

All of Marshfield's narrative, ostensibly designed as therapy, evolves into an elaborate act of seduction that once again merges the theological and the sexual. Like Ned Bork, Ms. Prynne, as the director of this institution, represents the theology of good works. So Marshfield's discursive performance is not merely a subversion of the therapy but an attempted conversion of Prynne to the Barthian way. He seeks to penetrate Prynne, both her consciousness and her body, which for Updike are doctrinally one and the same. Given the relation of the theological to the sexual, the four sermons that Marshfield "delivers" via his typescript on the four successive Sundays of his therapy are particularly telling. In his first journal entry, Marshfield plainly states his purpose, one that contradicts the purpose of those who have sent him away for rehab: "In *my* diagnosis I suffer from nothing less virulent than the human condition, and so would preach it" (8). And despite his rethinking of his tropes and imagined audience, he consistently preaches what he sees as a defining instance of the human condition—adultery.

Marshfield's first sermon is a straightforward defense of adultery as a matter of Christian doctrine. This sermon, like the second, is addressed to his New England congregation and represents what he might have said to that audience if he had been allowed to mount the pulpit after his public exposure. Marshfield's text is John 8:1–11, in which the Pharisees bring to Jesus the woman caught in adultery, an offense that in Mosaic law is punishable by stoning. Jesus frustrates the Pharisees' attempt to force him into contradicting the law by appearing to agree—but only on the condition that the one who is without sin should cast the first stone. Marshfield takes Jesus's refusal to condemn the adulterous woman, in conjunction with a number of other moments of biblical adultery, as the basis for his assertion that adultery "is our inherent condition" and therefore "not a choice to be avoided" but a "circumstance to be embraced" (56). Indeed, for Marshfield, "the sacrament of marriage, as instituted in its adamant impossibility by our Savior, exists but as a precondition for the sacrament of adultery" (58).

Strikingly, Marshfield, who elsewhere advocates the power of the author over the reader, reveals himself here as a practitioner of Barthes's "manly" reading. Marshfield's intricate close reading of Scripture collapses the difference between reading and writing that he would elsewhere maintain; the minister's reading of his text of pleasure, the Bible, is indistinguishable from his writing of this sermon. Thus, Marshfield's claim that "the Word is ever a scandal" resonates with Barthes's position "that the pleasure of the text is scandalous: not because it is immoral but because it is *atopic*" (*Pleasure* 23). Yet despite this apparent agreement, there is a difference in what Marshfield and Barthes mean by the scandal of writing.[21] For Marshfield, the scandal of God's Word is that it is alien to human ethics and morality: the biblical text scandalizes America's residual Victorian notions of the sanctity of marriage. For Barthes, the scandal of textual pleasure is that it is never there, properly speaking, because pleasure is not an identifiable formal element of the text; therefore, since this pleasure need not be repeatable, it points simultaneously to the intertextual nature of subjectivity and to the profoundly unstable nature of any text. Textual pleasure reveals identity to be scandalously adrift. Against his overt meaning of the scandal of the Word, Marshfield participates in Barthes's notion of textual scandal in the atopian nature of his first two sermons by "addressing" an audience, his former congregation, that he can never hope to address again.

It is precisely this drifting subjectivity that Marshfield hopes to secure through a bedrock of adultery: "Wherein does the modern American man recover his sense of worth, not as dogged breadwinner and economic integer, but as romantic minister and phallic knight, as personage, embodiment, and hero? In adultery" (58). Yet all the while Updike attempts to channel the reader's pleasure with *A Month of Sundays* through *The Scarlet Letter*, another canonical text—Eliot's *The Waste Land*—emerges as an intertext between and among Marshfield's four sermons. When Marshfield leaves for the Arizona desert, which (except for the facility's well-tended golf course) is a literal wasteland, he is yet another embodiment of the wounded Fisher King, rendered impotent in his last attempt at adultery with Frankie. He, like the Fisher King, needs a phallic knight to restore him to health and spiritual wholeness.

Marshfield's second sermon is delivered from his atopian space—situated in the Arizona desert, he again imagines his suburban congregation as his audience. This sermon, like the first, expresses his rage toward the people he had served. Their failing is their lack of faith, an inability to believe in Christ's miracles and to recognize, with Karl Barth, that "His way is not ours" (125). Taking particularly a verse from Matthew ("If ye have faith as a grain of mustard seed, ye shall remove mountains; nothing shall be impossible unto you" [127]), Marshfield challenges his congregation to pray for the annihilation of themselves and their church if a "single mustard seed of faith" cannot be found among them: "There is not. The walls stand. We are damned. I curse you, then, as our Lord cursed the fig tree; may you depart from this place forever sterile; may your generation wither at the roots, and a better be fed by its rot" (128). Like Eliot's, Marshfield's wasteland is not the actual desert but the spiritual desert of contemporary life where both authors see the possibility of faith as severely limited.

Marshfield's third sermon makes explicit the sense in which modernization has produced a wasteland: "The pavements of our cities are deserted, emptied by fear. In the median strips of our highways, naught but trash blows. In our monotonous suburbs houses space themselves as evenly as creosote bushes, whose roots poison the earth around" (193). But Marshfield's third sermon makes an interesting turn away from the thematics of the wasteland. Indeed, the desert becomes the site of almost miraculous regeneration as the last part of the sermon catalogs a range of flora and fauna that flourishes despite the harsh conditions of the desert. With this turn toward regeneration comes Marshfield's recognition of a new audience for his address: "What lesson might we draw from this undaunted profusion? The lesson speaks itself. Live. Live, brothers, though there be naught but shame and failure to furnish forth your living. . . . To those who find no faith within themselves, I say no seed is so dry it does not hold the code of life within it, and that except a corn of wheat fall into the ground and die, it abideth alone; but if it die, it bringeth forth much fruit" (196). Notable here is the way that, once again, faith and sexuality merge through figurative language. The mustard seed of faith from the second sermon becomes the seed of regeneration in the third. This seed in turn points back to the chapter preceding the third sermon, in which Marshfield tells of the end of his relationship with Frankie Harlow: "Distilling my ministry, I find this single flaw: Frankie Harlow never did get to feel my seed inside her, sparkling and burning like a pinch of salt" (187). In Eliot's dark vision of the postwar world, the mythic possibilities of male-female union had become degraded; sexuality had been reduced to the physical act, devoid of a deeper intimacy. For Updike, however, there is no such thing as casual sex—the sex act always carries the possibility for the spirit's regeneration—at least a man's spirit. Thus, the mustard seed of faith becomes conflated in Marshfield's discourse with semen, the male seed of generation. This veiled sexual imagery continues in the conclusion of the third sermon, which forecasts the dominant tropological strategy of the fourth sermon—the phallus, either flaccid or erect: "Brothers, we have come to a tight place. Let us be, then, as the chuckwalla, who, when threatened, *runs* to a tight place, to a crevice in the burning rock of the desert. Once there, does he shrink in shame? No! He puffs himself up, inflates his self to more than half its normal size, and fills that crevice as the living soul fills the living body, and cannot be dislodged by the talon or fang of any enemy" (196-97). The "tight place" that these men of the cloth find themselves in is, on the one hand, the disgrace in which they find themselves; but, on the other hand, it is also literally the omega/vaginal-shaped "motel"—with its tightly regimented schedule—in which they are housed. In Marshfield's case, Ms. Prynne, as the manager of this omega, embodies the tight place he wishes to fill, thereby reerecting his "living faith" in her living body.

One can understand why Prynne might be moved to mark Marshfield's text with a handwritten comment—if indeed it is her hand that produces the note Marshfield finds on his typed page.[22] No longer is Marshfield trying to justify his adultery to his congregation; he instead now ministers directly to his fellow men of the cloth, beginning simply: "My brothers" (243). But despite this rethinking of audience, his figurative language reveals that, doctrinally, his end is his beginning; for, far from modifying his position on adultery, he has decided, well, to let it stand, for his message is modulated through a thoroughly phallic set of imagery. Marshfield takes as his text Paul's letter to the Corinthians: "And if Christ be not risen, then is our preaching vain, and your faith is also vain" (243). Not only is Christ's resurrection the issue but also "Paul's carnal stipulation" (247) regarding the literal resurrection of the body on the Day of Judgment. For Marshfield (and for Updike, presumably), the clearest manifestation of this bit of "barbaric doctrine" can be found in the penis, the organ that repeatedly affirms the reerection of the flesh. Note the recurring figuration in Marshfield's sermon: "No man, unless it was Jesus, believes. We can only *profess* to believe. *We stand,* brethren, where *we stand,* in our impossible and often mischievously idle jobs, on a boundary of opposing urgencies where there is often not space enough to set one's feet—*we so stand as steeples stand,* as emblems. . . . In this Inbetweentimes let us take comfort at least from the *stiffness of our roles,* that *still stand though we crumple within them*" (249–50; emphases added except for "*profess*"). The tropological implications of this passage are at odds with Prynne's presumption of Tom's "cure" and reveal instead that he still justifies the "romantic minister and phallic knight" of the first sermon; in other words, even though "fallen" men, as ministers, they can still "rise to the occasion" and preach the human condition of adultery.

Marshfield figuratively penetrates Prynne precisely through his figurative language, so that his representation of a literal moment of penetration and physical climax with her—whether real or imagined—is actually anticlimactic. Marshfield has discovered a subversive discourse that will allow his audience to swallow the scandal of his reading of the Word. In this regard, Marshfield reverses the course of Dimmesdale; until the end of *The Scarlet Letter*, Hawthorne's minister speaks in a duplicitous fashion that makes his congregation take him to be holy while concealing his role as Pearl's father; Marshfield, however, only by his final sermon learns to suppress his urge to proclaim bluntly his sense of the true by disguising his unseemly convictions through figurative language.

Even in this final sermon—which serves as the subversive triumph of Updike's erect faith, figured on male arousal—that feared and fantasized specter of the male homosexual arises. Two chapters earlier, Marshfield describes what has moved him to minister to his homosocial community, and the comments about his homosexual golf partner, Jamie Ray, are particularly telling: "And to Jamie Ray I have listened even more intently, though smiling at his delicious Southernisms ('asshole slicker than a buttercup' comes to me out of many) and rejecting the sidling fear that any announced homosexual puts into me, trying to detect, for myself and for him, what holy thing it is men see in each other, what fear brings them to cling only to their own sex, though their bodies become, not manly, but mockeries, often fanatically skillful, of the despised feminine" (236). The passage emphasizes fear in two senses: first, Marshfield's fear of announced homosexuals, which he claims he is trying to think through; and, second, the fear that he believes motivates men to become homosexuals. Marshfield's fear of acknowledged homosexuals should be seen in relation to his liking Ned, whom Marshfield believed was a latent homosexual; to be able to identify Ned as latent helps Marshfield stabilize his own sense of masculinity, something that announced homosexuals disrupt. Although he poses the latter fear as a problem, he answers his own question. What homosexuals fear is "the despised feminine." Marshfield's thinking about homosexuality, obviously, remains conventional, especially his belief that all male homosexuals are effeminate; but what I would suggest is that this "despised feminine" tells us at least as much about Marshfield's role as a lady's man as it does about homosexuality. Earlier, Marshfield constructs an odd conceit regarding the metaphorical relation between sexual iden-

tity and golf: "Jamie Ray swings miserably but putts like an angel; I sometimes wonder if buggery hasn't made the hole look relatively huge to him.
Whereas us poor cunt men keep sliding off to the side" (217). Noteworthy
here is Marshfield's attempt to essentialize a particular sexual pleasure as
the defining feature of male heterosexuality (cunt men) and male homosexuality (asshole men). What this overlooks is a multiplicity of other
pleasures, particularly the pleasure that most readily collapses this distinction: namely, that heterosexuals and homosexuals can both be mouth
men. For example, Marshfield's description—via a gustatory adjective
("delicious")—of his pleasure at Jamie Ray's figuration of his presumptive
pleasure ("asshole slicker than a buttercup") serves to unhinge the opposition Marshfield wishes to maintain and simultaneously recalls his "abhorrent impulse" connected to his curate's mouth.

Tellingly, when Marshfield, thinking of Alicia, tries to imagine Prynne's
perspective on this all-male community, his language leads to a queer declaration: "At moments, in the bar afterwards, I let the rank maleness of my
fellows blow through me, and try to think their wrinkled whiskery jowls,
their acrid aromas, their urgent and bad-breathed banalities, into some
kind of Stendhalian crystallization. I cannot quite do it, I am less than half
queer" (229). Here is the panic once again—expressed as an inability to do
what he has just done. To express a love of maleness must simultaneously
be accompanied by a denial of homosexuality, else Marshfield fears he will
be hailed as homosexual.

Marshfield's relation to the "despised feminine" is evident in relation
even to the revelatory Alicia. "Enjoyed and dismissed" (80), she becomes
in the postcoital moment something repulsive that Tom feels he must defend himself from; Marshfield thinks of his clothes as armor to fend off her
naked body. The thought of her bodily fluids disgusts him: "She laughed
through her tears, snorting; I feared a sudden extrusion of phlegm, and
backed her face from my chest" (82). In addition to the hard/soft opposition, Marshfield also thinks of sexual difference between men and women
in terms of dry and wet. What occasions the excess of Alicia's fluidity
at this moment is Marshfield's own recent "sudden extrusion" of bodily
fluid, yet he figures—as we have previously seen—semen as dry (his dry
seed or spore, capable of burning). In the broader logic of the narrative,
when Marshfield has just about decided that the previously enjoyed Alicia
must be dismissed again—now from her position as church organist—she
once more produces unwanted bodily fluids: "wantonly the wench let her
bunny-pink eyes go teary" (168–69). This description links Alicia's emo-

tions to a negative representation of female sexuality, yet his own name (marsh-field, another type of wasteland) undercuts Tom's attempt to isolate fluidity as a negative attribute of the female.

What finally can one make of Marshfield's adultery with Ms. Prynne? Readers who see enlightened development in the course of Marshfield's four sermons doubtless may construe the consensual sex between Marshfield and Prynne as a moment manifesting God through this communion. Prynne, in this reading, seems to provide a spiritual revelation to Marshfield, a moment that restores faith as Marshfield loses his sexual "ache in the almost—nay, veritably—alarming liquid volume of the passage to [her] womb" (271). But Alicia in bed was also a revelation, and one can hear even in Marshfield's description of the pleasure of heterosexual intercourse what will become his postcoital disgust with female fluidity. Like Crick, Prynne is "enjoyed and dismissed": "You have brought me to an edge, a slippery edge. And nothing left for me to do, dear Ideal Reader, but to slip and topple off, gratefully" (271).

For Marshfield, then, both faith and heterosexual identity are as fragile and transient as the last erection; doubt returns as the phallus goes flaccid. Marshfield's extramarital sexuality is a displaced expression of a self-loathing regarding what he cannot escape—"the despised feminine" that is always already a part of his masculine identity. In the end, Updike's notion of the "instinctive" heterosexual collapses in the space of the "despised feminine," since on that point Updike's representations of male heterosexuality and male homosexuality become practically indistinguishable. But Marshfield knew this already: "Freud's darkest truism: opposites are one."

Updike's nod to Freud resonates within *A Month of Sundays* in a number of ways. To the extent Updike might wish the reader to register the homoerotic affect in Marshfield's character (an uncertain supposition about authorial intent, especially given Updike's lovingly detailed portrayals of heterosexuality), he domesticates that homoeroticism by casting it as all in the family. In good Freudian fashion, Updike, consciously or not, suggests that all sexual possibility is generated within the Oedipally constructed nuclear family, whether Marshfield's acts of heterosexual adultery or his homosexual tendencies. The way Updike contains the threat of queer possibility is through Marshfield's relationship with his senile father, who lives in a nursing home. Marshfield's father resides in a perpetual present where his memories of all prior relations with other men are triggered every time his son, Tommy, comes for a visit: "He confused me with his brother Erasmus, with an old Army mate called Mooney, . . . with several

interchangeable m.c.'s who ran daytime television quizzes and exhibi-
tions of middle-class pawkiness, with the obscure power behind and above
this slippery establishment in which he found himself, and, obscurer and
more ominous still, with some man who, he seemed to believe, threatened
to steal my mother from him" (148). The list of substitutions is worth
noting here because of the way it recalls the catalog of male-male relations
that Sedgwick sees as implicated in homoerotic desire. Sedgwick more recently has criticized "the theoretical parsimony of the Oedipal scenario" as
a model of the construction of gender and sexuality, since the psychoanalytic model "requires the assumption that individual gender and sexuality,
whatever may be their variations, are arrived at by some more or less complex routing of a child's identifications and desires through the circumscribed sexual dyad of a father and mother."[23] In short, from a Freudian
perspective, queer affect always originates from a presumptive heterosexual origin. In the passage from *A Month of Sundays* above, male heterosexual rivalry grows out of the father's experience of the Oedipal triangle—the
son does disrupt his affective relation with the wife. This point is reiterated
in Marshfield's last meeting with his father; his father says: "I gave her . . .
what comfort I could. Had you not appeared, she would have been contented enough" (204). The multiple possibilities of the Oedipal triangle
anticipate the triangulated desire of adultery; and in Marshfield's voyeuristic intrusion on Ned and Alicia's sexuality, the minister becomes little
Tommy, once again the "son," enjoying the insular Tahiti of the latency
period:

> From their bedroom, too, silence, once the mumble of my father's account of
> their day died, and with it the lighter music, mostly rests, of my mother's re-
> sponses, and her voluntary canticle of the household, a few chimed facts that
> primarily, I imagined, concerned me. Then, silence. So my pleasure in verifying
> that Ned and Alicia were screwing might be, deeply, pleasure in discovering that
> my parents in their silence were not dead but alive, that my birth had not chilled
> all love, that the bower of their union continued to flourish above me. (26)

Marshfield's thoughts find completion much later in his narrative: "Alicia's new car, blood-orange by sulphurous lamplight, appeared at his curb,
but not so often, and I imagined them talking, shoeless, through veils of
that desexing fumigant called grass. What would they be talking about?
Me, I imagined, and dropped into sleep like a shoe" (171). Through Updike's Freudian grid, Marshfield can be safely marginalized as "latent homosexual," someone who has unsuccessfully negotiated the Oedipal com-

plex; in his last meeting with his father, Tommy still "goes feminine" when his father accuses him of being the man who tried to steal the wife: "Daddy, I'm frightened. Tell me what to do. What shall I become?" (204). The cultural implications of homosexual panic are rendered less challenging to presumptive heterosexuality because Marshfield's case can be reduced to personal pathology.

In Updike's first retelling of *The Scarlet Letter*, every possible male-male social relation already has taken place between father and son, and every subsequent relation between men may be read as a displaced repetition of that primal relationship. To see in Updike's portrayal of Marshfield a masculinity uncertain of its identity is to be the kind of reader who, as Fredrick Crews might complain, tries to save the text from the author. One wishing to disavow homoerotic possibility in *A Month of Sundays*, however, must contend with Updike's figurative language that constantly points to a feared homosexuality, a language that recurs not only in *Roger's Version* but elsewhere in Updike's novelistic imagination.

Notes

1. See Jane Tompkins, "Masterpiece Theater: The Politics of Hawthorne's Literary Reputation," *Sensational Designs: The Cultural Work of American Fiction, 1790–1860* (New York: Oxford University Press, 1985), 3–39.

2. This is hardly the place to rehearse the history of psychoanalytic readings of *The Scarlet Letter*, but it safe to say that psychoanalysis has enjoyed a healthy place in Hawthorne studies at least since Fredrick Crews's subsequently repudiated *Sins of the Father* (New York: Oxford University Press, 1966) and has continued through more recent work such as Joanne Feit Diehl's "Re-Reading *The Scarlet Letter:* Hawthorne, the Fetish, and the (Family) Romance," *New Literary History* 19 (1988): 655–73. (A historical irony is that Bercovitch's essay "The A-Politics of Ambiguity in *The Scarlet Letter*" immediately precedes Diehl's in the same issue of *New Literary History*.)

3. In a 1995 review of contemporary fiction, for example, Updike wonders "why the insights of Freud, who drew upon imaginative literature and often presented his cases in narratives that have the color and the force of fiction, have in fact so little." His answer is that psychoanalysis "is a form of mechanistic diminishment . . . when what we seek, gropingly, in fiction is enlargement, a glorification of the furtive and secret and seemingly trivial, a valorization of human experience" ("Novel Thoughts," *New Yorker*, 21–28 Aug. 1995, 110).

4. Donald J. Greiner argues that Updike's other published thoughts on Hawthorne are a useful context for understanding the trilogy ("Body and Soul: John Updike and *The Scarlet Letter*," *Journal of Modern Literature* 15 [1989]: 475).

5. John Updike, *Odd Jobs* (New York: Knopf, 1991), 856.

6. John Duvall, "The Pleasure of Sexual/Textual Wrestling: Pornography and Heresy in *Roger's Version,*" *Modern Fiction Studies* 37 (1991): 81–95.

7. James Schiff, *Updike's Version: Rewriting "The Scarlet Letter"* (Columbia: University of Missouri Press, 1992), 39.

8. My use of the term "dissident reading" is borrowed from Jonathan Dollimore, *Sexual Dissidence: Augustine to Wilde, Freud to Foucault* (Oxford: Oxford University Press, 1991) and Alan Sinfield, *Faultlines: Cultural Materialism and the Politics of Dissident Reading* (Berkeley: University of California Press, 1992).

9. Nathaniel Hawthorne, *The Scarlet Letter*, 3d ed., ed. Seymour Gross et al. (New York: Norton, 1988), 175.

10. John Updike, *A Month of Sundays* (New York: Fawcett, 1975), 224. Subsequent references to this work will be included parenthetically in the text.

11. Eve Kosofsky Sedgwick, *Epistemology of the Closet* (Berkeley: University of California Press, 1990), 186.

12. Schiff briefly notes the homoerotic possibility in these novels but discounts it because "Updike's characters are decidedly heterosexual" (*Updike's Version*, 39).

13. Eve Kosofsky Sedgwick, *Between Men: English Literature and Male Homosocial Desire* (New York: Columbia University Press, 1985). Sedgwick's thinking on this male symbolic economy grows out of the anthropological work of Claude Lévi-Strauss and Gayle Rubin on the exchange of women.

14. Greiner, "Body and Soul," 477 (subsequent references to this work will be included parenthetically in the text). Schiff similarly reads the Hawthorne-Updike difference (*Updike's Version*, 10).

15. John Updike, "Barthes, Berlin, Cioran," *Hugging the Shore: Essays and Criticism* (New York: Random House, 1983), 580. Subsequent references to this work will be included parenthetically in the text.

16. John Updike, "Faith in Search of Understanding," *Assorted Prose* (New York: Knopf, 1965), 273–74.

17. Drawing on Roland Barthes's discussion of connotation and denotation near the beginning of *S/Z*, D. A. Miller argues that connotation, "the dominant signifying practice of homophobia," constructs "an insubstantial homosexuality" while "tending to raise this ghost all over the place"; connotation, of course, can always be denied, simply by uttering: " 'But isn't it just . . . ?' before retorting the denotation" ("Anal *Rope,*" *Representations* 32 [1990]: 118–19).

18. Schiff rightly notes the way Updike's characters move between the different possibilities created by Hawthorne's triangulated pattern of desire (*Updike's Version*, 37).

19. Roland Barthes, *The Pleasure of the Text*, trans. Richard Miller (New York: Hill and Wang, 1975), 27. Subsequent references to this work will be included parenthetically in the text.

20. Here I follow John T. Matthews, who notes that "Ms. Prynne is not a person but a creature of the manuscript, as her title might punningly suggest. The act of intercourse that takes place is really the climax of an act of discourse; Ms. Prynne's body . . . remains the emanation of writing and reading" ("The Word as Scandal: Updike's *A Month of Sundays*," *Arizona Quarterly* 39 [1983]: 380).

21. Matthews's "Word as Scandal" contains a brilliantly detailed reading of Marshfield's first sermon; however, he uses Kristeva rather than Barthes to talk about the issue of intertextuality.

22. The penciled comment ("Yes—at last, a sermon that could be preached" [251]) on Marshfield's typed page is insufficient to establish Ms. Prynne as an actual reader. Since his manuscript indeed is typed, any handwritten comment would appear graphically different and could make sense as Marshfield's own editorial comment that recognizes he has now found a discursive strategy that will allow him to continue his subversive ministry.

23. Eve Kosofsky Sedgwick, *Tendencies* (Durham, N.C.: Duke University Press, 1993), 78.

8

The Fascination of the Lesbian Fetish: A Perverse Possibility across the Body of Dorothy Allison's *Bastard Out of Carolina*

Mary M. Wiles

Dorothy Allison's novel *Bastard Out of Carolina* resembles Roland Barthes's "Text of Pleasure" insofar as it serves its reader as a fetish object: "The text is a fetish object, and this fetish desires me. The text chooses me, by a whole disposition of invisible screens, selective baffles: vocabulary, references, readability, etc.; and, lost in the midst of a text (not behind it, like *deus ex machina*) there is always the other, the author."[1] Allison's novel foregrounds its status as a fetish object, exposing a topography of sexual abuse that simultaneously denies and discloses a veiled meaning. The cycles of disavowal that unfold through the novel engage us as a textual fetish, inaugurating the production of pleasure and belief in which we are positioned in the space of structural plenitude. While the sexual topography of abuse scripted by the character Bone permits our indulgence in a fantasized mastery, the fetishization of the text is simultaneously subverted through our active construction of a perverse language of desire— the lesbian fetish. In the novel, the symptomatic language of sexual abuse is interlaced with the canonical language of hard-core pornography that points beyond itself to the production of a lesbian possibility—a poetic language of revolt and resistance that we may or may not be able to interpret. We might then describe the pleasure of reading as double-edged: "Two edges are created: an obedient, conformist, plagiarizing edge (the language is to be copied in its canonical state . . .) and another edge, mobile, blank (ready to assume any contours), which is never anything but the site of its effect: the place where the death of language is glimpsed" (Barthes, *Pleasure* 6). *Bastard Out of Carolina* allows us to envision the formation of a perverse lesbian sexuality as a subversive semiotic process in which the contingencies of both personal and social history produce the subject Bone as the shifting point of their intersection.

The Name

Bastard Out of Carolina begins by proposing an absence. The space of the central character and narrator of the fiction is circumscribed by a surplus of names that paradoxically signify her lack of identity. Ruth Ann (or Ruth Anne or Ruth Anna) is nicknamed Bone and branded by the state as a bastard out of South Carolina. Bone is thus "marked" from the outset, situated "outside" of the symbolic structures of institution and paternal family. Her mother was not present at her naming: "My mama didn't have much to say about it, since strictly speaking, she wasn't there."[2] She is situated within what psychoanalytic theorist Julia Kristeva has described in *Powers of Horror* as "abject space": "It is thus not lack of cleanliness or health that causes abjection but what disturbs identity, system, order. What does not respect borders, positions, rules. The in-between, the ambiguous, the composite. The traitor, the liar, the criminal with a good conscience, the shameless rapist, the killer who claims he is a savior."[3] The name "Bone" itself signifies a space outside the symbolic register of language—demarcating the maternal body and the phantasmic relation she maintains with it. Bone describes herself precisely in terms of the lack or loss of a female body: "Moving gave me a sense of time passing and everything sliding, as if nothing could be held on to anyway. It made me feel ghostly, unreal and unimportant, like a box that goes missing and then turns up but you realize you never needed anything in it anyway" (65).

Both Bone and her mother inhabit abject social space. Bone points precisely to the connection: "The stamp on that birth certificate burned her like the stamp she knew they'd tried to put on her. *No-good, lazy, shiftless*" (3). Indeed, her mother's pregnant body literally breaks apart in midair to give birth to Bone's own shattered subjectivity: "Mama still asleep with her hands curled under her chin, flew right over their heads, through the windshield, and over the car they hit. Going through the glass, she cut the top of her head, and when she hit the ground she bruised her backside. . . . she didn't wake up for three days, not till after Granny and Aunt Ruth had signed all the papers and picked out my name" (2). As Teresa de Lauretis points out in *The Practice of Love*, "what the absent mother generates is not fantasies of plenitude or a dream of pre-Oedipal bliss but rather the consciousness of a loss which is and will remain unrecoverable; an emptiness, a void, a lack on which is constituted the daughter's subjectivity."[4] This impossibility of identifying with the imago of the maternal body produces in Bone a desire that is absolutely unrealizable and thus consists in the desiring itself.

In the novel, the lack or loss of the female body is also a sociohistorical inscription that discloses the legacy of the Boatwright women, articulated across the bodies of both sisters Ruth and Alma. The abject body of Aunt Ruth imaged in the wardrobe mirror is refracted in Bone's specular reflection: "She [Aunt Ruth] used to stand in front of Granny's wardrobe mirror and stare at herself when she thought no one was looking. . . . I [Bone] remembered all the times I had stared in the bathroom mirror, knowing I wasn't pretty and hating it. I felt a cold chill go up my back, as if Aunt Ruth had just touched my spine" (231). In similar fashion, Bone is transfixed by Aunt Alma's demeanor, which mirrors that of her sister Anney: "Family they were, obviously related, clearly sisters. When I swallowed loud, they both turned to me with the same gesture and the same expression" (269). Alma's body image provides the specular refraction of abject lack inscribed across the bodies of all Boatwright women: "That was blood among the mud stains all over Aunt Alma's hands, dress, sweater, calves, and face. Her hair was matted with it. . . . There was glass everywhere, shattered, scattered, gleaming in the sun. I was standing barefoot in a yard of broken glass" (268). The social histories of the Boatwright sisters interpellate the subject Bone as the shifting point of their intersection: "I knew what I looked like . . . I had looked at myself in the mirror and known I was a different person. I had wanted to laugh at everyone . . . all of them watching me like some fragile piece of glass ready to shatter around boiling water" (301).

Color

In *Bastard,* abject space is not simply a psychoanalytic inscription across the body but a sociohistorical inscription that is color encoded in the text. The abjection of the maternal Boatwright family is signified by the color black, while the respectability and elevated social stature of the paternal Parsons clan is characterized by the color white. Bone's half-sister Reese inherited the Parsons' white-blond hair, for it was her father Lyle who "had been as pretty as a girl and so white blond he could have been a model in magazines" (59). The Parsons perfectly fit the image of what a family should look like; according to Bone, Reese's grandmother Mrs. Parsons "looked like a granny you'd read about or see in a movie" (55). Perusing the technicolor movie stills of *Gone with the Wind*, Bone spots screen star Scarlett O'Hara of the antebellum South and concludes that the Boatwrights conformed more closely to the abject representation of a darkened "wild zone": "I looked up from Vivien Leigh's cheeks to see Mama coming in from work with her hair *darkened from sweat* and her *uniform stained*. Emma Slattery, I thought. That's who I'd be, that's who we were. Not Scarlett with her *baking-powder cheeks*. I was part of the trash down in the *mud-stained cabins, fighting with the darkies*" (206; emphasis added). As whiteness signifies Reese's "insider" status within the symbolic structures of institution and paternal family, black becomes the privileged signifier of Bone's "outsider" status. The outlaw persona of Black Earle and the illegitimacy of her own paternal family cast a dark shadow across Bone's mien. While Bone's biological father, a "sorry excuse for a man," had lived near Blackburn, the infamous Black Earle Boatwright had earned his name, "for that black black hair that fell over his eyes in a great soft curl, but Aunt Raylene said it was for his black black heart" (24). With Bone, blackness indexically signifies not only her lack of status within the symbolic but her inscription within white southern society as a racial abject, a Cherokee crossbreed: "When I started school, one of the Yarboro cousins . . . had called me a nigger after I pushed her away from the chair I'd taken for mine. She'd sworn I was *as dark and wild* as any child 'born on the wrong side of the porch,' which I took to be *another way of calling me a bastard*" (54; emphasis added).

In this passage, the term "bastard" does not simply point to the psychosexual inscription of abject lack or loss across the female body. Its meaning is overdetermined by its intersection with color codification that carries sociosexual significance, indicating the integral role of social structuring in subject formation. The circulation of color codes in the novel allows us to envision how social history constituted in a configuration of discourses and representations—which are both familial and institutional, cultural and subcultural—interacts with personal history to produce the subject Bone as the shifting point of their intersection. The representation of Bone's mother Anney, perfectly poised between the bastardized Boatwright and privileged Parsons clans, is encoded in black and white: "Her [Mama's] face was like a photograph, black-and-white, her eyes enormous dark shadows and her skin bleached in that instant to a paper gloss, her open mouth stunned and gaping" (69). As the refracted image of the maternal imago, Bone will assume each color at different moments as her story unfolds.

As the signifiers black and white circulate through the text, their signifieds become inverted. The color white becomes encoded as abject; black is coded as beautiful. At Aunt Alma's new downtown apartment, the shiny black faces of neighborhood kids press against the windowpane and peer in at the new arrivals. Here, the beauty of African-American features is mirrored in Bone's face: "The cheekbones were as high as mine, the eyes large and delicate with long lashes, while the mouth was small, the lips puffy as if bee-stung, but not wide. The chocolate skin was *so smooth, so polished, the pores invisible*. I put my fingers up to my cheeks, looked over at Grey and then back down" (84; emphasis added). The smooth specular image of narcissism is here momentarily mirrored in the imago of the black face. Yet Bone's narcissistic identification is condemned in advance; as Kristeva reminds us: "The more or less beautiful image in which I behold or recognize myself rests upon an abjection that sunders it as soon as repression, the constant watchman, is relaxed" (*Powers* 13). The recto-verso relation between black and white that is intricately woven through the novel characterizes the relation of narcissism to the abject. Framed from within Bone's perspective, the white luminescence of the albino Shannon Pearl, restated by her name, provides the abject underside to the specular image of the black face: "No amount of Jesus' grace would make her even marginally acceptable, and people had been known to suddenly lose their lunch from the sight of the *clammy sheen* of her skin, *her skull showing blue-white* through the *thin, colorless hair*, and those *watery pink eyes* flicking back and forth, drifting in and out of focus" (156; emphasis added). As Bone's fascinated attention to the body of Shannon Pearl intensifies, she becomes what Kristeva would term "a devotee of the abject" who cannot "cease looking at what flows from the other's innermost being, for the desirable and terrifying, nourishing and murderous, fascinating and abject inside of the maternal body" (*Powers* 54). Bone characterizes her own perverse absorption in Shannon's image in terms of the anxiety she feels about her own body: "My fascination with her felt more like the restlessness that made me worry the scabs on my ankles. As disgusting as it seemed, I couldn't put away the need to scratch my ankles or hang around what Granny called 'that strange and ugly child' " (156).

Bone credits her covert obsession with the grotesque body to her more acceptable passion for gospel music. Shannon and the Pearls, who travel on the gospel circuit, bask in the respectability of their social class, Bible Belt religiosity, and gospel refrains that they sing whenever Bone accompanies them on tours. The lure of the gospel tour for Bone is the abject spectacle of the albino body, which is marked as such by the excess of color it carries. The sight of Shannon's body affirms for Bone the integrity of her own body image, allowing her to feel provisionally safe within the limits of her own marginal acceptability. The tenuous balance of this relationship is upset, however, in a recto-verso reversal of color codification, when Shannon unleashes her repertoire of racial and class codes—"Everyone knows you're all a bunch of drunks and thieves and bastards" (170)—and attempts to reinscribe Bone's darkened persona as abject: "The way Shannon said 'nigger' tore at me, the tone pitched exactly like the echoing sound of Aunt Madeline sneering 'trash' when she thought I wasn't close enough to hear" (170). Bone's discursive backlash brands Shannon as a physiological freak: " 'You bitch, you white-assed bitch.' I wrung my hands, trying to keep myself from slapping her pasty face" (170–71). The social structuring of the subject Bone, revealed in this exchange through the dynamic reversal of color codes, is inscribed as both an effect and a precondition of the process of sexual structuring.

During the confrontation between Shannon and Bone, the boundaries preserving the spatial integrity of identities become confused. Bone rests tenuously on the threshold, neither inside nor outside, neither completely identified with the abject nor completely distanced from it. Kristeva comments on the unstable ego of primary narcissism, the collapse of borders that constructs an abject space: "If dung signifies the other side of the border, the place where I am not and which permits me to be, the corpse, the most sickening of wastes, is a border that has encroached upon everything. It is no longer I who expel, 'I' is expelled. The border has become an object. How can I be without border?" (*Powers* 3–4). Death determines the "final" interpretant, the color black that migrates across the abject corpse of Shannon Pearl. Bone is witness to the dizzying spectacle of Shannon's blue-white body that is instantaneously consumed by the dancing flames, which leave behind only her charred and blackened features: "I saw the smoke turn black and oily. I saw Shannon Pearl disappear from this world" (201). This displacement of the abject signifier black onto a different body will permit the recodification of its signified. Bone will emblematically assume the color when she wields the "four-pronged blackened object trailing a chain," the fetish hook that will allow her to establish active human agency. The transmutations of color codification that we have traced through the text index the intersection of somatic, material, and historical forces that together overdetermine the subject formation of Bone.

Music

The narcissistic wound in Bone consists in not having a body such as her mother desires it. As de Lauretis points out, psychoanalysis has theorized that the child's wish to be the object of the mother's desire is a wish to be the phallus, as the latter is assumed to be the mother's only object of desire (*Practice* 241). But in the case of Bone, the relation of castration to the narcissistic wound appears to be based on a different maternal fantasy: the mother's narcissistic wish for a feminine body (in the daughter as in herself). Bone's nostalgia for "something she never had" is voiced in the gospel melodies she hears and sings: "It was as if I were mourning the loss of something I had never really had. I sang along with the music and prayed for all I was worth. Jesus' blood and country music, there had to be something else, something more to hope for" (152). As Kaja Silverman points out in *The Acoustic Mirror*, the image of the infant contained within the "sonorous envelope" of the mother's voice inaugurates a fantasy of origins, "a fantasy about precultural sexuality, about the entry into language, and about the inauguration of subjectivity."[5] In an "operatic" version of the maternal voice fantasy, Guy Rosolato in "La voix: entre corps et langage" characterizes the maternal voice as a sonorous womb enclosing the newborn infant: "The maternal voice helps to constitute for the infant the pleasurable milieu which surrounds, sustains and cherishes him. . . . One could argue that it is the first model of auditory pleasure and that music finds its roots and its nostalgia in [this] original atmosphere, which might be called a sonorous womb, a murmuring house—or *music of the spheres*" (qtd. in Silverman, *Mirror* 84–85). The high drama and metaphoric excess found in gospel music hold an irresistible lure for Bone, who remarks: "There was something heady and enthralling about being the object of all that attention. It was like singing gospel on the television with the audience following your every breath. I *could not resist it*" (150; emphasis added). Repeated "fourteen times—fourteen Sundays in fourteen different Baptist churches," the salvation ritual of the gospel service promises a moment of purification and plenitude that Bone paradoxically describes as a "dark chocolate terror in my throat" (151). As the moment of redemption arrives, Bone vacillates "on the line between salvation and damnation" (151). Swaying beneath the swell of the music and savoring the experience she wanted to "go on forever" in which "everything ran together," Bone's perceptual ambivalence is voiced in her ecstatic lament, "something hurt me, ached in me" (151). This blurring of spatial and perceptual boundaries that music alone makes available recalls Kristeva's description of the ego of primary narcissism as "uncertain, fragile, threatened, subjected just as much as its non-object to spatial ambivalence (inside/outside uncertainty) and to ambiguity of perception (pleasure/pain)" (*Powers* 62). The nostalgic ambience ends with the music, however, and Bone is condemned to gaze into the mirror once more, an instance of recognition in which "the magic . . . was absent, the moment cold and empty" (152).

The Body

This pre-Oedipal drama of mother and child is inscribed not only through the voice but across the body of Bone as lack. The phantasmic plenitude of an idealized female body image is situated as a storybook representation that Bone affirms is beyond her reach: "No part of me was that worshipful, dreamy-eyed storybook girlchild, no part of me was beautiful" (208). As Bone gazes into her mother's handmirror, she is repulsed by the reflection of her naked body precisely because it is phallic, "scary, stern and empty"— whereas the body she desires and mourns for is a feminine, female body, "like Uncle James's girls in their white nylon crinolines and blue satin hair ribbons. They were the kind of little girls people really wanted" (208). The fantasy of castration in this text is thus explicitly associated with the failure of narcissism and, consequently, figured as the lack of a (female) body that the mother can love. This lack and its consequent damage to the subject's libidinal relationship with her body image provide, in de Lauretis's terms, the possibility of a perverse lesbian desire (*Practice* 242). The mother's rejection of Bone's body is repeatedly made explicit: "Mama's hand moved automatically, stroking my head as if I were a wounded dog. I knew from the way she was touching me that if I had not come to her, pushed myself on her, she would never have taken me into her arms. I shuddered under that unfeeling palm, slapped her hand away, and ran for the bedroom" (252). After the brutal, violent rape of Bone by Daddy Glen, her mother again refuses to hold her, turning away to instead cradle him: "She was holding him, his head pressed to her belly. . . . I hated her now for the way she held him" (291).

In formulating a model of perverse lesbian desire, de Lauretis focuses on the failure of the mother's narcissistic validation of the daughter's body image (*Practice* 242). In de Lauretis's scenario, castration for the feminine subject means the lack of the female body, which the castration complex rewrites in the symbolic as a narcissistic wound (242). Yet, it remains unclear whether this model of perverse desire could account for the symbolic scripting of the narcissistic wound during childhood. For de Lauretis, what is formed in the process of disavowal for the female subject is not a phallic symbol or a penis substitute "but something of the nature of a fetish—something that would cover over or disguise the narcissistic wound (the loss of the female body), and yet leave a scar, a trace of its enduring threat" (242). She reasons that insofar as the phallus is both culturally and historically inscribed as the valorized signifier of sexual and cultural plenitude, visible signifiers of masculinity stand in for the denied but desired female body (242). While the male fetishist projects the phallus onto the female body, de Lauretis claims that the lesbian fetishist projects the phallus onto her own body. In this manner, de Lauretis moves from the origins of perverse lesbian desire, which she locates in the disavowal of castration, to its manifestation much later in the signifiers of masculinity across the female body. The formation of Bone's subjectivity in the novel provides us with the possibility of articulating a semiosis of perverse desire as formulated during childhood and thereby determining the theoretical liaison—between the disavowal of castration and its later manifestation in the lesbian masculinity fetish—that de Lauretis's model elides.

The failure of narcissism in Bone that derives from the lack of a lovable female body is reconfirmed for her in the sadistic sexual abuse of her by Daddy Glen. Sexual abuse scenarios are detailed as the locus of psychic trauma in which Bone's body is denied, vilified, made into a hole, into a body for the master: "It was like sliding down an endless hole, seeing myself at the bottom, dirty, ragged, poor, stupid" (209). Bone's denial and dissociation is mirrored everywhere in the world around her. An aural participant in the abuse, Anney disavows its reality: "When Daddy Glen beat me there was always a reason, and Mama would stand right outside the bathroom door" (110). The nurse who examines Bone's body actually apologizes to Anney for the doctor's confrontational accusation of abuse, citing his youth and inexperience. Aunt Ruth, who seems to understand the enormity of Bone's dilemma, probes—" 'Bone, has Daddy Glen ever . . . well . . . touched you? Has he ever hurt you, messed with you?' " (124)—but denies the truth, contenting herself with Bone's predictable negative response to her inquiry. Daddy Glen lies to Anney, sobs, begs for forgiveness, but invariably repeats his sadistic torment. The sexual abuse and beating scenes scripted by Daddy Glen not only confirm Bone's sense of dispossession but deepen her denial, forcing her dissociation from her female body. Bone's symptoms—her masochistic masturbation fantasies—"speak" of castration, annihilation, and symbolic disempowerment: "I would imagine being tied up and put in a haystack while someone set the dry stale straw ablaze. I would picture it perfectly while rocking on my hand. The daydream was about struggling to get free while the fire burned hotter and closer. I am not sure if I came when the fire reached me or after I had imagined escaping it. But I came. I orgasmed on my hand to the dream of fire" (63).

Bone's fantasies later escalate to include an audience of spectators on whom she inflicts the visual spectacle of the beating rituals that transpire between herself and Daddy Glen. In these fantasies, Bone becomes not only the masochistic heroine but the active agent who is sadistically imposing her scripted scenarios on others rather than a passive object-body:

> Someone had to watch—some girl I admired who barely knew I existed, some girl from church or down the street, or one of my cousins or even somebody I had seen on television. . . . *They couldn't help or get away. They had to watch.* In my imagination I was proud and defiant. I'd stare back at him with my teeth set, making no sound at all, no shameful scream, no begging. Those who watched admired me and hated him. I pictured it that way and put my hands between my legs. . . . Those who watched me, loved me. It was as if *I was being beaten for them. I was wonderful in their eyes.* (112; emphases added)

It seems reasonable to speculate that Freud's seminal essay " 'A Child Is Being Beaten' " (1919) provides the inspiration of this daydream. The psychoanalytic theorist David Rodowick has remarked on the importance of Freud's study of infantile beating fantasies, attributing its significance to the discovery of an elaborate system of desire where the subject forms multiple identificatory positions, which include those of onlooker, agent, and victim.[6] While I will not attempt to address the theoretical implications of Freud's essay here, I will propose that the multiple identificatory positions that Bone assumes within the framework of her fantasy point to the radical potential of fantasy as a site of revolt and resistance. In her daydream, Bone is allowed to play out her masochistic role of martyred heroine—a Joan of Arc who remains morally and spiritually victorious. The sex of the audience, designated as ungendered and/or female, as well as its impassivity recall the voyeuristic positions of both Bone and her mother during the beating and rape scenarios that transpire between Bone and Daddy Glen. Anney is explicitly or implicitly always situated as impassive onlooker. Bone dissociates from her own body, watching herself watching Daddy Glen's sexual overtures as if from the theatrical wings. The mise-en-scène of Bone's daydream gives expression to her voyeuristic desire, which film theorist Christian Metz reminds us maintains a stronger and more special relationship with the absence of its object than the other perceptual drives: "If it is true of all desire that it depends on the infinite pursuit of its absent object, voyeuristic desire, along with certain forms of sadism, is the only desire whose principle distance symbolically and spatially evokes this fundamental rent."[7] The voyeurism of mother and/or daughter inscribed in the dream scene is predicated on lack. The dreamwork gives formal and spatial expression to Bone's unconscious desire for the all-encompassing and adoring gaze of the mother that alone can confirm Bone as a lovable female body.

The Fetish

The novel works the structure of disavowal insofar as the sexual abuse of Bone is systematically denied within the diegesis. Bone's masturbatory fantasies reinscribe the discourse of denial, assuring the position of her subjectivity, the fiction of her self-identity. The dreamwork disavows her shattered subjectivity, constituted as such within the symbolic structures of family and societal institutions, while simultaneously allowing her to create and perversely to take pleasure in a phantasmic wholeness and unity of the self within scripted sadomasochistic scenarios. In similar fashion, cycles of disavowal that unfold within the novel's diegesis engage the reader as a textual fetish, inaugurating the production of pleasure and belief in which the anticipatory subject is positioned in the representational space of structural plenitude. Yet the incessant repetition of sadomasochistic rituals and dreams foregrounds the canonical stature of sexual abuse in the text. Desire is stated and overstated, as in the pornographic text, through a repetition of the same—both the sexual act and anatomical precision.[8] On the surface, nothing is withheld from the reader: "His hand dug in further. He was holding himself in his fingers. I knew what it was under his hand. I'd seen my cousins naked, shaking their things and joking, but this was a mystery, scary and hard. . . . He grunted, squeezed my thighs between his arm and his legs. . . . He brought his hand up to wipe it on the blanket, and I could smell something strange and bitter on his fingers" (47). I will suggest that in the novel the topography of sexual abuse is foregrounded as a textual fetish that serves to simultaneously deny and to disclose a veiled meaning that we may or may not be able to interpret. This telling by not telling defines the symptomatic language of a perverse lesbian desire.

I will argue that Bone discovers both a voice and a vision through Raylene, formulating the origins of a lesbian subjectivity. It is Raylene's voice that enables Bone to recast her own image: "I loved her praise more than the money, loved being good at something, loved hearing Aunt Raylene tell Uncle Beau what a worker I was" (182). Silverman points out that the mother's voice initially functions as the acoustic mirror in which the child discovers its identity and voice (*Mirror* 81). It is her voice that first charts space, circumscribes objects, explains and defines the external world (76). The voice of the mother is identified by the child long before her body is; thus, Silverman asserts that it remains unlocalized during the most formative moments of subjectivity (76). Raylene's voice and her music supplant gospel hymns as a source of fascination and identification for Bone: "Sometimes she'd hum softly, no music I'd ever heard. . . . I never imagined that out on the river I would suddenly find myself as fascinated with my reclusive old aunt as I had ever been with gospel music" (180). Its pure sonorousness evokes what Kristeva would term "the abject laced with the sublime," the language of a perverse desire that could be characterized as "a cluster of meaning, of colors, of words, of caresses, there are light touches, scents, sighs, cadences that arise, shroud me, carry me beyond the things that I see, hear or think" (*Powers* 11–12).

Bone is drawn to the bewitching music of Raylene, which provides her with access to a unique new vision on the river. I will suggest that the gleaming hook she retrieves at Raylene's serves her as a lesbian fetish— a metonymical signifier for the denied but wished-for female body. The hook is initially spotted in the murky water thanks to its shine, recalling Freud's celebrated reference in his essay "Fetishism" to the "*Glanz auf der Nase*"[9] that his patient had exalted into a fetishistic precondition for the establishment of potency: " 'Lookit the shine!' she yelled, almost sliding down in the mud" (183). Indeed, the shine becomes indispensable, the most heavily cathected aspect of the fetish-object. Bone will become inconsolable when the hook is camouflaged and covered in black paint by her cousin Grey: "He (Grey) squatted down and opened the sack, pulling out a four-pronged blackened object trailing a chain. 'You ruined it!' I hissed. . . . It was still sharp, but the scary razor-and-steel feeling was gone. I swallowed hard. I had really loved the shine of it" (219). Following the initial sighting, Aunt Raylene provides Bone with a powerful description of the hooks, which were used to drag the river bottom for drowned bodies.

Bone's access to the hook through Raylene's narration inaugurates the anguished vision of her body in bits and pieces: "When I tried to imagine my flesh in pieces it was like a cartoon, completely unreal, but in the night stringy terrible pieces of meat loomed in my dreams. The hooks got in my dreams too, dripping blood and river mud" (186–87). Under the sway of castration anxiety, Bone envisions hooks that give rise to the horrific spectacle of the *"corps morcelé"* that has been most precisely defined by feminist theorist Jane Gallop as "a violently nontotalized body image, an image psychoanalysis finds accompanied by anxiety."[10] Several weeks later, Bone's dreams isolate the hook as the privileged object of her voyeuristic and fetishistic gaze. Film theorist Stephen Heath depicts the theatrical mise-en-scène of fetishization as "a brilliance, something lit up, heightened, depicted, as under arc light, a point of (theatrical) representation; hence the glance."[11] Heath's "glance" is echoed in Bone's dreams: "But a few weeks later, I started to dream about them again. This time their razor points whistled when the wind blew, and *the steel edges reflected light where there was none.* I would wake up from those dreams with my teeth aching, my ears throbbing as if there were a wind blowing on me, stinking, cold and constant. I *wanted one of those hooks, wanted it for my own,* that cold sharp metal where I could put out my hand and touch it at any time" (187; emphases added).

In theorizing the lesbian fetish, de Lauretis relies on Michel Foucault's formulation of "reverse" discourse in *The History of Sexuality* to describe the psychic movement from fantasy scenario to the crystallization of the fetish object (*Practice* 308). According to Foucault, a representation in the world is subjectively assumed and reworked—through fantasy—in the internal world.[12] In Bone's dream, the hook is the interpretant, metonymically signifying the denied but desired body. It is at Raylene's that the representation of the hook is returned to the external world, resignified and rearticulated performatively: "After she [Raylene] was asleep, I snuck out to get the hook. I took it back to my room, pried the chain off, and cleaned and polished it. When it was *shiny and smooth,* I got in bed and put it between my legs, pulling it back and forth. It made me shiver and go hot at the same time. I had read in one of the paperbacks Daddy Glen hid in the garage about women who pushed stuff up inside them. I held the chain and thought about that, rubbed it against my skin and *hummed to myself"* (193; emphases added). The interpretant is here returned to the external world to be recast ritualistically as a fetish in the representation of an erect penis and its symbolic representation in the phallus. Bone's reference to

Daddy Glen's pornographic text seems to confirm de Lauretis's assertion that, insofar as masculinity is associated with sexual activity and desire in modern Western representations, visible masculine signifiers typically serve as lesbian fetishes (243). On the surface, the hook may seem a peculiar object choice; but, as de Lauretis has remarked, the inappropriateness as well as the singularity of the fetish object make it suitable to stand in for what is absent but phantasmically wished for (*Practice* 307). Freud points to the pleasurable sensation that the devotees of fetishes enjoy: "They are quite content with them [the fetishes] or even extol the advantages they offer for erotic gratification" ("Fetishism" 152). Indeed, it is through the fact of fetishization that Bone is able to discover the sensuality of her own voice. Bone's humming—which echoes Raylene's on the river—is harmoniously integrated with the erotic pleasure of the scene, a music that she creates and controls rather than the choral music of the gospel choir that had overwhelmed and controlled her.

The shine of the fetish serves Bone as a protective talisman against the dark: "It made me stand taller just to know it was there, made me feel as if I had suddenly become magically older, stronger, almost dangerous" (194). As Heath points out, the fetish serves not only to ease the erotic life of the subject but, more importantly, provides a token of triumph over the threat of castration and a safeguard against it ("Lessons" 106). For Bone, the fetish does, indeed, serve as a safety guarantee: "I used the lock I had found on the river bank to fasten the chain around my hips. . . . I put my head back and smiled. The chain moved under the sheet. *I was locked away and safe. What I really was could not be touched.* What I really wanted was not yet imagined. Somewhere far away a child was screaming but right then, it was not me" (193; emphasis added). Bone as fetishist projects the phallus onto her own body, disavowing the lack of the female body and the prohibition of access to it. Yet the fetish not only serves the passive function of protection but also takes on an active role in establishing human agency. After her humiliation at the hands of the Woolworth's manager (who bars her after her forced confession of theft), Bone and her cousin Grey plan the Woolworth's heist. The hook is the essential element in Bone's scheme of revenge, for it provides her with access to active human agency: "I swung the hook back and forth, back and forth—and let go, right into the nuts case. The glass shattered and the nuts poured out. I felt a shock of electricity shoot up my arm to my shoulder; a river of nuts was flooding out of the case, a tide of nuts, an avalanche" (223–24). The image of shattered glass that had previously indexed the abject legacy of the Boatwright women is recodified in this scene. The black fetish object provides Bone with the impetus to establish active agency in the world—she swings the hook and shatters the institutional glass strictures that had circumscribed her subjectivity and space as abject.

Lesbian Possibility

Bone comes of age after the violent rape by Daddy Glen and is repositioned in an identificatory space with the body of Raylene. Raylene has already aligned Bone's life with her own: " 'I made my life, the same way it looks like you're gonna make yours—out of pride and stubbornness and too much anger' " (263). After the rape, Bone attempts to force her mother to choose between her child and her lover, but the pathos underlying this family melodrama has determined an inversion of traditional roles. Anney chooses Daddy Glen—who occupies the place of whining, crying, pleading child—over Bone—who plays the role of unrequited lover: "Could she love me and still hold him like that?" (291). In this manner, the position of Bone mirrors that of Raylene, inscribed in the text precisely as "the desire to desire."[13] Raylene states: " 'But I was crazy with love, too crazy to judge what I was doing. I did a terrible thing, Bone . . . I made the woman I loved choose. She stayed with her baby and I came back here alone. It just about killed her. It just about killed me' " (300). The rape of Bone inaugurates the onset of a blackness that envelops her: "I heard a roar far off, a wave of night and despair for me, and followed it out into the darkness" (291). Yet the black horizon simultaneously serves as the backdrop against which she recasts a new image and identity. In Aunt Alma's scrapbook, Bone discovers her photographic image from the *Greenville News*: "I was leaning against Raylene's shoulder, my face all pale and long, my chin sticking out too far, my eyes sunk into shadows. I was a freshly gutted fish, my mouth gaping open above my bandaged shoulder and arm, my neck still streaked dark with blood" (292). Transmogrified here as a "freshly gutted fish" with its "mouth gaping open," Bone's body has ingested the hook that had previously allowed her active human agency. What remains is its black dynamism that is projected and displaced outward to inaugurate the sublime and seductive night of a lesbian possibility: "I wrapped my fingers in Raylene's and watched the night fold around us" (309). A blank, white birth certificate provides the tabula rasa for the inscription of a perverse lesbian subjectivity that extends beyond the bounds of institutional strictures.

Bastard Out of Carolina provides us with the possibility of articulating a semiosis of a lesbian desire as formulated during childhood and thereby determining the theoretical liaison between the disavowal of castration and its consequent manifestation in the lesbian fetish. In tracing the transmutation of color codification through the novel, we can bring to light the manner in which social history dynamically interacts with personal history to produce the sexual subjectivity of Bone as the shifting point of their intersection. In the novel, the psychosexual topography of sadomasochistic dreams and fantasies scripted by Bone serves as the language into which the possibility of a perverse lesbian desire is intricately woven. While her fantasies seem to be simply restating the topography of sexual abuse with pornographic precision, they actually are proposing a subversive language of lesbian desire. It is through the musicality of Raylene's voice on the river, functioning in the text as the acoustic mirror, that the subject Bone gains access to both her own vision and voice. The bewitching language of the lesbian fetish that is formulated through the dynamic interrelation between voice and vision in the novel might be envisaged as the scripting of a feminine poetics, which Eve Sedgwick has characterized as "always (though always differently) to be looked for *in* the tortuousness, in the strangeness of the figure made between the flatly gendered definition from an outside view and the always more or less crooked stiles to be surveyed from an inner."[14] In *Bastard Out of Carolina*, perverse lesbian sexuality and textuality are interlocked through sign systems produced through the pornographic language of sexual abuse that points beyond itself (Schwichtenberg, "Erotica" 28). As both sadistic voyeurs (searching for titillation in the sexual fantasies of Bone) and as masturbators engaged in our own lack (the sexual topography of abuse permits our indulgence in a fantasized mastery), we become quietly complicit with Bone in the construction of a semiotics of perverse lesbian desire.

Notes

1. Roland Barthes, *The Pleasure of the Text* (New York: Noonday Press, 1989), 27. Subsequent references to this work will be included parenthetically in the text.

2. Dorothy Allison, *Bastard Out of Carolina* (New York: Plume, 1993), 1. Subsequent references to this work will be included parenthetically in the text.

3. Julia Kristeva, *Powers of Horror: An Essay on Abjection*, trans. Leon S. Roudiez (New York: Columbia University Press, 1980), 4. Subsequent references to this work will be included parenthetically in the text.

4. Teresa de Lauretis, *The Practice of Love: Lesbian Sexuality and Perverse Desire* (Bloomington: Indiana University Press, 1994), 200. Subsequent references to this work will be included parenthetically in the text.

5. Kaja Silverman, *The Acoustic Mirror: The Female Voice in Psychoanalysis and Cinema* (Bloomington: Indiana University Press, 1988), 74. Subsequent references to this work will be included parenthetically in the text.

6. See Sigmund Freud, " 'A Child Is Being Beaten': A Contribution to the Study of the Origin of Sexual Perversions," in *The Standard Edition of the Complete Psychological Works*, ed. James Strachey. Vol. 17 (London: Hogarth Press, 1955), 179–204. See also David N. Rodowick, *The Difficulty of Difference* (New York: Routledge, 1991).

7. Christian Metz, *The Imaginary Signifier: Psychoanalysis and the Cinema*, trans. Celia Britton, Annwyl Williams, Ben Brewster, and Alfred Buzzetti (Bloomington: Indiana University Press, 1982), 60.

8. Cathy Schwichtenberg, "Erotica: The Semey Side of Semiotics," *SubStance* 32 (1981): 27. Subsequent references to this work will be included parenthetically in the text.

9. Sigmund Freud, "Fetishism," in *The Standard Edition of the Complete Psychological Works*, ed. James Strachey. Vol. 21 (London: Hogarth Press, 1961), 152. Subsequent references to this work will be included parenthetically in the text.

10. Jane Gallop, *Reading Lacan* (Ithaca, N.Y.: Cornell University Press, 1985), 79.

11. Stephen Heath, "Lessons from Brecht," *Screen* 15:2 (1974): 107. Subsequent references to this work will be included parenthetically in the text.

12. Michel Foucault, *The History of Sexuality*, vol. 1: *An Introduction*, trans. Robert Hurley (New York: Random House), 101.

13. Mary Ann Doane, *The Desire to Desire: The Woman's Film of the 1940s* (Bloomington: Indiana University Press, 1987), 1.

13. Eve Kosofsky Sedgwick, "A Poem Is Being Written," *Tendencies* (Durham, N.C.: Duke University Press, 1993), 209.

Part 3 "Culture"

"Not That There's Anything Wrong with That": Reading the Queer in *Seinfeld*

Katherine Gantz

The world of mass culture, especially that which includes American television, remains overwhelmingly homophobic. Queer theory offers a useful perspective from which to examine the heterosexism at the core of contemporary television and also provides a powerful tool of subversion. The aim of this article is twofold: first, it will outline and explain the notion of a queer reading; second, it will apply a queer reading to the narrative texts that comprise the situation comedy *Seinfeld*. The concept of the queer reading, currently en vogue in literary analysis, has evolved from a handful of distinct but connected sources, beginning with the popularization of the term "queer." In 1989, the AIDS activist group ACT UP created Queer Nation, an offshoot organization comprised of lesbians and gays dedicated to the political reclaiming of gay identity under the positively recoded term "queer."[1] The group was initially formed as a New York City street patrol organized to help counteract escalating hate crimes against gays. As Queer Nation gained visibility in the public eye, the use of "queer," historically a derogatory slur for homosexuals, entered into standard parlance in the gay and lesbian press.[2] Eve Kosofsky Sedgwick's *Epistemology of the Closet*[3] appropriated the term with a broadened interpretation of "queer," suggesting not that literature be read with the author's possible homosexuality in mind but instead with an openness to the queer (homoerotic and/or homosexual) contexts, nuances, connections, and potential already available within the text. The concept of "queerness" was elaborated once more in 1991, with the publication of *Inside/Out: Lesbian Theories, Gay Theories;*[4] within this assemblage of political, pedagogical, and literary essays, the term was collectively applied to a larger category of sexual non-straightness, as will be further explained.

As the political construction of "queer" became increasingly disciplin-ized in academia, the emerging body of "queer theory" lost its specifically homosexual connotation and was replaced by a diffuse set of diverse sexual identities. Like the path of feminism, the concept of queerness had been largely stripped of its political roots and transformed into a methodologi-cal approach accessible to manipulation by the world of predominantly heterosexual, white, middle-class intellectuals. It is with this problematic universalization of queer theory in mind that I undertake an application of queer reading.

In what could be deemed a reinsertion of the subversive into a "straight-ened" discipline, Alexander Doty's book *Making Things Perfectly Queer: Reading Mass Culture*[5] has taken the queer reading out of the realm of the purely literary and applied it to analyses of film and television texts. From this ever-transforming history of the queer reading, the popular situation comedy *Seinfeld* lends itself well to a contemporary application.

In the summer of 1989, NBC debuted a tepidly received pilot entitled *The Seinfeld Chronicles,* a situation comedy revolving around the mundane, ur-bane Manhattan existence of stand-up comic Jerry Seinfeld. Despite its ini-tially unimpressive ratings, the show evolved into the five-episode series *Seinfeld* and established its regular cast of Jerry's three fictional friends: George Costanza (Jason Alexander), ex-girlfriend Elaine Benes (Julia Louis-Dreyfus), and the enigmatic neighbor Kramer (Michael Richards). By its return in January 1991, *Seinfeld* had established a following among Wednesday-night television viewers; over the next two years, the show became a cultural phenomenon, claiming both a faithful viewership and a confident position in the Nielsen ratings' top ten. The premise was to write a show about the details, minor disturbances, and nonevents of Jerry's life as they occurred before becoming fodder for the stand-up monologues that bookend each episode. From the start, *Seinfeld*'s audience has been comprised of a devoted group of "TV-literate, demographically desirable urbanites, for the most part—who look forward to each weekly episode in the Life of Jerry with a baby-boomer generation's self-involved eagerness," notes Bruce Fretts, author of *The "Entertainment Weekly" "Seinfeld" Com-*

panion.[6] Such obsessive identification and self-reflexive fascination seems to be thematic in both the inter- and extradiegetic worlds of *Seinfeld*. The show's characters are modeled on real-life acquaintances: George is based on Seinfeld's best friend (and series cocreator) Larry David; Elaine is an exaggeration of Seinfeld's ex-girlfriend, writer Carol Leifer; Kramer's prototype lived across the hall from one of David's first Manhattan apartments.[7] To further complicate this narcissistic mirroring, in the 1993 season premiere entitled "The Pilot" (see videography for episodic citations), Jerry and George finally launch their new NBC sitcom *Jerry* by casting four actors to portray themselves, Kramer, and Elaine. This multilayered Möbius strip of person/actor/character relationships seems to be part of the show's complex appeal. Whereas situation comedies often dilute their cast, adding and removing characters in search of new plot possibilities, *Seinfeld* instead interiorizes; the narrative creates new configurations of the same limited cast to keep the viewer and the characters intimately linked. In fact, it is precisely this concentration on the nuclear set of four personalities that creates the *Seinfeld* community.

If it seems hyperbolic to suggest that the participants in the *Seinfeld* phenomenon (both spectators and characters included) have entered into a certain delineated "lifestyle," consider the significant lexicon of Seinfeldian code words and recurring phrases that go unnoticed and unappreciated by the infrequent or "unknowing" viewer. Catch phrases such as Snapple, the Bubble Boy, Cuban cigars, Master of My Domain, Junior Mints, Mulva, Crazy Joe Davola, Pez, and Vandelay Industries all serve as parts of the group-specific language that a family shares; these are the kinds of self-referential in-jokes that help one *Seinfeld* watcher identify another.[8] This sort of tightly conscribed universe of meaning is reflected not only by the decidedly small cast but also by the narrative's consistent efforts to maintain its intimacy. As this article will discuss, much of *Seinfeld*'s plot and humor (and, consequently, the viewer's pleasure) hinge on outside personalities threatening—and ultimately failing—to invade the foursome. Especially where Jerry and George are concerned, episodes are mostly resolved by expelling the intruder and restoring the exclusive nature of their relationship. The show's camera work, which at times takes awkward measures to ensure that Jerry and George remain grouped together within a scene, reinforces the privileged dynamic of their relationship within the narrative.

Superficially speaking, *Seinfeld* appears to be a testament to heterosexuality: in its nine-year run, Jerry sported a new girlfriend in almost every episode; his friendship with Elaine is predicated on their previous sexual relationship; and all four characters share in the discussion and navigation of the (straight) dating scene. However, with a viewership united by a common coded discourse and an interest in the cohesive (and indeed almost claustrophobic) exclusivity of its predominantly male cast, clearly *Seinfeld* is rife with possibilities for homoerotic interpretation. As will be demonstrated, the construction, the coding, and the framing of the show readily conform to a queer reading of the *Seinfeld* text.

Here I wish to develop and define my meanings of the word "queer" as a set of signifying practices and a category distinct from that of gay literature. Inspired by Doty's work, I will use "queer"—as its current literary usages suggest—as relating to a wide-ranging spectrum of "nonnormative" sexual notions, including not only constructions of gayness and lesbianism but also of transsexualism, transvestism, same-sex affinity, and other ambisexual behaviors and sensibilities. Queerness at times may act merely as a space in which heterosexual personalities interact, in the same ways that a queer personality may operate within an otherwise heterosexual sphere. In this system, "queer" does not stand in opposition to "heterosexual" but instead to "straight," a term that by contrast, suggests all that is restrictive about "normative" sexuality, a category that excludes what is deemed undesirable, deviant, dangerous, unnatural, unproductive. "Queer," then, should be understood not so much as an intrinsic property but more as the outcome of both productive and receptive behaviors—a pluralized, inclusive term that may be employed by and applied to both gay and nongay characters and spectators.[9]

The second point I wish to clarify about the use of the term "queer" as it relates to my own textual analysis of a mass culture text is the indirect, nonexplicit nature of the queer relationships represented in *Seinfeld*. Explicit references to homosexuality subvert the possibility of a queer reading; by identifying a character as "gay," such overt difference serves to mark the other characters as "not gay." Sexual perimeters become limited, fixed, rooted in traditional definitions and connotations that work contrary to the fluidity and subtle ambiguity of a queer interpretation. It is precisely the unspokenness ("the love that dare not speak its name") of homoeroticism between seemingly straight men that allows the insinuation of a queer reading. As Doty rightly notes, queer positionings are generated more often through the same-sex tensions evident in "straight films" than in gay ones:

traditional narrative films [such as *Gentlemen Prefer Blondes* and *Thelma and Louise*], which are ostensibly addressed to straight audiences, often have greater potential for encouraging a wider range of queer responses than [such] clearly lesbian- and gay-addressed films [as *Women I Love* and *Scorpio Rising*]. The intense tensions and pleasures generated by the woman-woman and man-man aspects within the narratives of the former group of films create a space of sexual instability that already queerly positioned viewers can connect in various ways, and within which straights might be likely to recognize and express their queer impulses. (8)

Of course, there is a multitude of possibilities for the perception and reception of queer pleasures, but, to generalize from Doty's argument, the implications in the case of the *Seinfeld* phenomenon suggest that while queer-identified viewers may recognize the domesticity between Jerry and George as that of a gay couple, straight viewers may simply take pleasure in the characters' intimate bond left unbroken by outside (heterosexual) romantic interruptions.

This is not to say that *Seinfeld* ignores the explicit category of homosexuality; on the contrary, the show is laden with references and plot twists involving gay characters and themes. In separate episodes, Elaine is selected as the "best man" in a lesbian wedding ("The Subway"); George accidentally causes the exposure of his girlfriend Susan's father's affair with novelist John Cheever ("The Cheever Letters"); and, after their breakup, George runs into Susan with her new lesbian lover ("The Smelly Car"). At its most playful, *Seinfeld* smugly calls attention to its own homosexual undercurrents in an episode in which Jerry and George are falsely identified as a gay couple by a female journalist ("The Outing").[10] Due to the direct nature of such references to homosexuality, these are episodes that slyly deflect queer reading, serving as a sort of lightning rod by displacing homoerotic undercurrents onto a more obvious target.

Such smoke-screen tactics seem to be in conflict with the multitude of queer-identified semiotics and gay icons and symbols at play within the *Seinfeld* text. Most notably, no "queer-receptive" viewer can look at the *Seinfeld* graphic logo (at the episode's beginning and before commercials) without noticing the inverted triangle—hot pink during the earliest seasons—dotting the "i" in "Seinfeld".[11] Although the symbol dates back to the Holocaust (used to mark homosexuals for persecution), the pink triangle has recently been recuperated by gay activists during ACT UP's widely publicized AIDS education campaign, "Silence Equals Death," and has consequently become a broadly recognized symbol of gayness.

Even if the pink triangle's proactive gay recoding remains obscure to the "unknowing" viewership (i.e., unfamiliar with or resistant to queerness), *Seinfeld* also offers a multitude of discursive referents chosen from a popular lexicon of more common gay signifiers that are often slurs in use by a homophobic public. In an episode revolving around Jerry and Kramer's discussion of where to find *fruit*—longstanding slang for a gay men—Jerry makes a very rare break from his standard wardrobe of well-ironed button-up oxfords, instead sporting a T-shirt with the word "QUEENS" across it. Although outwardly in reference to Queens College, the word's semiotic juxtaposition with the theme of fruit evokes its slang connotation for effeminate gay men.

Narrative space is also queerly coded. Positioned as Jerry and George's "place" (or "male space"), the restaurant where they most often meet is "Monk's," a name that conjures up images of an exclusively male religious society, a "brotherhood" predicated on the maintenance of masculine presence/feminine absence, in both spiritual and physical terms.

Recurring plot twists also reveal a persistent interest in the theme of hidden or falsified identities. As early as *Seinfeld*'s second episode ("The Stakeout"), George insists on creating an imaginary biography for himself as a successful architect before meeting Jerry's new girlfriend. Throughout the *Seinfeld* texts, the foursome adopts a number of different names and careers in hopes of persuading outsiders (most often potential romantic interests) that they lead a more interesting, more superficially acceptable, or more immediately favorable existence than what their real lives have to offer: George has assumed the identity of neo-Nazi organizer Colin O'Brian ("The Limo"); Elaine has recruited both Jerry and Kramer as substitute boyfriends to dissuade unwanted suitors ("The Junior Mint" and "The Watch"); Kramer has posed as a policeman ("The Statue") and has even auditioned under a pseudonym to play himself in the pilot of *Jerry* ("The Pilot"). Pretense and fabrication often occur among the foursome as well. In "The Apartment," Jerry is troubled by Elaine's imminent move into the apartment above him. Worried that her presence will "cramp his style," he schemes to convince her that she will be financially unable to take the apartment. In private, Jerry warns George that he will be witness to some "heavy acting" to persuade Elaine that he is genuinely sympathetic. Unshaken, George answers: "Are you kidding? I lie every second of the day; my whole life is a sham." This deliberate "closeting" of one's lifestyle has obvious connections to the gay theme of "passing,"[12] the po-

litically discouraged practice of hiding one's homosexuality behind a fa-
çade of straight respectability. One might argue that *Seinfeld* is simply a
text about passing—socially as well as sexually—in a repressive and judg-
mental society. It must be noted, however, that George and Jerry are the
only two characters who do not lie to each other; they are in fact engaged
in maintaining each other's secrets and duplicities by "covering" for one
another, thus distancing themselves somewhat from Kramer and Elaine
from within an even more exclusive rapport.[13]

Another thematic site of queerness is the mystification of and resulting
detachment from female culture and discourse. While Jerry glorifies such
male-identified personalities as Superman, the Three Stooges, and Mickey
Mantle, he prides himself in never having seen a single episode of *I Love
Lucy* ("The Phone Message"). Even Elaine is often presented as incom-
prehensible to her familiar male counterparts. In "The Shoes," Jerry and
George have no problem creating a story line for their situation comedy,
Jerry, around male characters; however, when they try to "write in" Elaine's
character, they find themselves stumped:

> Jerry: [In the process of writing the script.] "Elaine enters." . . . What does she
> say . . . ?
> George: [Pause.] What *do* they [women] say?
> Jerry: [Mystified.] I *don't know.*

After a brief deliberation, they opt to omit the female character completely.
As Jerry explains with a queerly loaded rationale: "You, me, Kramer, the
butler. . . . Elaine is too much." Later, at Monk's, Elaine complains about
her exclusion from the pilot. Jerry confesses: "We couldn't write for a woman." "You have *no idea?*" asks Elaine, disgusted. Jerry looks at George for
substantiation and replies: "None." Clearly, the privileged bond between
men excludes room for an understanding of and an interest in women; like
Elaine in the pilot, the feminine presence is often simply deleted for the
sake of maintaining a stronger, more coherent male narrative.

Jerry seems especially ill at ease with notions of female sexuality, perhaps
suggesting that they impinge on his own. In "The Red Dot," Jerry con-
vinces the resistant George that he should buy Elaine a thank-you gift after
she procures him a job at her office. Despite George's tightfisted unwillingness to invest money in such social graces as gift giving, he acquiesces. The
duo go to a department store in search of an appropriate gift for Elaine.
Jerry confesses: "I never feel comfortable in the women's department; I feel

like I'm just a *little* too close to trying on a dress." While browsing through the women's clothing, George describes his erotic attraction to the cleaning woman in his new office:

> George: . . . she was swaying back and forth, back and forth, her hips swiveling and her breasts—uh . . .
> Jerry: . . . convulsing?

George reacts with disdain at the odd word choice, recognizing that Jerry's depiction of female physicality and eroticism is both inappropriate and unappealing. (It should be noted that the ensuing sexual encounter between George and the cleaning woman ultimately results in the loss of both their jobs; true to the pattern, George's foray into heterosex creates chaos.)

Although sites of queerness occur extensively throughout the *Seinfeld* oeuvre, the most useful elucidation of its queer potential comes from a closer, more methodical textual analysis. To provide a contextualized view of the many overlapping sites of queerness—symbolic, discursive, thematic, and visual—the following is a critique of three episodes especially conducive to a queer reading of *Seinfeld*'s male homoerotic relationships.

"The Boyfriend" explores the ambiguous valences of male friendships. Celebrated baseball player Keith Hernandez stars as himself (as does Jerry Seinfeld among the cast of otherwise fictional characters), becoming the focal point of both Jerry's and, later, Elaine's attentions. Despite Elaine's brief romantic involvement with Keith, the central narrative concerns Jerry's interactions with the baseball player. Although never explicitly discussed, Jerry's attachment to Keith is represented as romantic in nature.

The episode begins in a men's locker room, prefiguring the homoerotic overtones of the coming plot. The locker room is clearly delineated as "male space"; its connection to the athletic field posits it as a locale of physicality, where men gather to prepare for or to disengage from the privileged (and predominantly homophobic) world of male sports. The locker room, as a site of potential heterosexual vulnerability as men expose their bodies to other men, is socially safe only when established as sexually neutral—or, better still, heterosexually charged with the machismo of athleticism. This "safe" coding occurs almost immediately in this setting, accomplished through a postgame comparison of Jerry's, George's, and Kramer's basketball prowess. As they finish dressing together after their game, it is the voracious, ambisexual Kramer who immediately upsets the precarious sexual neutrality, violating the unspoken code of locker-room decorum:

Kramer: Hey, you know this is the first time we've ever seen each other naked?

Jerry: Believe me, *I* didn't see anything.

Kramer: [With disbelief.] Oh, you didn't sneak a peek?

Jerry: No—did you?

Kramer: Yeah, I snuck a peek.

Jerry: Why?

Kramer: Why not? What about you, George?

George: [Hesitating] Yeah, I—snuck a peek. But it was so fast that I didn't see anything; it was just a blur.

Jerry: I made a conscious effort *not* to look; there's certain information I just don't want to have.

Jerry displays his usual disdain for all things corporeal or carnal. Such unwillingness to participate in Kramer's curiosity about men's bodies also secures Jerry firmly on heterosexual ground, a necessary pretext to make his intense feelings for Keith "safe." The humor of these building circumstances depends on the assumption that Jerry is straight; although this episode showcases *Seinfeld's* characteristic playfulness with queer subject matter, great pains are taken to prevent the viewer from ever believing (or realizing) that Jerry is gay.

After Kramer leaves, Jerry and George spot Hernandez stretching out in the locker room. With Kramer no longer threatening to introduce direct discussion of overtly homoerotic matters, the queer is permitted to enter into the narrative space between Jerry and George. Both baseball aficionados, they are bordering on giddy, immediately starstruck by Hernandez. Possessing prior knowledge of Keith's personal life, Jerry remarks that Hernandez is not only a talented athlete but intelligent as well, being an American Civil War buff. "I wish *I* were a Civil War buff," George replies longingly. Chronically socially inept, George is left to appropriate the interests of a man he admires without being able to relate to him more directly.[14]

Keith introduces himself to Jerry as a big fan of his comedy; Jerry is instantly flattered and returns the compliment. As the jealous and excluded George looks on (one of the rare times that Jerry and George break rank and appear distinctly physically separated within a scene), Keith and Jerry exchange phone numbers and plan to meet for coffee in the future. Thus, in the strictly homosocial, theoretically nonromantic masculine world of the locker room, two men have initiated an interaction that becomes transformed into a relationship, consistently mirroring traditional television representations of heterosexual dating rituals. The homoerotic stage is set.

Later, at Monk's, Jerry complains to Elaine that three days have passed without a call from Keith. When Elaine asks why Jerry doesn't initiate the first call, he responds that he doesn't want to seem overanxious: "If he wants to see me, he has my number; he should call. I can't stand these guys—you give your number to them, and then they don't call."

Here, in his attempts not to seem overly aggressive, Jerry identifies with the traditionally receptive and passive role posited as appropriate female behavior. By employing such categorization as "these guys," Jerry brackets himself off from the rest of the heterosexual, male dating population, re-inforcing his identification with Elaine not as Same (i.e., straight male) but as Other (Elaine as Not Male, Jerry as Not Straight). Elaine responds sympathetically:

Elaine: I'm sorry, honey.
Jerry: I mean, I thought he liked me, I really thought he liked me—we were get-
    ting along. He came over to *me*, I didn't go over to *him*.
Elaine: [Commiserating.] I know.
Jerry: Here I meet this guy, this *great* guy, ballplayer, best guy I ever met in my
    life . . . well, that's it. I'm *never* giving my number out to another guy again.

Jerry is clearly expressing romantic disillusionment in reaction to Keith's withdrawal from their social economy. Elaine further links her identity—as sexually experienced with men—to Jerry's own situation:

Elaine: Sometimes I give my number out to a guy, and it takes him a *month* to
    call me.
Jerry: [Outraged.] A *month*? Ha! Have him call *me* after a month—let's see if *he*
    has a prayer!

Thus, Jerry's construction of his relationship with Keith is one bound by the rules of heterosexual dating protocol and appropriate exchange; the intensity of his feelings and expectations for his relationship with Keith have long surpassed normative (that is, conventional, expected, toler-able), straight male friendship. By stating that Keith's violation of protocol will result in Jerry's withdrawal, it is clear that Jerry is only willing to con-sider any interactions with Keith in terms of a romantic model—one that, as suggested by Keith's relative indifference, is based in fantasy.

Elaine suggests that he simply put an end to the waiting and call Keith to arrange an evening out. Jerry ponders the possibility of dinner but then has doubts:

Jerry: But don't you think that dinner might be coming on too strong? Kind of a turnoff?

Elaine: [Incredulous.] Jerry, it's a *guy*.

Jerry: [Covering his eyes.] It's all very confusing.

Throughout the episode, Jerry is content to succumb to the excitement of his newfound relationship, until the moment when someone inevitably refers to its homoerotic nature (terms such as "gay" and "homosexual" are certainly implied but never explicitly invoked). Elaine's reminder that Jerry's fears about a "turnoff" are addressed to a man quickly ends his swooning; he covers his eyes as if to suggest a groggy return from a dream-like state.

To interrupt and divert the narrative attention away from Jerry's increasingly queer leanings, the scene abruptly changes to George at the unemployment office, where he is hoping to maneuver a thirteen-week extension on his unemployment benefits.[15] There, George evades the questions of his no-nonsense interviewer Mrs. Sokol until she forces him to provide one name of a company with which he had recently sought employment. Having in truth interviewed nowhere, he quickly concocts "Vandelay Industries," a company, he assures her, he had thoroughly pursued to no avail. Further pressed, he tells Mrs. Sokol that they are "makers of latex products." His blurting-out of the word "latex" must not be overlooked here as a queer signifier directly associated with the gay safe-sex campaigns throughout the last decade. Whereas "condoms" as a signifier would have perhaps been a more mainstream (straight) sexual symbol, latex evokes a larger category of products—condoms, gloves, dental dams—linked closely with the eroticization of gay safe-sex practices. When Mrs. Sokol insists on information to verify his claim, it is telling that George provides Jerry's address and phone number as the home of Vandelay latex. George's lie necessitates a race back to Jerry's to warn him of the impending phone call; once again, he will depend on Jerry's willingness to maintain a duplicity and to adopt a false identity as the head of Vandelay Industries.

As if to await the panicked arrival of George, the scene changes to Jerry's apartment, where he is himself anxiety ridden over his impending night out with Keith. In a noticeable departure from his usual range of conservative color and style, he steps out of his bedroom, modeling a bright orange and red shirt, colors so shocking that they might best be described as "flaming." Pivoting slightly with arms outstretched in a style suggesting a fashion model, he asks Elaine's opinion. Again, she reminds him: "Jerry, he's a guy." Agitated (but never denying her implication of homoerotic attraction), he drops his arms, attempting to hide his nervous discomfort.

Jerry's actual evening out with Keith remains unseen (closeted) until the end of the "date"; the men sit alone in the front seat of Keith's car outside of Jerry's apartment. In the setup that prefigures the close of Elaine's date with Keith later in the episode, Jerry sits in the passenger seat next to him; a familiar heterosexual power dynamic is at play. Keith, as both the car owner and driver, acts and reacts in his appropriate masculine role. Jerry, within the increasingly queer context of an intimate social interaction with another man, is left to identify with what we recognize as the woman's position in the car. As the passenger and not the driver, he has relinquished both the mechanical and social control that defines the dominance of the male role. In a symbolic interpretation of power relations, Jerry's jump into the feminized gender role is characterized by the absence of the steering wheel:

> Jerry: [Aloud to Keith.] Well, thanks a lot, that was really fun. [Thinking to himself.] Should I shake his hand?

This anxiety and expectation over appropriate and mutually appealing physical contact expresses the same kind of desire—that is, sexual—that Keith will express with Elaine later on; whereas Keith will long for a kiss, Jerry's desires have been translated into a more acceptable form of physical contact between men. It would seem that part of Jerry's frustration in this situation comes from the multiplicity of gender roles that he plays. Whereas in his interactions with George, Jerry occupies the dominant role (controlling the discourse and the action), he is suddenly relegated to a more passive (feminine) position in his relationship with the hypermasculine Keith Hernandez. Part of the tension that comprises the handshake scene stems not only from Jerry's desire to interact physically *and* appropriately but also from wanting to initiate such an action from the disadvantaged, less powerful position of the (feminine) passenger's seat. I would suggest that the confusion arising out of his relationship with Keith is not strictly due to its potentially homosexual valences but is also the result of the unclear position (passive/dominant, feminine/masculine, nelly/butch) that Jerry holds within the homoerotic/homosexual coupling.

Once again, the humor of this scene is based on the presupposition that Jerry is straight and that this very familiar scene is not a homosexual recreation of heterosexual dating etiquette but simply a parody of it. Nonetheless, Jerry's discomfort over initiating a handshake betrays the nature of his desire for Keith. From behind the steering wheel (the seat of masculine power), Keith invites Jerry to a movie over the coming weekend. Jerry is elated, and they shake hands: a consummation of their successful social interaction. However, Keith follows up by telling Jerry that he would like to call Elaine for a date; the spell broken, Jerry responds with reluctance and thinly veiled disappointment.

Back in Jerry's apartment, George jealously asks for a recounting of Jerry's evening with Keith. Again, the handshake is reinforced as the symbol of a successful male-to-male social encounter:

George: Did you shake his hand?
Jerry: Yeah.
George: What kind of a handshake does he have?
Jerry: Good shake, perfect shake. Single pump, not too hard. He didn't have to prove anything, but firm enough to know he's there.

George and Jerry share a discourse, laden with masturbatory overtones, in which quantifying and qualifying the description of a handshake expresses information about the nature of men's relationships. This implicit connection between male intimacy and the presence and quality of physical contact clearly transcends the interpretation of the handshake in a heterosexual context. Upon hearing that Jerry had in fact shaken hands with Keith, George follows with the highly charged question: "You gonna see him again?" Here, the use of the verb "to see," implying organized social interaction between two people, is typically in reference to romantic situations; George has thus come to accept Jerry in a dating relationship with Keith.

Elaine enters and immediately teases Jerry: "So, how was your date?" Not only has she invaded Jerry and George's male habitat, but she has once again made explicit the romantic nature of Jerry's connection to Keith that he can only enjoy when unspoken. Jerry is forced to respond (with obvious agitation): "He's a guy." Elaine quickly reveals that she and Keith have made a date for the coming Friday, perhaps expressing an implicit understanding of a rivalry with Jerry. Realizing that such plans will interfere with his own "date" with Keith, Jerry protests with disappointment and resentment. Elaine mistakes his anger as being in response to some lingering romantic attachment to her:

Elaine: I've never seen you jealous.
Jerry: You weren't even *at* Game Six—you're not even a fan!
Elaine: Wait a second . . . are you jealous of *him* or are you jealous of *me*?

Flustered and confused, Jerry walks away without responding, allowing the insinuation of a queer interpretation to be implied by his silence.

Jerry steps outside of the apartment just as Kramer enters; he sits alone with Elaine as George disappears into the bathroom. Predictably, it is just as Kramer finds himself next to the phone that the call from the unemployment bureau arrives; Kramer, the only one uninformed about George's scheme, answers the phone and responds with confusion, assuring the caller that she has reached a residential number, not Vandelay Industries. Having overheard, George bursts from the bathroom in a panic, his pants around his ankles. Despite his frantic pleading with Kramer to pass him the phone, Kramer is already hanging up; the defeated George collapses on the floor. Precisely at this moment, Jerry reenters the apartment. In a highly unusual aerial shot, the camera shows us Jerry's perspective of George, face down, boxer shorts exposed, and prone, lying before him on the floor in an obvious position of sexual receptivity. Jerry quips: "And you want to be my latex salesman." Once again, Jerry's reinvocation of latex has powerful queer connotations in response to seeing George seminude before him.

The next scenes juxtapose Elaine and Keith's date with Jerry's alternate Friday night activity, a visit to see his friends' new baby. Elaine, the focal point of a crowded sports bar discussing Game Six of the World Series with Keith, has occupied the very place (physically and romantically) that Jerry had longed for. In the accompanying parallel scene of Jerry, he seems both out of place and uncomfortable amid the domestic and overwhelmingly heterosexual atmosphere of the baby's nursery. The misery over losing his night on the town to Elaine is amplified by his obvious distaste for the nuclear family, the ultimate signifier of "straightness."

The scene again changes to Keith and Elaine alone in his car, this time with Elaine in the passenger seat that Jerry had previously occupied. Elaine, comfortable in her familiar and appropriate role as passive/feminine, waits patiently as Keith (in the privileged masculine driver's seat) silently wonders whether or not he should kiss her, mirroring Jerry's earlier internal debate over suitable intimate physical contact. Although they kiss, Elaine is unimpressed. Later, just as George had done, Jerry pumps Elaine for information about her date. When Elaine admits that she and Keith had kissed, Jerry pushes further: "What *kind* of kiss was it?" Incredulous at Jerry's tactlessness, Elaine does not respond. Jerry at last answers her standing question: "I'm jealous of everybody."

Keith calls, interrupting one of the few moments in the episode when Jerry and George share the scene alone. After hanging up, he explains with discomfort that he has agreed to help Keith in his move to a new apartment. George seems to recognize and identify with Jerry's apprehension over this sudden escalation in their rapport. "This is a big step in the male relationship," Jerry observes, "the biggest. That's like going all the way." Never has Jerry made such a direct reference to the potential for sexual contact with Keith. Of course, Keith has by no means propositioned Jerry, which makes the queer desire on Jerry's part all the more obvious in contrast with the seemingly asexual nature of Keith's request. However, Jerry has made clear his own willingness to homoeroticize his friendship with another man. By likening "going all the way" to moving furniture, Jerry is able to fantasize that Keith shares Jerry's homosexual desire. Ingeniously, he has crafted an imaginary set of circumstances that allow him to ignore Keith's preference for Elaine as a sexual object while tidily completing his fantasy: Keith has expressed desire for Jerry, but now Jerry has the luxury of refusing his advance on the moral ground that he will not rush sexual intimacy. Once Keith arrives, Jerry tells him that he cannot help him move, explaining that it is still too soon in their relationship. Again, by positing Keith in the masculine role of sexual aggressor, Jerry in turn occupies the stereotypically feminine role of sexual regulator/withholder.

Kramer and Newman arrive just as Jerry declines Keith's request; not surprisingly, Kramer jumps at the opportunity to take Jerry's place. As he and Newman disappear out the door to help Keith move his furniture, Jerry commiserates with Elaine over the phone: "You broke up with him? Me too!" Even as Jerry's homoerotic adventure has drawn to a close, Kramer's last-minute appearance lends an air of sexual unpredictability to end the episode on a resoundingly queer note.

In contrast to "The Boyfriend," in which the queer subtext is exploited as the source of the humor, "The Virgin" and its companion episode "The Contest" present an equally queer narrative expressed in subtler and more indirect ways. Within these interwoven episodes, the "knowing" spectator—one familiar with gay culture and receptive to potentially homoerotic situations—is essentially bombarded by queer catchphrases and code words, gay themes, and gay male behavior, while the "unknowing" spectator would most likely only recognize a traditionally "straight" plot about heterosexual dating frustrations. "The Virgin" drops its first "hairpins" almost immediately;[16] Jerry and George are drinking together in a bar when Jerry spots Marla, a beautiful woman whom he recognizes across the room. "She's in the closet business—reorganizes your closet and shows you how to maximize your closet space. She's looked into my closet." In the same instant that we are introduced to a potential female love object for Jerry, she is immediately identified with the closet, a widely recognized metaphor referring to a gay person's secret sexual identity. Queerly read, Marla could be interpreted as (and will in fact become) a nonthreatening, nonsexual female object. Having "looked into his closet," Marla functions as a woman who is aware of Jerry's homosexuality and will be willing to interact with him in ways that will permit him to pass while still maintaining the homoerotic connections to the men around him. By allowing him this duplicity, she will indeed maximize Jerry's "closet space."

While at the bar, George bemoans the fact that he is miserable in his relationship with television executive Susan, his first girlfriend in some time. He is instead more interested in the new partnership that he has developed with Jerry, writing his new situation comedy pilot for NBC. The ostensibly platonic nature of such privileged male-male relations becomes further queered by Jerry's insistence that George "maintain appearances" with Susan until she has persuaded the network to pick up their pilot. The Seinfeldian recurring theme of hidden identities and guarded appearances puts into place the knowing viewer's suspicions about the homosexual potential between George and Jerry.

In the following scene, the spectator is given a rare view of Jerry's bedroom, made even more rare by the presence of a woman with him. Although the scene employs the standard formula for a possible sexual encounter (a man and woman alone in his bedroom), the couple remains perpetually framed inside Jerry's open closet; Jerry's coded homosexuality, symbolically surrounding the couple as they speak, prevents the sex scene from occurring.

To further complicate Jerry's interaction with Marla, his friends start to invade the apartment, interrupting the potential for intimacy. First, Kramer intrudes, taking over the television in the living room. (He is desperate to see *The Bold and the Beautiful,* a show whose soap opera genre is largely identified with a female viewership.) Jerry kicks Kramer out only to have Elaine buzz over the intercom a moment later. In the few private moments left, Marla confesses that the reason for her breakup with her ex-boyfriend was his impatience with her virginity. Elaine arrives before they can discuss it.

Marla and Elaine, Jerry's current and past romantic interests, stand in stark contrast to one another. The timid, traditional, and virginal Marla is further desexualized in the presence of the heterosexually active Elaine; this contrast is intensified by Elaine's crass description of her embarrassment at a recent party when she accidentally let her diaphragm slip out of her purse. As she laughs knowingly, Jerry winces, sensing Marla's shock at Elaine's casual remark: "You never know when you might need it." This exaggerated reference to female sexuality makes Marla's virginity even more pronounced; she is unable to hide her discomfort any longer and excuses herself in haste. It seems that Jerry, socially and romantically attached to a woman horrified by even the discussion of sex, could himself not be further from heterosexual activity.

Upon hearing that her indiscretion has lost Jerry a potential girlfriend, Elaine chases after Marla in hopes of repairing the damage. Over coffee at Monk's (clearly a female invasion of Jerry and George's male space), Elaine tries to dissuade Marla from her horror of sex with men. However, her lecture quickly dissolves into a listing of male failings: their thoughtlessness, manipulations, and fear of emotional attachment after sex. Despite Elaine's outward intentions to reunite Jerry and Marla, she has instead instilled an intensified mistrust of men. Once again, Jerry's friends have been the cause of his distancing from women; he remains insulated in the homoerotic network of his male friends and is ushered through acceptable straight society by his platonic female friend.

In a strange reversal of roles, George is still engaged in a romantic relationship with a woman (even if he is unwillingly "maintaining appearances" with Susan). At the crucial meeting with the NBC executives, George greets Susan with a kiss, an appropriate and public gesture of straightness. However, by exposing Susan as his girlfriend, George compromises her professional standing with the network. Not only is she fired, but she also breaks off her relationship with George (and consequently later "becomes" a lesbian).[17] Despite George's delight at having inadvertently rid himself of Susan, the overall message is clear: straying out of his queer context sparks destructive results in the straight world.

Juxtaposed with George's ultimately disastrous straight kiss is one of Jerry's own; he and Marla, back in his bedroom, are finally embracing passionately. The (hetero)sexual potential suggested in this scene is diffused, however, by the viewer's instant recognition that the couple is not only framed by Jerry's closet but in fact that they are embracing inside of it. Marla, as a nonsexualized female object with knowledge and access to

Jerry's closet(edness), poses no threat of engaging in "real" sexual intimacy with Jerry. Their embrace is made comically awkward by the clutter of Jerry's hanging clothes around them; the encounter is again cut short as Marla recalls Elaine's unflattering depiction of typical male behavior after sex. Even in absentia, Jerry's friends precipitate the woman's departure and his own separation from the possibility of (hetero)sex.

"The Contest" follows up on this storyline; Jerry is still patiently dating the virginal Marla while, as usual, spending the bulk of his social time with George, Kramer, and Elaine. As George arrives to join them for lunch at Monk's, he announces sheepishly (yet voluntarily) that he had been "caught" by his mother. Although never explicitly mentioned, George is clearly making reference to masturbation. Believing himself to be alone in his mother's house, he was using her copy of *Glamour* magazine[18] as erotic material when his mother entered and discovered him masturbating. In her shock, Mrs. Costanza had fainted, hurt herself in the fall, and ultimately wound up in traction. It is essential to note the homosexual underpinnings of masturbation as a sexual act; the fetishization of one's (and in this case, George's) own genitalia is often closely linked in psychoanalytic theory to the narcissism and reflexive fixation associated with same-sex desire. Mrs. Costanza was not reacting so much to her recognition of her son as sexual but instead to his inappropriate sexual object choice, the (his) penis. George has paid dearly for being exposed to straight eyes while practicing queer pleasure.

Traumatized by his experience, George announces that he is swearing off such activity for good. Jerry and Kramer are skeptical of the claim, and the three men find themselves in a contest—regulated by the "honor system"—to see which of them can abstain the longest from masturbating. The wager is steeped in homoerotic potential; in fact, the three *Seinfeld* men have entered into a kind of sanitized "circle jerk" in which they monitor (and consequently augment) each other's sexual tension, voyeuristically waiting to see who will be the first to "relieve" himself. When Elaine, who has been listening to their conversation from the periphery of their queer circle, wants to enter the contest as well, the men protest that she would have an unfair advantage. As Kramer explains: "It's easier for women—it's part of *our lifestyle*." By creating a stiff binary opposition between women and "our lifestyle," he not only employs a phrase closely associated with the "alternative lifestyle" of homosexuality, but he also demonstrates an obvious ignorance and detachment from female sexuality, perpetuating myths about the limited appetite and imagination of the female sexual drive. Despite her protests, Elaine is forced to stake fifty dollars extra to even the odds before entering into the contest.

In the next scene, the foursome returns to Jerry's apartment, where Kramer immediately spots a naked woman in the window across the street.[19] The sexually ravenous Kramer is unable to control himself; he excuses himself immediately and returns to announce what we had been led to predict: "I'm out." Of the three male characters, Kramer takes on the most ambisexual valence, moving freely from the homoerotic circle shared with Jerry and George to the distinctly heterosexual desire he expressed for the naked woman. While highly sexualized, neither Kramer's intimate and often seductive relationship with Jerry and George nor his frequent erotic encounters with women serve to posit him in clear homo- or heterosexual territory. Functioning as a sort of sexual fulcrum depending on the social context, Kramer may well be acting as *Seinfeld*'s embodiment of queerness.

The three remaining contestants are left to their own frustrations. In her aerobics class, Elaine finds herself positioned behind John F. Kennedy Jr., the popular object of white, privileged heterosexual female desire. George is disturbed and aroused by his discovery that the privacy curtain separating his mother's hospital bed from her beautiful roommate's creates an erotic silhouette of the stranger's nightly sponge bath.[20] Locked in a passionate embrace in the front seat of Jerry's car, Marla pulls back and asks Jerry to "slow down"; he politely acquiesces, assuring Marla that her virginity is not hindering his enjoyment of their relationship.

On the surface, Marla's virginity is posited as an intensifying factor of her attractiveness; the withholding of not only sex but also of her sexuality seems to make the possibility of physical intimacy even more inaccessible— and thus desirable. In fact, Marla's virginity is a crucial element to balance (and perhaps camouflage) the more important discussions and representations of masturbation. Marla's introduction to the periphery of Jerry's bet with Kramer, George, and Elaine serves a twofold purpose. First, her virginity becomes both a presence and an obstacle between Jerry and Marla, impeding any progress toward a heterosexual encounter. Second, without Marla as Jerry's ostensible love object, the "masturbation episode" would take on a glaringly homosexual tone. Marla's presence serves to divert attention away from what is more or less a circle jerk among homosexualized men: a collective and voyeuristic study of each other's (auto)erotic activity, focusing—if we may momentarily exclude Elaine's participation—on the male orgasm brought on reflexively by the male participants. As a virgin,

Marla serves to deflect the queerness of the contest away from Jerry while never threatening the homoerotic trinity of Jerry, George, and Kramer.

Elaine, by comparison, is indeed a heterosexually active female. Why is Elaine allowed to participate in the otherwise queerly coded masturbatory abstinence contest? In effect, she never truly is cast as an equal participant. Throughout the episode, she is consistently figured as the "odd man out"; at the restaurant table where the triangulated male bodies of Jerry, George, and Kramer construct the terms of the bet, Elaine is seated in the corner of the booth. Within the frames, she appears either alone or with her back partially turned to the camera, surrounded by the men who look toward her, clearly separated from the intimate boy talk of the others who share the booth with her. As mentioned before, the men's misconception that women are naturally predisposed to such masturbatory abstinence works to further distance female sexuality—and thus females—from their own collective experience of (same-sex) desire. Perhaps most importantly, Elaine's strongest connection to the trio is through her relationship with Jerry, a friendship that is predicated on their previous failure as (hetero)sexual partners. Her potentially menacing role as Straight Female is mitigated by her position as Not Love Object. Elaine may participate in the contest from the sidelines without truly interrupting its homosexual valence.

Despite the remaining contestants' boasts of being "queen of the castle" and "master of my domain," their sexual frustrations are evident in the four juxtaposed scenes of their private bedrooms: Jerry appears restless in his bed of white linens; George thrashes beneath his sheets printed with cartoon dinosaurs;[21] Elaine is sleepless in her darkened room; Kramer, however, long having satisfied his desire, snores peacefully.

Grumpy from his sleepless night, Jerry tells Kramer that he can no longer tolerate the view of the naked neighbor across the street. As he prepares to go over and ask the woman to draw her shades, the infuriated Kramer tries to stop him, doubting Jerry's sanity for wanting to block their view of a beautiful nude woman. Kramer has called into question Jerry's priorities, which seem to be clear: Jerry privileges his participation in the queerly coded contest over the visual pleasure Kramer experiences from the nude woman.

In the next series of juxtaposed bedroom shots, the viewer discovers from Elaine's restful sleep that she has given in. The next morning, as she sheepishly relinquishes her money, she explains that rumors of JFK Jr.'s interest in her had prompted her moment of weakness. Jerry marvels that "the queen is dead," thereby leaving only himself and George to compete for the pot.

In the following scene, two embracing figures are stretched out on the couch in Jerry's dark apartment. In the close-up shot, we see that Marla is on top of Jerry; not only does this physicality suggest a heightened potential for sexual intimacy between the ordinarily distant couple, but Jerry's positioning on the bottom of the embrace casts him in the stereotypically feminine, passive role of a woman in a straight couple (a role evocative of the one he occupied in his relationship with Keith Hernandez). In keeping with the episode's (and indeed the show's) pattern, such menacing circumstances should surely create chaotic results.

Taking her cue from Jerry's receptive position, the previously hesitant Marla becomes the aggressor, initiating a (masculine) invitation to have sex: "Let's go in the bedroom." From beneath her, Jerry's somewhat timid voice sounds unsure: "*Really?*" Now too close for comfort, Jerry must find a way to disengage from the heterosexual situation in which he is now entangled; Marla's virginity is no longer a sufficient buffer. When Marla asks why he looks so tense, he thoughtlessly (or so it would appear) recounts the details of the contest to explain his (ostensible) relief at the chance to have sex with her. Marla reacts with horror and disgust and quickly exits, leaving Jerry alone.

On the street, Marla bumps into Elaine, who is eagerly awaiting the arrival of JFK Jr. for their first arranged meeting. Marla pulls away from Elaine in revulsion: "I don't want to have anything to do with you or your perverted friends. Get away from me, you're horrible!" Having clearly identified Jerry, George, and Kramer as sexually deviant (i.e., not "straight"), Marla leaves, removing the safe, female heterosexual anchor that her presence provided to the otherwise transparently queer contest.

Believing that JFK Jr. stood her up, Elaine complains to Jerry only to hear from George that Kennedy had just driven away with Marla. As they look out the window, Jerry spots Kramer in the arms of the beautiful woman across the street.

In the final series of four bedroom shots, Jerry and George are at last also enjoying a restful sleep; Kramer snores next to his new lover, and Marla compliments "John" on his sexual prowess. Whereas the two latter scenes depict the postorgasmic satisfaction of the two heterosexual partners that share it, the two former scenes are ambiguous by contrast: no explanation is provided for how or why Jerry and George relieved their pent-up sexual energies at the same time. With no female love object available (no recent viewings of the erotic sponge bath for George, and Jerry's potential lover has left him) to dehomosexualize Jerry and George's two-member circle jerk, the viewer is left with the suggestion that they have satisfied their sexual frustrations together. Intensified by the "success" of the hypervirile JFK Jr. in the face of Jerry's sexual failure with Marla, the narrative closes with individual shots of George and Jerry—alone and yet paired off. Quite apart from the strong homoerotic sensibility of "The Contest'"s construction, the simple and familiar plot resolution—the duo's inability to sustain a romantic relationship with a woman leaves them again alone with each other—marks the episode as incontrovertibly queer.

Seinfeld's narrative design would, at first glance, seem to lack the depth necessary in character and plot to facilitate a discussion of the complexities of homoerotic male relationships. The sort of nonspecific, scattered quality of the *Seinfeld* text, however, makes it well suited to the fluid nature of a queer reading, whose project is more concerned with context than fixity, more with potential than evidence. Nonetheless, *Seinfeld* is full of both context and evidence that lead the text's critics toward a well-developed queer reading. *Seinfeld* enjoys a kind of subculture defined by a discursive code that unites its members in a common lexicon of meaning. The narrative restricts its focus to the foursome, containing and maintaining the intimate bonds between the show's three men and its one woman (the latter being clearly positioned as sexually incompatible and socially separate from the others). Directly related to this intense interconnection, the foursome often causes each member's inability to foster outside heterosexual romantic interests.

Jerry and George share the most intimate relationship of them all; they aid each other in perpetuating duplicities while remaining truthful only with one another. They are the two characters who most frequently share a frame and who create and occupy male-coded narrative spaces, whether in the domestic sphere of Jerry's apartment or in the public sphere at Monk's.

All of these relationships are in motion amid a steady stream of other discursive and iconic gay referents. Their visibility admits the "knowing" viewer into a queerly constructed *Seinfeld* universe while never being so explicit as to cause the "unknowing" viewer to suspect the outwardly "normal" appearance of the show.

Reading the queer in *Seinfeld* sheds a revealing light on the show's "not that there's anything wrong with that" approach to representations of male homoeroticism. While sustaining a steadfast denial of its gay undercurrents, the text playfully takes advantage of provocative semiotic juxta-positions that not only allow but also encourage the "knowing" specta-tor to ignore the show's heterosexual exterior and instead to explore the queerness of *Seinfeld*.

Selected *Seinfeld* Videography

(*Seinfeld*. Created by Jerry Seinfeld and Larry David. NBC-TV, 1989–98.)

"The Apartment." Writ. Peter Mehlman. 4 Apr. 1991.
"The Boyfriend." Writ. Larry David and Larry Levin. 12 Feb. 1992.
"The Café." Writ. Tom Leopold. 6 Nov. 1991.
"The Cheever Letters." Writ. Larry David. 28 Oct. 1992.
"The Contest." Writ. Larry David. 13 Nov. 1992.
"The Dog." Writ. Larry David. 9 Oct. 1991.
"The Junior Mint." Writ. Andy Robin. 18 Mar. 1993.
"The Limo." Writ. Larry Charles. 26 Feb. 1992.
"The Outing." Writ. Larry Charles. 11 Feb. 1993.
"The Phone Message." Writ. Larry David and Jerry Seinfeld. 13 Feb. 1991.
"The Pilot." Writ. Larry David. 20 May 1993.
"The Red Dot." Writ. Larry David. 11 Dec. 1991.
"The Shoes." Writ. Larry David and Jerry Seinfeld. 4 Feb. 1993.
"The Smelly Car." Writ. Larry David and Peter Mehlman. 15 Apr. 1993.
"The Stakeout." Writ. Larry David and Jerry Seinfeld. 31 May 1990.
"The Statue." Writ. Larry Charles. 11 Apr. 1991.
"The Subway." Writ. Larry Charles. 8 Jan. 1992.
"The Virgin." Writ. Larry David. 11 Nov. 1992.
"The Watch." Writ. Larry David. 30 Sept. 1992.

Notes

All dialogue quoted in this essay, unless otherwise indicated, comes from my own transcriptions of the television programs in question.

1. Dave Walter, "Does Civil Disobedience Still Work?" *Advocate*, 20 Nov. 1990, 34–38.
2. For further discussion of the political and semiotic history of the word "queer," see Ernesto Laclau, *New Reflections on the Revolution of Our Time* (London: Verso, 1990); Teresa de Lauretis, "Queer Theory: Lesbian and Gay Sexualities," *differences* 3:2 (1991): iii–xviii; Michelangelo Signorile, "Absolutely Queer: Reading, Writing, and Rioting," *Advocate*, 6 Oct. 1992, 17.
3. Eve Kosofsky Sedgwick, *Epistemology of the Closet* (Berkeley: University of California Press, 1990).

4. Diana Fuss, ed. *Inside/Out: Lesbian Theories, Gay Theories* (New York: Routledge, 1991).

5. Alexander Doty, *Making Things Perfectly Queer: Reading Mass Culture* (Minnesota: University of Minnesota Press, 1993).

6. Bruce Fretts, *The "Entertainment Weekly" "Seinfeld" Companion* (New York: Warner Books, 1993), 12.

7. Bill Zehme, "Jerry and George and Kramer and Elaine: Exposing the Secrets of *Seinfeld*'s Success," *Rolling Stone* 660–61 (6–22 July 1993): 40–45, 130–31.

8. As evidence of this Seinfeldian shared vocabulary, I offer one of my primary resources for this paper, *The "Entertainment Weekly" "Seinfeld" Companion*. Author Bruce Fretts creates a partial glossary of these terms, situating them in their episodic contexts, cross-referencing them with the episodes in which the term recurs, and finally providing a chronological plot synopsis of episodes 1–61, ending with the 1993 season premiere, "The Pilot."

9. Doty outlines the political and semiotic complexities of the term "queer" in his insightful introduction to *Making Things Perfectly Queer.*

10. My essay takes its title from this episode; while combating the rumor of their homosexuality, the phrase "not that there's anything wrong with that" serves as Jerry and George's knee-jerk addendum to their denials. The catchphrase becomes a running joke through the episode, being echoed in turn by Jerry's and George's mothers and, later, by Kramer as well.

11. During the 1994 season, the *Seinfeld* triangle suddenly switched to blue. Might this suggest that the show's creators wished to distance themselves from an overly gay-identified icon, or does a queer interpretation suggest that Jerry is simply attempting to be more butch during that period? The 1995 season was marked with an ambiguous green triangle; the icon continued to change in each following season. One can only speculate that the shift away from the pink triangle is meant to mirror the shift away from the queerness of the early seasons—as evidenced by Susan's abrupt renunciation of lesbianism and subsequent return to George (my thanks to colleagues Melinda Kanner and Steve Bishop for their insightful ideas on this subject).

12. A particularly useful example of this theme occurs in "The Café," in which George, terrified of his girlfriend Monica's request that he take an IQ test, fears that he will not be able to pass. Out of desperation, he arranges for the more intelligent Elaine to take the test for him by passing it out to her through an open window. Jerry too has approved their secret plan to pass George off as an intelligent, appropriate partner for Monica: "Hey, I love a good caper!" Despite their best efforts to dupe Monica by presenting George in a false light, she discovers their duplicity and breaks up with him.

13. When questioned, Jerry makes no secret about the intensity of his "friendship" with George; in "The Dog," he confesses that they talk on the

phone six times a day—coincidentally, the same number of times a day that he gargles.

14. A queer reading of the social differences between Jerry and George reveals a substratum of conflict: within the homoerotic dynamic that groups them together as a couple, George is constantly portrayed as crude, unrefined, and in need of direction. When George is paired with Jerry in the intimate, caretaking relationship they share, their connection suggests a domestic partnership in which Jerry, the more successful and refined of the duo, acts as their public voice, correcting George's social missteps, allowing them to "pass" less noticeably through acceptable, urban, upper-middle-class society.

15. It should be noted that George's presentation as both unemployed and desperate accentuate the clear class differences between him and Jerry, the successful stand-up comic being courted by a celebrity athlete.

16. In *Gay Talk* (New York: Paragon Books, 1972), Bruce Rodgers defines the expression "drop hairpins" (also "drop beads" or "drop pearls") as "to let out broad hints of one's sexuality" (69). Historically rooted in gay male culture, this expression is useful here to express the texts' many links to gay icons and lexicon. It should be noted, however, that the intentionality suggested by the phrase "drop hairpins" is problematic in the context of this paper, as I am not entering into an analysis of whether or not the creators of *Seinfeld* have knowingly or inadvertently produced a heavily queer text.

17. In "The Smelly Car," George runs into Susan for the first time since their breakup and is shocked to see her with Mona, her new lover. Although Susan alludes to her longstanding attraction to women, George makes multiple references to how he "drove her" to lesbianism. After Mona is inexplicably seduced by Kramer's mystique, Susan makes a new romantic contact in Allison, another of George's ex-girlfriends. The implication is not only that George is a failure as a heterosexual but also that, even in his attempts to connect romantically with women, he is attracted to inappropriate (or equally conflicted) female object choices.

18. George's use of *Glamour,* a women's fashion magazine, is a notably odd choice for visual sexual stimulation. In contrast to such heterosexual pornography as *Playboy,* in which nude women are presented in ways to elicit sexual responses from men, George has instead found sexual pleasure from a magazine whose focus is women's beauty culture—fashion, health, cosmetics—and not women themselves. It is essential to recognize that George's masturbatory activity was not in response to heterosexual desire for women's bodies but instead connected to something only indirectly related to their appearances.

19. In contrast to George's interest in *Glamour,* Kramer provides us with a more familiar example of an "appropriate" erotic stimulus for the heterosexual male; the sight of a nude woman directly and immediately enacts Kramer's sexual response.

20. This visual joke is revived in "The Outing": having been falsely identified in the newspaper as Jerry's lover, George attempts to set his shocked and still-hospitalized mother "straight." However, the tempting silhouette of the beautiful patient and her nurse has been replaced by the erotic shapes of a muscular male attendant sponge-bathing a brawny male patient.

21. Again, the spectator is privy to a subtle material reference to the class distinctions apparent within the coupling of Jerry and George; the contrast in their choices of bed linens—Jerry's tasteful white and George's childish, colorful pattern—provide a point of reference from which to understand the power dynamic between them as middle- to upper-middle-class (Jerry) and lower-middle- to working-class (George) gay men.

10

Mediating the Taboo:
The Straight Lesbian Gaze

Jane Garrity

Not that long ago, Ellen Morgan's coming out was heralded as the most significant breakthrough for gays and lesbians in television history—tantamount to Bill Cosby's smashing of the color barrier in the 1960s—earning the nation's applause and even Vice President Al Gore's endorsement.[1] Since then, the sitcom *Ellen* has offered an unprecedented weekly look at lesbian life in mainstream America, tackling a range of controversial issues such as lesbian parenting, internalized homophobia, and homoerotic desire. It is precisely the show's candor—in addition to inflammatory moments such as Emma Thompson's hilarious line, "let's go out and terrify some Baptists"—that has prompted the ABC television network to post a homophobic "parental discretion advisory" during episodes in which the same-sex content was deemed inappropriate.[2] That *Ellen* is the first television show in history to insist on lesbian visibility—and implicitly presume a lesbian spectator—arguably explains why, despite all the fanfare, the sitcom was not renewed by the network. Although the audience seemed poised to embrace *Ellen*, the program's inconsistent ratings demonstrated a much more complicated and ambivalent attitude toward lesbian visibility. Oprah Winfrey's reassuring presence as the therapist on the coming-out episode presaged that viewers might be resistant to Ellen's open homosexuality. I would argue that it was not Ellen's lesbian identity per se that was unassimilable but rather the unmediated representation of lesbian experience and desire that was threatening, if not objectionable.[3]

The fate of Ellen Morgan is instructive and speaks directly to the central issue of this essay: the problematics of lesbian visibility in contemporary Hollywood film. The public's short-lived love affair with *Ellen* demonstrates mainstream America's conflicted cinematic posture: allegedly ready to embrace an out lesbian character but resistant to what that representation might require it to "see."

The Prime-Time Lesbian

Clearly, the making of lesbian meaning is a contested process, determined as much by the parameters of historical variability and the location of the "lesbian reader" as by the content, whether real or imagined, of the "lesbian text."[4] In contemporary feminist film theory, the debate concerning the question of "lesbian spectatorship" rages over not only who constitutes the "lesbian viewer" but what, ultimately, qualifies as a "lesbian" film.[5] At this particular moment, with lesbian theory in vogue but still at an early stage of critical discourse, this seems like a good question to be posing. For experimental filmmaker Barbara Hammer, the form must be radical and innovative for a film to qualify as "lesbian"; thus, more traditional movies like *Personal Best* (1982) and *Desert Hearts* (1985)—despite their homosexual content—are denounced as conventional cinematic forms. According to Hammer, a lesbian cultural feminist, such films offer "no lesbian to deconstruct, as the discourse of the gendered subject is within a heterosexist authority system."[6] And yet, while one might justifiably celebrate Hammer's explicit, iconoclastic work as a crucial contribution to the history of lesbian cinema, it is still possible to argue that other pleasures are to be found in seemingly conventional narrative structures. By "other pleasures," I mean not only the viewer's identification with overt lesbian content (i.e., watching Sandra Bernhard play Nancy on *Roseanne*) or the conspiratorial delight of reading for a homoerotic subtext that appears invisible to other viewers (e.g., *Fried Green Tomatoes*) but the process by which the lesbian spectator has been able to claim as queer such cinematic heroines as Thelma and Louise, Linda Hamilton in *Terminator 2: Judgment Day*, Sigourney Weaver in the *Alien* movies, or Jamie Lee Curtis in *Blue Steel* (Tasker, "Pussy" 175).[7] Each of these performances, as critics have observed, plays with gendered and sexual identities, rendering their characters ambiguous, uncertain, and thus open to a range of possible interpretations. The spectatorial pleasure in this kind of viewing is very different in kind from the experience of watching a lesbian-produced and lesbian-directed feature film such as Nicole Conn's *Claire of the Moon* (1992), a low-budget romance burdened by the goal of sustaining "positive" images of lesbian sexuality. Drained of any complexity, this predictable coming-out story is notable primarily because it contains sex scenes between women, but the film is too didactic, melodramatic, and invested in proselytizing political categories to be much fun. Lesbianism as pedagogical enterprise, this film conveys, is not a very pleasurable medium.[8] One might reasonably object, however, that at least this classic "girl meets girl" formula is better than the representation of the lesbian as psychopath or killer in two mainstream Hollywood movies that were released the same year, *Single White Female* and *Basic Instinct*.[9]

Despite the apparent deviance of the lesbian characters in such enormously popular films or the gratuitous inclusion of a lesbian sex scene in *Crash*, Hollywood also appears, at least most recently, to be distributing a less monolithically "perverse" perspective on same-sex relations between women. Perhaps this development is in response to popular culture's embrace of what *New York* magazine dubbed "Lesbian Chic," or maybe it simply speaks to the studios' sense that, because lesbians are fashionable, they will increase revenue.[10] *Vogue's* 1993 announcement that "lesbians are the Hula-Hoop of the nineties" appears to be borne out by prime time's embrace of lipstick lesbians: in addition to *Ellen,* recurring lesbian characters have been cast on the weekly television programs *Friends* and *Mad about You* and were regulars on the now-defunct *Roseanne* and *Relativity*.[11] The butch-femme staging of the August 1993 *Vanity Fair* cover, on which k.d. lang is being rapturously shaved by a scantily clad Cindy Crawford, invites the visual pleasure of the voyeuristic gaze, underscoring the degree to which lesbian eroticism functions as a fantasy for the (male) heterosexual viewer.[12] Yet despite this pop cultural evidence that lesbian sexuality is hot—and despite what some might herald as a new era in lesbian visibility—it is important to recognize that most television programs contain lesbian characters who are virtually asexual, with barely a single kiss between two women such as occurs regularly between heterosexuals.

One need only recall the uproar caused by the infamous smooch between C.J. and Abby on *L.A. Law* in 1991; so few kissing lesbians have surfaced on television since that storyline was dropped that it is easy to track the evolution of the same-sex kiss.[13] *Roseanne* dared to show its star receiving a kiss from a lesbian character, played by Mariel Hemingway, in 1994; but the degree to which this kiss was visually occluded speaks volumes, as does the fact that a parental advisory was broadcast before this episode aired. More than one same-sex kiss has made its way onto *Ellen,* prompting

ABC News (in October 1997) to poll America electronically with the question: "Would you allow your child to watch a lesbian kiss on television?"[14] *Ellen's* kisses have ranged from the comedic to the sexually reticent and tender, but none compares to the lesbian kiss on *Relativity* in 1997. There, the lesbian sister, Rhonda, engaged in what I would call television's landmark lesbian kiss: tender, sexy, visually unobscured, and lengthy.[15] However, this twentysomething show's equation of gay and straight romantic angst was atypical. More representative is *Xena, Warrior Princess*, which flirts with homoerotic passion while keeping the exact nature of Xena's relationship to Gabrielle ambiguous. When lesbian desire is more than subtextual, it is likely to be pathologized, as it was during the fall 1997 season of *Melrose Place*, when a visiting lesbian character, Connie, preyed on one of the show's straight regulars, Samantha. Television's response to the sexualized lesbian is exemplified by its treatment of the beautiful, predatory teenager in a 1994 *Beverly Hills, 90210* storyline. Her flirtatious advances to heterosexual teen-queen Kelly Taylor are met with disgust and reproach, and the young woman's body is eventually burned to a near-smoldering crisp in a fraternity-house fire; quite a price to pay for unconsummated lesbian passion.

Lesbians may have taken up residence in the world of prime-time television, but the space they inhabit is heterosexually conceived and circumscribed by strictly enforced restrictions on their sexuality; as a result, the mainstream endearments between women are few, and any chaste overtures are always in the service of foreclosing any specifically sexual lesbian possibilities. The sanitized depictions of same-sex desire in two recent made-for-television movies, *Serving in Silence: The Margarethe Cammermeyer Story* (1995) and *Two Mothers for Zachary* (1996), a Hallmark production about a lesbian custody battle, illustrate the representational limits of lesbian passion. Both movies tentatively explore the issue of lesbian self-discovery within the context of a same-sex relationship; but in each instance, the romance is subordinated to issues more palatable to a mass audience: military service and maternity.[16] A notable exception to this trend is the representation of Helen Mirren's physical intimacy with Kyra Sedgwick in the cable network Showtime's recent movie *Losing Chase* (1996), about a middle-aged, married woman's mental breakdown and her subsequent sexual awakening—and recovery—through the intervention of a young woman. In contrast to the sterile depictions of lesbian desire on network television, in *Losing Chase*, the dialogue and the representation of growing affection between the two women are erotically charged (if framed within the context of a mother-daughter dyad). Early in the film, Mirren's character, Chase Phillips, stages a scene that is both flirtatious and imperious, asking her new "mother's helper," Elizabeth (Sedgwick), to retrieve a cigarette from her breastpocket. Elizabeth hesitates but complies—a dynamic that is replayed throughout the film—and Chase responds by giving her paid companion another directive: "You can put that back where you found it." The maternal breast here functions as a sign of control and unarticulated desire, for what is foregrounded in this narrative is not the child's insatiability but the mother's homoerotic longing for the daughter's body.[17] At another erotically charged moment, Chase demands that Elizabeth strip off her pants so that she can try them on; Elizabeth hesitantly complies while Chase gazes at her naked legs and remarks, "you play sports I see," then coos, "oh—still warm," as she slides on Elizabeth's garment.

What is remarkable about this film is the degree to which heterosexuality is represented as disease: for marriage, in effect, is what appears to be the sole catalyst for Chase's mental breakdown. Lesbianism, in this scenario, becomes the magic antidote for a woman's heterosexual repression. After the climactic beach scene in which Chase kisses Elizabeth several times on the lips, she confesses to her horrified husband Richard: "I love her . . . she's made me feel alive again . . . she's brought me back in a way that you never could." Despite the critique of heterosexuality and the desirability of same-sex passion that the movie sustains, lesbianism is eventually relegated to the margins and has to be contained because, as Richard puts it, "this perversion" threatens the integrity of the family. Although *Losing Chase* does not equate lesbianism with perversion, it unwittingly enacts complicity in this paradigm by banishing Elizabeth from the narrative and ending with a final frame of Chase on the beach with her two young sons, thereby recuperating the mother as a marker of heterosexuality. The movie sustains an ambivalence about the sexualization of the mother-daughter coupling, both inviting and refuting its possibility by allowing for the charged expression of same-sex desire between women but ultimately denying its consummation.

It is precisely this tension between the depiction and denial of lesbian sexuality that I want to examine in this essay by raising questions about both the limits and the possibilities of mainstream representations of the lesbian body in Hollywood film. While audiences will undoubtedly not be seeing any explicit lesbian bedroom scenes on prime-time television anytime soon, one would have to be a real naysayer not to acknowledge that there has been a conspicuous paradigm shift for lesbians in the world of representation and visibility. Just in the last few years, with the incarnation of queer theory and the institutionalization of gay and lesbian studies, the literature on the representation of lesbians in mainstream and independent cinema, television, and popular culture has proliferated.[18] And yet, one television executive's cautious remarks—regarding the probable squeamishness of prime-time advertisers for *Ellen*—underscore the limits of the media's embrace of lesbian visibility: "Ellen and a girlfriend hanging around the house in funny situations would be fine, but I don't think they'd want Ellen in bed with another woman. Anything sexual would be a real problem" (Jacobs, "To Be" 25).[19] This observation encapsulates lesbianism's media problem for the 1990s: how to capitalize on the current fascination with lesbian chic and at the same time expand the representational parameters to sidestep, if not overcome, middle America's presumed distaste for lesbian sexuality?

Tracking the Straight Lesbian Gaze

The central question that the increased visibility of lesbianism raises is this: Do depictions of the lesbian in mainstream, heterosexual movies of the 1990s reflect a new visibility for homosexual women, or do they merely reinscribe, and thus perpetuate, what we might call the old voyeurism?[20] To put the question somewhat differently, is all this exposure good for lesbians, or does it merely reflect the media's cannibalization of lesbian sexuality? In contrast to the portrayal of lesbian subjectivity on *Dyke TV* (which airs on cable television), where identity is inexorably tied to some notion of the body as not only knowable but eminently visible, the representation of the lesbian self in today's mainstream movies is less transparent, her body a site of ideological contradiction. This cinematic contradiction is symptomatic, I would argue, of a larger cultural anxiety about the dangers of the lesbian body, exemplified by the simultaneous embrace of the "new femme" as cutting edge and the denunciation of real-life lesbians as perverse and depraved.[21] One need think only of the well-publicized Sharon Bottoms custody battle of 1995, in which the Virginia Supreme Court ruled that Bottoms was an unfit parent because she is a lesbian; or of the 1996 Florida case in which a state appeals court ruled that John Ward, convicted of murdering his first wife in 1974, was a more fit parent than his ex-wife Mary, a lesbian.[22] These two examples are by no means anomalous events, but they do typify what we might term the schizophrenic plight of today's lesbian: battling for her civil rights against the repressive strategies of the Right while at the same moment riding the cultural wave of what Helen Eisenbach has dubbed Hollywood's "lesbian invasion."[23] We can see this dichotomous split reflected in two recent mainstream films, the anti-lesbian *G.I. Jane* and the homoerotically suffused *Romy and Michelle's High School Reunion*. The "malicious allegation" of lesbianism haunts Demi Moore's character, Jordan O'Neil, from the outset, but *G.I. Jane* never challenges the assumption that such imputations of character are inherently homophobic. Although O'Neil acts butch, her heterosexuality is repeatedly confirmed. In contrast, Romy (Mira Sorvino) and Michelle (Lisa Kudrow) are femmes who claim to desire heterosexual love, but they vow to give each other a try if they have not found male mates by thirty. The homoeroticism of their relationship is tenderly conveyed during the scene in which they slow-dance at the prom, and it culminates in the film's final triangulated sequence, in which the two women dance with Sandy, a male partner. That their dyad is central is underscored by Michelle's assertion that she will only dance with Sandy if Romy is able to join them.

The 1990s mainstream movies I examine here—*Three of Hearts, Boys on the Side, Sirens, Diabolique,* and *Henry and June*—reveal a tension between the desire to promote—or at least engage—dominant heterosexual paradigms and at the same time to represent—if only to suppress—lesbian desire. In contrast, as I will argue at the end of this essay, *Bound* offers an alternative model, one that attempts to configure a different spectatorial position for the lesbian viewer. Although not marketed to an explicitly lesbian audience, the movies I refer to differently explore the lesbian viewer's erotic attraction to female characters on the screen, reflecting a range of representational possibilities—and the lack thereof—for lesbian visibility. What ultimately is at stake in each of these films is some form of triangulation through which lesbians (both onscreen and in the audience) are able to negotiate their desire for seemingly heterosexual cinematic subjects. These movies raise important questions about lesbian representation and spectatorship, inviting us to rethink the implications of what we mean when we say "the lesbian gaze."[24] Although Laura Mulvey's phrase "the male gaze"—as a kind of metaphor of patriarchal relations—has become a cliché used to identify the way that men look at women, most of the recent analysis of what happens when women look at classic narrative cinema still relies on an idea of male identification.[25] Within Mulvey's analysis, there is little space, as critics have observed, to conceptualize active lesbian relations of looking or to explain changes in some contexts where women's experience cannot be incorporated into the psychoanalytic discourse of heterosexual relations (Evans and Gamman, "Gaze" 19–23, 32–36; Roof, "View").[26] The mainstream movies I consider here provide an interesting counterpoint to the perspective that female spectatorship is only a form of masculinization, illustrating that same-sex desire cannot always be explained away by recourse to what Mulvey terms "visual transvestitism"—cross-identification with the opposite sex. For the lesbian spectator, the pleasures of looking at a woman on the screen are not equivalent, or reducible to, the male viewing position; yet some concept of cross-identification is, I want to argue, precisely what is at stake in attempting to characterize the "lesbian content" of movies that foreground a heterosexual narrative.

While no one has posited an adequate model of lesbian spectatorship to date, the production of an interpretation that privileges the erotic contemplation of women by women arguably rests on some notion of the "spectatorial fluidity" of lesbian identification (Evans and Gamman, "Gaze" 45).[27] Within the conventions of psychoanalysis, as Teresa de Lauretis has observed, desire and identification typically are considered to be mutually exclusive.[28] Desire (wanting to possess the other) is deemed implicitly heterosexual, while identification (the desire to be the other) has a homosexual valence. The representations of lesbianism in the movies I consider here differently reveal the inadequacy of this dichotomy, illustrating the various ways that lesbians negotiate the double possibility of both desiring and identifying—at times simultaneously—with their object choices. Carol Clover's work on mainstream horror films, in which she has demonstrated the mobility of cross-gender identification in her analysis of the "Final Girl," a figure who alternately functions at different points in the film as an icon of feminine and masculine identity, has important implications for lesbian film theorists who seek to carve out a place for lesbian desire within the context of nominally straight movies.[29] Clover explores the dynamics of both cross-gender identification and its sexual consequences to speculate about the mobility of sexual identities and identifications, providing a useful model for talking about spectatorship beyond the binarism of psychoanalytic film theory. The mutability of such sexual positioning may provide some insight into the current utility of the lesbian as cultural sign, in which questions of desire and social marginalization can be temporarily engaged—or identified with by viewers—but without assuming the full gravity of their social significance. The conventional alternatives for the lesbian spectator, narcissism or transvestitism, do not allow for the plurality, variability, and mobility of the lesbian gaze, nor does the psychoanalytic model take into account identificatory dynamics other than gender—such as sexuality, race, ethnicity, and class.[30] Like Tamsin Wilton, I want to recognize and deploy the category of "the lesbian" as a strategic sign, remaining attentive to both the social content and cultural difference of the cinematic character's experience as a means of tracking a range of spectatorial identifications (*Invisible* 5).

This essay foregrounds the utility and limitations of "the straight lesbian gaze" as a privileged site of inquiry in which lesbians derive pleasure from mainstream movies. In contrast to de Lauretis, who condemns mass-audience "lesbian" features as "outright obnoxious commercial products" on the grounds that they do not adequately engage with the problem of representation, I want to suggest that the movies I consider here reveal a much more complicated relation to the problem of lesbian visibility than this dismissal warrants (de Lauretis, "Film" 256–57). Specifically, what interests me is how these mainstream movies differently negotiate the relation between identification and desire, which is today still a preoccupying issue in lesbian film theory. Sharon Stone's character in *Basic Instinct*, Catherine Trammell, may be a ruthless killer, but at least she, unlike the majority of big-screen lesbians I examine, gets to have a lot of sex.[31] Trammell both embodies and enacts the most extreme example of the male fear of the female deviant: insatiably promiscuous yet ultimately unavailable, invested in undermining the heterosexual status quo, and sexually gratified through the murder of her sexual conquests. The movie's eroticization of the deadliness of female desire is amplified by Trammell's lesbian involvements; but by end of the film, lesbianism has been exiled from the story and what viewers are left with is a sexualized image of Trammell choosing Nick over her ice pick. Despite the ambivalence of this move, what the gesture conveys is that, with the restoration of heterosexuality, there exists a possibility (however slim) for the recuperation of Trammell's character. To the extent that *Basic Instinct* situates lesbianism within the context of a heterosexual triangle (Catherine pursues Nick at the same time that she is involved with Roxy), the movie can be seen as a part of a group of recent films that feature erotic triads in which lesbian desire is ultimately suppressed, if not completely displaced. Largely, what happens to lesbianism when it is marketed to a mass audience is either the deeroticization or hypersexualization of the lesbian body; in either case, the film's failure to engage with the problem of lesbian representation hinges on the containment and regulation of the lesbian gaze. Moreover, as we shall see, the straight lesbian gaze privileges whiteness, even when it appears as though racial difference will intersect with sexuality.

The 1991 comedy *Switch*, about a transgendered man trapped in a woman's body, in many ways encapsulates this dilemma. The movie, which stars Ellen Barkin as the female incarnation of a sexist and homophobic philanderer, has a lesbian subplot in which Barkin becomes involved with the out lesbian Sheila Faxton (played by Lorraine Bracco), the beautiful president of a cosmetics company. Barkin initiates the first sexual move and Bracco lustfully responds, but the movie cannot sustain the possibility of lesbian consummation. In the midst of the seduction scene, Barkin suddenly faints, preserving her lesbian virginity and underscoring the fact that, although this woman is in fact a heterosexual man, the illusion of lesbian passion—for what one "sees," after all, is the staging of same-sex desire—must necessarily be contained. This one scene is the film's only direct engagement with lesbianism, but the idea of lesbian eroticism—as filtered through a straight, male desiring body—fuels much of the heterosexual narrative. Significantly, Barkin later gets drunk, has sex with, and is impregnated by her male best friend (played by Jimmy Smits), illustrating that the "truth" of the body (that is, this staging of heterosexuality) is ultimately more believable than the psychic reality that is repressed—that is, the fact that this coupling is, in effect, a male homosexual encounter. *Switch* flirts with lesbian desire but only to illustrate that this taboo must forever be denied representation. What *Switch* and several other recent movies that feature triangulation reveal is that the most effective way to interfere with same-sex desire between women is to insert a male figure into the narrative. To this extent, the films I examine demonstrate the prevalence of what Judith Roof calls "narrative heteroideology," her proposition that sexuality and narrative are mutually constitutive and fulfill a reproductive function that works to naturalize heterosexuality.[32]

Enforced Celibacy: Regulating the Lesbian Body

While the movies that I consider foreground lesbianism as a possibility in different ways, they all utilize male heterosexuality as a frame to divert attention away from and delegitimate the lesbian, even as lesbian desire itself functions as a catalyst for male voyeuristic pleasure. Mainstream movies are informed by the conventions of heterosexuality so that, as Chris Straayer puts it, "simultaneous actions take place in the [film's narrative] to eroticize the women's interactions and to abort the resulting homoerotics."[33] In the commercial features I examine, what is ultimately at stake—if the seductiveness of lesbianism is to be granted both articulation and representation—is some concept of mediation. It is precisely in this space of contradiction and conflicting intentions, I suggest, that ambiguity functions as possibility, allowing for the erotic investiture of both the lesbian spectator and "the lesbian" within the narrative. In the romantic sex comedy *Three of Hearts,* released in 1993, William Baldwin plays Joey, an obnoxious male escort, who is hired by Connie (Kelly Lynch) to seduce—and then dump—her ex-girlfriend, Ellen (Sherilyn Fenn), so that the women can reconcile after a breakup. The patently offensive premise of the film is that, because men are louses, women will take refuge in lesbian relationships. The problem with this, however, is that Ellen falls for Joey, who reciprocates her affection, thereby illustrating the heterosexual truism that the only thing a lesbian needs is a good lay. The most troubling aspect of this triangulated matrix is the degree to which the women's history is categorically effaced throughout; although Connie's "love" for Ellen is the supposed impetus for the story, we never know the most basic things about them: why the women were together, what that was like, why they broke up, or why Connie (despite her profuse whining) would want Ellen back. Ellen declares to her sister at one point: "I loved Connie and she loved me. I wasn't trying on a new perm"; but the only time we see the two women together is when they are breaking up.

The only evidence we have that a lesbian romance transpired at all comes from the scenes of Connie, obsessively identified with her ex-girlfriend, sitting on her sofa, teary-eyed, watching home videos of their relationship. The movie is problematic on a variety of levels, not the least of which is the fact that lesbianism is never figured directly in the film—that is, we never unmediatedly see these cosmetically perfect women kiss, embrace, or caress each other—but, rather, is restrictedly framed within a frame. The lesbian relationship is relegated to video; and, even then, we get only fleeting glimpses of these so-called happy domestic moments. In contrast, we have several sexualized encounters between Ellen and Joey so that lesbianism is multiply displaced: it is denied representational status on a par with heterosexuality and functions only as an escapist fantasy; even then, it can be represented only through the mediation of a "screen" memory rather than through the immediacy of actual flashbacks.[34] Moreover, the use of video as the privileged medium through which lesbianism is framed suggests a kind of voyeuristic prurience (what one watches is inevitably someone watching). This particular kind of spectatorship, marked by titillation and eavesdropping, recapitulates both Joey's and the male heterosexual viewer's relation to lesbian sexuality in *Three of Hearts*. The video becomes a stand-in for lesbianism itself, which realistically functions only in the realm of fantasy, propelling male heterosexual desire.[35]

Another recent movie that situates lesbianism within a heterosexual context and privileges identification over desire is *Boys on the Side* (1995), which stars Whoopie Goldberg as grumpy lesbian rock singer Jane DeLuca. Mary-Louise Parker plays uptight, Carpenters-worshiping WASP Robin Nickerson, who suffers from AIDS, and Drew Barrymore is Holly, the innocent yet sensual pregnant girlfriend of an abusive drug dealer. Each woman is fleeing from her past in this movie, which begins as a feel-good, road-trip story that eventually slides into melodrama. The three women wind up living together in a southwestern hacienda, where they set up a postnuclear family, one based on personal affections rather than blood. Reviews of the film hailed *Boys on the Side* for its boldness in tackling the risky themes of lesbianism, AIDS, and spousal abuse; but, like *Three of Hearts,* this movie strips the lesbian body of desire, invoking lesbianism only to displace it. The emotional focus of the story is Jane's love for Robin, who, as both terminally ill and straight, is from the start established as an unobtainable object of desire. The viewers learn through a dialogue between Holly and Robin that Jane once had a crush on Holly, thus conveying early on that Jane is the kind of lesbian who falls in love with "straight girls." Holly's view of lesbianism is a humorous stereotype, which the movie invokes to illustrate her limited perspective: "They're very emotional, they love uniforms . . . especially UPS. Not that I'm an expert. [Jane's] the only one I've ever seen except for the girls in the porno films Nick used to rent." This reference to lesbian sexuality functions not as a prelude to a series of eroticized scenes between Jane and any of the other characters but rather to establish a dramatic contrast between "that" kind of (promiscuous) lesbian and the asexual sort of woman that Whoopie Goldberg portrays. *Boys on the Side* participates in the policing of lesbian desire at the same time that it refuses to engage the politics of race, even though the discourses of lesbianism and race are often intertwined—only to be disavowed— throughout the narrative.

In one of the first lines of the movie, Jane explodes to an unidentified man: "You get the fuck out of my way, go back to Pakistan." This is a throwaway line—neither the man nor Pakistan ever materialize as relevant to the story—but its content suggests that Jane will be a character for whom race is a preoccupying issue. To the extent that Jane makes reference to racial categories, this is true; but race itself is never engaged by the film as a fully realized discursive category. Jane's racist comment—"go back to Pakistan"—also introduces into the narrative the idea of bounded categories of racial difference that are sustained throughout the movie.[36] At the movie's outset, Jane refers to Robin as "the whitest woman on the face of the earth," a seemingly charged observation that does not initiate a dialogue about interracial lesbian attraction but instead serves merely to polarize the two women. Blackness only serves to further stigmatize Goldberg's character as other; and, cumulatively, the comments about race remain suspended without ever working toward any resolution about racial difference. A good example is the scene in the hospital, where Robin has just been admitted for AIDS-related pneumonia. It is only from her hospital bed that Robin finally discloses that she knows Jane is gay; quickly, Jane reassures her that she is not "after [her]," provoking Robin to say: "I'm not worried. Why aren't you after me?" Jane's response, "you're not my type," prompts Robin to counter with "this is a black-white thing," but Jane refuses to engage that possibility, only responding by saying: "No, it's more like a blondes-Carpenters thing." Of course, even the indirection of her response reveals that race indeed is an issue; but here, as elsewhere, the movie does not examine the racially coded dynamic of sexual desire between the two women. The conversation ends with Jane's assurance to Robin, "you're safe," thereby crystallizing the movie's greatest anxiety: that it is not AIDS, but lesbianism, that is the real source of contagion.

Robin is the one who races toward a premature death, but Jane is the character whose sexuality must be contained in this film. As a result, both Robin and Holly are allowed lustful heterosexual encounters, while Jane remains unquestionably celibate, permitted only to pine for straight women she can never have. And yet, the intimacy of the two women's conversations suggests that homoeroticism is certainly in play. At one point, in the kitchen, the two discuss what words they use to describe the female genitals, an intimate dialogue that both calls attention to the female body's sexual zones and—precisely because the linguistic task is so difficult for Robin—underscores the degree to which lesbian desire can never be represented. Robin's initial resistance—"I'm not going to say that"—is broken down by Jane, and she eventually discloses her private signifiers to be "hoo-hoo . . . [and] sissy." Jane proceeds to make fun of this childish language and urges her friend to say aloud the worst word she can think of. Jane's promise, "say it, it'll free you," prompts Robin to whisper, then spell, shout, and finally sing the unspeakable: "Cunt." Goldberg's character bursts into an exuberant response: "You free, Miss Scarlett, you free! Cunt!" again calling attention to, but immediately dropping, the issue of racial opposition. This scene is significant not only for the way in which the topic of female genitals, for a moment, eclipses all other concerns in the movie, but because the women's conversation concretizes the film's most conspicuous absence: the location of lesbian desire and the problem of its articulation. In the following scene, Jane plays the piano that Robin has given her as a birthday gift, singing the words to the Carpenters' song "Superstar" as a sign of her affection while Robin stands on a balcony, out of her immediate view, listening to the lyrics: "Don't you remember you told me you loved me baby?" The script's selection of the Carpenters underscores Robin's receptivity to romantic schmaltz (we elsewhere see her watching *The Way We Were* and *An Officer and a Gentleman*), but it also works to signal her whiteness, her fixed difference from Jane. When Robin hears the line "I love you," she leaves the scene and Jane stares off into her empty space. The framing of this scene—the song's dialogue standing in for Jane's sentiments and the fact that the two women never directly meet one another's gaze—underscores the degree to which the inscription of lesbian desire must always be narratively mediated. Significantly, this scene's confession-of-love through the Carpenters is sandwiched between the women's conversation about female genitalia and Jane's attempt to find a man for Robin—a gesture that conveniently constructs a third term through which Jane's desire can be displaced. It is only through Jane's intervention that Robin almost has sex with this male character, but the passionate interlude abruptly ends when Robin realizes that Jane has secretly disclosed her HIV status to him. Robin accuses him of pity—"bringing sex to the unfuckable"—a self-description that is accurate not because she is HIV positive but because this is really a lesbian love story, and Jane is the only character Robin truly wants.

The use of a male figure as a sexual intermediary occurs only once, but it literalizes the displacement of lesbian desire that occurs repeatedly throughout the film. After the scene following Robin's abortive heterosexual encounter, Robin explodes at Jane, demanding that she stay out of her love life because, as she puts it: "You're the one who's in love with somebody you can never have." While this observation is certainly true, the statement also works to characterize Robin's own repressed feelings about her friend. During a dinner-table conversation between Robin and her mother, the issue of Jane's lesbianism arises, and Robin flatly states: "I'm not into lesbians"; Hollie intervenes by saying: "I think she's not being honest. It's the black thing, too." That the mother knows nothing of Jane's existence is evidenced by her scandalized response: "She was a black lesbian, and she was living here?" Again, the issue of racial difference is raised only to be immediately dropped; as elsewhere, Jane's blackness is invoked here only to mark her as other. Although Robin is the woman who is about to die from AIDS, it is the black lesbian body that is most clearly pathologized in this movie.

The exchange between Jane and a homophobic lawyer in a melodramatic courtroom scene (in which Holly is being tried for the murder of her ex-boyfriend) illustrates this point. Jane takes the stand as a character witness for her friend, and the lawyer attempts to discredit her testimony on the grounds that she is a lesbian, asking her if her friendship with Holly is "romantic" and demanding to know if she is really gay. Robin's testimony revisits the question of Jane's sexuality when she is asked about the nature of their relationship. Robin directs her gaze to Jane and unequivocally declares her affection—"you are my family, and I love you"—responding to the interrogation of her sexuality by saying that, although she is not gay, she certainly "understands the impulse," claiming that "like speaks to like." Robin's confession of same-sex desire hinges on an identificatory impulse—"there's something that goes on between women"—but this declaration is not followed by a plot twist in which the women go off together. The next scene does feature the two women and a bed, but it is the hospital bed in which Robin is rapidly dying. As a displaced gay signifier, AIDS facilitates the affective involvement of the two women at this final moment, allowing the expression of intimacy to flourish. The imminence of death liberates Robin to confess a youthful crush on another girl and enables her to ask of Jane: "It was me you loved, wasn't it?" Jane's frank and tender response—"yes, and still"—is in direct contrast to her behavior during a previous hospital-bed scene, in which she had recoiled from Robin's attempt to take her hand. Robin's AIDS status ensures that lesbianism—as act—will forever be denied, even though her illness facilitates this final exchange of love. Robin dies because the narrative cannot accommodate the women as an interracial lesbian couple; in this movie, same-sex desire is relegated to the spectral and mediated margins, unimaginable as literal embodiment.

Tracking the Lesbian Libido

This anxiety surrounding lesbian desire is the centerpiece of another recent mainstream movie, *Sirens* (1994), in which lesbianism is again represented in terms of mediation. But unlike *Three of Hearts* and *Boys on the Side*, lesbian libido in this film figures prominently, even though it relies on identification and is seemingly in the service of maintaining the heterosexual status quo. I would argue that *Sirens* invites a multiplicity of spectator positions, including the pleasures of the lesbian viewer—both within the film and from the audience's perspective. The narrative of this Australian movie centers on Estella (Tara Fitzgerald), the sexually inhibited wife of the nice but repressed clergyman Tony (Hugh Grant); together, this English couple travels to the Australian outback, stopping at the rural estate of painter Norman Lindsay (Sam Neill) at the behest of the church, which seeks to prohibit the artist from exhibiting his paintings of naked women. The story, set in the 1930s, is easily summarized: Estella enters Lindsay's libertine household and gets her inhibitions loosened by a trio of young, beautiful, and often nude female models; she eventually experiences an erotic awakening under the influence of the sexually provocative Sheila (Elle Macpherson) and through the intervention of a crude, but apparently virile, laborer named Devon. The Australian setting is exoticized from the outset, especially through shots of roaming koala bears, kangaroos, and snakes slithering through grasses and into domestic spaces—obvious signs that this is "dangerous" country. The fundamental danger, however, is not the remarkable landscape but the bohemian enclave's atmosphere of diffused lesbian eroticism: the models spend much of the movie either nude or draped in gauze, teasing and flirting with one another, while Sheila in particular is constantly doing things like gazing invitingly at Estella while sucking Stilton cheese off her finger or encouraging the repressed woman to strip for a swim by exposing her own voluptuous body.

Of course, it is not surprising that the situation that allows Estella's libido to flourish—an abundance of beautiful, sexually aggressive, bisexual women—just happens to be the one that heterosexual men find extremely titillating. Because lesbian sex scenes in heterosexual pornography are ubiquitous preludes to straight sex, lesbian homoeroticism in a mainstream movie like *Sirens* may be read by some as exploitative or at least as delegitimizing lesbian sexual difference and pleasure.[37] While such an interpretation of this film is perhaps possible from a male scopophilic perspective, for the lesbian spectator, I would argue, *Sirens* provides an alternate possibility, a less conventional space from which to read against the heterosexual grain. The question of whether or not, in the end, the sexual status quo in this movie remains unchallenged is not foreclosed; for although Estella is indeed reunited with her husband Tony, the terms of that reconciliation are extremely unstable. Desire, for this clergyman's wife, is

...ys triangulated—always mediated through her fantasies surrounding the exquisite Sheila. The two women are often framed returning one another's gaze, particularly during moments when Sheila models nude for Norman. This is a movie preoccupied with the scopophilic pleasures of voyeurism: Sheila gazes at Estella as she sleeps; Tony watches the women posing nude; Norman watches Estella gaze at the models' naked bodies, and so on, repeatedly. At one point, two of the models spontaneously start caressing the body of the youngest, Giddy, by raising her gown and exposing her legs to the camera; within seconds, Estella—who had been watching the scene unfold—joins the group and, as if in an erotic trance, similarly begins to gaze on and touch the young woman's body. To say that *Sirens* is invested in looking as a form of pleasure is to state the obvious, but the issue of whose pleasure—and what, exactly, one "sees" when one looks here—remains to be theorized. *Sirens* poses a challenge to the contention that spectators are always forced into the masculine subject position, for while certainly women function as spectacles for the pleasure of men here, this model does not account for the sexual desire of women in the audience for women on the screen, nor does it adequately address the nature of the lesbian gaze between women in the film itself.

That *Sirens* is interested in privileging the seductiveness of lesbianism arguably rests on both the fluidity of identification, in which spectatorial positions are variable and mobile, and the instability of heterosexuality, which provides a space for the film's lesbian erotic content. Estella's sexual interest in Sheila throughout the film is ultimately mediated through the laborer, Devon, whom Estella also gazes on at regular intervals. At one point, after Tony makes dispassionate love to her, Estella creeps out of bed and slips into Devon's room, where he subsequently makes love to her. But at this moment, the movie appears to escape the tyranny of a heterosexual reading in two important ways: first, although Estella does transgress here by having extramarital sex with another man, because Devon is blind— and therefore arguably cannot objectify her with "the male gaze" in the same way that the other characters, or the viewer, might—she seems to circumvent the economy of visual exchange between the sexes, in which men look and women are looked at. The staging of the scene works to suggest that the representation of female desire need not necessarily be constructed in relation to a male spectator. It is, moreover, significant that what Estella looks at through a window as Devon makes love to her is the voluptuous spectacle of Sheila, on a swing, floating back and forth through the air. Devon's blindness facilitates Estella's homosexual identification, allowing her to desire the other woman without actually transgressing sexual boundaries. While *Sirens* seems to be invested in both a critique of heterosexuality and an argument about the potency of lesbian passion—albeit necessarily sublimated—a brief scene near the end of the movie complicates this reading. Norman tosses a ball to Devon, who catches it without hesitation, thus conveying that this "blind" man can actually see. Although Norman functions primarily as a "blank screen" through which lesbian desire is mediated, the viewer now knows that blindness was merely a ruse utilized to ensure Estella's loss of inhibition. And yet, Estella is never privy to the viewer's insight; one might argue, therefore, that although from the audience's perspective, the movie is complicit in a kind of heterosexual appropriation of lesbian imagery, from Estella's point of view, what is privileged is an eroticism between women.

Ultimately, the movie is rather ambiguously situated in relation to the question of "whose" desire gets represented. Near the end of the film, Estella has a sexual dream in which she floats, Ophelia-like, in a pool of still water among lily pads; slowly, hands appear and begin to caress her limp body, and soon the hands are transformed into the three nude models. Estella's eyes are closed throughout this dream, again suggesting that lesbian desire can never be directly experienced or represented in this movie but must always be somehow mediated. This is certainly true of the final scene, in which Estella's toes rub her husband's groin on a moving train while she visualizes herself, along with the artist's models, posing naked in the midst of spectacular natural scenery for the camera. This ending works in two ways: on the one hand, Estella's lesbian sex fantasy is clearly the catalyst for her renewed sexual relationship with her husband, thus suggesting that a woman's return to heterosexuality is the culminating stage in her sexual exploration. But, from a different perspective, it is possible to argue that the ending unravels the dominance of heterosexuality precisely because lesbianism is privileged as the destabilizing force, complicating Estella's sexual allegiances and providing a space for the lesbian viewer to experience a final moment of erotic identification, appropriative desire, or both. The last shot of the group of women posing provocatively for the camera's eye reinstates the fact that, in this movie, naked women still function as objects for the voyeuristic male gaze; however, if the spectator of this final frame is a lesbian, then perhaps the conventional reading no longer makes sense precisely because the traditional heterosexual model of objectification necessarily breaks down. Lesbian sexuality still functions as mediation in this film, but *Sirens* does provide a series of narrative gaps that repeatedly foreground the fact that there is no heterosexual resolution here, thereby allowing for the intervention of lesbian visual pleasure. *Sirens* may hold out more for lesbian spectators than its conservative storyline can possibly deliver, but it nevertheless allows us to examine the dynamics of sexual desire and its relation to multiple identifications.

Lesbian Desire and the Phallus

When Hollywood does create a space for the visibility of same-sex desire between women, that desire is always predicated on the presence—whether actual or imaginary—of the phallus.[38] The recent remake of the French movie *Diabolique* (1995) clearly articulates the degree to which Hollywood lesbianism hinges on both triangulation and this central signifier of desire. This is the story of an unlikely murder conspiracy, in which the odious headmaster of a boy's preparatory school, Guy (Chazz Palminteri), is killed off by his wife, Mia (Isabelle Adjani), a sexually inhibited former nun prone to coronary attacks, and his disgruntled mistress, Nicole (Sharon Stone), an unlikely math teacher who smokes, smolders, and looks spectacular in form-fitting 1950s outfits. Guy's abuse and humiliation of Mia provide ample reason for her desire to kill him off, but Nicole's motivation is more difficult to discern. The film provides the missing link by flirting with lesbian passion, suffusing the women's relationship with what amounts to a series of homoerotic moments—kisses on the face, various meaningful glances, more than one caress, an embrace from behind—all initiated by Nicole.[39] The killer-as-lesbian-bombshell persona that Stone created in *Basic Instinct* is in evidence here in her stylized portrayal of Nicole, who is a sexual predator—her last name is "Horner"—compared to the literally fainthearted Mia. At one point, Mia is shown teaching French, parsing the verb "to desire"; in another sequence, her students watch a sexual education film on sperm and testicles. These classroom scenes are comic because the viewer knows from Guy that Mia, "a fucking angel," is both sexually repressed and religiously inclined. But when considered in relationship to Nicole, Mia's "sexually frigid" body is more open to alternate readings; she never recoils from the other woman's advances, instead exhibiting receptivity. After Guy has been drowned by the two women in Nicole's bathtub, there is a scene of them in bed together—Mia in flannel, Nicole in a leopard bra and red toreador pants—in which Mia wraps her arms around Nicole. Later, it is Mia who proposes that they confess to the police and present themselves as lovers, a possibility that is not lost on Nicole—"well, you can take the girl out of the convent"—the prep school boys (who call them dykes), or the lesbian spectator, who fully registers the homoerotic subtext. Nothing explicit ever transpires, but it is the sexual suggestiveness of Stone's character and the accumulation of many homoerotic moments that fuel a lesbian reading of the women's relationship.

The movie, however, ultimately works against this interpretation despite its fetishization of lesbian sexuality, utilizing the erotic charge between the two women to encourage the viewer's fantasy but then ultimately denying its possibility when we learn that Guy has been alive all along, conspiring with Nicole against Mia. In the end, what *Diabolique* does is reassure the male viewer that heterosexuality has never really been displaced, while conveying to the lesbian spectator that the women's eroticized relationship has only been a ruse. The movie's self-consciousness about vision and visibility—for example, Mia's repeated insistence that Guy "is watching," Nicole's loss of her glasses in the pool, the detective's surveillance of the women—does not extend to the issue of lesbian representation. Although *Diabolique* foregrounds the question of what can be "seen" (and by whom), it is precisely because Guy has always been alive that the question of lesbian visibility becomes moot. In retrospect, the fantasy of lesbian coupling necessarily reads like a hallucinatory interlude; although the film is critical of Guy, it never contradicts the heterosexual frame of reference. The way the movie accomplishes this specifically is through the invocation of the phallus, which is metaphorized through a series of displaced references to male erection. The first time that Mia and Nicole believe that they have drowned Guy, his body pops up out of the water and sits rigidly in the tub. Later, after they have dumped him in the pool of stagnant water at the prep school, they wait for days for the body to rise, literally, to the surface. Mia's incessant question—"why hasn't he risen yet?"—has both sexual and religious connotations, for Guy, like Christ, is eventually resurrected. By recuperating Guy, the narrative reinstates the primacy of the male member in the ménage à trois. The name "Guy" itself functions as a substitute for any man, underscoring the degree to which lesbianism in *Diabolique* is unimaginable outside the circulation of heterosexuality. Even though this privileging of heterosexuality is momentarily destabilized when Nicole and Mia join forces to kill Guy, the women part immediately following this hyperbolic drowning scene because lesbianism cannot be sustained without the phallus. For the lesbian spectator, what this ending evokes is an earlier scene in which Mia is publicly coerced by Guy to ingest something she finds disgusting to humiliate her. His imperative, "swallow it for once in your life," is an obvious allusion to fellatio, but the line can also be read as the movie's message to the lesbian viewer: swallow the fact that you have been supplanted by the phallus and vaporized from this narrative.

Whereas the phallus functions in *Diabolique* as a marker of lesbian absence, in *Henry and June* (1990), we find a much more ambivalent and complicated representation of the relation between lesbian desire and phallic intervention. Because this film offers a more subtle perspective on the overlap between lesbian desire and identification, I want here to devote more space to a reading of some of the movie's crucial scenes. Set in 1930s Paris, this film (the first to earn an NC-17 rating) is a steamy adaptation of Anaïs Nin's (Maria de Medeiros) account of her triangulated relationship with writer Henry Miller (Fred Ward) and his wife June (Uma Thurman). Although the movie draws attention to lesbianism as a resurfacing narrative element, propelling the dramatic focal point of the story through Anaïs's passion for June, the film also presents a series of shifting triangular alliances: Anaïs and her husband Hugo (Richard E. Grant); Anaïs and Henry; Anaïs and, briefly, her cousin Edouardo; and, of course, Henry and June. As a writer, Anaïs wants above all to expand her experiential horizon, and the primary way she accomplishes this is by identifying with Henry as well as June. This is a film that foregrounds a woman's sexual mobility and fluidity of identification, suggesting that an underlying basis for this oscillation is narcissism, the desire to see the self variously reflected, and amplified, in the other. Anaïs is drawn to Henry's sexual frankness, his outspoken objective to "liberate literature" from prudish conventions; she decides at the outset that Henry "is like me, but he doesn't know it yet," an identification that has everything to do with the fact that he is a writer and a self-fashioned sexual rebel. At the same time, Anaïs's interest in June is also fueled by an identificatory impulse: "I'm just like you," she declares in the scene in which she and June almost make love, while June concludes that Anaïs is actually "just like Henry"—that is, interested in other people only as material for future books. For both Anaïs and Henry, writing is in some sense the real source and stimulus for erotic pleasure; sex happens repeatedly between the two, but what each of them fetishizes is the literary representation of that practice. (This is in particular evidenced by the many scenes of Anaïs recording her illicit encounters in her diary.) By the end of the movie, Henry and Anaïs's sexual exploits appear to be over, but the linguistic account of those adventures will proliferate through the circulation of the books they have written during their affair: both Miller's *Tropic of Cancer* and Nin's *House of Incest* explore the issues of sexual prohibition and risk. Like Henry, Anaïs draws from her experiences with June to redefine the literary boundary of what constitutes "the obscene"; yet, unlike heterosexuality, which is endlessly replayed and therefore endlessly recounted, lesbianism proves to be a much more elusive narrative topic.

June is represented from the outset as a transgressive figure; the child of a magician and a trapeze artist, she is an actress, a ventriloquist, a bisexual woman with a shady string of past lovers who represents, for Anaïs, the greatest forbidden danger. In contrast to Henry and June, for whom writing and sexuality are inseparably linked, June's liaisons do not result in narrative; consequently, she flounders throughout the movie with no clear purpose or motive, sailing to New York for an audition only to return an alcoholic, without money or ambition. The confession June makes to Anaïs after her return—"I don't know who I came back for"—crystallizes her indeterminacy and underscores the degree to which she perceives herself to be a malleable entity. Lacking a substantial identity, June's primary function in the movie is to provide others with a projection screen for their own fantasies. For Anaïs, who is obsessed with the transcription of her own "erotic imaginings," June is the perfect object of desire precisely because she not only lacks definition but also willingly submits herself to authorial analysis. It is not surprising, therefore, that both Henry and Anaïs are preoccupied with telling June's story; but because June lacks a discrete self, no biographical account can ever be satisfying to her. As a result, she is unable to recognize herself either in Henry's work, which she perceives to be an ugly distortion of her character (even though he protests, "it's the you inside me"), or Anaïs's, which she rejects on the basis of its lack of realism. June's objection to Henry's portrait of her is specifically a critique of perception—"you can't see me, or anyone as they are"—a theme that is repeatedly invoked as a gendered standard of comparison throughout the movie.

The film presents a complex nexus of cross-gendered identifications but also suggests that what is ultimately privileged is some notion of "women's ways of knowing." In contrast to Henry, who consistently mispronounces Anaïs's name throughout the film (calling her "Annis"), June articulates her name correctly. This level of attention is recapitulated in Anaïs's pronouncement, "I am going to write a book about June from a woman's perspective—inside out," which claims for femininity the vantage point of authenticity. What this privileging of women's relationships establishes is the expectation that lesbianism will surface as the unassailable source of authority. The problem with this presumption, and what ultimately thwarts its realization, is the movie's compromised relation to the issue of lesbian visibility. As the story's only marked lesbian, June is the figure who embodies this ambivalence. The black-and-white photograph of her face that flashes intermittently throughout the movie works to convey her status as beautiful image, providing visual affirmation of the fact that she is indeed an object to be looked at. But at the same time, June's eyes are also fixed on the spectator, sending out an eroticized look that positions her as a desiring subject.

The viewer's initial exposure to June occurs in a movie theater, where we watch Anaïs observe Henry as he watches her cinematic image kiss another actor. This series of multiple displacements initiates the voyeurism that will fuel much of the narrative, but the situation also literalizes June's function as a projection screen for others. Later, when June is first introduced to Anaïs and Hugo, her image repeatedly appears and dissolves in a moody sequence that is staged to signal her elusiveness and draw attention to the question, What can be seen? For this is, in effect, the central preoccupation of the movie. Both of these introductions to June underscore her inscrutability (is she real or an illusion?) and presage the way that lesbianism will function in the movie: through the simultaneous affirmation and denial of its visibility. Although the representation of lesbian desire poses a problem, June is by no means a static icon, for she both returns Anaïs's gaze and initiates most of the homoerotic moments between the two women. In one suggestive scene, June sits beside Anaïs in a robe, drying her wet hair as she provocatively exposes a gartered leg and gazes wordlessly at the other woman, who furtively returns her look. Immediately following this interlude, the two are shown at the cinema, watching the most explicitly lesbian moment in *Mädchen in Uniform*—the scene of Fraulein von Bernburg's kiss, full on the lips, of the schoolgirl Manuela. It is at this instant that June takes Anaïs's hand and whispers to her, "You're like the schoolteacher, I'm like the young girl," positioning herself in the role of the passionate student whose incipient homosexuality drives her to desire what is expressly forbidden.[40] June is the one who takes them both to a lesbian bar that is packed with gorgeous dykes in drag, an episode that makes explicit the homoeroticism that has fueled their relationship. Whereas earlier, Anaïs had asked June if she loved women, yet received no answer, here June openly declares her affection on the dance floor: "so many things I wish I could have done with you. . . . I wanted to hold you. . . . I wish I could have taken opium with you." This confessional moment is facilitated by both the lesbian context and the alcohol that June has imbibed, but it nonetheless is a clear exhibition of lesbian subjectivity and desire. June takes a bracelet off her arm and clasps it onto Anaïs as an erotic token, the two exchanging several seductive kisses as their intertwined bodies move to the music. The phrase that June whispers and Anaïs echoes—"I am innocent now . . . you are innocent"—does not deeroticize the moment but rather situates lesbian libido in a primary position, outside the presumed defilement of heterosexuality. The word "innocence" suggests that what June retrieves here is some aspect of an uncontaminated lesbian self.

What is unique about this bar scene is its staging of lesbianism within a context that is not subordinate to heterosexuality; but it is precisely this unbounded possibility of lesbian desire that is so problematic. This is the only scene in which lesbian eroticism is not mediated in some way by the phallus; it is therefore not coincidental that we do not see the women leave the bar and make love. Because the movie's primary interest is not lesbian libido per se but the triangulation of desire that lesbianism animates, female sexuality in *Henry and June* must necessarily be contained within a heterosexual context. This is not to say that desire between women does not exist but rather that lesbianism cannot exceed the bounds of heterosexual convention. As a result, what one finds in this movie is an obsession with phallic sexuality, even in scenes that appear to be privileging lesbian desire. A good example of this is the interval in which Anaïs has sex with Hugo but demands that he pretend to be "making love to [June], to her voluptuous body." As Hugo lies on top of her, Anaïs is distracted by thoughts of the other woman: "she's so perverse, so naked; tell her that you love her, possess her like a man." At this moment, Anaïs switches from an identification with June (as the object of masculine desire) to an identification with Hugo—"I want to fuck her like a man"—that resituates her in the position of the desiring subject. It is not surprising that Hugo finds this momentary usurpation disconcerting (he tries to silence her), but Anaïs quickly reverts back to an identification with June, crying out, "fuck her, Hugo!" What this scene makes clear is Anaïs's desire both to be and to possess June, a dual position that, despite its lesbian referent, is ultimately in the service of heterosexuality. Yet from Anaïs's point of view, the moment is subversive precisely because June initiates her desire.

As the narrative unfolds, what becomes more apparent about Anaïs is her investment in what one might call "transgressive heterosexuality." The movie contains multiple examples of copulation that are in some way illicit: Anaïs has sex with Henry several times while Hugo is nearby—but out of immediate earshot; the two lovers repeatedly have sex in public, in spots where they could easily be discovered—at a nightclub, in a garden, standing in an alley. All of these erotic interludes are exciting for Anaïs, but none arouses her desire as intensely as the carnival scene in which Hugo, his body painted bright blue and his face completely masked, in effect rapes her. While the viewer registers this scene as a violation, what it does for Anaïs is act as a stimulant, propelling her even more urgently into a search for unfamiliar sexual pleasures. Thus, at her instigation, they visit the same bordello Henry had visited earlier in the movie. Like Henry, Anaïs selects the June look-alike, as well as another dark-haired woman who is intended as a proxy for herself. As she and Hugo watch transfixed, the two women perform a lesbian "exhibition," parodying a heterosexual encounter in which one of the women simulates resistance while the other plays the aggressor.

Although the scene is expressly intended to exploit its voyeuristic possibilities, Anaïs's gaze undoes the gender opposition that aligns male spectatorship with mastery, for she herself is a desiring subject here. When at one point the blonde performer pauses to ask, "would you like anything else?" Anaïs responds by saying: "yes, stop making love like a man." Following this directive is a brief moment in which the woman appears to be taking off a harness, and then—almost too quickly to see what has transpired—a pink dildo flashes in the upper-left-hand corner of the screen. This moment is surprising not because the woman removes a dildo but because Anaïs objects to its presence; given the earlier scene in which Anaïs had reimagined herself with a phallus, it is perhaps surprising here to find her reject this prosthesis. Heather Findlay observes that, for many lesbians, the dildo's transgressive possibilities hinge on a downplaying of its referentiality—that is, denying that the instrument actually represents a penis.[41] In contrast, for Anaïs, the dildo here has no substitutive or transgressive function but operates instead to mark lesbianism as simulated heterosexuality. The simulacrum must be refused in order to make space for the unknown, and what is presumed to be more "authentic," lesbian lovemaking. Immediately following the removal of the dildo, June's proxy performs cunnilingus on the Anaïs-substitute, an action that makes visible what has up to now, for both Anaïs and the spectator, been unseen. But when the blonde looks up at Anaïs and invites her to participate, Anaïs refuses the offer, betraying her ambivalence and illustrating the movie's inability to imagine lesbian sexuality as anything other than imitation. This lesbian sex scene does not compel Anaïs to seek out a female lover; instead, we watch her seduce and have sex with her cousin Edouardo where she had earlier had sex with Henry. Once again, lesbianism's narrative function is to enhance the desirability of heterosexuality. Soon after this, Anaïs recounts a dream about June to Edouardo as the spectator watches the sequence unfold; we see the two women in bed together, naked to the waist, as June smokes a cigarette and they kiss. Anaïs recalls: "I asked her to let me see between her legs," and as June lays on top of her, she continues: "I felt a penis touching me." At this moment June remarks, "aren't you glad?" just before she metamorphoses into the bordello proxy, echoing the words that had earlier been said when Anaïs refused to join the exhibition: "commes vous voulez."

The dream is significant because it once again posits lesbianism in terms of simulated heterosexuality, subordinating same-sex desire to masculinity by reinscribing the primacy of the phallus. Edouardo's cautionary remark, "be careful Anaïs, abnormal pleasures kill the taste for normal ones," speaks directly to this anxiety that lesbian sexuality is merely a pretender of the "real" thing. That lesbianism must be mediated by heterosexuality is conveyed most explicitly in the anticlimactic scene in which June and Anaïs finally do go to bed together. In contrast to the many instances of explicit heterosexual coupling—and compared even to the voyeuristic lesbian exhibition—this soft-core sex scene is a massive disappointment in terms of lesbian visibility. Like every other scene of lesbian eroticism in the movie, this one is framed in terms of phallic intervention; thus, as the two women begin to make love, June expresses fear that Henry will overhear them, and the interlude ends with neither consummation nor resolution. The phantom phallus, invoked as a possible interlocutor, once again demonstrates that lesbian sexuality is unimaginable outside the triangulation of heterosexuality. In the end, Anaïs returns to her husband, proving that lesbianism has been merely a phase in her sexual odyssey. Following in the tradition of *Henry and June*, the recent low-budget *Chasing Amy* (1997) demonstrates that erotic triangles that feature beautiful young lesbians but privilege heterosexuality continue to be a preoccupying narrative. This film is objectionable for the way it repeatedly essentializes lesbian identity only to reveal at the end that its "lesbian" character, Alyssa (Joey Lauren Adams), has been bisexual all along. Although *Chasing Amy* does not explore the politics of bisexuality, it does confirm the view upheld by its most homophobic character, Banky (Jason Lee), that "all a woman wants is some serious deep dicking." More blatantly than any other recent film that invokes female homoeroticism, *Chasing Amy* illustrates that lesbianism is not only the best conduit to good heterosexual sex but can even facilitate male homoerotic desire.[42]

Desire Beyond the Closet

While today's mainstream cinematic lesbian is certainly a subject of heterosexual fantasy, what remains to be "seen" is whether or not her representation will ever intersect with a version of desire that is not based on a heterosexual model of specular mediation. That Hollywood is perhaps moving in this direction appears to be evidenced by *Bound* (1996), a noir thriller-comedy whose premise is that a lesbian couple joins together to outwit the Mob—provided that they can trust each other to carry out their scheme. Gina Gershon is Corky, a butch dyke ex-con who works as an apartment building "handywoman"; Jennifer Tilly plays her lover, Violet, a sultry, provocatively dressed femme who is also the moll of a high-strung Mafia money launderer named Caesar (Joe Pantoliano).[43] The pleasure of watching this movie is its self-conscious manipulation of noir and gender conventions, such as the scene in which Caesar literally handwashes and irons a large bundle of bloodstained money; but if the spectator is a lesbian, then the film provides additional layers of visual and semantic gratification. This is a commercial feature that, perhaps surprisingly—given that it was cowritten and codirected by two men (Larry and Andy Wachowski)—also exhibits repeated self-consciousness about the issue of lesbian visibility. *Bound* opens, literally, in a closet, where the first thing the viewer sees is a wardrobe full of stiletto-heeled shoes. The next shot is of a bound woman, Corky, from whose perspective much of the movie is narrated in flashback. The first sound we hear inside this closet is Violet's sexy voice—"I have this image of you, inside me, a part of me"—a reference to Corky, although the viewer does not register this until later, and a sign that this is yet another lesbian movie that will invoke the trope of identification. The use of the closet playfully illuminates the movie's interest in exploiting multiple layers of meaning: if you are a lesbian viewer, this enclosure already has a charged meaning, while the voice-over (the final phrase that Violet utters is "I want out") signals that this is a narrative that intends to invert the dynamic of lesbian invisibility. The two women's initial meeting is in another enclosed space, an elevator; there, unbeknownst to Caesar, who is also present, they exchange conspicuous, lingering looks. Caesar's inability to detect the women's mutual attraction here is but one example of the movie's self-consciousness regarding the problem of articulating lesbian subjectivity. Soon after this visual interchange, Violet plays the role of a helpless housewife who has lost her earring down the drain, calling Corky to come to her aid; here, the scene borders on lesbian camp as we watch the camera linger in slow-motion on Corky's grease-stained hand, unscrewing the kitchen pipes, as Violet stands poised beside her in a skintight cocktail dress.[44] The scene is both serious—because it is loaded with sexual suggestiveness—and funny—because its tongue-in-cheek parody of the heterosexual scenario invites the lesbian spectator to participate in its critique of gender asymmetry. In particular, Violet's excessive flaunting of femininity foregrounds her performance as parody, for the movie ultimately demonstrates that it is the seemingly helpless femme, rather than the butch Corky, who masterminds the plot to steal the Mob's money. Violet begins her seduction of Corky by fondling her labrys tattoo, a symbol whose queer significance is lost neither on Violet nor the lesbian spectator. As she sits on Corky's lap caressing her arm, Violet invites Corky to explore her own tattoo, which is conveniently located on her partially exposed breast. The seduction scene continues hot and heavy until it is interrupted by Caesar, who walks in unannounced, convinced that Violet has been "screwing someone" in the living room. Blind to the possibility that lesbianism might pose a sexual threat, Caesar relaxes once he registers that Corky is a woman, commenting to her, "you must be good with your hands" when he learns about her maintenance job.

For the lesbian viewer, this double entendre is funny because it reveals a sexual secret and exposes the relation between heterosexual privilege and lesbian invisibility; Caesar's fatal mistake throughout this movie is his inability to see that Violet has clearly fallen for another woman. The women eventually do have sex following this interruption in an interlude that is not only sexy but manages to dodge the standard scenario in which lesbian eroticism is only a prelude to heterosexual sex. The lovemaking scene "works" for the lesbian spectator largely because the movie is so self-conscious about how its own cinematic operations intersect with the issue of lesbian visibility. And unlike the soft-focus, conventionally "romantic" depiction of love scenes in so many lesbian features, the sex in this movie clearly conveys that what draws the women together into their larcenous plot is lust.[45] Corky's remark the following day to Violet, "I can see again," can be read as an address to the lesbian audience, for whom the inscription of lesbian visibility remains such a central concern. By calling attention to the question of what can be seen, *Bound* situates itself in a very different position, vis-à-vis the issue of lesbian representation and spectatorship, than the movies I examined earlier. Unlike those movies, this film acknowledges that heterosexuality is the dominant code, fully registering that lesbians are inextricably bound up with that discourse.

Yet, despite its many pleasures, the danger of this movie is in believing that the film's in-jokes about handheld "power tools" signify anything revolutionary about lesbian subjectivity. In the end, the pleasure of the tongue-in-cheek performances by Gershon and Tilly does not make up for the movie's emotional vacuity; the women's relationship is about as authentic as Sharon Stone's commitment to her girlfriend Leilani Sarelle in *Basic Instinct.* To the extent that this is a movie preoccupied with surfaces, one can dismiss it as just one more commercial feature interested in exploiting the trendiness of beautiful dykes. To do so, however, would be to miss the movie's attempt to carve out a different spectatorial position by locating itself in the space between what can and cannot be seen.[46] This, for the lesbian viewer, is what separates *Bound* from the other commercially viable features about lesbians; despite its limitations, this film does subvert the dominant paradigm, in which lesbian desire is possible only through heterosexual mediation. In this feminist revenge fantasy, the lesbian couple gets to escape the closet, have great sex, run off together—with the money—and not die in the end. Ultimately, however, the movie is unable to move beyond a model of lesbian desire that is defined outside of identification. Sitting in her red getaway truck in the final frame, Corky asks Violet: "do you know the difference between you and me?" Violet's answer, "no," prompts Corky to respond, "neither do I," thereby illustrating once again that, in the popular imagination, lesbian sexuality is incompatible with the idea of difference. What remains conspicuously absent in the realm of mass-entertainment lesbian features is a representation of lesbian subjectivity that does not subsume desire into identification but allows images of difference to circulate concurrently with the visibility of same-sex desire.

Notes

I am grateful to Mary Pat Brady, Kate McCullough, and especially Karen Jacobs, each of whom generously read and commented on earlier drafts of this essay. All dialogue quoted in this essay, unless otherwise indicated, comes from notes I made while viewing the television shows and films in question.

1. Following a storm of media attention, Ellen's coming out, titled "The Puppy Episode," aired 30 April 1997 (during May sweeps month), featuring cameos by Melissa Etheridge, k.d. lang, Laura Dern, Demi Moore, Dwight

Yoakam, Billy Bob Thornton, and Oprah Winfrey. Across the country, thousands of people celebrated the event with "Coming Out with Ellen" home-party kits supplied by the Gay and Lesbian Alliance Against Defamation. The hour-long episode, watched by 36.2 million viewers, was carried by 224 of the 225 stations in the ABC network; only the Birmingham, Alabama, affiliate (WBMA) declined to broadcast the show on the grounds that it was inappropriate family viewing. Despite conservative opposition, Al Gore applauded the sitcom for demonstrating that Ellen the perceived heterosexual was not all that different from Ellen the lesbian. The simultaneous coming out of the show's eponymous star, Ellen DeGeneres—highlighted by the 14 April 1997 *Time* cover story, "Yep, I'm Gay"—further fueled the hype surrounding the sitcom's big event. In a series of media moves that appeared to validate the openness of *Ellen*, the program's star was singled out as "Entertainer of the Year" by *Entertainment Weekly* (26 Dec. 1997) and was named one of *People* magazine's "Twenty-five Most Intriguing *People* of the Year" (29 Dec. 1997). Barbara Walters named DeGeneres one of the "Ten Most Fascinating People of 1997" on her ABC special (2 Dec. 1997), and *Vanity Fair* inducted the star into its "Hall of Fame" (Dec. 1997)—complete with a sexy photo spread by Annie Leibovitz. Most recently, *Ms.* magazine named DeGeneres one of their thirteen "Women of the Year" (Jan.–Feb. 1998).

2. A thorough analysis of *Ellen* requires more attention than I can offer in the space provided here. On the 19 November 1997 episode, Emma Thompson played a lesbian whose dark secret was not that she was gay but that she was a closeted American from Dayton, Ohio. The Southern Baptist Convention boycotted Disney (ABC is an affiliate) in large part because of Ellen's coming out. The highly controversial, on-again, off-again "parental warning" was denounced by several critics, including DeGeneres, for its double standard. (Six of the season's twenty-one episodes carried the advisory.) For example, the advisory appeared before the episode in which a humorous same-sex kiss was exchanged between Ellen and her best friend Paige (Joely Fisher), even though ABC's *Spin City* featured a similar comedic kiss between Mike (Michael J. Fox) and Carter (Michael Boatman) without any such warning. Similarly, the episode in which Ellen and her girlfriend Laurie (Lisa Darr) are shown walking into the bedroom carried the parental warning, while NBC's *Mad about You* showed its lesbian couple—Joan (Suzie Plakson) and Debbie (Robin Bartlett)—in bed together several times during the 28 October 1997 episode with no advisory. In an interview with Diane Sawyer on *PrimeTime Live* (6 May 1998), DeGeneres argued that the advisory's double standard was due to the fact that she herself is gay—unlike other television actors who merely simulate homosexuality. Although the president of ABC, Richard Iger, claimed to Sawyer that the fact that DeGeneres is lesbian "had absolutely nothing" to do with the network's decision to cancel her sitcom, he simultaneously betrayed the dis-

ingenuousness of this position by admitting that the star's "inner passion" for gay rights—in particular her refusal to "slow down" her character's overt lesbianism—is ultimately what killed the show.

3. The mainstream view that since *Ellen* began to foreground its lesbian content it has been a "bomb creatively"—as television critic Joanne Ostrow (*Denver Post,* 10 Mar. 1998, E-1) puts it—suggests two things: either a straight audience has been unable to read its gay humor (e.g., inside jokes to the Michigan Wymen's Music Festival, the Dinah Shore Open), or mainstream viewers simply do not want to watch a show that focuses on the experiences of a homosexual character. The view that *Ellen* was "too gay" was interrogated by Diane Sawyer in her "Ellen Uncensored" interview. That same week, the topic was also foregrounded by *Entertainment Weekly,* which put DeGeneres on its cover with the caption, "Yep, She's Too Gay" (8 May 1998). For some lesbian and gay viewers, the fear is that the fate of the sitcom (which averaged an audience of 12.4 million) will be seen as a referendum on homosexuality. For DeGeneres's candid account of what happened to her sitcom, see the BRAVO documentary *The Red Ellen,* which first aired on cable television during the summer of 1998.

4. Valerie Traub's question "What is a 'lesbian'?" speaks to the heart of this issue: "Whatever a 'lesbian' 'is' is constantly negotiated—a matter of conflicting and contradictory investments and agendas, desires and wills. . . . The terms by which 'lesbian' is interpreted, and thus given cultural meaning and presence, alter in relation to the shifting fortunes of gender ideologies and conflicts, erotic techniques and disciplines, movement politics, fashion and consumer trends, media representations, and paradigms of mental illness and physical disease—to name just a very few" ("The Ambiguities of 'Lesbian' Viewing Pleasure: The [Dis]articulations of 'Black Widow,'" in *Out in Culture: Gay, Lesbian, and Queer Essays on Popular Culture,* ed. Corey K. Creekmur and Alexander Doty [Durham, N.C.: Duke University Press, 1995], 115–36, quote on 115).

5. The question "What Is a 'Lesbian Film'?" that launches Yvonne Tasker's essay "Pussy Galore" underscores the central issue that lesbian film theorists are grappling with at this critical juncture in the attempt to categorize, classify, and determine the parameters of what constitutes the lesbian cinematic image. See "Pussy Galore: Lesbian Images and Lesbian Desire in the Popular Cinema," in *The Good, the Bad, and the Gorgeous: Popular Culture's Romance with Lesbianism,* ed. Diane Hamer and Belinda Budge (London: Pandora, 1995), 172–83 (subsequent references to this work will be included parenthetically in the text). While there is no unified perspective on what qualifies as "lesbian" cinematic representation, the "primal question" (as Tamsin Wilton puts it) of how to define a lesbian film informs the introductory chapters in *Immortal Invisible: Lesbians and the Moving Image,* ed. Tamsin Wilton (New York: Rout-

ledge, 1995), and *A Queer Romance: Lesbians, Gay Men, and Popular Culture,* ed. Paul Burston and Colin Richardson (New York: Routledge, 1995). Subsequent references to Wilton's *Immortal Invisible* will be included parenthetically in the text.

6. Cited in *Immortal Invisible,* ed. Wilton, 4. For a discussion of Barbara Hammer, see Richard Dyer, "Lesbian/Woman: Lesbian Cultural Feminist Film," *Now You See It: Studies on Lesbian and Gay Film* (London: Routledge, 1990), 174–210. Liz Kotz also discusses the experimental filmmaker in "Anything but Idyllic: Lesbian Filmmaking in the 1980s and 1990s," in *Sisters, Sexperts, Queers: Beyond the Lesbian Nation,* ed. Arlene Stein (New York: Plume, 1993), 67–80.

7. See also Penny Florence, "Lesbian Cinema, Women's Cinema," in *Outwrite: Lesbianism and Popular Culture,* ed. Gabriele Griffin (Boulder, Colo.: Pluto Press, 1993), 126–47. Ros Jennings writes about lesbian spectatorship and the Sigourney Weaver character, Ripley, in "Desire and Design—Ripley Undressed," in *Immortal Invisible,* ed. Wilton, 193–206.

8. Of course, since the release of *Claire of the Moon,* there has been a small explosion of lesbian-themed romantic features such as Christine Vachon's *Go Fish* (1994), Marita Giovanni's *Bar Girls* (1995), Maria Maggenti's *Incredibly True Adventure of Two Girls in Love* (1995), Patricia Rozema's *When Night Is Falling* (1996), and Cheryl Dunye's *Watermelon Woman* (1996). While I do not mean to suggest that *Claire of the Moon* is the measure by which lesbian films are to be judged, my experience has been that the movie functions as a kind of Rorschach test among lesbians. A good example of the disparate range of emotions that this movie has elicited is the reaction of two critics, Cherry Smyth, who calls it "the turkey of independent features," and Judith M. Redding, who gives *Claire of the Moon* the highest rating. For Redding's review, see "Sapphic Screen-O-Meter," *Deneuve,* July–Aug. 1995, 15. Smyth's comment appears in "Beyond Queer Cinema: It's in Her Kiss," in *Daring to Dissent: Lesbian Culture from Margin to Mainstream,* ed. Liz Gibbs (London: Cassell, 1994), 195. In general, however, the relative silence on the part of lesbian academics has been striking, particularly given the passionate responses that *Claire of the Moon* has generated among lesbian audiences.

In contrast, two earlier lesbian romance films, John Sayles's low-budget *Lianna* (1983) and Donna Deitch's commercial hit *Desert Hearts* (1985), have received some critical attention. See Jackie Stacey, " 'If You Don't Play You Can't Win': *Desert Hearts* and the Lesbian Romance Film," in *Immortal Invisible,* ed. Wilton, 92–114. Mandy Merck devotes a chapter to *Lianna,* in *Perversions: Deviant Readings* (New York: Routledge, 1993), 162–76. Judith Roof discusses her disaffection for both *Lianna* and *Desert Hearts,* arguing that neither film ever "exceeds the bounds of familiar heterosexual activity" despite the seemingly explicit rendering of lesbian sex ("View to a Thrill," *A Lure of Knowledge: Lesbian Sexuality and Theory* [New York: Columbia University Press, 1991], 14–

89; subsequent references to this work will be included parenthetically in the text). For a popular overview of new and recent films by lesbian filmmakers, see Abramowitz's "Girl Gets Girl," *Premiere*, Feb. 1996, 81–85, 95–97, and "Dyke Directors," *Girlfriends*, Nov.–Dec. 1994, 20–21, 44.

That the *Claire of the Moon* school of lesbian sensibility has not been completely superseded is evidenced by Conn's latest venture, a short video entitled *Cynara, Poetry in Motion* (1996), and Sharon Pollack's *Everything Relative* (1996). Set in 1883, *Cynara* is a melodramatic period piece that sets out to merge lesbian romance with erotica; the result is an abysmally clichéd film that is, dare I say it, even more painful than *Claire of the Moon*. (At least this film lasts only thirty-four minutes.) Less disappointing but still problematic is *Everything Relative*, a kind of modern-day lesbian *Big Chill*. The dialogue of this "womyn's" movie, shown in 1996 at the San Francisco Gay and Lesbian Film Festival, has a 1970s cultural-feminist feel to it—quite a regressive switch, I would argue, from the fresh, witty, self-conscious representation of contemporary dyke life in *Go Fish*.

9. Lynda Hart devotes separate chapters to the lesbian content of *Single White Female* and *Basic Instinct* in *Fatal Women: Lesbian Sexuality and the Mark of Aggression* (Princeton, N.J.: Princeton University Press, 1994). renée c. hoogland reads the lesbian in *Basic Instinct* as an aspiring straight male in *"Basic Instinct:* The Lesbian Spectre as Castrating Agent," *Lesbian Configurations* (New York: Columbia University Press, 1997), 24–42. Although, as Hart observes, there has been a recent proliferation of films depicting lesbian and bisexual women as predatory murderers, I would also suggest that a very different kind of lesbian-as-killer movie is currently in circulation. Three such releases— *Heavenly Creatures* (New Zealand, 1994), *Butterfly Kiss* (Britain, 1994), and *Sister My Sister* (Britain, 1995)—sensitively explore the intersection of violence and passion between women. Space does not permit an elaborate reading of these films here, but I would argue that, in contrast to the mainstream movies that Hart denounces, these art films are beautifully shot, intelligently rendered, and nonhomophobic interrogations of the relation between lesbian desire and murderous impulses. Notably, none of these movies is an American production.

10. The cover of the 10 May 1993 issue of *New York* magazine featured the lesbian icon k.d. lang staring directly into the reader's eyes above the headline "Lesbian Chic: The Bold, Brave New World of Gay Women." Danae Clark discusses lesbians as both objects of the advertising industry and as consumers of popular culture in "Commodity Lesbianism," in *Out in Culture*, ed. Creekmur and Doty, 484–500. For another analysis of mainstream women's magazines and lesbian visual pleasure, see Reina Lewis, "Looking Good: The Lesbian Gaze and Fashion Imagery," *Feminist Review* 55 (Spring 1997): 92–109. For those who think that lesbian chic is on the wane, the publication of the following

books should confirm that the trend is still with us: Helen Eisenbach, *Lesbianism Made Easy* (New York: Crown, 1996); Shelley Roberts, *Roberts' Rules of Lesbian Living* (Duluth, Minn.: Spinsters Ink, 1996); Liz Tracey and Sydney Pokorny, *So You Want to Be a Lesbian?* (New York: St. Martin's/Griffin, 1996).

11. Alexis Jetter, "Goodbye to the Last Taboo," *Vogue*, July 1993, 86–88, 92. A. J. Jacobs, "To Be or Not to Be?" *Entertainment Weekly*, 4 Oct. 1996, 19–25 (subsequent references to this work will be included parenthetically in the text), examines primetime network's representation of homosexuality. Jacobs includes a poll that asked 1,003 Americans, "Would you be personally offended if a lead character on a TV program were gay?" Although 23 percent of those polled said "yes," an impressive 72 percent answered "no." Yet, of this polling sample, only 15 percent believed that the lead character on *Ellen* is a lesbian, a fact that perhaps explains in part why the mainstream audience eventually rejected the show.

12. Of course, the image reads differently from the perspective of a lesbian viewer. Whereas eroticized pleasure for a straight male has arguably to do with the objectification of the female body, from the lesbian spectator's perspective, the sexualized image of k.d. lang and Cindy Crawford can be said to fuel both an identificatory and a proprietary fantasy. In other words, for the lesbian reader of *Vanity Fair*, what one wants is not only to be k.d. lang (or Cindy Crawford) but to have that object of desire. For another discussion of the lesbian gaze and fashion magazines, see Reina Lewis and Katrina Rolley, "Ad(dressing) the Dyke: Lesbian Looks and Lesbians Looking," in *Outlooks: Lesbian and Gay Sexualities and Visual Cultures*, ed. Peter Horne and Reina Lewis (New York: Routledge, 1996), 178–90.

13. Roseanne Kennedy refers to the kiss as "restrained to the point of being asexual" ("The Gorgeous Lesbian in 'LA Law': The Present Absence?" in *The Good, the Bad, and the Gorgeous*, ed. Hamer and Budge, 132–41, quote on 133).

14. According to the Gay and Lesbian Alliance Against Defamation's *GLAADAlert*, 15 Oct. 1997, a radical religious group attempted to stuff the electronic ballot box during the polling period. While the answer was strongly affirmative throughout the voting period, the final tally—even with the homophobic ploy to "fix" the election—was 69 percent who voted "yes" and just under 33 percent who voted "no," out of 15,000 polled.

15. Rhonda was what I would call a television first, a smart, hip, sexy, vulnerable Jewish dyke whose sexual orientation was not pathologized in any way but was instead represented as matter of fact. It is refreshing that *Relativity* did not stage the traditional coming-out scene but instead began by narrating Rhonda's complicated breakup with her girlfriend of two years, Sylvie. Moreover, several attempts were made on the show to illustrate parallels between Rhonda's romantic longings and those of her straight peers. While this "normalizing" of lesbian desire is a welcome shift, the episode (11 Jan. 1997) in

which Rhonda's lesbian kiss occurs is not without its problems. The program opens with the main characters, Leo and Isabel, enjoying an extended and (for television) explicit scene of soft-core sex; a Los Angeles earthquake occurs in the midst of all this passion, and the couple assumes that it is their amazing lovemaking that has instigated the giant quake. In contrast to this, the lesbian kiss between Rhonda and her new girlfriend is extremely tame, and the context in which it occurs is problematic. The two women sit inside an earthquake simulator as the new girlfriend, a Cal Tech graduate student in seismology, regulates the intensity of the tremor for Rhonda—who is terrified of quakes. The catalyst for the kiss is a huge simulated tremor, a fact that inevitably situates lesbianism in the position of the simulacrum. Whereas the straight couple's passion is equated with the intensity of a "real" earthquake, for the lesbian couple, desire is only a form of simulation, something expressed through a virtual medium. For a discussion of Rhonda Roth and the actress, Lisa Edelstein, who played her on the television program, see Katie Sanborn, "The Lesbian Theory of *Relativity*," *Curve*, Oct.–Nov. 1996, 24–26.

16. In the dramatization of the Sharon Bottoms custody battle, Valerie Bertinelli's character exchanges a brief kiss with her girlfriend early in the movie; in *Margarethe Cammermeyer*, Glenn Close and Judy Davis do not kiss until almost the end of the story, despite several earlier "romantic" scenes that establish that the women are physically intimate. Even when the couple finally does kiss, this event (which is filmed from a side-view perspective) is partially occluded by Glenn Close's hand, which covers over the women's mouths. The dialogue between Close's character and a male army officer during her security clearance epitomizes the movie's desire not to make lesbian sexuality an issue. Cammermeyer is here asked if she has "ever engaged in immoral activity"; she responds "no," then counters with a question: "what's immoral activity?" When the officer reads her a laundry list of army taboos that includes homosexuality, she confesses that she's a lesbian, thus prompting the officer to ask her whether she's "an active lesbian." Cammermeyer responds that she "connects emotionally to women," claiming that "it doesn't have anything to do with sexual activity," even though the viewer already knows that it is her sexual involvement with another woman that has prompted this confessional moment. When the officer presses her by asking, "then what makes you a lesbian?" Cammermeyer responds by emphasizing the emotional and suppressing any traces of the erotic: "my feelings, it's more about myself; it's who I am."

17. The staging of lesbian passion in terms of a mother-daughter dyad is not news, but the movie does waffle on how it wants readers to interpret this structural frame. Early on, Chase proposes to her family and Elizabeth that they "play the Ramsays," a reference to Virginia Woolf's novel *To the Lighthouse* that Richard misses (because, as his wife points out, he's a "literary ignoramus") and Elizabeth comprehends. Chase adopts the role of Mrs. Ramsay

and assigns Elizabeth to be Lily, thus drawing a parallel between the novel's homoerotic elements (e.g., Lily's longing for Mrs. Ramsay; Mrs. Ramsay's solitary, masturbatory moments) and the women's own relationship. This allusion is repeatedly signaled throughout the film as the camera lingers intermittently on a lighthouse shining at night, recalling Mrs. Ramsay's sexually charged response to her own lighthouse beam. Yet, while the novel privileges the daughter's desire for the mother, *Losing Chase* stages the mutual longings of the two women even as it foregrounds the mother's erotic awakening. Elizabeth's interest in Chase is clearly fueled by her problematic relation to her own mother, who (like Chase) had a nervous breakdown and (unlike Chase) committed suicide. But at one critical point in the movie, when Elizabeth—in a flashback—confuses Chase with her dead mother, Chase refuses the Oedipal conflation, clearly stating not once but twice, "I'm not your mother."

For a discussion of the relation between lesbianism and maternity within classic psychoanalytic narratives of female homosexuality, see chapter 4 of Teresa de Lauretis's *Practice of Love: Lesbian Sexuality and Perverse Desire* (Bloomington: Indiana University Press, 1994), 149–202. For a film analysis of lesbianism within the context of mother-love, see Lizzie Thynne, "The Space Between: Daughters and Lovers in 'Anne Trister,'" in *Immortal Invisible,* ed. Wilton, 131–42. The most recent attempt to situate lesbianism in relation to the maternal occurs in the 1998 HBO movie *Gia* about the lesbian-junkie-supermodel Gia Carangi (played by Angelina Jolie).

18. See Burston and Richardson, *A Queer Romance;* Creekmur and Doty, *Out in Culture;* Hamer and Budge, *The Good, the Bad, and the Gorgeous;* Griffin, *Outwrite;* and Wilton, *Immortal Invisible.*

19. For a similar sentiment, see Frank Bruni, "It May Be a Closet Door, but It's Already Open," *New York Times,* 13 Oct. 1996, 1, 40.

20. Laura Cottingham problematizes the issue of lesbian visibility, focusing on popular culture, in *Lesbians Are So Chic . . . That We Are Not Really Lesbians at All* (London: Cassell, 1996).

21. It is crucial to recognize, as Arlene Stein observes, that, "generally speaking, the 'new lesbian' face peeking through today's mass culture is young, white, and alluring, fiercely independent, and nearly free of the anger that typed her predecessors as shrill and humorless" ("All Dressed Up, but No Place to Go? Style Wars and the New Lesbianism," in *Out in Culture,* ed. Creekmur and Doty, 476–83, quote on 477).

22. See Barbara Kantrowitz, "Gay Families Come Out," *Newsweek,* 4 Nov. 1996, 56.

23. Helen Eisenbach, "If the Plot Is Girl Meets Girl, Is That Enough?" *New York Times,* 10 Nov. 1996, 10. While the gay press is overwhelmingly better about reporting crimes against gays and lesbians than is the mainstream media, the news program *20/20* did air a segment entitled "Mom, I'm a Lesbian"

(27 Sept. 1996) that attempted to address the issue of violence against lesbians. The program recounted the story of a teenager, Lynn Doff, who was locked up in the Rivendel psychiatric facility near Salt Lake City by her own mother, allegedly for the treatment of disruptive behavior but in fact because the daughter exhibited "homosexual tendencies." Although the segment was constructed as a sympathetic portrayal of the trauma sustained by this teenage girl, Barbara Walters's wrap-up statement—"homosexuality is a condition you are born with"—merely served to repathologize the lesbian body.

24. See de Lauretis *Practice of Love*, Roof, *Lure of Knowledge*, and Wilton, *Immortal Invisible*. Caroline Evans and Lorraine Gamman also discuss the lesbian gaze in "The Gaze Revisited; or, Reviewing Queer Viewing," in *A Queer Romance*, ed. Burston and Richardson, 13–56. Subsequent references to this work will be included parenthetically in the text.

25. Laura Mulvey's much-cited psychoanalytic perspective in "Visual Pleasure and Narrative Cinema," *Screen* 16:3 (1975): 6–18, formulates the gaze as gendered and discusses the pleasure of the male spectator. A more recent article by Mulvey, while adhering to the idea of the gaze as gendered (i.e., male), nevertheless asks whether or not something different happens when women look at classic narrative cinema. See "Afterthoughts on 'Visual Pleasure and Narrative Cinema,'" *Visual and Other Pleasures* (Bloomington: Indiana University Press, 1989), 29–38. As Lewis and Rolley argue in "Ad(dressing) the Dyke": "there is no room in Mulvey's formulation for a woman to make an active identification as female let alone to actively desire a woman from a female perspective" (182).

26. For additional gay and lesbian responses to Mulvey's framework that extend the parameters of the discussion about gendered spectatorship to include questions about identity politics, see Cherry Smyth, "The Transgressive Sexual Subject," in *A Queer Romance*, ed. Burston and Richardson, 123–43. Also in the same volume, see Steven Drukman, "The Gay Gaze; or, Why I Want My MTV," 81–95.

27. Critiquing what they call "the fixity of Mulvey's analysis," Evans and Gamman write: "Although we would argue against the idea of an essentially gay or lesbian gaze, we do not want to make the case for the 'queer gaze' either. Rather, we want to make the case for identifications which are multiple, contradictory, shifting, oscillating, inconsistent and fluid" ("Gaze Revisited," 45). Judith Roof's phrase "oscillating identifications" provides another way of theorizing the lesbian spectator without reinstating her as male-identified (*Lure of Knowledge*, 36).

28. Teresa de Lauretis foregrounds the question of lesbian desire, contrasting it to simple narcissistic identification, in "Film and the Visible," in *How Do I Look? Queer Film and Video*, ed. Bad Object Choices (Seattle: Bay Press, 1991), 223–76 (subsequent references to this work will be included parenthetically in

the text). For another discussion of the "fundamental indissociability of identification and desire" and its relation to gendered spectatorial positions, see
Diana Fuss, *Identification Papers* (New York: Routledge, 1995), 12.

29. Carol Clover, "Her Body, Himself: Gender in the Slasher Film," *Representations* 20 (Fall 1987): 187–228.

30. Lewis and Rolley discuss the possibilities for the lesbian spectator within
the conventions of psychoanalytic theory and also provide an alternative
model based on the "shifting spectatorship" of the lesbian gaze ("Ad[dressing]
the Dyke," 181–84).

31. Although I am well aware of the fact that Catherine Trammell is bisexual, I have chosen to refer to her (as well as the other characters who could
qualify as bisexual here) as a lesbian on the grounds that, for the purposes of
my argument, it is this aspect of her sexuality that is most salient. Judith
Halberstam's reading of *Basic Instinct* brings to mind a line from the 1968
British movie *The Killing of Sister George,* in which one character says, "Not all
girls are raving bloody lesbians, you know," and another responds, "That is a
misfortune that I am perfectly well aware of." Halberstam's claim that she
"would rather see lesbians depicted as outlaws and destroyers than cozy, feminine, domestic, tame lovers" does not invite consensus, but her observations
speak to the heart of what I am trying to argue here: that "positive" portrayals
of mainstream lesbians never intersect with explicit representations of female
sexuality. Halberstam interprets the queer protest against *Basic Instinct* as misguided, arguing instead that the film is really about "the objectification of
men . . . [and] the 'lesbianization' of straight sex" (review in *The Ultimate Guide
to Lesbian and Gay Film and Video,* ed. Jenni Olson [New York: Serpent's Tail,
1996], 30–32, quote on 31). Catherine Trammell is perhaps a psychopath, but
she is also powerful, hot, beautiful, and utterly in control of her own sexuality—both homo- and heterosexual. In contrast to Halberstam, who reads all of
the women in *Basic Instinct*—plus Michael Douglas—as lesbians, Lynda Hart
claims in *Fatal Women* that there are no lesbians in *Basic Instinct,* thus inval-
idating the assumption that the movie is homophobic (134).

32. Judith Roof, *Come as You Are: Sexuality and Narrative* (New York: Columbia University Press, 1996), xxviii.

33. Chris Straayer, "The Hypothetical Lesbian Heroine in Narrative Feature
Film," in *Out in Culture,* ed. Creekmur and Doty, 56.

34. On the issue of lesbian erasure, an interesting postscript to the American
distribution of *Three of Hearts* is offered by Raymond Murray: "Before the film
was released on home video, store owners around the country were given the
unprecedented chance to change the film's ending. The two endings, in which
Baldwin gets the girl and other where he does not, amazingly left out the
option of Lynch getting the girl! The original theatrical (and much better, but

not best) ending was eventually chosen" (*Images in the Dark: An Encyclopedia of Gay and Lesbian Film and Video* [Philadelphia: TLA Publications, 1994], 368).

35. It is worth mentioning that, shortly after this movie was released, a gay male version of triangulation soon appeared, called *Threesome* (1994). In this film about a sexually confused college student, Eddy (played by Josh Charles), male homosexual desire is much more overt, both visually and verbally, than is lesbian desire in *Three of Hearts*, although the movie is certainly not devoid of problems. Despite Eddy's obvious crush on his straight roommate Stuart (Stephen Baldwin), for most of the film, he only has sex with women and rebuffs the advances of a gay student. During the climactic "threesome" sex scene (between the two men and their third roommate, Alex, played by Lara Flynn Boyle), the only explicitly homoerotic gesture is when Eddy, whom we understand to be a gay virgin, gingerly places his hand on Stuart's back. Although there are no overt expressions of sexual passion represented between the two men, the mere fact that the ménage à trois is staged for the viewer suggests that the depiction of male homoerotic desire is not as subject to erasure as is the repressed lesbian content of *Three of Hearts*.

36. The other important element at work in this film is the choice of Whoopie Goldberg as the lesbian character; intertextually speaking, Goldberg's lesbianism in *Boys on the Side* is, for the knowing viewer, informed by her portrayal of Miss Celie in *The Color Purple* and by her role as the medium Oda Mae in *Ghost*. The latter film contains a scene in which Oda Mae's black body functions as an intermediary for the reunion of a young white couple, Sam (Patrick Swayze), who has been murdered, and his bereaved wife, Molly (Demi Moore). Oda Mae surrenders her body to Sam, allowing him literally to merge with her in order to enable him to have a moment of physical contact with his wife, who is able neither to "see" nor hear his ghostly communications. Oda Mae grasps Molly's hands as the camera moves toward her face, where her eyes are, significantly, closed so as not to directly register that the erotic tension that builds for her occurs through the intercession of another woman. In the next instant, Sam's body is substituted for Oda Mae's; and when he kisses Molly, there remains no discernible trace of the black medium—except, of course, in the minds of lesbian viewers who have fully registered the erotic possibilities that this channeling situation presents. The simultaneous affirmation and denial of racial difference that this scene stages is recapitulated in Goldberg's portrayal in *Boys on the Side* of Jane, for whom blackness functions as both a marker of difference and a conspicuous absence. Similarly, the concomitant presentation and denial of lesbian possibility that Oda Mae's and Molly's bodies hold out is reflected in *Boys on the Side*, where Jane's and Robin's negotiation of desire remains "ghostly" throughout the film, discernible only through an interrelated series of mediated associations. Z. Isiling Nataf dis-

cusses *Ghost* within the context of a larger argument about race and lesbian visibility in "Black Lesbian Spectatorship," in *A Queer Romance,* ed. Burston and Richardson, 69–72.

37. For a discussion of lesbian sexuality within the context of soft-core pornography, see Roof, *Lure of Knowledge,* 15–37.

38. For a psychoanalytic reading of the relation between lesbianism and the phallus, see Elizabeth Grosz, "Lesbian Fetishism?" *differences* 3:2 (Summer 1991): 38–54. In *The Practice of Love,* de Lauretis also discusses the significance of the phallus, arguing that "to reject it altogether or to refuse to rethink its terms is to leave the lesbian subject without symbolic means to signify desire" (202). For an additional discussion of the phallus within a cinematic context, see Roof, "Coming Apart," *Come as You Are,* 93–97.

39. The original French *Diabolique* (1955) was based on Boileau and Narcejac's *La Femme qui E'tait,* a book whose premise is that the two women are lesbian lovers; the film, however, omitted any reference to the lesbian content. The closest that the French *Diabolique* comes to suggesting anything "perverse" in the women's relationship is a man's observation: "I may be old-fashioned, but I find that friendship of theirs revolting. The wife drying the tears of the mistress—really."

40. For a detailed analysis of the lesbian implications of this film, see B. Ruby Rich, "From Repressive Tolerance to Erotic Liberation: *Madchen in Uniform,*" in *Out in Culture,* ed. Creekmur and Doty, 137–66.

41. Heather Findlay, "Freud's 'Fetishism' and the Lesbian Dildo Debates," in *Out in Culture,* ed. Creekmur and Doty, 329.

42. To this extent, *Chasing Amy* supports Shameen Kabir's view that contemporary filmmakers, "feminist and otherwise, lesbians or not, have not broken adequately with the phallic frame of reference" ("Lesbian Representations in Film: Mermaids in the Desert . . . Must Be Seeing Things," in *Volcanoes and Pearl Divers: Essays in Lesbian Feminist Studies,* ed. Suzanne Raitt [New York: Harrington Park Press, 1995], 201–39, quote on 203). Arguably, an even more objectionable representation of triangulated desire appears in the 1998 thriller *Wild Things,* a soft-porn mainstream release that features a three-way sex scene between Sam (Matt Dillon), Suzie (Neve Campbell), and Kelly (Denise Richards). The sex scene is initiated by Sam, who asks the women to kiss, pushes their heads together, and then watches them go at it. This staged titillation between Richards and Campbell is later replayed during a steamy pool scene, which begins as a cat fight but then shifts into lovemaking. Although Sam is absent from this scene, it is still triangulated by a male figure; we watch the women engage in "lesbian" sex through the video camera of the detective (Kevin Bacon), a voyeuristic move that demonstrates, once again, that the representation of same-sex desire between women is only possible through mediation. Although the movie is filled with shifting triangular alliances, les-

bianism can only be sustained through the presence of a male gaze—either direct or technologically mediated.

43. Gershon's lesbianism in this movie is in stark contrast to her earlier portrayal of a lesbian character, Cristal, in the Paul Verhoeven/Joe Eszterhas bomb *Showgirls*. In this film, Gershon plays the star of a glitzy Las Vegas stage show, "Goddess," who, unlike Corky, has only a rivalrous flirtation with one of the other women, a stripper named Naomi (Elizabeth Berkley). For all of its promise of a lesbian subplot, *Showgirls* only illustrates, yet again, that the primary function of female homoeroticism in popular culture is to fuel male pornographic fantasies.

44. For a discussion of lesbian camp and femininity as performance, see Sue-Ellen Case, "Towards a Butch-Femme Aesthetic," *Discourse* 11:1 (Fall–Winter 1988–89): 55–73.

45. This is perhaps indebted to the fact that Susie Bright, the self-styled lesbian "sexpert," was a screenplay consultant to *Bound*. Stephen Holden, in "Hollywood, Sex and a Sad Estrangement," *New York Times*, 3 May 1998, argues that the love scenes between Gershon and Tilly are "among the hottest to be found in American film this decade," but he recognizes that lesbianism here still functions as "titillation for heterosexual male audiences" (39).

46. My argument here has been influenced by de Lauretis's essay "Film and the Visible," in which she reads Sheila McLaughlin's film *She Must Be Seeing Things* (1987) as a text that self-consciously engages the problem of representation, foregrounding the "complexity and difficulty of lesbian visibility" (255). While I do not want to suggest that *Bound* is as nuanced or sophisticated at sustaining the critique of "what can be seen and the relations of seeing" (228), I do believe that this mainstream movie is similarly attempting to foreground its frame of reference in a way that allows viewers to pose questions about spectatorship and its implications for lesbian visibility.

11

Undressing Crazy Jane: Queer Acts from Yeats to Hollywood and Mine

Joseph O. Aimone

Playing Queer

Why in the world would anyone want to do that?

I had come to consult a scholar fairly well known for her involvement in queer theory debates. A conference paper I had submitted had been turned down, but the panel organizer had asked me to perform as respondent on the panel, which was to address the "Straight with a Twist" theme. I wanted some advice from her about what to expect from this event, since I had only just begun to read queer theory about a year before in one of her seminars.

Her reply ("Why in the world . . .") surprised me. Was it not obvious? Did not the necessity of men thinking about feminism, the inevitability of whites thinking about antiracism, and so on, have their cognate forms in the need for the straight-identified to think about queer theory? Had I not been "doing" queer theory in her seminars, by the mere fact of participating in them, already? Or did she really wonder what my motives were, had been, all along? Was she asking what I stood to gain? Or what good it would do society (or queer society) for me, or any straight, to "play" at queer thinking? Might one assume I may be edified by the study of queer theory but could never contribute to it or even anything near it?

I am very suspicious of any "speaking for," even any "speaking for myself." To authenticate utterance is intractably difficult, certainly not solvable by means of identifying who is speaking. At a minimum, we must know (assuming we can at least temporarily put aside the difficulties of the term "know") what is being said, to whom, and in what tone of voice. Message, audience, and attitude are as important as identity, though identity is certainly indispensable to beginning interpretation. Certainly, the deflating question, "Why in the world would anyone want to do that?" covers with doubt the issues of identity, "anyone," and attitude, "why," while presuming message, "that," and leaving unspoken the name of the audience. And that silence rhetorically implies the nonexistence of any audience for messages of "that" sort and from such speakers.

So while the ethical imperatives of an approximately radical pluralism seem to suggest that I, or any other straight-identified thinker, might need to respect the possibility of the claims of queer theory, the blank unimaginability of any claims we might make in or even around that area leaves uncertain the merits of proceeding with any scholarly—or otherwise "public"—interrogation by me in this light.

Recognizing the blurry quandary of my position, I had to proceed unadvised, as it were, to comment on the papers presented at the conference. The odd thing was, all of them seemed to leave unanswered the polyvalent question my queer theory had made me brook. Some simply celebrated "catching" straights being queer. Some tried to universalize queer as a salient point of allegiance for all antihierarchic politics. Some naturally analyzed the appropriation of queer by the dominant culture. But none offered a motive for straights being queer that did not either undo their being straight or else undo their being queer. The discursive universe seemed unable to produce a conjunction of straightness with an absence of hostility to homosexuality.

And, oddly enough as well, the paper I had submitted, which had provoked the invitation to be respondent on the "straight" queer theory panel, seemed dogged with essentially the same question. Many writers have been "queered" in recent years, and certain theoretical views (most notably Eve Kosofsky Sedgwick's[1]) have implicitly "queered" straight identity itself by excavating its presumed foundations in an anxiety of loss of gender identity. But few readings have surfaced that at once identify straights voicing queer thoughts without also implicating those processes of voicing as either evidence of the suppression of queerness or part of the very mechanism of its suppression. Bluntly, nobody queers a text without queering the author or else "making" him or her as a "homophobe." Yet I had been trying to do just this, to queer William Butler Yeats without queering him.

And in trying to queer him without queering him, I was trying, as I am here, to queer myself without queering myself.

(Of course, it will always be possible to read my reticence to queer myself in the process of queering myself as either a repressive gesture or an attempt to co-opt queerness for the stability of straightness, no matter how I disclaim. And this parenthesis itself may reinforce the impression of my bad faith rather than exculpate me. It seems to me there is no way out of this problem. I can only take the risk of speaking with a certain blindness and hope for the best.)

In this essay, I present the substance of my argument to "queer" Yeats. But Yeats's case is not sufficiently similar to the case of the critic, myself, writing about him to allow exercise of the important issues of who can say what about what and to whom. For Yeats, if his text is indeed as queer as I make it, "passed," remained "in the closet," until now. But being "in the closet" may not be clearly inferior to "coming out." David Van Leer argues why within the purview of the queer-identified in *The Queening of America:* "Uncertain that sexual reticence [the reticence to reveal homosexuality] is necessarily a form of self-hatred, I treat 'the closet' and 'coming out' not as problem and solution, but more neutrally as two different strategies for dealing with the dominant culture."[2] But Van Leer's project, as a queer analysis per se, cannot say whether the possibility of coming out, once valorized and now seen more neutrally as only one option, would be more or less neutral for the straight writer who is queered without being queer. Such a project cannot imagine any answer to "Why in the world would anyone want to do that?" To imagine why, I find it necessary to consider both the straight found out as queer, while not queered (as in Yeats found out as queer by me but not queered himself) and the straight as deliberately self-queered, while not queer (as in myself self-queered while not queer). My analysis of the pop-genre film *To Wong Foo, Thanks for Everything! Julie Newmar*[3] makes it the example-text of the latter, with all the dangers I court in writing this essay writ large in the reception the film invites. In both cases, the use of playing queer is to smuggle back into play a kind of masculinity ruled out by the discursive assumption of the work in question. For Yeats, his early, repressed, lushly sensual and sensitive late Romantic masculinity returns in the guise of dragged-out drag queen; in the commercial pop film *To Wong Foo,* a masculine code ruled out by the presupposition of tolerance that the integration of drag queens into mainstream cinema implies reerupts as the code of "true" drag-queen behavior itself.

The Pink Angel

Queer things happen to the straightest people. Waiting on the curb, nose steaming gently into the night, she opened my door and paid the cabbie through the window as I climbed out into the gutter. Overhead, italic lettering is bracketed by downward-pointing triangles, all shown in pink neon: The Pink Angel. Movie title? No, that was *Pink Flamingos*. I jerked the brass club sticking from the door, but it opened inward; I pirouetted awkwardly into a blur of smoke, thinking: "This is not a pipe. Turkish. Cured in shit." Cowboy hats and college sweatshirts, punk safety pins and black-pearl-studded shirt fronts—even a wing collar—what a dump. She strode past me. The wings of her shoulder blades arched and folded under the black leather motorcycle jacket. My eye spiked by a gleam off her boot buckle, I glided into her wake. We sat. "Cointreau." Cointreau? She usually drank boiler-makers. I thought hard and called for Hennessy. Erect, the waitress swivelled off. (Backless gown—*very* backless.) Music erupted: gypsy stuff—major key, snatches of altered minors superimposed—not straight-ahead jazz. The spot came forward, lighting an explosion of hair around a green-eyed sneer, a perfect Greek nose. I itched but couldn't move, a pounding in my ears. An abrasive contralto taunted, aggressively sexy. My date leaned over the table, whispering floating words: "Isn't he wonderful?"

Undressing Crazy Jane

Like Gallimard in *M. Butterfly* or the IRA gunman Fergus in *The Crying Game,* I was shocked to discover the signs of my own blind desire. But I should not have been surprised entirely. Every actor that creates a woman's part impersonates a female. So does every writer. Yeats may have seen female impersonators on stage at the Abbey Theatre—Raymond Browne-Lecky played there in the late 1890s and early 1900s, and even hostile reviewers, according to Roger Baker's *Drag: A History of Female Impersonation on the Stage,* found him not "unconvincing."[4] The accompanying photo, I believe, vindicates that possibility. Yeats was well acquainted with the most celebrated textual transvestite of his day, William Sharp, alias Fiona Macleod. And Yeats, in a letter to Dorothy Wellesley, admired her poetry thus: "What makes your work so good is the masculine element allied to so much feminine charm—your lines have the magnificent swing of your boyish body. I wish I could be a girl of nineteen for certain hours that I might feel it more acutely."[5] His postscript to the same letter should re-

Crazy Jane, watercolor by Richard Dadd. Reproduced from Patricia Allderidge, *The Late Richard Dadd, 1817–1886* (London: Tate Gallery, 1974), 109 (pl. 151).

move any doubt about the reasonableness of at least looking for male homosexuals expressing femininity in the works of his mind: "Have you noticed that the greek androgynous statue is always the woman in the man, never the man in the woman? It was made for men who loved men first" (*Letters* 875). And that Crazy Jane in particular might be a transvestite is perhaps suggested by Yeats's experience, for an exhibition in London in 1913 of paintings by artists from Bedlam is conjectured to have included the watercolor *Crazy Jane* by Richard Dadd, reproduced in the Tate Gallery's *The Late Richard Dadd,* by Patricia Allderidge. A close look at the painting, even in the photographic reproduction, will unsettle any conviction that the figure represented is simply a female: as Allderidge's catalog notes, "the figure is obviously drawn from a male model."[6]

Of the Crazy Jane poems in "Words for Music Perhaps,"[7] "Crazy Jane Talks with the Bishop" has been the most popular for expatiating critics enamored of Crazy Jane's sharp tongue and her contrarian philosophy— two virtually stereotypic characteristics of theatrical female impersonations. But the textual suggestion that Crazy Jane may have homoerotics in mind is palpable to one prealerted by that risky suggestion: "A woman can be proud and stiff / When on love intent" (Yeats, *Variorum* 513). And what otherwise might seem merely a bit of Blakean metaphysics changes dramatically when so highlighted: "But Love has pitched his mansion in / The place of excrement" (513). Such a radically reoriented reading would tease out some differences from "Crazy Jane and the Bishop":

Bring me to the blasted oak
That I, midnight upon the stroke,
(*All find safety in the tomb.*)
May call down curses on his head,
Because of my dear Jack that's dead.
Coxcomb was the least he said:
The solid man and the coxcomb.

Nor was he Bishop when his ban
Banished Jack the Journeyman,
(*All find safety in the tomb.*)
Nor so much as parish priest,
Yet he, an old book in his fist,
Cried that we lived like beast and beast:
The solid man and the coxcomb.

> The Bishop has a skin, God knows,
> Wrinkled like the foot of a goose,
> (*All find safety in the tomb.*)
> Nor can he hide in holy black
> The heron's hunch upon his back,
> But a birch-tree stood my Jack:
> *The solid man and the coxcomb.*
>
> Jack had my virginity,
> And bids me to the oak, for he
> (*All find safety in the tomb.*)
> Wanders out into the night
> And there is shelter under it,
> But should that other come, I spit:
> *The solid man and the coxcomb.* (508–9)

Perhaps the coxcomb here is Crazy Jane, and the Bishop's remonstration exaggerates sodomy rather than mere heterosexual fornication into bestiality, as "beast and beast" are notably the same. The Bishop himself may be reduced to a symbol of phallic impotence, with his flaccid skin "wrinkled like the foot of a goose," and his own form hunched like the heron with neck unextended, unlike the erect "birch tree," Jack the Journeyman, who responds to "her." And what kind of journeyman is Jack? Perhaps, the term suggests, one of the gay sailors whose tales for which the Bishop does not care for and who tempts Jane to try "bestiality" like Europa in "Crazy Jane Reproved" (509).

Crazy Jane's secret is never fully revealed—she is "naked and hidden away," eschatology notwithstanding ("Crazy Jane on the Day of Judgment," *Variorum* 510). But we may have a clue to it in "Crazy Jane Grown Old Looks at the Dancers," where she longs equably to have "the limbs to try" either part: the male who strangles the female with the sign of her own fatal femininity, the mane of "coal-black hair"; or the female who fatally penetrates the male body with her hidden blade.

Yeats invented Crazy Jane in a manic period he described as "exultant," though he later wanted to exorcise her: ultimately, then, Yeats was ambivalent (*Variorum* 831). What are we to make of all this gender-bending by a major male poet? A happy androgynization of the phallogocentric voice? A misogynistic invasion of the Feminine Imaginary? A chance irruption of that vacant-eyed Necessary Angel of Deconstruction? A fugitive carnival act displaced from the Political Unconscious? (Possible—Yeats reprised

Raymond Browne-Lecky performed at the Abbey Theatre Dublin, in the late 1890s and early 1900s. Reproduced from Roger Baker, *Drag: A History of Female Impersonation on the Stage* (London: Triton, 1968), 128.

Crazy Jane in *On the Boiler,* ensconcing her with Cuchulain and "great bladdered Emer" [*Variorum* 628] to lament the fate of Ireland, and only Crazy Jane weeps.) What does this fan-dance in *The Winding Stair* signify?

I want to suggest a hypothesis, more than half serious, that Crazy Jane is something like the madwoman in Yeats's attic—the return of the repressed, specifically the return of a masculinity at work in Yeats's early poems in the decadent mode of the 1890s, one that he vigorously repressed to achieve the style of his middle period. The theoretical implications of this hypothesis are indeed troublesome: one assumes that the articulation of virtual genderings in the textual process of the poetry works in some sense the same way as does the articulation of gender in the life of the mind. Further, one assumes the explanatory model for the life of the mind—the broadly Freudian/Bloomian/Gilbert and Gubarian[8] narrative with which I am by no means entirely at ease. But, as with the basic interpretive point on which this paper is based—that one can see that Crazy Jane is a transvestite male homosexual—the proof will be in the plausibility of the picture once seen.

Crossways opens Yeats's poetic construction of masculinity. Yeats preserved and revised his first published poems as a matter of self-definition, claiming: "Every time I have reprinted them I have considered the leaving out of most, and then remembered an old school friend who has some of them by heart, for no better reason, as I think, than that they remind him of his own youth" (*Variorum* 841). He answered critics objecting to his revisions in a famous, untitled epigram that suggests these early poems do more than simply remind him:

> The friends that have it I do wrong
> When ever I remake a song,
> Should know what issue is at stake:
> It is myself that I remake. (778)

Yeats remakes the early poems, remaking the early Yeats, retroactively imposing a mold of prolepsis on the protean past.

The year he turned thirty, 1895, Yeats issued *Poems,* which collected the work of his previous two books: *The Wanderings of Oisin and Other Poems,* issued six years earlier; and *The Countess Cathleen and Various Legends and Lyrics,* issued three years earlier. In the new book, the long narrative of Oisin, much revised, and the drama of Cathleen were extracted and positioned separately from the lyrics, which remained divided in two sections:

one called "The Rose," reproducing with few changes the poems that had originally appeared with *Cathleen*; and one called "Crossways," reproducing the lyrics from *Oisin,* with major deletions—about half the poems as well as sections of poems preserved—and revisions. He described the composition of *Crossways* as a period when he took many directions before finding his true one, yet he preserved and revised these poems, feeling, as he said, "compelled to leave unchanged many lines he would have gladly re-written, because his present skill is not great enough to separate them from thoughts and expressions which seem to him worth preserving" (*Variorum* 845). Thus, he made *Crossways* a site of something indispensable (I hesitate to say essential) as well as a site of supplementation and repression.

Number 6 in the *Collected Poems* illustrates these three superimposed images. Here is the original version, "An Indian Song," reconstructed from the variorum edition:

Oh wanderer in the southern weather
Our isle awaits us; on each lea
The peahens dance in crimson feather
A parrot swaying on a tree,
Rages at his own image in the enamelled sea.

There dreamy Time lets fall his sickle
And Life the sandals of her fleetness,
And sleek young Joy is no more fickle,
And Love is kindly and deceitless,
And all is over save the murmur and the sweetness.

There we will moor our lonely ship
And wander ever with woven hands,
Murmuring softly, lip to lip,
Along the grass, along the sands—
Murmuring how far away are all earth's feverish lands:

How we alone of mortals are
Hid in the earth's most hidden part,
While grows our love an Indian star,
A meteor of the burning heart,
One with the waves that softly round us laugh and dart

Like swarming bees, one with the dove
That moans and sighs a hundred days;

—How when we die our shades will rove,
Dropping at eve in coral bays
A vapoury footfall on the ocean's sleepy blaze.

Compare the final revision, "The Indian to His Love":

The island dreams under the dawn
And great boughs drop tranquillity;
The peahens dance on a smooth lawn,
A parrot sways upon a tree,
Raging at his own image in the enamelled sea.

Here we will moor our lonely ship
And wander ever with woven hands,
Murmuring softly lip to lip,
Along the grass, along the sands,
Murmuring how far away are the unquiet lands:

How we alone of mortals are
Hid under quiet boughs apart,
While our love grows an Indian Star,
A meteor of the burning heart,
One with the tide that gleams, the wings that gleam and dart,

The heavy boughs, the burnished dove
The moans and sighs a hundred days:
How when we die our shades will rove,
When eve has hushed the feathered ways,
With vapoury footsole by the water's drowsy blaze.

The title shifts from "An Indian Song" to "The Indian to His Love." Note that the poet no longer considers this a set piece, openly generic, but instead a unique and possibly a definitive statement. Also note that he feels obligated to announce the nature of his speaker's relationship to the nominal audience, perhaps suggesting that this might not obviously seem a love poem without that announcement. The suppression of the second stanza, with its Keatsian capitalized personifications and the vague allusion to postcoital languor, where "all is over save the murmur and the sweetness," collaborates in the exclusion of explicit love compensated by the title. The revision of the first two lines elides the beloved in favor of the mystic place of satisfaction, which the now more confident speaker only longs for in the original but has already achieved in the revision, as the shift of adjective from "there" to "here" at the beginning of the following stanza indicates. The character of this place has changed also, though subtly, as the center of verbal action of the clause describing the parrot in the tree shifts from the emotional—the raging of the bird—to the pacific inanimate—the swaying motion of his seat. This new speaker is coolly imaginative, not passionately distracted—his word for the mundane world the lovers leave behind is the understated, cerebral "unquiet" rather than the visceral "feverish." He suppresses the hyperbolic precursor who would hide in "earth's most hidden part," hiding instead "under quiet boughs," just as he had substituted the restraint of the "smooth lawn" for the flamboyance of the "crimson feather" in stanza one. He suppresses the happy atonement of the lovers with a nature imagined as a community where waves "laugh." He substitutes for bucolic bees a dove that is "burnished"— as if artificial, clay or metal. Finally, as he describes the two lovers imagining themselves after death, he offers an evening ghost walk along the shore, erasing the image of spiritous footprints on the water found in the original—a much less sublime haunting. To sum up, the revised lover confidently eschews the sensual, the emotional, and the natural and oceanic in favor of the cerebral, the restrained, and the artificial and terrene.

These are two kinds of poet and two kinds of masculinity. If we subtract the repressions and the revisions, the residue is a boat trip by two lovers to the island, but what kind of man is it? Only the fact of desire remains, a desire for a permanent companion, "lip to lip" intimate—a desire Yeats would not give up. Later in his career, in 1912, Yeats would say: "I have not again retouched the lyric poems of my youth, fearing some stupidity in my middle years" (*Variorum* 848). And even later, in 1927, when he extensively revised other poems, saying, "one is always cutting out the dead wood" (848), he would leave these untouched. Perhaps these early revisions definitively accomplished something crucial for poetic masculinity, salvaging abandoned youth with manly redress.

But is this repressed masculinity the masculinity of Crazy Jane? Sensual, passionate—and bitter in old age—surely it seems possible to me, at any rate. And what are the implications of assuming this explanation—that Crazy Jane's homosexuality reflects the repression, that it is a symptom? That the early, sensuous, and decadent masculinity is already if not essentially a homosexual masculinity? Is it possible to do a straight reading of a gay figure, even if the figure is inscribed by a straight poet? Can a straight poet create a gay-affirmative figure—and one as acrid as Jane? And what does the long interval between her appearance in print and the recognition of the nature of her performance say about Yeats's readers?

Jane smuggles in a style of masculinity that Yeats had long edited out of his poetic persona. Whether he consciously worked Jane to represent his repressed affects is not clear; that Jane carries affects like the ones he repressed is. But the fact that Jane passed, that we experience an uncanny moment of surprise in seeing under her clothes, while capturing one side of the predicament of the straight writer writing queer as I am doing it now, does not capture the peculiar additional dimension of expectation I cannot escape: that I know I will be recognized (though perhaps doubted) to be what I am, straight writing queer. A little closer to this predicament is a bit of popular Hollywood film.

Imitations and Intimations:
Macho Drag Queen in *To Wong Foo, Thanks for Everything! Julie Newmar*

I have little stomach for realistic gore or high-tension movies and none for the theoretically interesting genres of hard-core porn. Serious film can interest me, but I often find myself preferring films that palpably offend the enlightened with conventionality or other mildly perverse pleasures. Such pedestrian taste is often apparently at odds with my intellectual preoccupations in philosophy, psychoanalysis, and literature. This difficulty is particularly trenchant when it comes to theorizing masculinity and to doing what I have recently heard called, half in jest, "straight man theory." Occasionally, a film or two procures a happy agreement in my nature.

Rob Epstein and Jeffrey Friedman's *The Celluloid Closet*[9] is a good example. The film offers a wide-ranging retrospective of clips from mainly popular, if sometimes serious, film—clips that demonstrate the recurring eruptions of homosexual characters, characterizations, topics, and topoi in one of the main fictions of twentieth-century American culture. Marlene Dietrich looks great in a tuxedo, and she kisses women as well as men (to the titillation of both). Stan Laurel and Oliver Hardy indulge in pillow talk: Oliver complains that his wife assumes he cares more about Stan than her, to which Stan replies, "you do, don't you?" Interviews are interlarded with the clips. We learn from Gore Vidal how Charlton Heston was kept in the dark about the intentional homoeroticization of his dialogue in *Ben Hur*, when Ben Hur's childhood friend Messala, now a Roman centurion, returns, and the two men engage in a spear-throwing contest. From the 1940s through the 1970s, the agon of representation, explicit and honest treatment of homosexuality, is excerpted in poignant highlights. And *The Celluloid Closet* closes on an optimistic, perhaps bromidic note, claiming that a new era of tolerance and serious treatment of queer subjects in film, mainstream film even, was initiated in the mid-1980s.

Indeed, queer is hot at the box office as well as in the seminar room: *The Crying Game; M. Butterfly; Torch Song Trilogy; Paris Is Burning; Priscilla, Queen of the Desert; Philadelphia; Le Cage aux Folles* (in both the original and the Robin Williams–as-secret-ingredient remake, *The Birdcage*). One film that might go in the foregoing, very incomplete list—and which did not do well with reviewers or at the box office—is Beeban Kidron's *To Wong Foo, Thanks for Everything! Julie Newmar.*

A typical review: "The film promotes stereotypes about so-called 'typical' gay lifestyles, and in the process unfairly denigrates the liberating potential of drag as a satirical swipe at heterosexual society and its value systems (both in the treatment of women and how heterosexual society ascribes effeminate behavior to gay men)."[10] Admittedly, this critic's dismissal takes place in passing, and the reviewer elsewhere admires the acting and deft cinematic allusion and quotation of the film. But note the clear anticipation that the film will offend for its failure to do enough progressive political educating.

Perhaps the problem is that this film occupies a discursive universe ruled more by television (and even comic books), in particular by the logic of the action-hero male, than by movies. The title—excessive as a drag queen's mascara—is the clue to something colorful; it is the inscription on a photograph of actress Julie Newmar. This photo hangs in a restaurant called the China Bowl, where two drag queens, stage-named Vita Boheme (Patrick Swayze) and Noxeema Jackson (Wesley Snipes), have gone to "be seen" following their tie-victory in the New York Drag Queen of the Year pageant. Vita has determined, over the unsuccessful protests of her onetime protégé Noxeema, to take under her wing the young Chi Chi Rodriguez, a "little Latin boy in drag" who lost the contest, and whom the two have brought with them to the China Bowl. After trading off the prize airline tickets from the contest for road money and advice from one John Jacob Jingleheimer Smith (played by Robin Williams months before his appearance in *The Birdcage*), Vita notices this photograph, hanging over her shoulder, in her compact mirror. After a campy speech, she steals the photo off the wall to carry with them as their "sovereign token" on their journey west to Holly-wood, where they will compete in the Drag Queen of America Contest.

So much for the plot setup: it is a road movie and a drag queen's bil-dungsroman in which Chi Chi learns from Vita and Noxeema how to be a drag queen, which, as I will explain, is—in this case, anyway—how to be a man. But, as I said, the photograph is a clue to a comic-book, television, action-hero Imaginary. In her apostrophe to the photo, Vita says of Julie Newmar: "You are the *only* Catwoman." That is, the recent film remakes of the Batman business are nonexistent; the campy 1960s *Batman* television series is not.

What's the difference? Aside from providing a tie to the world of action heroes in tights, their speech and actions highly stylized, why bring up the embarrassing foolishness of Adam West and Julie Newmar? Let me indulge in a bit of amateur psychoanalysis. In the television series, Batman's en-counter with Catwoman is a queer Oedipal triangle. Catwoman competes with Robin for Batman's affection. Robin, note, also dresses in tights, and in bright colors: yellow, green, and red. And he wears what preteens in the 1960s called "fairy boots." To triangulate the erotic politics roughly: Cat-woman is the phallic mother with which the drag queen identifies, at once abjectly failing to win Batman away from Robin (a half-consoling result, since Robin is the Oedipal boy in drag as well) and potently renewing a conflicted and perennial love-hate relationship with Batman, which the caped crusader nobly—but reluctantly—disavows. The more recent film versions dispense with the Catwoman problem before ever bringing Robin into the picture. So, does *To Wong Foo* resuscitate a queer economy from the matrix of action-hero identity politics? (Julie Newmar *is*—or *was*—an action hero, only syllables—nay, mere phonemes—removed from Batman as Catwoman. She is Batman's mirror image, for they are clad in almost identical cowls with pointed ears.) Or does it resurrect an economy of masculine, action-hero codes amid the current cachet of queer identity politics? Is not Julie Newmar–as-Catwoman always already Batman as drag queen?

I will maintain that the latter is the case. This is, in fact, what is so offensive about the film. But by extracting the codes of the action hero from this unlikely seeming source, one may end up turning a denuncia-tion of a film that appropriates the queer subject for straight masculinity into a partial recuperation of the action hero's mainstream masculine ethos—a theorization of how to be a straight man in a queer world—with-out mucking things up too badly, at least as a critic, though it involves the doubtful idea that straight men can teach a novice drag queen how to be what he/she wants to be.

It also involves, as I said, reading the film as a bildungsroman for Chi Chi. Vita and Noxeema teach Chi Chi how to be a queen. But Vita and Noxeema are not credible as female impersonators themselves. The film opens with scenes of Patrick Swayze and Wesley Snipes doing their makeup, pulling on their sheer stockings, adjusting their corsets and falsies, trying on pumps, and giggling. But both are such clearly male-seeming bodies: no subcutaneous fat cultivated to disguise a testosterone-driven metabolism—rather, muscles rippling like those of a steely action hero under taut skin, the body itself as a kind of armor, a phallic presence under the petticoat. If one puts aside the notion that a drag queen may wish to be identified easily as such, to play with our recognition of the deception, and instead assumes that the masquerade is to some degree in earnest, these two hunks are miserable failures—purely at the level of costume and makeup. They are action heroes dressed up as drag queens, not drag queens dressed up as women.

Yet they are vulnerable. Noxeema is quite aware of the danger of queer beaters, as well as racism, on their odyssey to Hollywood. She says to Vita, as the trio consider what hotel to try, somewhere early in their journey: "It could get violent. We've seen it before. You know that, Vita." And Vita is still quite capable of emotional injury from her own mother, who comes to the door of the palatial home in a Philadelphia suburb where Vita grew up when the crew drive by on the first leg out of New York City. Vita has come to show her friends her childhood home, perhaps hoping that, if she tries one more time, her parents will accept her for what she is. But the white-haired matron who comes to the door and scans the bright Cadillac across a quarter-acre front yard slowly recognizes that one of the occupants is her son Eugene, now Vita Boheme, and turns away in disgust and dismay. Vita, in the driver's seat in this scene (as she is in the plot), tears up her road map and tosses it from the convertible, slams the yellow land-yacht around in a violent U-turn, and speeds recklessly out of the neighborhood, obviously hurt.

And they have to improvise a code by which to educate Chi Chi, the Four Steps to Drag Queendom, a code that will, on inspection, say more about how a straight man acts like a man than about how a queer man acts like a lady.

The code originates as a pretext for reconciliation when the volatile Chi Chi, not for the last time, threatens to part company with the charitable Vita and her reluctant co-auntie Noxeema. Noxeema lectures Chi Chi, with interspersed agreements from Vita (the ensemble playing in this film is on a par with some of the best Cary Grant–vehicle, screwball-comedy dialogue), about how Chi Chi is not actually a drag queen but simply "a little Latin boy in a dress." Chi Chi readily agrees: "When a straight man dresses up like a woman and gets his sexual kicks, that is a transvestite." She also acknowledges: "When a woman is trapped inside a man's body and has the little operation, that is a transsexual." Noxeema continues: "When a *gay* man has way too much fashion sense for one gender, that is a queen. But when you put a little Latin boy in a dress, what you have is just that: a boy in a dress." This insult upsets Chi Chi, who forces Vita to stop the car by threatening to jump out of it and then storms off the road into an empty field in a huff. Vita cajoles Chi Chi back into the car by allowing that she is, at any rate, a "drag princess" if not a full-fledged queen. Chi Chi says, from the back seat, that she would rather be a princess anyway: "They're so much younger." Noxeema retorts: "Is everything a joke with you? This is not a game. This is real. There are steps to being a queen." As Vita adds: "You will know them when you reach them." "How many?" queries Chi Chi. Hesitating, Noxeema offers: "Four. There are four steps."

Satisfied, Chi Chi offers a frankly parodic version of the serenity prayer: "God grant me the serenity to accept being a boy in a dress, the courage to change with the fashions, and the wisdom to look different." In the untroped versions of the serenity prayer, wisdom ironically caps the series, arbitrating between courage and acceptance: "God grant me the serenity to accept the things I cannot change, the courage to change the things I can, and the wisdom to know the difference." In Chi Chi's version, wisdom accentuates with vigilance and yet partly contradicts the force of an agreement between courage and acceptance in what might be a fashion designer's creed: wear a dress, change with the fashions, and yet look different. The illusion of individual integrity and uniqueness on which the standardization of the women's "looks" trades is fully endorsed. Yet it comes down to centering the creed on courage rather than wisdom. Rather than mixing a degree of acceptance with a degree of bravery, acceptance joins bravery to demand wisdom in the service of bravery, all of which has a queerly straight male feel to it.

To this profession, Vita says, "That's it. Step One." Noxeema agrees: "That's right. Step One: Good thoughts be your sword and shield." The subtext matters: sword and shield. A serenity made up of bravery, a state of mind full of heavy defense and deadly, penetrative, severing, violent aggression.

The remaining three steps toward Queendom also have complementary chivalric allusions. When Chi Chi disregards Noxeema's fears about how they will be treated at their first hotel stop, and the threesome end up crashing a women's basketball league convention, Noxeema and Vita, blandished by the hotel's amenities, rationalize Chi Chi's rash parade into the hotel lobby by admitting that their protégé has passed Step Two: "Ignore adversity." Courage, sword and shield, ignore adversity—something familiar to action-hero fans is accumulating.

An action hero has a characteristic set of virtues regarding sex. He will act violently to suppress violence against women. A pudgy local cop, Sheriff Dollard (played by Chris Penn, with a badge where his name is misprinted as "Dullard"), stops the flashy Cadillac on a deserted country road. Oddly fooled by their drag attire, he gets Vita out of the car and makes a pass at her. Vita responds brutally—"Get your hand off my dick, buddy!"—and crashes the hapless minion of abusive patriarchal authority to the ground. They leave their victim for dead, driving away in a complete panic. Later on, in the highway-eyeblink town of Snydersville, where the queens are stuck waiting for their car to be repaired, Vita thoroughly thrashes a wife-beating auto mechanic.

The action hero may get the girl—but never by deceit. Near the end of the film, Vita confesses her secret to Carol Ann, whose husband Vita had pummeled, so that the friendship between Vita and Carol Ann will not be tainted by falsehood. And when young Bobby Ray takes a shine to Chi Chi, she turns him loose for local girl Bobbie Lee to capture after a prolonged exchange in which Chi Chi presses Bobby Ray to concede: "True lovers could keep just one big secret from each other, no?" Which, of course, Chi Chi refuses to do. This magnanimous declination of Chi Chi's, while it might seem simply to ensure the "proper" matching up of the heterosexual boy and girl and to write the queer Chi Chi out of the picture (as far as sex is concerned), also imbricates a male action hero's virtue, Step Three: "Abide by the rules of love." Love is voluntary, honest, and unconstrained. So, bravery, sword and shield, ignore adversity, honor love with violence and gentility . . . what action hero could dispute this code?

Chi Chi learns Step Four only at the end, when she wins the Drag Queen of America contest and receives her crown from none other than Julie Newmar herself: "Larger than life is just the right size." That all action heroes are larger than life goes without saying. That drag queens tend to be larger than life is also worth noting: men tend to be larger than women, and men who play action heroes certainly are, physically. Courage, sword and shield, ignore adversity, honor love with violence and gentility, be larger than life: a fair definition of an action hero.

Certainly, this summary has left untouched certain piquant details of the film: the queens launch what they call "Operation Decorator Storm" to make the little town of Snydersville tolerable for a weekend. The film is also replete with delicious cinematic allusions: the stand-up confrontation borrowed from *Spartacus*, where every member of the community claims to be a drag queen to face off the vengeful Sheriff Dollard, who has hunted the queens to ground after trying every flower shop, antique store and beauty parlor in his rural demesne; the brief allusion to Bergman's *Wild Strawberries*, in which the town's dull and depressed ladies discuss with the queens how to make the town's annual Strawberry Social into something more interesting than a day when everybody bakes a strawberry pie and eats it.

What needs more reflection is how this dragging of the codes of the action hero into the drag film sits with the identity politics it plays with. It is easy enough to say that, since one can decode the film into an action-hero affair, and since all action heroes are implicated in the troublesome drama of the reproduction of patriarchal privilege, this film is not only momentarily insulting but fundamentally pernicious. But I am not satisfied with that dismissal, and I will have my satisfaction if I can get it.

As a queer film, this one might be defended as Harvey Fierstein (of *Torch Song Trilogy* fame) defends the character of the Sissy in Hollywood film in his interview in *The Celluloid Closet:* "Visibility at any price. Plus, *I'm* a Sissy." However, I have argued that *To Wong Foo* is not principally, though it is explicitly, a film about being queer but a film about being straight. Still, I could insist, in parallel terms, on the value of a straight film—an action-hero film—that embraces queers and queerness, even fearlessly taking on the supposedly dangerous equation of the action hero with the drag queen. And some might think that I, comfortable in my assurances of the straightness of the heroes, had denied my implication in the patriarchal oppression that trades on homophobia.

A more subtle approach to the matter of writing the straight man in criticism might, as Calvin Thomas has suggested in his recent book *Male Matters,*[11] celebrate its own failure to be convincing in the current critical climate. This abjection is the only place from which to be heard. I may not have succeeded at such abjection here any more than action heroes succeed as drag queens. But we do try, bravely.

Coda: The Pink Angel (Reprise)

I remember, just before that devastating little question from my date that revealed to me the dressing game onstage, the words of the nightclub singer and their torchy irony: " 'O no, my dear, let all that be; / What matter, so there is but fire / In you, in me?' " ("The Mask," *Variorum* 263). Interesting what you can do with lyrics by Yeats.

Notes

All dialogue quoted in this essay, unless otherwise indicated, comes from notes I made while viewing the films in question.

1. See Eve Kosofsky Sedgwick, *Between Men: English Literature and Male Homosocial Desire* (New York: Columbia University Press, 1985) and *Epistemology of the Closet* (Berkeley: University of California Press, 1990).

2. David Van Leer, *The Queening of America: Gay Culture in Straight Society* (New York: Routledge, 1995), 5.

3. Beeban Kidron, dir., *To Wong Foo, Thanks for Everything! Julie Newmar* (MCA/Universal, 1995).

4. Roger Baker, *Drag: A History of Female Impersonation on the Stage* (London: Triton, 1968), 128.

5. William Butler Yeats, *The Letters of W. B. Yeats*, ed. Allen Wade (London: Hart-Davis, 1954), 875. Subsequent references to this work will be included parenthetically in the text.

6. Patricia Allderidge, *The Late Richard Dadd, 1817–1886* (London: Tate Gallery, 1974), 106. *Crazy Jane* is plate 151, page 109.

7. William Butler Yeats, *The Variorum Edition of the Poems of W. B. Yeats*, ed. Peter Allt and Russell K. Alspach (New York: Macmillan, 1957). Subsequent references to this work will be included parenthetically in the text.

8. See Sandra M. Gilbert and Susan Gubar, "Cross-Dressing and Re-Dressing: Transvestism as Metaphor," *No Man's Land*, vol. 2: *Sexchanges* (New Haven, Conn.: Yale University Press, 1989).

9. Rob Epstein and Jeffrey Friedman, dirs., *The Celluloid Closet* (Telling Pictures, 1995).

10. Carrie Gorringe, 1995 Internet review of *To Wong Foo, Thanks for Everything! Julie Newmar* at http://www.nitrateonline.com/rtowong.html.

11. See Calvin Thomas, *Male Matters: Masculinity, Anxiety, and the Male Body on the Line* (Urbana: University of Illinois Press, 1996).

Afterword(s):
A Conversation

Calvin Thomas and Catherine A. F. MacGillivray

The following dialogue took place on 26–28 May 1998 at Catherine MacGillivray's home in Cedar Falls, Iowa (with Merlin Ganter MacGillivray, age 2½ months, in attendance).

The Word "Queer": Merely Academic?

CT: A character in your friend Sarah Schulman's novel *Rat Bohemia* says that the word "queer" is used only by academics. Of course, the comment comes from one of her characters: I don't know if it represents Schulman's opinion or not, but do you think this is true? Do you think that this word has any kind of positive valence or utilization outside of the academy?

CM: Having recently moved here from New York, where I was slightly involved in and even more so aware of activism going on, I would have to say that I don't agree, because, historically speaking, the taking up of this word in a positive way was first proposed by the activist group Queer Nation. And I'm pretty sure that that precedes any academic usage. Certainly around New York there was a period of time when Queer Nation, an offshoot of ACT-UP, made T-shirts and you started seeing Queer Nation T-shirts all over the place. On the other hand, I would agree that, as is so often the case, the word has been taken up by the academy with a vigor such that you tend to lose sight of its activist beginnings. But I really think that the original impulse was an activist one.

CT: The first instance I remember reading of any kind of queering of the straight, any use of the term "queer" to describe a people who don't neces-sarily have sex with people of the same sex, was in the *Village Voice* article about Queer Nation that I cite in my essay. It came from an activist, not an academic.

CM: I think the other reason you're going to see a character in a Sarah Schulman novel saying that is that, historically speaking, in terms of de-bate around the use of the term "queer" and the category that it is propos-ing, there has been more lesbian critique of the term and the category than there has been a gay male critique.

CT: Why do you think that is?

CM: Well, I think it's for the same reason that there's been more critique of the term "gay" by women than by men; like "gay," "queer" is a nongen-dered term, supposedly a neutral term, whereas we know from feminism that, under patriarchy, the neutral is really the male subsuming the female. I know a lot of lesbians who find "queer" a somewhat suspect term for that reason, who therefore prefer the word "lesbian." The advantage of con-tinuing to insist on the use of the term "lesbian" is that it's a female term. Of course, what I'm mentioning is more a critique of the term "queer" than of queer practice, but I also think there's more of a critique on the part of lesbians of queer practice than on the part of gay males because of the notion, discussed in this volume, that queer doesn't necessarily have to do with sexual practice; that, too, has been a problematic issue in lesbian feminism.

CT: There's Adrienne Rich's "lesbian continuum". . .

CM: Well, even before that—Adrienne Rich's proposal of the concept of the lesbian continuum to a certain extent comes out of the practice and discussion during the seventies within feminism of political lesbianism—and that's related to one of the things I want to ask you about in your text, so maybe we could turn to that next. But to finish up, for a lot of lesbians, this notion that lesbianism can have something to do with a practice other than a sexual practice is problematic, because it's very different for women to be asexed or unsexed than it is for men—and especially gay men. Gay male sexuality has often been figured—rightly or wrongly—as a kind of hypersexuality, whereas lesbian sexuality has often been figured as this quasivirginal, platonic, or emotional friendship type of thing that is less sexual than any of the sexualities, the least sexual of all the possibilities.

CT: But that notion of asexual homosexuality occurs in mainstream rep-resentations of gay men as well, particularly in recent movies like *As Good As It Gets*, in which the Greg Kinnear character is completely desexualized.

CM: Yes, I suppose there are examples of that, too, but I think that the mainstream understanding of male homosexuality is much more along the lines of the recent George Michael fiasco; in other words, that it's gay men who are, in keeping with notions of male sexuality in general, highly sexed—but that much more so because they're doing it with other men. So then you have two hypersexed people—it's like a doubling phenomenon, whereas straight men are figured as having to prod (pun intended) their little woman into doing it, because, according to this logic, women as a rule aren't all that interested in doing it. In this sense, lesbian sexuality functions in opposition to gay male sexuality: in lesbian coupling, you have two people who are not that interested in doing it, making them, as it were, less interested in doing it than anyone! I think that this problematic but not untypical way of figuring lesbian sexuality is another reason why lesbians have a greater investment in remaining suspicious of the whole queer category, to the extent that it veers off into the "sex is not what it's about" arena, thus obscuring the sexiness of lesbian sexuality yet again!

CT: This argument occurs a number of times in Teresa de Lauretis's critiques and in Leo Bersani's argument that "queer" poses the threat of a dangerous despecification and desexualization of the homosexual terrain. The erasure of gender is evident in this sort of maneuver as well. One of the things my essay in this volume addresses is the parallels between the move from feminism to gender studies and the move from gay/lesbian to queer studies, and the potential these moves imply for just these sorts of erasures. I mention, for example, Cornell's advertising a position back in '94 that was described as being for someone who did gay/lesbian studies *or* queer theory. I found that "or" rather interesting, though I really wonder if any job in this nation that was advertised as queer theory has ever gone to anyone who wasn't gay or lesbian. I've even thought of sending out a questionnaire to different departments to ask if this has happened.

CM: Well, if it hasn't happened, I'm sure it's going to; there certainly have been men hired for feminist studies positions. I guess I feel about the gay/lesbian versus queer split similarly to the way I feel about the gender studies versus women's studies split: I'm interested theoretically in what the notion of gender studies opens up; for example, the possibility of looking at constructions of masculinity from a feminist perspective, of gendering the masculine, and so on. At the same time, I will fight for the continued use of the term "women's studies" instead of "gender studies," because there's no reason why you can't do a study of masculinity in the context of a discipline that's called "women's studies," and I think there are very good reasons for doing precisely that. Furthermore, I don't want to lose the term "women's studies"—for the sake of the word "woman" and so as not to lose the focus on a feminist point of view. And the same thing goes, in my view, for the use of the word "queer": I think it's very important, precisely to the extent that it opens up nonsexual possibilities, but you have to be sure that opening something up doesn't close the door on something else. For example, I certainly would want to insist on the continued use of the word "lesbian"—because it is gendered feminine—and on making sure that the opening up of the term "queer" is not going to mean losing the use of the word "lesbian." Look at the Ellen DeGeneres phenomenon, for example—that's a very good example.

CT: Does she ever say "lesbian"?

CM: She doesn't.

CT: When she comes out over the airport microphone in the celebrated episode, she specifically says "gay" rather than "lesbian."

CM: Exactly, but this is the case not only in that moment. In all the interviews that were done with her before and after that particular segment, she said numerous times that she herself uses the term "gay" because she doesn't feel comfortable with the term "lesbian." She basically has a straight world's reaction to the word "lesbian"—it makes her feel squeamish and so she's much more comfortable with the word "gay." I think that is a growing trend, a very problematic and dangerous one to my mind, especially when you've got the most public lesbian in America afraid to use the word "lesbian," finding it a kind of icky, embarrassing word.

CT: Maybe she hasn't heard of the word "queer."

CM: If she thinks the word "lesbian" is embarrassing, she'd probably have the same hesitations about "queer."

CT: Unless she found out that certain straight people are using it, then maybe it would be OK for her. The crux here seems to be that some productive possibilities are opened up by a specific sort of nomination like "queer" or "gender." Some possibilities for critique, analysis, and intervention arise—the study of masculinity, for example, that was left untouched for so long. But with those possibilities comes also the possibility of retrenchment and reaction and normalization, the evacuation of specifically feminist inquiry and intervention. As a man who does masculinity studies, I try to keep in the foreground that the point of my intervention into masculinity is to help bring about change in the way women are treated in patriarchal society, since masculinity in its present construction depends on and is fortified by the domination of women. There's much discussion within masculinity studies about why men should study masculinity, and there are basically two rationales to consider. The first is the "justice" angle: it's just the right thing to make interventions into masculinity for the sake of women's rights. The other rationale is that such interventions will ultimately benefit men as well, because masculinity dehumanizes them. Michael Kimmel argues that profeminist men should strategically adopt the latter rhetoric because most men really don't care about gender justice anyway; they only want to understand what's in it for them. Although the benefits of changing masculinity to men should be considered, I'm more strongly tied to the justice argument, both in terms of feminism and queer theory. But I wonder in what ways an argument that queer theory benefits straights would work. You can certainly argue that masculinity deforms the men it interpellates, but can you in the same way suggest that all the privileges that are afforded to straights by virtue of their being straight in any way harms them? "Try queering yourself, folks—it will add years to your lives!"

CM: I think you could argue just that, particularly on the level of sexual practice, on the level of *jouissance*, in the same way that one argues that the damage done to men by patriarchy is, granted, not social but psychic. In this way, I think there is a parallel. Yes, in terms of social position, to the contrary of there being harm, there's great benefit to being straight; but, on the level of sexual practice, there is harm, since I for one would suggest that heterosexuality is based on a repression of all unsanctioned sexual impulses, which most—if not all—of us feel.

CT: I was reading Holly Hughes's *Clit Notes* recently; and, in her introduction to that book, she talks quite a bit about her family history. She remembers being out for a drive with her family somewhere in Michigan and thinking: "This isn't a family—it's four pieces of sliced cheese in a car." And, of course, for her, quite rightly, this cheesiness has everything to do with her family's straightness. If straightness turns people into processed cheese, then obviously it's more humanizing for people to interrogate straightness and try to work their way out of it.

There's another problem here, though, and that's the question not only of straight social advantage in general but of academic advantage in particular. Just as some feminist women are justly suspicious of men doing feminism because they see a motivation to encroach on a particular terrain or to gain some sort of academic advantage, there's also the suspicion that straights are talking up queer theory as the latest trendy bullet to add to one's theoretical (or careerist) ammo belt. Jacqueline Foertsch discusses this problem in her essay.

CM: That's why your survey on whether anyone straight has gotten a queer theory job would be interesting.

CT: To know if that's happened.

CM: To continue with the parallel between straightness and masculinity, I think the other thing that needs to be pointed out is that women can also study masculinity and, indeed, are doing so more and more. And I'm sure the same thing will happen and has happened in terms of queer theorists who are gay or lesbian asking the kinds of questions about straight people that are being asked in this volume. We could also then talk about the parallel with regard to race studies and thinking about constructions of whiteness, which is happening more and more, too.

CT: Actually, I think it's happening more than straight interrogation—there's much more white interrogation of whiteness than there is straight interrogation of straightness, it seems to me.

CM: And I think the same central problems arise. Personally, I think the risk is worth the benefit; in all these arenas, it's the case that you have to proceed with caution, be vigilantly autocritical as well as constructively critical of what everyone else is doing. As I know we're aware in terms of publishing this volume, if you're going to risk throwing yourself into this arena as a straight person, you've got to expect that you're going to get some criticism from practicing gays and lesbians; but, whatever those critical slings and arrows might be, the fact remains that, on another level, on the level of the street and the supermarket, when we go out in the world every day as straight people, we're not under attack.

CT: The point I try to make in the preface is that whatever the risks with being charged with appropriation are, they don't stack up to much compared with the risks of being denied citizenship and humanity in a homocidal world. Criticism of *SWAT,* as we've come to call this volume, is expected and welcomed, and I hope that our blind spots will be pointed out and that those of us interested in this kind of critique will continue to work on them. However, too often, I think, the charge of appropriation is made as a way of not having to think about or deal with specific arguments and issues.

CM: And it's also the case that if because of the fear of being labeled as appropriators we didn't make a foray into these areas, we would be succumbing to the pressure of various assumptions about identity and identity formation, and that's a danger in and of itself. I think we're juggling all the time.

On Your Deathbed, If Someone Asks You, "What Are You Most Proud of?" Are You Going to Say, "That I Never Got Fucked!"?

CM: I was very interested in note 18 in your essay in this volume, where you say: "I find problematic, anyway, the notion that subjects can voluntaristically 'change' their sexual practices. Certainly, change is possible; but such voluntarism plays all too well into the right-wing religious rhetoric of homosexuality as a perverse but alterable 'lifestyle choice' and pseudo-therapeutic efforts to convert gays and lesbians to 'healthy' heterosexuality. Moreover, though I agree with Bersani that there are salutary political *possibilities* inscribed in anti-identitarian sexuality, per se, it isn't clear to me, or to him, that any specific sexual practice has an *intrinsic* political value in itself nor, correspondingly, that any change in sexual practice has intrinsic political value." I was very interested in this argument. There's a way in which you're in disagreement with some of the things Jane Garrity is arguing in this volume, and that seemed inevitable to me, because, it seems to me, the way you're positioning yourself here is similar to the way many gay men position themselves with regard to this issue, in contradistinction to the way many lesbians position themselves. In other words, I see this, too, as a gendered split.

One of the ways this split has manifested itself is around recent coverage of the scientific community's search for the gay gene. Queer reactions to this research have been gendered, not exclusively of course, but what I mean to say is that a majority of gay men have inscribed themselves as looking forward to such an eventual discovery, precisely so that they can then use the gene as a defense whereby one says: I was born gay, I can't help or change it. Whereas a majority of lesbians are more suspicious of and less interested in this search for the gay gene, for the opposite reason. Which is to say, once again, that since feminism has impacted on lesbian practice, particularly in the last forty years, and since one of the main points about sexuality that feminism has been trying to make since its theoretical beginnings is that it is constructed, then biology or genetics have little to do with it. So when I read something like your note 18, my reaction is to think: No, it's exactly the opposite: not only is it possible to change one's sexuality, it's crucial that one at least think about doing so—it's at the very least possible to experiment, and why shouldn't such experimentation be part of one's feminist and queer self-interrogations? For me, as a feminist, I see something politically reactionary and dangerously limiting about arguing that voluntarism can't play a part in one's sexuality. And we could also note that the gendered split I'm noticing here parallels a similar gay/queer split: I think it is the queer, along with the lesbian feminist, who would argue for voluntarism as an important sexual politics. In fact, this might be an appropriate moment for me to say that there are many ways in which I see the category of the queer championing ideas lesbian feminists have been developing and arguing for for decades, but not many outside the feminist community were listening. Maybe the queer and queer theory have had the impact they have in part because they are gendered as *male* and therefore more valuable.

Furthermore, for you to argue against choice as a straight man registers differently for me than were a gay man to similarly argue, for the reasons I've just mentioned—obviously, were he to do so, it could save his life. Whereas reading you saying it, I understood it more as a hidden proclamation: And that's why I don't ever have to sleep with a guy. Because that desire is not in me, and I can't change that. But maybe I'm reading too much into it. Still, I would venture to wager that, in a group of people such as the people who are writing in this volume, people who are asking questions about issues of sexuality, you'll find many more women who have had, no matter how they live otherwise or how they self-identify, lesbian sexual experiences than you'll find men such as yourself in this theoretical arena who have had similar homosexual experience. And I guess I should add, in an effort to clarify, that when I say men such as yourself I mean adult males, since we know, thanks to Kinsey, that many if not most men have some kind of homosexual contact as teenagers. But to get back to your argument, I guess I wonder to what extent it is not a protective gesture.

CT: The reason I question voluntarism is mainly for the reason given—concern about the right-wing use of that rhetoric—but I appreciate your pointing out the difference in valence with regard to voluntarism in terms of straight men, gay men, and straight and lesbian women. There are several places in my essay where I question the extent to which a straight-queer politics is necessarily predicated on a voluntarism that would indicate that one must have sex with a man, if you're a man, to be able to say anything about this politics at all. It seems to me that if I were to have sex with another man and not say anything about it, not tell anyone about it, keep it in some way discrete or secret, that could be considered much less of a political act than the exercise of walking down the street holding hands with a man with whom I was not actually having sex.

CM: I agree. Do I agree? I'm not sure if I agree. I'll have to think about it.

CT: There's a place in my essay where I say quite specifically that I am, in effect, keeping my straight ass covered.

CM: You do, and I was impressed with how self-critical and honest you are in your essay in general, and it is your obvious ability to be so that prompts me to ask you about this. So I'm asking you, Do you think your note 18 has any protective function?

CT: To an extent, it does. Just quickly to amplify this business about the possibility of finding the gay gene, though. Right-wing homophobes are just as interested in finding the gay gene as some gay men are but for a completely different reason: so it can be transformed, eradicated, or excised, et cetera.

But in terms of my essay and its protective gestures, the question that I bump up against is this: If, in the end, I have to have sex with another man in order to have any legitimacy to speak about these issues, then I might as well just shut up, because in the context of my specific sexual configuration and desires—and my specifically monogamous relationship with my partner Liz—it's not going to happen. If to have any legitimacy at all as a speaker or interrogator here I need to point back to the sexual encounters I had with men earlier in my life, then I can say that, yes, I've had some rather limited experiences. But it seems to me that if "queer" is going to mean both the sexually specific and the elaboration of nonsexually specific areas, then those elaborations have to be followed and granted some legitimacy. But if, in the final instance, it all comes back to the question of specific same-sex practices—and whether or not one is having them—then what, finally, does the word "queer" amount to?

CM: Well, I'm not bringing this discussion up in terms of one's right to make any intervention at all on the subject. I'm trying to make two separate points: on the one hand, if you look at, let's say, a group of straight people, men and women, who are interested in questions like the questions posed by this volume, I would argue that the men in that group are less interested in pursuing the actual sexual possibilities opened up by those very questions and, therefore, perhaps as a protective gesture, are more invested in talking about queerness in its nonsexual manifestations. Whereas my experience has been, and perhaps this is merely anecdotal— obviously we're not doing a sociological study here—that straight women who are interested in these same kinds of questions are also more likely to be actively interested in having sexual experiences of the queer sort. And then, of course, we might also wonder why this is. Maybe because women have less to lose in the realm of power than men do? But again, I'm not talking about one's right to talk about any of this stuff.

The other point I'm trying to make . . . with regard to what you're saying in note 18 about sexuality is that I just don't agree with it. Precisely because, as a feminist and from a political point of view, I have a problem with anything that says that people can't change their desires and therefore have no reason to waste their time thinking about the possibility of changing their actual sexual practice.

And, of course, I don't agree with your note 18 first and foremost because it's contrary to my experience. For example, before I came to Iowa—of course now all bets are off—but before I came to Iowa, one of my goals in the women's studies' classroom was to convert someone to lesbianism in the course of the year—and I was always successful at this, just by talking about how sexuality is a construction and heterosexuality an institution and by simply posing the question, by asking my students: How do you identify yourself sexually? And if they would respond: I'm heterosexual, then I would say: How do you know? How can you be so sure? thus provoking them to question their sexuality in certain fundamental ways. Result? Conversions right and left. And let me just say this about the whole issue of conversion: when the right wing accuses homosexuals of trying to convert everyone, I prefer to respond by saying: Exactly, exactly, because if you're convertible, this just shows that the whole premise on which your sexuality was based was coming not from you, but from . . .

CT: I think that this is very complicated. I agree with what you're saying. My suggestion is not that voluntarism or conversion or transformation is not possible but that voluntarism always takes place within specific cultural, discursive, and rhetorical contexts. There are some instances in which I might reserve the right to be suspicious of the discourse of voluntarism and other instances, like those you allude to, where I wouldn't want to question it but would join you in insisting upon it. When Judith Butler talks about gender and sexuality as performative, she makes the point that people don't just wake up and say, "I'm going to wear this sort of identity today" and that we can't change gender or sexuality as simply as we change our clothes or our hairstyles, because things are much more profoundly intricated than that. So I don't mean to suggest that voluntary transformation or conversion is not possible. I'm convinced that the kinds of interrogations and interventions that we want to make here will lead, for many people, particularly in the classroom, to the kinds of pedagogical practices that you're talking about, that what you're talking about will lead to these confirmations.

CM: At the same time, we could go back to other kinds of questions that you raise in your essay, such as the question of penetrability. I think the reason why straight men, albeit interested in these issues, are less interested in seeing their interest serve as a bridge to any kind of practice is exactly because of this question of penetrability.

CT: Yes. One point that I stress when I talk in my classes about sexual practices is that the very idea of homosexuality between men is problematized by the fact that, in some cultural contexts, some Latin-American cultures, some African-American cultures as well, men can have sex with other men as long as they're the *active* participant, because then their masculinity is not in question at all. It's only if you're penetrated orally or anally that you are a "queer" in the derogatory sense. So those differences have to be taken into consideration as well. So, yes, I agree with you that penetrability is the issue, and that's why I say in one of my notes that whatever my particular *discursive* adventures or contortions in self-identification and interrogation may be, at the end of the day, my ass is still covered.

CM: Yes. And, of course, the issue of penetrability obviously is not merely a sexual one—it has become one of the cornerstones—if not the very foundation—for current constructions of masculinity in our culture. So, for me, from my position as a woman who's interested in deconstructing this particular kind of masculinity—it's obviously overly simplistic to say it this way—but there is a way in which I could say the "bottom" line for me is: How many of you guys are going to allow yourselves to be penetrated? Because until you are willing to do that, as far as I can tell, a certain kind of masculinity is going to remain intact, no matter how many questions you ask.

CT: I think that you're right, and there's . . .

CM: And I'm not just saying this in a theoretical way—this is something that I have said to my partners in the context of our sexual relationships: When are you going to let me penetrate you? And/or let someone else do it? Are you going to go to your grave without ever having had this experience? I would find that really weird, in part because I agree so much with Bersani's notion of *jouissance* as equating to self-shattering by, among other things, penetration.

CT: Among other things. For him, it's the preferred avenue but not the only one.

CM: Again, I think that there are so many more women, especially femi-nist women, who, if you asked them, would say that they would hold some measure of regret if they went to their graves without ever having had any sexual practice with another woman. Whereas if you ask the average guy . . .

CT: He'd say: "I'm so happy to have made it to my grave without ever having had sex with a man."

CM: On your deathbed, you know, if someone asks you . . .

CT: "What are you most proud of?"

CM: Are you going to say . . .

CT: "That I never got fucked!"

CM: Exactly. In a way, as a woman, I'm glad that penetration has just always been a part of my sexuality, that it hasn't become an obsessed-about limit, my body this fortress that needs to be protected.

CT: You're focusing on the real difference—that for a woman to have sex with another woman is not specifically as self-shattering as it would be for a straight man to be fucked by a man. Because the woman's self, her ego, is not based upon that impenetrability.

CM: I wouldn't say that it's not as self-shattering, I would say that femi-nine *jouissance* is already so much defined as an ego-loss experience, as a self-shattering experience, that . . .

CT: Whereas male identity, heteromasculine identity, is already defined against that.

CM: And now we have the answer to the question of where the harm is in heterosexuality—remember, I was saying that the harm lies in the realm of *jouissance,* especially if we agree with Bersani that *jouissance* is a self-shattering experience, and we agree that straight male sexuality is com-prised by all the attempts and maneuvers to maintain ego cohesiveness, which is the antithesis of *jouissance.*

I really think that if we said, Hey, let's get up tomorrow and make this world a better place, configure gender differently, configure power rela-tions between men and women differently, and what's the one thing we could do to accomplish this? my answer would be: Get these guys to open up their anterior spaces!

CT: One of the undergraduate-classroom gender exercises that I do is to put the words "masculine" and "feminine" on the board in a column A, column B sort of thing and then get the students to tell me everything they associate with these terms. After they've exhausted themselves, after they've put down everything they can possibly think of on the board, I'll go down the list and say: Raise your hand if you've never felt this, if you've never experienced that. And, of course, everybody identifies with everything that's on the board.

CM: That's because you don't include penetration on the list. That would be the standout.

CT: That would be the standout.

CM: It would stand out as the holdout.

CT: But then it does get back, I think, to a right-to-speak issue, a qualification, or legitimization, of a specific interrogative discourse. If you're dealing with a straight man like me who's trying to let queer theory interrogate the boundaries of his identity, unless I have had this specific experience, whence comes my legitimation to speak at all?

CM: I agree that some people might say this; I'm not invested in that question. I think it's better for everyone to just speak, and then someone else can come along and say, What right do you have to speak? And that's interesting. Whereas if that person were never to speak in the first place, we wouldn't get to think about whether or not they should have spoken, let alone about what they've said. I'm giving you a hard time because you've shown yourself in your work to be honest and, if I may say so, sincere about your own practice and your own limitations. Don't get me wrong, I do think, in this kind of simplistic, rosy-eyed way, that the world would be a better place if everyone had at least one same-sex sexual experience in their lives. But, by the same token, I don't mean to say that this issue of penetrability, male penetrability, only has to take place with another man, because I don't think it does. Again, I'm giving you a hard time because you were so up-front about your own sexual practice in your essay, whereas that's why Clyde Smith's essay frustrated me. Reading it, I felt, OK, this guy's talking a good game, but I want to know, has he ever allowed himself to be penetrated? C. Smith doesn't say anything about this—or anything else about his sexual practice for that matter. So I think you should call him and ask him.

CT: Well, I think we should have sent out a questionnaire to all the male contributors. I agree with you. But I think there is—for most men there would be—a huge difference between being penetrated by a man and being penetrated by a woman.

CM: Well, yeah, obviously there is a difference, psychically, at the same time that I do think there is an issue of physical boundaries and of where/

how you police those boundaries that would be interrogated regardless of who's on the other end.

CT: There's also the issue of the specific context of a specific monogamous relationship. If my partner were to put on a strap-on, then I could be penetrated without being "unfaithful." Since it would be in the context of our relationship.

CM: Yes—and this is what I'm proposing! Don't get me wrong, I'm not asking you to be unfaithful! That's what I'm saying! Get the strap-on!

CT: OK, OK, OK! . . . That is, I take your point.

CM: Look at Merlin. Is all this sex talk making you sleepy, baby? [Responsive coos from Merlin.]

CT: So your argument would be that there is an intrinsic political value to penetration?

CM: I think I am saying that. I'd have to think about it a little bit more to be absolutely sure, but. . . . But the more I think about it, the more I think that I am arguing this. That there is an intrinsic value.

CT: Well, I would still hold on to the idea that voluntarism, per se, is a complex issue that has to be considered within a specific context.

CM: You're absolutely right, because at the same time that I've just said all this stuff about how great experimentation is, I have to add that many in the lesbian community have felt used as the objects of straight women's . . .

CT: . . . objects of experimentation.

CM: So you're absolutely right, it is a complicated issue, because there is such a thing as sexual dilettantism. Which can be very negative.

CT: If there can be a discourse encouraging straight women to experiment or convert, there's also the possibility of a homophobic discourse that would say to lesbians and gay men: Oh, come on, give heterosexuality a try. You haven't given it its fair shot. [Indeed, not long after this dialogue, a religious-right "conversion" organization took out full-page advertisements featuring "ex-gays" and "ex-lesbians" in the *New York Times* and other national newspapers.—CT]

CM: That's a good point. I guess what I disagreed with was, it's one thing to wonder what the value of or problem with voluntarism is, which is what we're talking about now, but that's different from saying . . . whatever it is that you say there . . .

CT: What I say specifically is that I find problematic the notion that the subjects can voluntaristically change their sexual practices. Certainly, change is possible, I do say, but voluntarism can play into right-wing religious rhetoric.

Oh, the Norm, the Norm—How Boring Is That?

CT: I remember an interview with Fran Liebowitz about a year ago in *Vanity Fair* . . .

CM: I love her . . .

CT: She was talking about how some in the straight world used to look to gay culture for style and the lessons of the cutting edge, whereas now, she laments, gays want to have babies and join the army . . .

CM: And get married.

CT: And get married.

CM: Although that's rather gendered too: more gay men want the marriage thing than do lesbians . . .

CT: Why do you think that is?

CM: Again, I think this is related to the fact that feminism and lesbianism, at least for the current generation, have always been so closely intertwined. To value the patriarchal institution of marriage, for a feminist, lesbian or not, is complicated.

CT: One of the arguments for gay marriage is that marriage in general tends to stabilize relationships—though, of course, that could be for good or ill. Because marriages take more effort to get into, you have to make more effort to get out of them. This is perhaps a bad generalization, but I think that lesbians have already the reputation of being more invested in monogamous relationships, anyway. Whereas there's the whole discourse about gay male promiscuity. It could be argued that more gay men want to get into marriage, not simply because it's reinforcing a patriarchal institution to begin with and they're men, but because they see the greater need for legitimization of their monogamy or commitment.

CM: That's a point. I think it's also the case that it's easier for gay men to romanticize marriage. What I've noticed is that the marriage issue is twofold. On the one hand, it's a political goal for the sake of the benefits, and few are against that. When I say that lesbians in general, particularly political or activist lesbians, are not invested in the issue of marriage (and that's a huge generalization of course), I don't mean to say that they're against it. But even when they did surveys about the Hawaii situation, asking who would rush over there to do it if gay marriages were legalized in Hawaii, it was a majority of men who said they would take advantage of the right.

Yes, everyone wants the benefits, but it's also easier for a gay man who hasn't had any investment in feminism to romanticize the ceremony: the public declaration, the vows, the party, and the clothes and all that, whereas it's more difficult for a lesbian, particularly one who has been influenced by feminism, to get off on a romantic fantasy about marriage—marriage being the quintessential patriarchal institution devised for the benefit of men at the cost of women. There's a similar division around the issue of gays in the military. That's another one where lesbians were like, Yeah, sure, anyone should be allowed to be in the military who wants to be, but I'm not willing to work on this issue politically, because it's a horrible thing to be in the military, so why should we care? It's a question of priorities. There're only so many hours in the day, is this what we should be focusing on?

CT: Liebowitz suggests an increasing investment of gay and lesbian people, maybe more gay than lesbian, in occupying the position of the norm. That foregrounds the tension between "gay"/"lesbian" as nominations and "queer" as a nomination, if queer is taken as an interrogation into, or a hostility against, the norm.

CM: And that's another reason why people like us should be rigorously self-critical. Because it's easy for us to say, Oh, the norm, the norm—how boring is that?

CT: Because we're it.

CM: Exactly.

CT: And we enjoy its privileges.

CM: So, yes, from our perspective, it's boring and disappointing that there are more and more gay people who want to be just like us, but it's not our place to criticize them, either. Your essay was interesting for me in terms of thinking about my own subject position, because I realized that part of my dilemma is that, given my past homosexual experience—I self-identified as a lesbian, was out to my family as a lesbian, and so on, in college—they have a word for that now . . .

CT: You're a L.U.G.!

CM: OK, that's what it is. What does that stand for?

CT: Lesbian Until Graduation!

CM: Exactly! And so it was interesting for me, because when I read lesbian theory, I still so identify with the lesbian position, although it's gotten more complicated by virtue of this little critter Merlin here, I've noticed. For example, I call myself—because it really best describes how I feel as a subject—a lapsed Lesbian. Like a lapsed Catholic: always still kind of a Catholic. It was the perfect nomination for me. So, anyway, when I read a text like Butler's, I still feel totally identified. As a lesbian. At the same time that when I realize I'm having this lesbian identification, I also realize how problematic it is, too. It's all very good and well for me to read an essay and put myself into the lesbian reader position or, with regard to film, the lesbian spectatorial position, and there's some validity to that: because of my past experience, I think I do have access to those positions in some real way. At the same time, from a critical position, in terms of what I might write, or what we might talk about, or what I might talk about in the classroom, all that is complicated by the fact that I now lead a totally heterosexual life with all the privileges therefrom. So that's what I feel. A divide. Kind of a parallel to the divide that you talk about in your essay.

And that's certainly something that I've had to think about, especially here and now, walking around Iowa with this kid. How am I perceived, how does the right wing perceive me now, now that I'm a mother?

CT: I make the point in my essay that one can have established one's heterosexual credentials, marriage and children and all that, and still end up at the end of the day to have been "living a lie."

CM: That's one thing that I think about a lot being here in Iowa: the number of people that I meet here who I think right away are closeted. I never have that feeling, in New York, of running across these real-life examples of exactly what you're talking about. Married with children, and yet it's like, Hello! When are you coming out of the closet? In that 1950s kind of way that we live with in Iowa.

CT: Particularly in your case, with your relationship with your students, I was thinking that, even though they know you're married, and even though they know you've had Merlin, they probably think of you still as more queer than straight—in the way that they understand "straight."

CM: Well, I hope so. It was because of my pregnancy that I "came out" as a married person to my students. You'll remember that, in the fall semester, before I was showing, I got stuck in New York because of pregnancy complications. That was before my students knew I was pregnant—all they knew was that I had some sort of medical complication that kept me in New York. And remember how, when I got back, I discovered that my absence from the classroom had provided them with an opportunity to ask each other the question that had been burning on their tongues since the first day of class, which was, Is she a lesbian? And then from there, the next obvious question—according to their logic—was, Does she have AIDS? Is that why she's suddenly having to take this medical leave? When I came back and discovered this, I made a point of telling them, in an effort to gently point out their utter ignorance, If you're afraid of AIDS and want to make virtually sure you don't get AIDS, become a lesbian!

"The Lesbianization of Masculine Desire" . . . Oh, It's Fraught!

CT: You've made a positive reference to this section in my essay: "What I am suggesting, in other words, is the possibility of obversing the 'masculinization of the lesbian' that obtains in classical, normative psychoanalysis and working toward what might be called a 'lesbianization' of masculine desire."

CM: I found that really interesting. I thought it was very provocative.

CT: One of the things that Jane Garrity's essay refers to a number of times is this phenomenon in porn—and in mainstream movies like the recent *Wild Things*—of women having sex with each other as spectacle for the male gaze. I think that's at least potentially more complex than is generally allowed. I think the whole issue of spectatorship and voyeurism in pornography is really complicated in a number of ways, in terms of the potential disruption of gender and sexuality identity/spectator categories. Of course, there's certainly a vast difference in those types of representations which are staged for mainstream viewerships and those that aren't (like in *On Our Backs*). In the mainstream scenes, there's usually a boundary assumed between identification and desire, but I wonder to what degree that boundary is blurred sometimes in the diversity of spectator positions, even when the spectator is a straight man—a diversity internal to the straight male viewer. On the part of the men who are aroused by these scenes, which are usually called "two-girl" rather than "lesbian," is there a place where there's a moment of identification with the women? Though, obviously, this is still contained within completely normative terms. But is there some moment within those identifications that could be recuperated in some productive way? This isn't exactly what I was thinking about when I suggested a lesbianization of masculine desire, but I think those moments of viewership could be interrogated and subverted in some way.

CM: I think that's true, and I think one could argue that this is why, in certain constructions of masculinity, performing oral sex on women is considered less than ideally masculine.

CT: Because it's something a woman could do.

CM: It seems almost specifically defined as a lesbianization of male desire.

CT: On the other hand, in straight porn, fellatio scenes function as safe ways for men to get up close to other men's cocks while at the same time having the intimacy heterosexualized by the mediating presence of a female sex worker. But in terms of the anxieties about appropriation, a phrase like "the lesbianization of masculine desire" is one that seems fraught . . .

CM: Oh, it's fraught! That's why I think it's worth the risk. It's worth thinking about.

CT: I agree it's worth thinking about. And, obviously, I think it's made possible by formulations by people like Butler, whom I've quoted in a note as saying: "And if a man desires another man or another woman, is his desire homosexual, heterosexual, or even lesbian? And what is to restrict a single individual to a single identification?" This ties back into the question of voluntarism. There's still the question of how particular people might identify within or experience their desire, even in the context of a specifically heterosexualized bodily act.

CM: Especially to the extent that if you say that the quintessential heterosexual act is coitus, then anything that is not that might be considered queer. You could even go further than that and say that the quintessential heterosexual act is coitus for the sake of procreation.

CT: I do say that.

CM: Then anything that is not that would be a queering of heterosexual practice. And I think you can argue that there are plenty of people out there, men in particular, for whom there is no other sexual practice. The whole area of what is bounded thus becomes much bigger than merely the question of penetrability we were talking about before; it becomes every other kind of sexual practice. Not that those in question would be able to articulate it as: I don't do this and that because it's queer. But psychically, that's what it's about.

CT: One of the very interesting avenues of critical inquiry for me is this connection between sexuality and narrative. Teleologically narrativized sex is sex which leads to an end purpose. But the way that this narrative, in a sense, can become perverse is by a veering away from the path that leads toward a specific, normative goal. So this is a way in which queer sex is nonnarrativized sex.

CM: Don't look at Merlin when you say that, because we didn't create him through sex, I'll have you know. We made him—like any good lesbian—through artificial insemination.

CT: Really?

CM: Yes!

CT: Well, that is a bit of news. Was that a specific decision? To separate sex from procreation?

CM: It was in a way. It was too much of a pain. It was wrecking our sex life to have teleological sex, as a matter of fact, plus it wasn't working. It just ended up being so much easier, not to mention more efficient, to do a husband-as-sperm-donor artificial insemination. And, indeed, we did it once and that was that.

Fight the Future

CT: There are a number of places in my essay where I suggest that there may be something potentially queering about a het couple's decision to remain child-free. Correspondingly, it could be argued that there is nothing more "straightening" than parenting. My partner and I are child-free, as I stress in the essay. When I first realized that I was probably never going to parent, I realized that there wasn't, in conventional English, an expression for not wanting to have a kid that, particularly for women, didn't inscribe that desire as a negative or as an absence: there was only the word "childless." So learning to reinscribe that desire was a step towards queering it.

But you have Merlin now, born in March. This is the end of May. Is he straightening you out?

CM: I agree with you that this might be the case, on the level of social inscription; but, as usual—and that's the point of talking about these things— it's more complicated than that. So, do I think he's straightening me out? Yes, on the level of how I appear in the world. I would say yes. Because, and that's similar to what you mean when you say that being child-free, on that social-inscription level, queers you. Because of the scene at the supermarket or wherever. I feel very much now, and that's an odd and uncomfortable experience for me, that I am looked at by the other breeders here in Iowa as one of their group, whether I want to be or not, just by virtue of having this babe in arms. And that's what I don't like about it, the extent to which I feel that I have lost control of my own identity expression.

At the same time, of course, like anything else, if you have a queer agenda, you can always find opportunities for queering. So, I also find that— whether it's around the question of his gender, or the fact that we didn't give him his father's last name, or the ways in which variously gendered adults relate to him—there are opportunities, which I certainly try to grab, for inscribing the fact that although I may look like I'm now one of them, let me point out that that's not how it is for me.

But I also think that the question of the child has more than one level. And in terms of a more psychoanalytic level, I think that being child-free cannot be so easily inscribed as a queer or antipatriarchal move by someone like you.

CT: To some degree. It's problematized by the fact that I'm male, because wanting to be child-free is for the masculine subject a completely different issue.

CM: That's why I say that I agree with you on the social level, but then there's the other level where there's something decidedly not queer about it, to the extent that there's a patriarchal tradition by which the straight male doesn't want to have kids. I certainly know plenty of straight men whose position in relation to their female partners is that they are the ones who don't want to have kids, don't want to have to deal with the child and stuff like that.

Then there's also the level of the maternal in relationship to the masculine. And I can tell that this will be another queering issue for me. For example, I can already tell—Merlin's only two-and-a-half months old—and I am starting to get, as I'm sure I will continue to get more and more, patriarchal pressure as his mother to separate and distance myself from him, the male child. So as not to make him queer. So as not to make him into a mama's boy. So as not to make him into a sissy. And that is something that is completely against my notion of the maternal. To me, the maternal has to do with attachment, not with distance and separation. So, as I say, given my child's biological maleness, I'm gearing up for all the implicit, and sometimes explicit, claims that I am sissifying him by insisting on maintaining the closeness of the maternal bond instead of at a certain point deciding, OK, now I'll take my distance. Push him into the world. Let him be a little man on his own. That day is not going to come in this household. And I know we're going to get flak for that.

And it's interesting, of course, because, had he been a girl, we could have gotten away for many, many years with pushing her to be a tomboy. Because that would be understood and accepted. Whereas with Merlin, the specter of the sissy is what we're going to have to contend with. The sissy is not acceptable now, won't be at age three, at age seven, at any age. We could have gotten away with raising a tomboy girl until she was sixteen, seventeen. At some point, she would have been expected to negotiate a transition to femininity; but at least we could have gotten away with a good fifteen, sixteen years of encouraging her to develop her "masculinity."

CT: There's a rich vein of psychoanalytic feminist discourse on these issues of maternity. On the maternal and differentiation or nondifferentiation. Kristeva, of course. Jessica Benjamin in *The Bonds of Love*. There's the feminist analysis of the constitution of fledgling masculinity through the beating back of the maternal. Not only the maternal but the maternal as a subject position, so as to transform the mother into an object or conduit, which is the way that patriarchy constructs maternity, as this sort of function. I think of the issue of dependence, also, for the masculine, since one of the ways in which the masculine subject constitutes itself is through its disavowal of any dependence upon the maternal, any subjection to maternal power. I agree with you that there's a completely different valence for me as a straight male to say that I want to remain child-free. But what I try to do with that is to let my commitment to child-freedom be in some sort of solidarity with women who want to remain child-free. Because there's no end of pressure on women to reproduce and to be mothers, certainly much more of a pressure on women to be mothers than there is on males to be fathers. I hope to inscribe my own resistance to those pressures as a feminist as well as a queer project.

CM: How do you feel that you do that? How does that project manifest itself for you?

CT: Well, not always very effectively or conspicuously. The classroom is one site, particularly when I have first-year students who seem barely adolescent who come up to me and say that they can't come to class tomorrow because they have to take their child to the doctor. I try to get students to consider the essentialism according to which womanhood and motherhood are coconfigured or coimplicated. So many female students here are anxious to get married and have kids as quickly as possible. So one thing I do in class is to ask, How many of you actually have children? Some hands go up. And: If maternity is figured as the essence of womanhood by patriarchy, do those of you who don't have children yet feel like you're not completely women yet? And that leads to some discussion of the pressure to reproduce, where it comes from—the long history of women's forced economic dependence on men—and how it is maintained.

Sometimes, though, to be honest, with me, I feel like I'm some sort of Beckett character, like in *Endgame*, where Hamm says something like: "Oh my god, it's a fly, kill it! The whole human race might start again from that." I sometimes feel I have this kind of Beckettian aversion to the reproduction of life. It's certainly a non- or antibreeding stance, but I'm not sure if it's exactly queer, in Beckett or in me.

CM: I don't know, either.

CT: That is to say that I sometimes feel, your case included, a tinge of sadness when I hear that somebody's pregnant.

CM: I think that's probably a deep-seated psychic issue with you. I would, for example, refer you to the work of the French psychoanalyst Antoinette Fouque. The central argument of her work is that it is precisely maternality that is the object of patriarchal misogyny. And that forms the raison d'être of patriarchy. Fouque argues that the male subject is both threatened by and, in a reversal of Freud, envious of the woman's ability to produce what Fouque calls *de la chair pensante*—thinking flesh.

CT: So that the target of misogynistic violence is maternality.

CM: The maternal is the specific feminine economy that patriarchy is most concerned with repressing. Even more so than with what one might call femininity. I think you've put it very well, this kind of sadness you feel about the reproduction of life. And I think it has more to do with a patriarchally defined male identity and masculine ego formation than with the queer.

CT: You're probably right. I would say, though, that what I would like to be able to do is to take this deep-seated thing that is part of my constitution through patriarchy and see if it can't be queered in some way. To let it bleed out into other areas of discourse and intervention, where it might be more usefully reinscribed.

To change the subject slightly, though: since you have in fact reproduced, what are you going to do to make sure Merlin is queer? Or, to allude to the subtitle of this summer's *X-Files* movie, what are you doing to fight the future?

CM: I've been trying to influence him since he was in the womb! It's interesting, especially being here in Iowa, to come to realize, more and more with trepidation and anxiety, what a big project that is going to be.

CT: Bigger, perhaps than any other . . .

CM: Exactly. It's been amazing to me, for example, to see the extent to which men—happily, not including his father—want to gender him masculine in a patriarchally defined way and have done from the day he was born. Luckily, of course, he can't yet understand their discourse, although I'm sure he senses something about their affect—I'm sure there's something about the tone of voice and the underlying affect that is being communicated to him. At the same time, it's a fascinating lesson, and one that I will certainly be able to call upon the next time a student—or anyone else— wants to argue for the "naturalness" of gender. Because I'm certainly seeing how, as I say, from the moment the babe is born, it's talked to in a gendered way. I find that especially with regard to the men who relate to him or talk to him; women don't gender him half as much as men do. And this is another gendered phenomenon that, if it proves to be more than anecdotal, we would need to wonder about. Why is this? It's really like the guys want him for their camp!

CT: How specifically do they do this?

CM: Very specifically. Like by calling him a "little man." I think that is so bizarre. To call a two-month-old little baby, "Hey, little man!" or "How are you today, guy?" Or the other day, a guy we know said: "Hey, you're getting some flab on those arms, little man, you gotta go to the gym and lift some weights." He's two months old! And then there are the comments on the way he's dressed. The fact that he sometimes wears a sun bonnet instead of a midget baseball cap. And, of course, I've had a couple of comments on our choice of last name for him—his mother's name, which is my mother's name. So I've decided, from now on, whenever anyone comments on the way he's dressed or our choice of last name, I'm going to say: "Yes, deconstructing patriarchy: *scary!*" That's going to be my new slogan. Because that's exactly what it is. At the same time, what is amazing to me is that people would care. One little, teeny, tiny baby in the universe, why do you care? Then I realize—they see it as a huge threat.

CT: There's a continuum between what these people are doing and the case of the woman in Nebraska. From three or four or five years ago.

CM: Brandon Teena.

CT: Yes. She was passing as a man in high school. She was dating the homecoming queen; and when the homecoming queen's male friends found out that she was really a woman, they "put her in her place" by raping and murdering her. Obviously, gendering is something that some people take as seriously as death.

I don't know specifically what you're planning to do with Merlin educationally, but one of our colleagues who has kids was telling me recently that he had a conference with one of his daughter's teachers, and the praise that this teacher had for his daughter was that she really wants to fit in, that she's successfully fitting in.

CM: Nightmare.

CT: And our colleague, to his credit, was thinking: I don't want her to fit in. Why is this praised? I want the teacher to tell me my daughter is distinctive and unique, not that she's fitting in.

CM: I think that that is a very good answer to your question of how are we going to try to make Merlin queer. Well, first and foremost, by valorizing the queer. By making it a value to be different. And to not fit in. And by trying to bring to bear any resources that we have towards the realization of this goal. For instance, we're lucky that he's half German. I figure I can always say to him, when he is getting any kind of pressure or flak for not fitting in at school, I'm just going to teach him to say, I'm not an Iowan. I'm different because I'm not from here. I was made in New York! Because here, in Iowa, any encouragement that he develop his femininity is going to be seen as very queer. And not just in Iowa.

CT: I think it's significant that we're having this dialogue, in this particular town, in this particular state. It has become a convention when you're talking about, say, young gay people who are growing up in a place without any support whatsoever that "Iowa" becomes the primary signifier for that particular plight and that particular place. A number of times I've heard spokespeople for PFLAG [Parents and Friends of Lesbians and Gays] or some other organization say: "Think about these kids who are growing up in Iowa." "Iowa" becomes a metaphor—a very appropriate metaphor—for a certain kind of plight whereby the project of the queer is particularly threatened.

CM: At the same time, being here makes it easier to be queer, in an ironic sense, in that you can do just a minor thing—like wear black—and you're . . .

CT: Exactly. It's easier to be figured as queer. You don't have to step too far out of the line of the normative.

CM: The fitting-in space is very small.

CT: Well, I don't know if you're planning to have more offspring . . . oh, you're not? Well, that will queer you—here you have to have seven.

CM: And preferably all at the same time.

CT: I think I made the comment earlier in this conversation that you're probably not going to fool too many people here. Particularly not your students.

CM: Why do you think that?

CT: You could walk into your classroom with Merlin in tow, and you're still not going to signify maternity for them in the way that they understand it. Simply because of the discourse you've presented in class. And your demeanor and so forth. They're not going to buy you as straight.

CM: On the one hand, as I've said, I feel having a kid makes me less queer. On the other hand, I've never felt so strongly, even with regard to femininity, to women's issues, the pressure of patriarchy. In my relationship to him. In the sense that I can hear people thinking: Poor little boy, trapped in the claws of this feminist mother.

CT: This man-hating feminist woman.

CM: Exactly! Who's just going to sissify him and fuck him up and make him wear girls' clothes—as in bright and pretty colors! It's child abuse! We should get him away from her! Call the child protective services! In that sense, yes and no to the question of do I feel he's straightening me out.

CT: I think that you probably feel the pressures so strongly because you're at the very crux of the reproduction of patriarchy and heteronormativity. It's all up to you!

CM: It is a big responsibility. A couple of years ago, *Ms.* magazine had a cover story entitled "What If It's a Boy?" about feminists having boy children. And it was, critically speaking, a very disappointing issue, because it was a big cop-out: most of the feminists writing for it just said stuff like, My son, I love him, he's a boy, but who cares? The only person who took raising a son on as a project in any serious way—and these were a handful of very famous feminists—was Robin Morgan, who had raised a child, a son, now an adult. She did make it into a project in the way that we're talking about, she took very seriously her responsibility, but she was the only one.

CT: Were the other women being just sort of naive about the pressures, or oblivious, or what?

CM: To a certain extent, they were buying into the cop-out narrative about hormonal differences, the whole "boys will be boys" rhetoric, and so on. And, in another way, they were personalizing their relationships, refusing to see their sons and their relationships with their sons in a more sociopolitical context.

It was just last year I think that Gloria Steinem, in an editorial piece—she's been doing editorial pieces all over—I think it was in a mainstream publication where she was talking about the question, What should be the feminist focus for the twenty-first century? Looking back, what have we done, and what do we still have to accomplish? And she was saying she feels that feminists have really blown it, copped out, when it comes to changing the reproduction of masculinity. We have done reasonably well in terms of getting mainstream America to think differently about constructions of femininity, such that you will now see the average American concerned with raising daughters to want to have careers, be financially independent, get involved in sports, and the like. But you see very little change or movement when it comes to the way that we raise boys. So Steinem was putting this latter forth as the next big project. And what it's going to take to accomplish such a goal is precisely people like myself taking seriously their responsibilities and seeing boy-raising as the daunting, important project that it is. And making a commitment to doing that in a feminist way, regardless of the pressures—and the pressures will be enormous. Queering a little boy is going to be met with a lot more hostility—and violence, for that matter—than trying to do the same with a little girl. Which is one reason why there has been so little progress made in this direction.

CT: What you're describing, particularly in terms of what you're saying about the inadequacy of the response of women besides Robin Morgan, is that the straightening effect for these women, or for women who have had male children, is that they forget social structures. Things get naturalized. Things become merely personal again.

CM: I think this has to do with the threat of the queer. People don't say this, but implicit in all those *Ms.* essays was, for example, the message: With a girl, it's one thing; but with a boy, you've got to be careful not to turn him into a homosexual. So, bottom line, as a feminist, you may have problems with certain constructions of masculinity, but if you go too far with your own son, that's the risk you'll be taking, and it's not worth it. Better he be a patriarch than a queer. That was the kind of position that was implicitly being taken.

CT: And that could be figured as protectiveness, in a sense, because if he is a patriarch, he will be safer in the world than if he's a queer.

CM: Not only safer but more successful. And that reminds me of something Freud says about women: Women don't have a penis and they regret this their whole lives, and the only way that they can mollify this regret is by having a male child who will carry the penis on their behalf in a patriarchal society. There was definitely some of that going on in those *Ms.* essays, too. I'm going to raise him to be a patriarchal man because, thereby, he's going to have all the privileges that I didn't have and that I resented not having.

CT: And that helps ensure that women in the future will not have those privileges.

CM: You personalize because it's your child—the world of women and feminism becomes very abstract, and what you want for your child becomes very concrete. This is probably an appropriate moment to talk about how, in addition to Gloria Steinem's arguing, and very laudably so, that this is an important feminist issue for the next century, we could say it's become even more vital because of what we have recently seen in this country: the series of school and parental shootings by young boys. I trust that if I ever feel weakened by any of the patriarchal arguments about why I should let my son be a man, I can just remind myself: Catherine, don't fall for this; because, if you do, he might end up killing you one day. And if not literally, metaphorically. Symbolically. He's going to kill you. That's how he's going to succeed at finding his place in the realm of patriarchically defined masculinity.

CT: Or, at least, abject you.

CM: And I don't want to be abjected! For selfish as well as political reasons. . . . But I'm sure you have something you want to say about these killer boys . . .

CT: The women that you're talking about who are, shall we say, not recognizing their responsibility to reconfigure their son's subjectivity in a queer, productive, feminist way. When they want their sons to be successful, what that means, or risks meaning, as the shootings in Springfield and Jonesboro and Paducah would attest, is: I want my son to learn that the best way, the most manly way, to resolve problems is through violence. He must learn two things: first, that he must make it to his deathbed without having been penetrated; second, and relatedly, that the best way—the most manly way—for him to solve his problems is through violence and domination. If domination doesn't work, violence. That is what's being reproduced at this moment in masculinity. And when the rhetoric of wanting what's best for my boy comes up, it's a completely different level of violence altogether in terms of the child, but the women on the African continent who submit their daughters to genital mutilation also, on that conscious level, want what they think is "best" for their daughters, because they believe that the daughters are unmarriageable without having undergone the mutilation. Like I say, it's a different level of violence altogether, but it is still a mutilation of the son's humanity to want to inscribe him into that ideal.

CM: Which goes back to what you were saying about looking for the benefit for men in queer masculinity, and there is a benefit, as we have said. There is a psychic benefit. Plus, it's a great way to stay out of jail!

CT: Yes. [Coos of concurrence from Merlin.]

Contributors

Joseph O. Aimone received a Ph.D. degree from the University of California at Davis in 1996 and teaches at Olivet College in Michigan. His publications include poetry in literary journals and critical writing on modern poetry and poetics and on aesthetic theory.

John N. Duvall is an associate professor of English at Purdue University and the associate editor of *Modern Fiction Studies*. In addition to his book *Faulkner's Marginal Couple: Invisible, Outlaw, and Unspeakable Communities* (1990), he has published numerous essays exploring the ideological work of contemporary fiction in such journals as *Novel, Modern Fiction Studies, Contemporary Literature, Arizona Quarterly,* and *College Literature.*

Jacqueline Foertsch received a Ph.D. degree in twentieth-century literature from Tulane University in 1998 and teaches at Auburn University. Her publications include an article in *The South Central Review* (forthcoming) on the role of women in selected novels and plays of the AIDS era and an article in *Genre* (forthcoming) on the "alterapocalyptic" in nuclear literature. She is working on a book project in gender theory that investigates the connections among gay, lesbian, and straight feminist schools of thought.

Katherine Gantz received a Ph.D. degree in French from the University of Michigan and is an adjunct professor of French at Wittenberg University. She has published articles in the areas of queer theory and French cultural studies and is completing a manuscript on women's oppositionality and visibility politics.

Jane Garrity is an assistant professor of English at the University of Colorado at Boulder, where she teaches twentieth-century British literature and culture as well as Anglo-American lesbian literature and theory. She has published essays on Anna Kavan and Sylvia Townsend Warner and is at work on a book entitled *Step-Daughters of England: British Women Modernists and the National Imaginary.*

Catherine A. F. MacGillivray is an associate professor in the Department of English Language and Literature and the Women's Studies Program at the University of Northern Iowa. She is a prominent scholar and translator of the work of the French writer Hélène Cixous and has published, among others, translations of Cixous's books *Manna for the Mandelstams for the Mandelas* (1994) and *First Days of the Year* (1998). She is working on a book on feminism, maternity, and the construction of masculinity.

Richard Nemesvari, an associate professor of English at St. Francis Xavier University, has published articles and reviews on Hardy, Braddon, Emily Brontë, Conrad, and Stevie Smith in such journals as *Studies in the Novel, Victorian Newsletter, Journal of English and Germanic Philology, Victorian Review,* and *Dalhousie Review.* His edition of Hardy's novel *The Trumpet-Major,* with introduction and notes, was published in 1991. His coedited text of Braddon's *Aurora Floyd* appeared in 1998, and his edition of Brontë's *Jane Eyre* will be published in 1999.

Clyde Smith, who danced with The High Risk Group in San Francisco (1989–92) and earned a master's degree in dance studies from the University of North Carolina at Greensboro in 1995, is a doctoral candidate in cultural studies, with a focus on dance, gender, and education, at Ohio State University. His dissertation considers power relations in the dance classroom.

Lauren Smith is a poet, essayist, and scholar teaching English and women's studies at Eastern Illinois University. She is a coeditor (with Jessie Grearson) of *Swaying: Essays on Intercultural Love* (1995).

Goran V. Stanivukovic is an assistant professor of English at Saint Mary's University in Halifax, Nova Scotia. He has published articles on Shakespeare, Fletcher, Emanuel Ford, Renaissance homoeroticism, and Renaissance rhetoric, and his edition of Ford's prose romance *Ornatus and Artesia* is forthcoming. He is working on a project tentatively titled "Bodies and Sexualities in Early Modern Prose Fiction, 1580–1640."

Calvin Thomas teaches critical theory and cultural studies at Georgia State University and has been an Emerson Distinguished Faculty Fellow in Modern Letters at Syracuse University and an associate professor of English at the University of Northern Iowa. He is the author of *Male Matters: Masculinity, Anxiety, and the Male Body on the Line* (1996) and of critical essays and fiction in *Men and Masculinities, Genders, Novel, New German Critique, Literature and Psychology, Georgia Review, Kansas Quarterly,* and other journals.

Mary M. Wiles is a doctoral candidate in the English department at the University of Florida. She received M.A. degrees in French and film studies from the University of Iowa and has also studied at Paris III, Sorbonne in France. Her research and writing interests are in the articulation of homosexual desire in film and literature.

Index

Typeset in 9.5/13 Stone Serif
with Helvetica Neue Heavy Extended display
Designed by Dennis Roberts
Composed by Keystone Typesetting, Inc.

University of Illinois Press
1325 South Oak Street
Champaign, IL 61820-6903
www.press.uillinois.edu